The STEAM LOCOMOTIVE

The STEAM LOCOMOTIVE

Luciano Greggio

Translated and adapted by Peter Kalla-Bishop

Artwork by Guido Canestrari

Hamlyn

London · New York · Sydney · Toronto

Illustrations and original text
Copyright © Arnoldo Mondadori Editore S.p.A. Milano 1977
English translation
Copyright © The Hamlyn Publishing Group Limited 1980

First English edition published 1980 by
The Hamlyn Publishing Group Limited
London · New York · Sydney · Toronto
Astronaut House, Feltham, Middlesex

ISBN 0 600 38428 4
Printed in Italy

Contents

Foreword

The steam locomotive story can be told in many fashions, all of them pertinent and interesting, despite the different viewpoints from which this major feat of engineering by man may be seen and discussed. Rail transport's story over a century and a half is rich and involved, at once highly technical, and a key to the socio-economic scene and its customs. The purpose of this book is to tell the story of far-seeing men who, starting with Trevithick's invention and Stephenson's development, handed down their ideas and their enthusiasms, as well as their delusions, to the evolution of the most recent steam locomotives – locomotives that almost all of us have admired from close quarters.

It is an account that begins with the crude efforts of the pioneers and ends with the major achievements and perfections of the last generation of designs. For space reasons a selection has had to be made from the many schools of locomotive constructions that have from time to time helped the advance of steam locomotion. The most significant technical advances have been singled out and the contribution made by each school to the evolutionary process has been described in the simplest terms possible, with due regard to historical accuracy.

In many parts of the world the steam locomotive has an extraordinary fascination, beyond any logical and plausible explanation. Today, when the steam locomotive is far along the road to its disappearance, that fascination is more alive than ever and as fresh as at any time in the past. Evocative of many things, even in the eyes of the young, the steam locomotive brings warm and even painful feelings of nostalgia to those who have followed and shared in the last years of its almost legendary existence.

P. M. K-B.

The Heroic Age

At the end of the 18th century the time was ripe for something revolutionary to happen in the great coal and mineral fields of England, which supported a network of railways on which horse-drawn convoys of wagons travelled.

In many and diverse fields, the work of such men as Newcomen, Watt and Cugnot had given rise to a ferment of ideas and hopes, so rich in eventual fulfilment that within a century the brothers Wright were embarking on the first airborne venture. But it was much earlier–in Cornwall–that enlightened men made the first step towards steam traction, appropriately in the area where John Watt's first fixed steam engines were used for pumping and the working of incline-plane funiculars: William Murdoch, an apprentice of Watt, by 1784 had tried moving a three-wheeled vehicle by spirit-lamp generated steam.

The great debate of the day, not without its abrasive aspects, turned on the dangers of high pressure steam compared to the large and heavy low pressure stationary-plant boilers of the era.

The mining engineer Richard Trevithick, another Cornishman, took out the first patent– registered on 24 March 1800–for a new stationary engine plant that was sufficiently light and compact for Trevithick to extend its use to vehicles on wheels. He carried out road vehicle experiments and was trying to build a rail steam locomotive at Coalbrookdale in 1803 when he proposed a similar machine to Samuel Homfray, the owner of the Pen-y-Daren foundry in South Wales. The idea was for an experimental steam-powered self-propelled machine, capable of hauling iron ore wagons on an existing horse-powered tramway that ran to a canal at Abercynon.

As at Coalbrookdale, Trevithick designed a machine with a horizontal boiler and cylinder, the latter almost entirely enclosed within the boiler barrel. The firebox was carried inside the boiler, as was a great horizontal U-tube for the high-temperature gases, a form of construction that greatly improved heat exchange with the water.

The to-and-fro action of the piston in its cylinder was converted into rotary movement by a connecting rod and crank, while a gear train transmitted the movement to the wheels. Trevithick told the Royal Society that his locomotive, when tried out, weighed about 5 tonnes, water included, that it hauled a train of five wagons loaded with 10 tonnes of iron ore

Murdoch *By 1784 William Murdoch, who had worked as an apprentice in James Watt's workshop, had appreciated that steam could be used to turn the wheels of a vehicle. This crude tricycle was a first and successful experiment, but it was not followed up.*

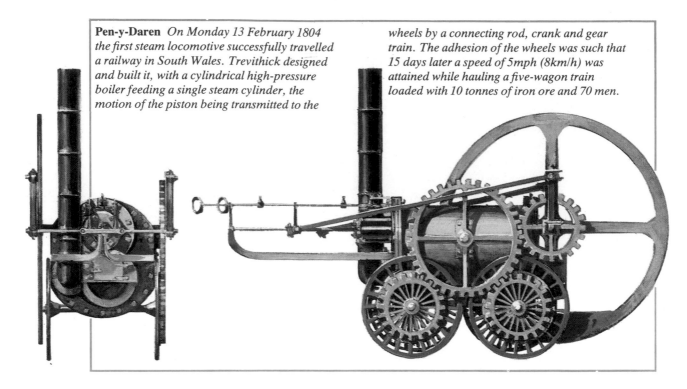

Pen-y-Daren *On Monday 13 February 1804 the first steam locomotive successfully travelled a railway in South Wales. Trevithick designed and built it, with a cylindrical high-pressure boiler feeding a single steam cylinder, the motion of the piston being transmitted to the* wheels by a connecting rod, crank and gear train. The adhesion of the wheels was such that 15 days later a speed of 5mph (8km/h) was attained while hauling a five-wagon train loaded with 10 tonnes of iron ore and 70 men.

and 70 men with ease, and that it ran the 9 miles (14.5km) from mine to canal in 4 hours 5 minutes. This included halts to chop away overhanging tree branches and to clear stones from the track. The speed attained was about 5mph (8km/h).

Several years were to pass before the imperfect functioning and temperamental behaviour of this, the world's first steam locomotive, were cleared up, and the potential of steam traction realised. The weight of the locomotive also smashed the track and something had to be done

about strengthening the latter. In fact, the Pen-y-Daren track was badly laid and sometimes sank into soft ground, under the weight of the train, occasionally leading to derailment.

The fact that a single-cylinder engine was used had the drawback that when the piston was on dead-centre and the locomotive stationary, it would move neither forward or backwards, unless the wheels were levered along the rails or the flywheel could be forced round. This would move the piston into a suitable position so that steam could enter the cylinder to provide the

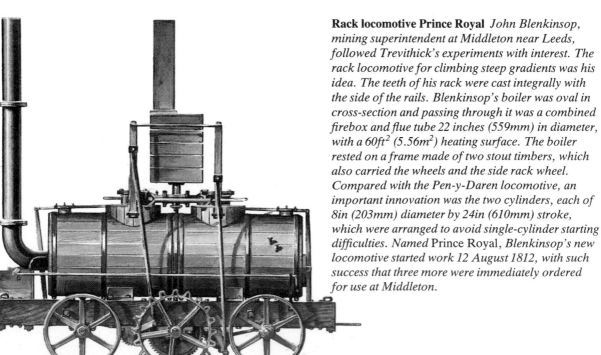

Rack locomotive Prince Royal *John Blenkinsop, mining superintendent at Middleton near Leeds, followed Trevithick's experiments with interest. The rack locomotive for climbing steep gradients was his idea. The teeth of his rack were cast integrally with the side of the rails. Blenkinsop's boiler was oval in cross-section and passing through it was a combined firebox and flue tube 22 inches (559mm) in diameter, with a 60ft^2 (5.56m^2) heating surface. The boiler rested on a frame made of two stout timbers, which also carried the wheels and the side rack wheel. Compared with the Pen-y-Daren locomotive, an important innovation was the two cylinders, each of 8in (203mm) diameter by 24in (610mm) stroke, which were arranged to avoid single-cylinder starting difficulties. Named* Prince Royal, *Blenkinsop's new locomotive started work 12 August 1812, with such success that three more were immediately ordered for use at Middleton.*

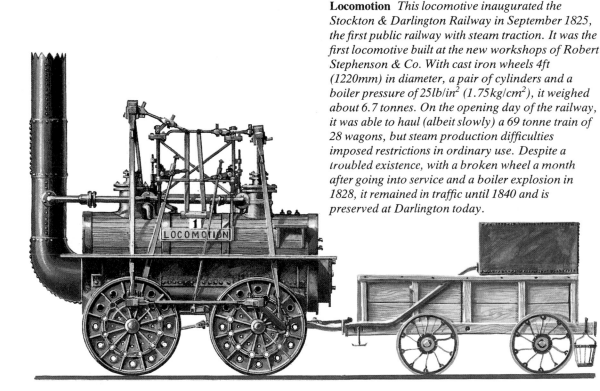

necessary force for movement. In addition, despite its weight, there were occasions when the locomotive wheels lost their adhesion and revolved uselessly on one spot.

Trevithick's steam locomotive encountered much adverse comment and gained little approval or support. Nevertheless it encouraged those who held that its principles were valid and who realised the exceptional importance of continuing along the road thus pioneered.

Among the supporters was John Blenkinsop, who in 1812 tried installing a rack along the track, which together with a pinion on the locomotive gave assured adhesion to the wheels. He was followed by William Hedley in 1813, who maintained and demonstrated that a rack was quite unnecessary for adequate adhesion. Then George Stephenson designed and built the successful series of Killingworth locomotives (named after the mine where he worked). He introduced the concept of coupling driving axles together with a chain as well as

Puffing Billy At Wylam Colliery, Hedley made experiments to show that a non-rack locomotive had sufficient adhesion to haul a train of wagons. Starting from Blenkinsop's designs, he built an engine in which vertical cylinders were disposed outside the boiler on either side, to drive the wheels through levers and a gear train. The firebox and flue tube was U-shaped to give a greater heating surface. Exhaust steam was directed up the chimney, giving rise to the name Puffing Billy *because of the distinctive noise.*

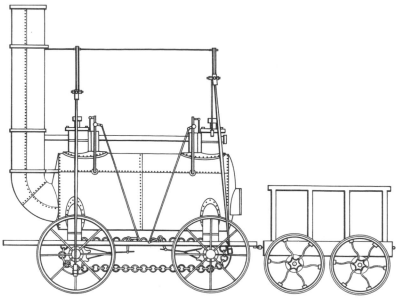

putting a crank on the wheel itself so that the connecting rod could be joined to the wheels direct. It was Stephenson, with his locomotive *Locomotion*, who inaugurated the train service on the Stockton & Darlington Railway in 1825, the world's first public railway using some steam traction.

In 1827, Timothy Hackworth first used exhaust steam blasting up the chimney to force the fire on his locomotive *Royal George*.

These were years filled with great enthusiasm and often with bitter disappointment, tense years in which effort was devoted to overcoming the huge obstacles which the undeveloped technology and materials of the day placed in the path of innovators. Bold technical solutions fell foul of these limitations again and again.

Though the steam locomotive had not been as successful as it had first promised to be, George Stephenson and his son Robert were well on their way towards convincing their country that the widespread adoption of steam traction was of the first importance in establishing Great Britain's world economic and military supremacy. Their ideas were confirmed decisively at the Rainhill trials in October 1829, which were held to confirm by a practical demonstration the overall steady performance and re-

George Stephenson *is known universally as the father of the steam locomotive, even if the description is not strictly correct historically. While observing* Puffing Billy *in traffic at Wylam he saw the necessity of simplifying its machinery and characteristics. In his first locomotive he used a fresh design for which he obtained a patent. The four wheels were driven directly by the connecting rods from the cylinders, instead of through a gear train, while the two driven axles were connected by a chain drive to improve adhesion. On this locomotive of 1816 the admission of steam to the cylinders was controlled by a regulator for the first time.*

Lancashire Witch *Built by Stephenson in 1828 for the Bolton & Leigh Railway, this locomotive design abandoned the vertical cylinders and placed them at an angle. Each piston drove a front wheel, alternately on each side, and due to the cylinder position it was possible to spring the axles. The boiler had a large firebox and flue tube with two small lateral tubes to augment the heating surface and improve steam production. For the first time steam admission to the cylinders could be adjusted by the driver.*

Royal George *The idea of coupling rods between axles to increase a locomotive's total rail adhesion is attributed to Timothy Hackworth, who had worked alongside Stephenson for some years. The* Royal George *of 1827 had two vertical cylinders alongside and above the boiler, and directly above the rear axle, while coupling rods drove two more axles. In the blast pipe, also attributed to Hackworth, a jet of exhaust steam from the cylinders was directed vertically up the inside of the chimney to force the fire. This helped make* Royal George *the most powerful locomotive of its day; it could haul 130 tonnes at 5mph (8km/h), the highest speed then permitted.*

liability of the still-developing steam locomotive.

The Liverpool & Manchester Railway organised the Rainhill trials and the terms set out for the competition were a severe challenge to the locomotive builders, whose products previously had run only on the shaky tracks of provincial railways. The complication of many of the designs were such that, as often as not, there was a call for horses by nightfall to haul the machines back to the starting point. Despite continuous modification and improvement these standard machines of the day failed to assert supremacy at Rainhill. Victory went to the Stephensons' *Rocket*, which was such a great step forward in locomotive engineering, both in principle and construction, that it is now considered to be the vital link between the slow-moving mineral railway engines then in general use and the modern steam locomotive.

At the end of 1829 steam locomotive euphoria was spreading throughout Great Britain, although across the Channel the idea aroused no interest at all. Sporadic and unsuccessful attempts had been made to use the new form of traction, notably in France, but these served merely to confirm its rôle as an extravagant curiosity.

Novelty *When it arrived at the Rainhill trials in 1829 this locomotive was a sensation. Ericsson, the designer, was born in Sweden in 1803 and was one of the most original locomotive engineers of his day.* Novelty *introduced the idea of a light versatile locomotive, in contrast to the bulky and heavy construction common at the time. The boiler was shaped like a 'T' laid on its side. The coils of a combustion gas tube, leading to the chimney, ran through the horizontal arm. The vertical part included a firebox (fired from above) while the whole was cantilevered out beyond the frames at the rear. The two cylinders drove one axle by rods and levers, the arrangement proving to be a weak point during the trials. Carrying both coal and water,* Novelty *can be considered the world's first tank locomotive. It attained the highest speed in the trials until a boiler fault caused it to be withdrawn.*

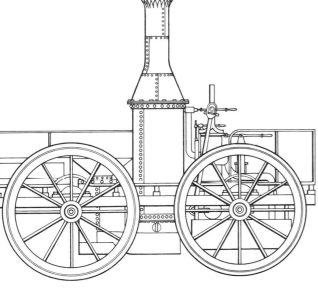

Perseverance *Built by Burstal of Leigh for the Rainhill trials, this locomotive had an accident two days before they started and was unable to take part. Of all the entrants, it was most obviously derived from the traditional horse-drawn carriage.*

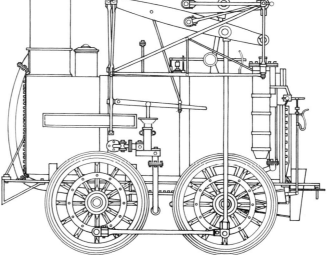

Agenoria *Foster Rastrick & Co built this locomotive for the Shutt End Colliery Railway in 1829. It was a typical traditional mineral railway locomotive, with vertical cylinders, outside coupled wheels, heavy construction and modest speed. The same year an almost identical locomotive was exported to the United States, the* Stourbridge Lion. *Trials there proved disappointing and it was withdrawn for scrap.*

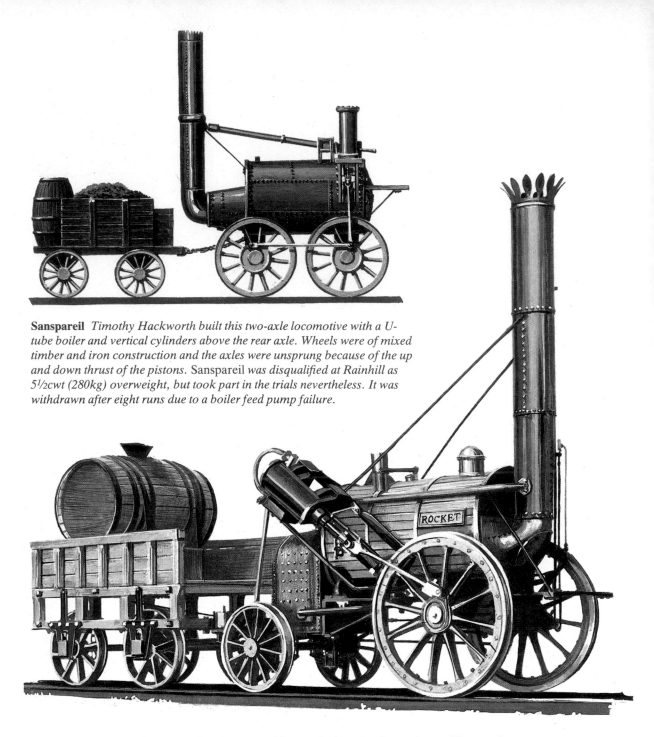

Sanspareil *Timothy Hackworth built this two-axle locomotive with a U-tube boiler and vertical cylinders above the rear axle. Wheels were of mixed timber and iron construction and the axles were unsprung because of the up and down thrust of the pistons. Sanspareil was disqualified at Rainhill as 5½cwt (280kg) overweight, but took part in the trials nevertheless. It was withdrawn after eight runs due to a boiler feed pump failure.*

Rocket *Built in 1829 by George Stephenson and his son Robert, Rocket is the world's most famous steam locomotive, because the design marked the transition from pioneering efforts to the modern steam engine. Designed expressly for the Rainhill trials, Rocket incorporated the new ideas tried out in* Lancashire Witch *a year before, with the addition of a water tube boiler (25 tubes through the barrel). The firebox and grate were separate from and placed at the rear of the boiler. Exhaust steam was used as a blast up the chimney to force the fire. Stephenson adopted a light single-driver design with two cylinders mounted at a 35° angle. The working weight of the locomotive was 4.3 tonnes. At Rainhill, Rocket attained a record speed of 30mph (48.5km/h) on 6 October 1829, while hauling a 12.9 tonne load.*

Steam Car *This German design of 1816 evidently took its inspiration from Blenkinsop's locomotives in England, for his frames and the final drive through a rack wheel were adopted.*

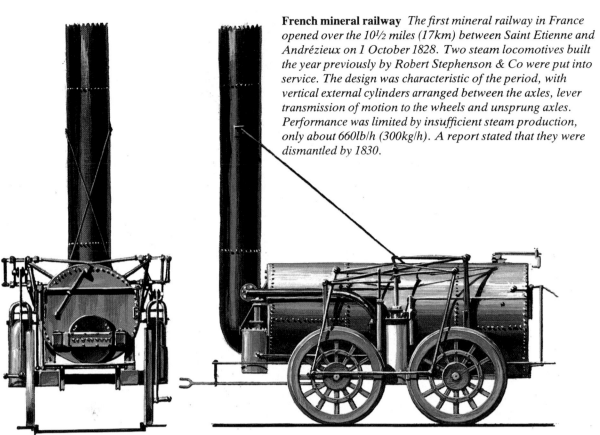

French mineral railway *The first mineral railway in France opened over the 10½ miles (17km) between Saint Etienne and Andrézieux on 1 October 1828. Two steam locomotives built the year previously by Robert Stephenson & Co were put into service. The design was characteristic of the period, with vertical external cylinders arranged between the axles, lever transmission of motion to the wheels and unsprung axles. Performance was limited by insufficient steam production, only about 660lb/h (300kg/h). A report stated that they were dismantled by 1830.*

Marc Seguin, *who ordered the Stephenson locomotives for the Saint Etienne-Andrézieux found that their low steam production was not to be remedied and designed a new type of boiler for himself. In this, some 43 tubes carried combustion gases through the barrel, the gases first passing through a combustion chamber under the boiler proper, which increased the heating surface. In addition, iron tanks arranged on either side of the boiler assembly allowed the boiler feed water to be preheated. Seguin held that increased draught was needed to force the fire and he placed blower outlets under the grate. Two large fans on the tender, driven from an axle by pulleys and belts, provided the draught through flexible ducts. The locomotive hauled a 19 tonne load up gradients on 9 November 1829, but achieved a speed of less than 2.5mph (4km/h). This modest performance was compounded in the months that followed by a continual series of mechanical failures.*

ACROSS THE ATLANTIC

At the start of the 19th century the United States seemed a sleeping giant; plains and forests were undisturbed, there were vast unexplored territories, few pioneer settlements and only the Atlantic coastline could boast any considerable population. Congress approved the construction of the National Road in 1806, a broad and well-paved highway to allow coaches to connect the important centres of the great new nation. Distances were great: from Washington to Wheeling, West Virginia, took 59 hours and Boston to New York took 41 hours. Freight travelled in large gaily-painted Conestoga wagons, each covered by a canvas roof and drawn by three pairs of horses.

At the beginning of the 19th century, however, there was less prejudice against the steam engine in America than there was in Great Britain. In the latter country the rulers feared that railways would upset an established social order in which inherited riches were taken for granted. Across the Atlantic there was less discrimination and more pioneering spirit, which took men of all classes across the Allegheny mountains towards the American West.

Thus when the locomotive arrived in America it was to a different climate of opinion and the far-seeing activities of Colonel John Stevens, who is considered to be the father of American railroads, had a different outcome. Stevens experimented with railway building for some years and in October 1824, he demonstrated a small circular line on his own farm in Hoboken, New Jersey. On this he ran a little steam locomotive with a vertical boiler and rack rail propulsion. Although it never ran outside the confines of the Stevens' farm, it aroused the greatest interest and gave a strong impetus to the building of America's first true railroad. Also contributing to this was another pioneer, Horatio Allen, who imported a locomotive from Foster & Rastrick in England and put it on rails at Honesdale, Pennsylvania, in August 1829. Allen himself drove this locomotive, named *Stourbridge Lion*, along three miles of railway, which included a bridge on a curve of 112yd (102m) radius. This trial was a success, but it was soon realised that, just as had been the case with Trevithick's locomotive of 1804, *Stourbridge Lion* was too heavy for main line service. The machine found itself relegated to shunting duty in the coal yards of the Delaware & Hudson Canal Co.

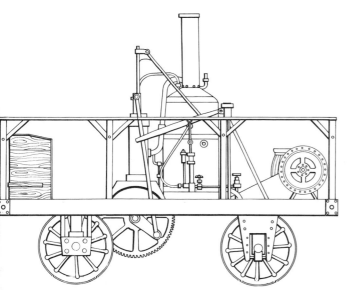

Tom Thumb *The Baltimore & Ohio company was authorised to build its first stretch of railroad in February 1831, and planned to run light horse-drawn vehicles on it. Peter Cooper persuaded the company's directors to consider the possibility of steam traction. He built a strange machine at his own expense, with a vertical boiler and two vertical cylinders. The movements of the pistons were transmitted to a pair of wheels through a gear train. It was hardly a locomotive, for it weighed little more than one tonne and developed scarcely more power than a horse, but* Tom Thumb *was the first locomotive to haul a wagon loaded with passengers in the United States.*

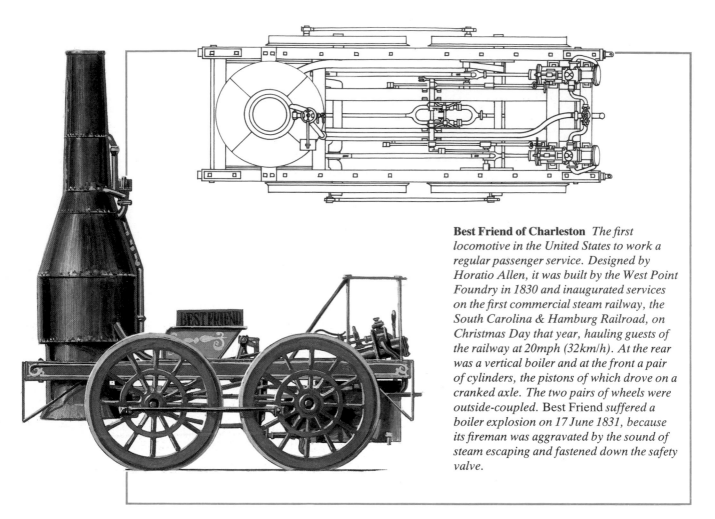

Best Friend of Charleston *The first locomotive in the United States to work a regular passenger service. Designed by Horatio Allen, it was built by the West Point Foundry in 1830 and inaugurated services on the first commercial steam railway, the South Carolina & Hamburg Railroad, on Christmas Day that year, hauling guests of the railway at 20mph (32km/h). At the rear was a vertical boiler and at the front a pair of cylinders, the pistons of which drove on a cranked axle. The two pairs of wheels were outside-coupled.* Best Friend *suffered a boiler explosion on 17 June 1831, because its fireman was aggravated by the sound of steam escaping and fastened down the safety valve.*

West Point *was put into service on the South Carolina Railroad before* Best Friend of Charleston's *boiler exploded. Designed by E L Miller, this was the first American locomotive with a horizontal boiler and was also built by the West Point Foundry. The inside cylinder and coupled wheel design of the* Best Friend *was adopted without any important modifications.* West Point *first hauled a train on 5 March 1831 and attained 17mph (27km/h) with four wagons carrying 117 passengers, and a van loaded with bales of cotton ahead of them as a safety precaution in case of collision.*

Nevertheless railway fever gripped the country and numerous railway construction proposals were made. Among the early organisations was the Baltimore & Ohio, which opened its first track on 4 July 1828, and this was soon followed by the Philadelphia & Columbia and many more. Peter Cooper of New York built the *Tom Thumb*, which, true to its name, was too small to be considered as a proper locomotive. Its construction was improvised to a degree, musket barrels being used as tubes in the vertical boiler while the two cylinders were those of a small stationary engine. The locomotive went to the Baltimore & Ohio in 1830 and in August of that year had a famous race with a horse-drawn coach on an adjacent track. The locomotive lost because of a broken belt driving the fan which provided draught for the fire.

Elsewhere, the tenacity and dynamism of Horatio Allen persuaded the citizens of Charleston to build a railway as an answer to the canal that brought cotton bales from the interior to the rival port of Savannah. This railway, the South Carolina Railroad, was the first in the

United States to run a regular passenger service by steam, using the historic *Best Friend of Charleston*. The *Best Friend* was built by the West Point Foundry in 1830, with a large vertical boiler overhanging the wheelbase at the rear. At the front were two inclined cylinders inside the frames, which drove the rear crank axle, and the two pairs of wheels were coupled. On Christmas Day 1830, *Best Friend* (considered to be the *Rocket* of America) hauled a train with over 40 passengers at 20mph (32km/h), and on 15 January 1831 it inaugurated the first train service.

De Witt Clinton *The West Point Foundry, which had become experienced in building locomotives, delivered* De Witt Clinton *to the Mohawk & Hudson in 1831, the first locomotive to run in the state of New York. Designed by John B Jarvis, it followed established practice, except that the boiler was provided with a large rivetted dome, and the tender platform was provided by the top of a water tank. It took the first train 14 miles (22.5km) from Albany to Schenectady on 9 August 1831, covering the distance in 46 minutes.*

York *Designed by Phineas Davis, this locomotive had a large vertical boiler with a vertical cylinder on each side of it. The pistons transmitted their motion to the wheels through a double-triangle coupling rod on each side.* York *started service in July 1831 and hauled the first train from Baltimore to Ellicott's Mills.*

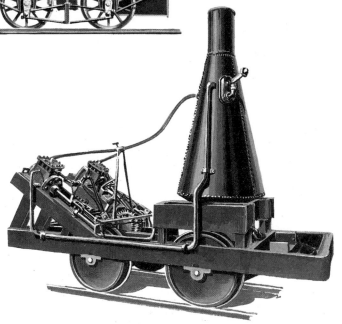

James the First *Designed by William James of New York, this machine took part in the Baltimore & Ohio's locomotive contest in 1831. The coned vertical boiler fed steam to two vertical cylinders, the pistons of which drove a jackshaft with triangular connecting rods to the wheels. The locomotive is shown here in rebuilt form, with cylinders inclined at 30° at the end of the frames, and a single driven axle to which motion was transmitted by a gear train.*

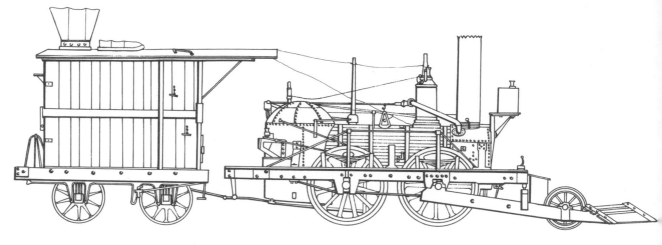

John Bull *Robert Stevens of the Camden & Amboy (running between Philadelphia and New York) imported a British Stephenson-type locomotive for the first Camden-Bordentown section. After modification, the dismantled locomotive was sent for re-assembly in the United States in July 1831. It had a Stephenson boiler, engine and wheels, with a Bury circular domed firebox added. To help in running through curves, coupling rods between the axles were removed in the United States, and a leading axle in a timber frame was added. For the first time a wedge-shaped cowcatcher was mounted at the front of the timber frame.* John Bull *started work 12 November 1831 and was withdrawn in 1866.*

South Carolina *Designed by Horatio Allen and built by West Point Foundry in 1832, this was the world's first articulated locomotive. Boiler barrels on each side were served by a large central firebox, the barrels being supported on four-wheel bogies. Each bogie had a driving wheel, and inside cranks were connected to a single cylinder at each end.*

Following the example of the Liverpool & Manchester Railway, the Baltimore & Ohio organised a locomotive contest and offered a first prize of $4 000 and a second of $3 000 for the best designs. The conditions published in January 1831 followed the customary technical requirements of the day. Maximum weight in working order, haulage capacity and the speed to be attained were all specified, together with boiler feed arrangements, safety fittings, and so on. To these was added a supplementary requirement: a candidate for a prize had to run in service for 30 days without a major breakdown. The victor was *York* designed by Phineas Davis, a clockmaker of Philadelphia, which was to be the prototype of a series of locomotives known as the Grasshoppers.

No history of steam in America would be complete without the name of Matthias Bald-

Experiment *John Jarvis designed this locomotive, which was built at the West Point Foundry and delivered to the Mohawk & Hudson in 1832. For the first time a front bogie appeared, in the form of a truck pivotted on a pin, separately from the main frames. A bogie helps a locomotive to run through curves and to negotiate roughly-laid track.* Experiment, *later known as* Brother Jonathan, *had a boiler and firebox similar to Stephenson's Planet locomotives, but the driving axle was moved to the rear of the firebox and the cylinders were placed under the smokebox. Results were excellent, except that the firebox had not been designed for the anthracite fuel used and so was soon replaced. It is claimed that* Brother Jonathan *attained 60mph (96.5km/h).*

Monster *Robert Stevens and Isaac Dripps combined to produce this complicated design in an attempt to increase power using low-price, small anthracite fuel. Built around 1834, it was an eight-coupled locomotive without a frame, the boiler taking its place and carrying the cylinders. Connecting rods from a rocking lever drove the third axle, the latter pair being coupled, as were the two front axles. A gear train coupled the third and second axles to allow some play for rounding curves. The firebox was extended inside the enormous boiler, but steaming was not satisfactory.*

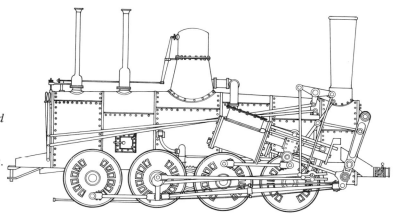

win, a brilliant and tireless constructor of locomotives. The works bearing his name built some 59,000 before the advent of the diesel, and the rapid leap forward of railway technology and technique was in great part due to his research into new methods of construction to reduce cost of building and maintenance, into ways of making a locomotive more versatile and into increasing its safety. Baldwin's contribution was a major factor in taking the locomotive out of the pioneering age and into the age of industrial expansion.

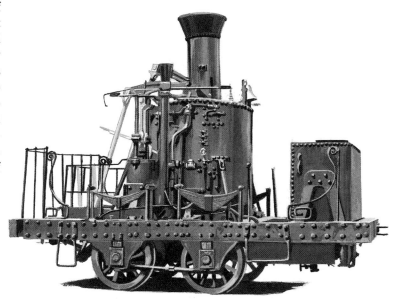

Atlantic *Based on his experience with* York, *Davis designed a machine with a large-diameter vertical boiler containing about 400 tubes. The fire was blown by exhaust-steam powered fans at first, altered later to an exhaust steam blast up the chimney in the manner then becoming universal. Entering service in summer 1832,* Atlantic *took the first train from Baltimore to Parr's Bridge. It was nicknamed Grasshopper, as it was front heavy and moved with a pitching motion that put it in danger of overturning if derailed. Withdrawn in 1892.*

Mazeppa *Ross Winans, an assistant to Davis on the Baltimore & Ohio, modified the Grasshopper design because of the poor riding of* Atlantic, *which was mainly due to the up and down motion of the pistons. Named after the hero of Byron's poem,* Mazeppa *had horizontal cylinders outside the frames and went into service in 1837. Crab was its nickname, as it gave the impression of going backwards when moving forwards.*

Buffalo *This, the last of the Grasshopper type, marked the end of the vertical boiler. Ross Winans had Baldwin build several Crab-type locomotives in 1842, but with four axles instead of two. The boiler was carried low in the frames between the second and third axles, to reduce the centre of gravity and overall height. Buffalo was the world's first eight-wheel outside-coupled locomotive, but performance was disappointing and it was out of service by 1850.*

Campbell *The engineer Henry R Campbell, searching for an improved locomotive at the end of 1836, adopted the Jarvis bogie from* Experiment *and combined it with four-coupled wheels. The first Campbell 4-4-0 was built by James Brooks of Philadelphia in 1837 and delivered to the Philadelphia, Germanstown & Norriston railroad. Among its features was the bogie springing, which lacked primary suspension for the two axles and relied on secondary suspension from the frames only. In addition, the front pair of driving wheels, 4ft 6in (1370mm) diameter, lacked flanges so as to help on curves.*

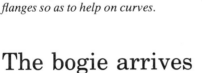

The bogie arrives

There was a great need for an idea to enable locomotives to run easily round curves, which were not of great radius in pioneering days and were not super-elevated. Entering a curve abruptly could lead to derailment and a device was sought to smooth such entries. A first experiment gave the leading axle some transverse play, but there was no significant improvement as the possible play was limited. Then it was considered that locomotives might be guided into curves by leading wheels articulated to the main frames in such a way that the engine was pulled towards the inside of the curve. This idea is attributed to Isaac Dripps, the master mechanic who re-erected *John Bull* on its importation to America from England (see

page 20). It was he who added the leading wheels in their prominent timber frame. The four-wheel leading bogie was a further improvement on this and, at the suggestion of Robert Stephenson, first appeared on *Experiment* of 1832 (see page 20). Railways in the United States were built in a rough and ready way compared with those of Europe. Indeed, in many cases there was little or no preparation of the ground beforehand. Track was often so uneven that it endangered trains and the lives of the passengers travelling over it. Later, the haste with which track was pushed across the great prairies of the West had similar consequences. Thus, in America more than elsewhere, the ability of a bogie to guide an engine over

Norris locomotives

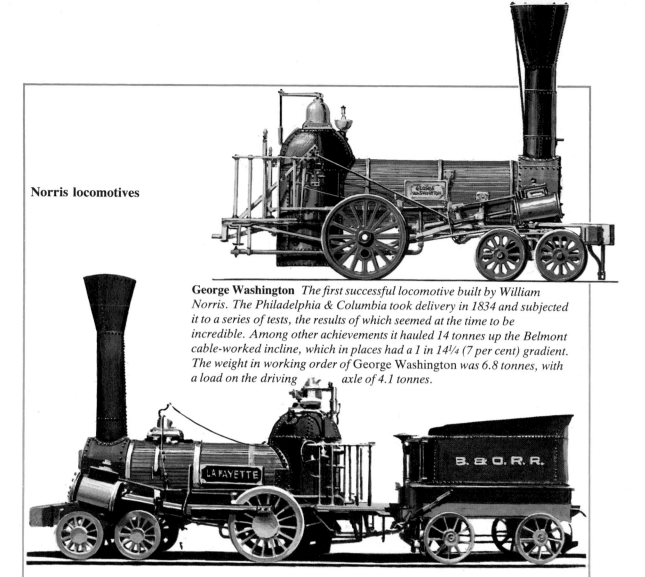

George Washington *The first successful locomotive built by William Norris. The Philadelphia & Columbia took delivery in 1834 and subjected it to a series of tests, the results of which seemed at the time to be incredible. Among other achievements it hauled 14 tonnes up the Belmont cable-worked incline, which in places had a 1 in 14¼ (7 per cent) gradient. The weight in working order of George Washington was 6.8 tonnes, with a load on the driving axle of 4.1 tonnes.*

William Norris occupied a prominent place among American locomotive pioneers. His designs had a characteristic appearance and were sufficiently simple, robust and versatile to see service almost everywhere in the United States, as well as having an influence on European locomotive practice. The most famous type was the Norris 4-2-0, which incorporated many important technical innovations, some of which had been first used elsewhere. Among these were bar frames, outside cylinders at the smokebox, the Bury firebox and a driving axle in front of the firebox to improve adhesion. By the end of 1840 Norris had built 135 locomotives, of which 41 were exported.

Virginia *William Norris realised that the success of his 4-2-0 locomotives was likely to be short-lived, so he designed a four-coupled machine, his first 4-4-0 locomotive being built in 1839. Virginia, built in 1842, was of particular importance because of the means adopted to give lateral play to the two coupled axles.*

Lafayette *Put into service by the Baltimore & Ohio in 1837 this locomotive was their first with a horizontal boiler. It was a typical Norris 4-2-0, with inclined cylinders, a large, domed firebox and a short-wheelbase bogie. Boiler pressure was 60lb/in² (4.2kg/cm²), driving wheel diameter 4ft (1220mm) and weight in working order 12.5 tonnes, of which 5.8 tonnes was on the driving wheels.*

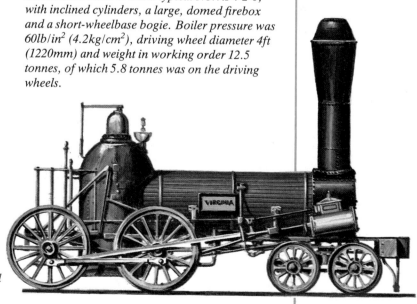

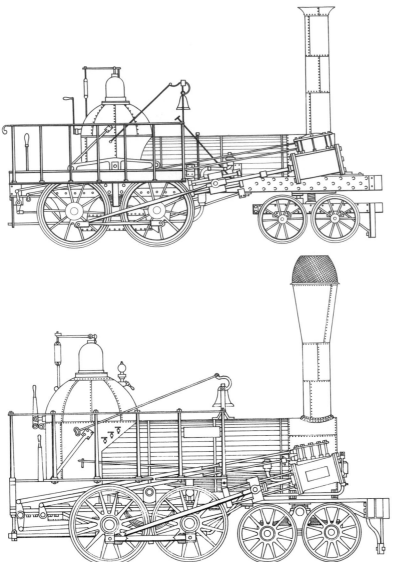

Hercules *Following very successful trials with Campbell's 4-4-0, it was realised that this wheel arrangement was the best of the time. Joseph Harrison Jnr., of the locomotive builders Garrett & Eastwick, patented various features to improve locomotive weight distribution, and incorporated his patents in* Hercules, *built in 1837 for the Beaver Meadow railroad. The two coupled axles had compensated springing, with a great cast iron compensation lever each side, while the bogie had a transverse spring above it, anchored at the centre. The locomotive frame thus had three-point suspension to give the best possible weight distribution and hence good riding characteristics.*

irregularities was seen as a real revolution and it was used from the earliest days. One of the engineers who spread its use was William Norris, who introduced it to Europe as well.

A decorative as well as functional feature of American locomotives which was to be retained for years to come appeared in 1831. This was the locomotive bell, mounted by Dripps on *John Bull* and then adopted by Baldwin on his second locomotive *E L Miller*. To Dripp also is attributed the first oil-burning headlight, evolved after Horatio Allen had tried to light the way ahead at night with a fire carried in a wagon in front of the locomotive.

A problem of the pioneers was the spark-throwing propensities of their locomotives, especially when fired with wood fuel. The sparks landed on the locomotive crews and passengers continuously, notwithstanding the

Gowan & Marx *A development of* Hercules *with increased grate area, obtained by raising the firebox above the frames so that its width was no longer restricted by the distance between them, and it could rest on them. Eastwick & Harrison delivered it to the Philadelphia & Reading in 1839 for freight traffic. As this road was comparatively level,* Gowan & Marx *succeeded in hauling a 423 tonne load of 101 wagons in 1840. It had a life of 20 years and news of its performance reached Europe, so that its builders received an order from Russia for similar locomotives to work the St Petersburg-Moscow railway. The rather mysterious name is not that of an inventor or locomotive builder, but that of a London banking house.*

Central of Georgia *Another great pioneer of the American railway, Matthias W Baldwin built an 0-6-0 with an articulated frame for the Central of Georgia railroad in 1842. The two leading axles were mounted in a kind of flexible parallelogram frame and thus, although the axles were coupled, could follow curves in the same fashion as Campbell's bogie. The arrangement was a success and Baldwin built 155 locomotives of this type by 1855. The locomotive was the first ever to haul a train of over 1000 tonnes, (consisting of 150 wagons).*

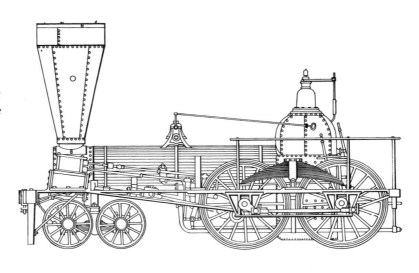

Camden & Amboy *Baldwin built an interesting locomotive for the C & A Railroad in 1846, although he had to acknowledge the patents of Campbell and Harrison to design this passenger 4-4-0. The outside frame was entirely metal and for the first time the coupled-axle box-frame brackets were made of cast iron. The two driving axles were sprung by enormous inverted leaf springs, while at the front the bogie had primary longitudinal springs. The large firebox was dropped between the two driving axles and still followed the design introduced by Bury 15 years before.*

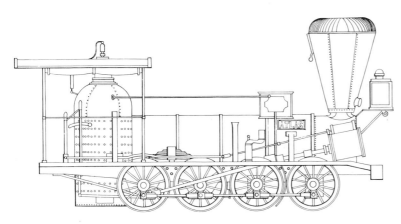

Atlas *Baldwin took out a patent in 1842 for an eight-coupled locomotive, based on his six-coupled design (which was then being received with approval) with an auxiliary frame. Baldwin delivered* Atlas *to the Philadelphia & Reading in 1846. It was a wood-fired inside-framed locomotive, with large inclined outside cylinders fixed to the smokebox. However, because of poor weight distribution its stability was not good, accentuated by the firebox's position outside the wheelbase at the end of the frames. It was claimed to be the first locomotive to have a shelter for the enginemen.*

Chesapeake *Septimus Norris built this locomotive in 1847 for the Philadelphia & Reading, at the time one of the most forward-looking railroads in America.* Chesapeake *was the first American 4-6-0 and the prototype of many others carrying the celebrated name Ten-Wheeler. The very long wheelbase made for difficulties when running through curves, so the first two coupled axles had no flanges on their wheels. When tried out on 19 March 1847,* Chesapeake *easily hauled 100 wagons in a train of 723 tonnes.*

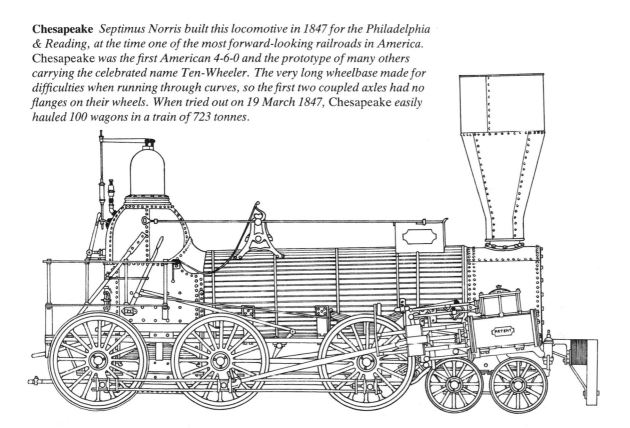

Chicago, Milwaukee, St. Paul & Pacific Railroad – 1848

Milwaukee & Waukesha Railroad – 1848

The American type

From about 1850 this legendary 4-4-0 locomotive type became a symbol of America's expansion towards the West. The picture of a locomotive crossing the boundless prairie at the head of a mixed train has entered the traditions and history of the United States. It was a universal type, used by all railroads for more than 30 years, hauling every sort of train. Some 25 000 were built. Its fame was not, however, limited to the New World, for the type found strong supporters – and fierce detractors – in Europe as well. Among evident qualities were its versatility and adaptability to heavy loads and all routes, its simple construction and its ready maintenance. The story of the American type, in all its fascinating technical, social and military aspects,

was crucial to the conquest of the West and is rich in anecdote. It is a matter of discussion if Campbell's 4-4-0 was the progenitor of the American type, but it was certainly the first 4-4-0. Three locomotives of the type are illustrated here: *Bob Ellis* built by Norris in 1848 for the Chicago, Milwaukee, St Paul & Pacific Railroad and which was the first locomotive to run in Wisconsin; *Fred Merril*, again built by Norris, was delivered to the Milwaukee & Waukesha Railroad in 1848 and is very similar to *Bob Ellis*. The last shown had distinctive variations and was also designed for the 6ft (1829mm) gauge used by the New York & Erie Railroad. It was the product of Swinburne in New Jersey, a small builder who disappeared in 1857. It was in these years that the familiar outline of these locomotives was developed, an outline that was seen from coast to coast until the end of the 19th century.

New York & Erie Railroad – 1848

Camel *Ross Winans of the Baltimore & Ohio designed a locomotive for heavy coal trains to replace the outmoded vertical-boiler two- and four-axle Crab machines. He had an eight-coupled locomotive built with a horizontal boiler and outside cylinders, a type that became known as the Camel because of the ample driver's cab mounted on top of the boiler. With its great area of glazed lights this cab gave full protection and an optimum view. The fireman was given scanty shelter on the tender, however, and could enter the cab only by climbing a staircase alongside the firebox. The first Camel was delivered in March 1848.*

great height of locomotive chimneys in those days. Again Dripps provided a solution. He tried a downward-pointing cone mounted inside the chimney in 1833, the cone bouncing back most of the sparks into the smokebox. This solution entailed the use of enormous smokestacks, the top circumference of which was often larger than that of the boiler. For greater protection, a fine metal mesh was fixed across the mouths of these smokestacks.

Among the many new ideas that Dripps introduced with *John Bull*—one which became common American locomotive practice—was the use of the cowcatcher. This prominent front-end fitting was designed to throw animals caught on the track clear of the wheels, and it is still placed on many American locomotives to this day.

Baldwin *This 0-8-0 of 1850 was an improved version of* Atlas. *Like the latter it had the articulated frame for which the builder had obtained a patent eight years before. In this 0-8-0, the wheelbase was increased and the axles of the two pairs at each end were farther apart, sufficient in the case of the rear pair to allow the insertion of the firebox between them. Connecting and coupling rods were of the maximum length acceptable, because the locomotive had to use track laid in haste and poorly ballasted. The locomotives served many years in North America, and Baldwin built a total of 150.*

Amoskeag *This express locomotive was built in 1851 by the Amoskeag Manufacturing Co of Manchester, New Hampshire. Although a 4-4-0 it differed from the near standard American type—it had outside frames, inside cylinders under the smokebox and a domed firebox. From the middle of the 19th century, a timber cab for the engineman became the usual thing.*

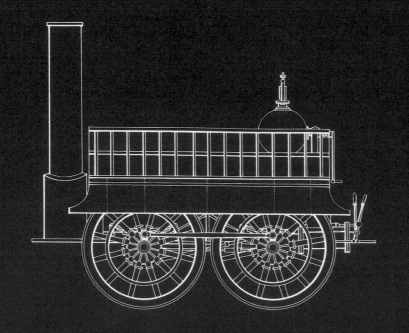

Pioneer Locomotive Building Schools

The Rainhill trials of 1829 aroused enormous British interest in both public and scientific circles. It was the first time that the steam locomotive had captured the attention of all social classes. Apart from their technical interest, the trials became a sporting event and it was estimated that 15000 spectators attended. The triumphant progress of Stephenson's *Rocket* at Rainhill was a great technical step forward and it marked not only the beginning of the end of the purely experimental period in the steam locomotive's brief history, but also the opening of a new phase of the story, the commercial exploitation of a revolutionary machine.

Robert Stephenson noted that *Rocket*–and its successor *Northumbrian*–showered water from the chimney. This led him to the conclusion that the steam inside the cylinders was being cooled excessively during the stroke of the pistons, so tending to condense. In his new locomotive *Planet*, built in 1830, he moved the cylinders' position and placed them horizontally under the smokebox, which permitted boiler steam to be used more rationally and

Wilberforce *Designed by Hackworth in 1833,* Wilberforce *was a development of* Royal George, *the latter having run successful trials on the Stockton & Darlington Railway. In* Wilberforce *all the axles were sprung, made possible by the main connecting rods from the pistons in the vertical cylinders driving a jackshaft, which in turn was coupled to the driving wheels. Smoke tubes were placed about the large firebox tube to aid steam production (as adopted by Stephenson and Seguin previously). Hackworth locomotives were not as advanced technically as those of Stephenson, but they were well-made, simple to maintain, and tough enough for heavy duty.* Wilberforce *and its sisters stayed in service hauling long coal trains for many years.*

productively. In making this move one major construction difficulty was met, the absolute necessity for an inside crank axle, which the metallurgists of the period found difficult to forge or to build up. *Planet* and its sisters, as well as *Samson* (a more powerful freight version) and the highly-successful *Patentee*, built shortly afterwards and discussed below, always had trouble with their crank axles. These were comparatively fragile and if one broke while the locomotive was running it could cause a bad accident, especially in the case of a two-axle locomotive (2-2-0 or 0-4-0).

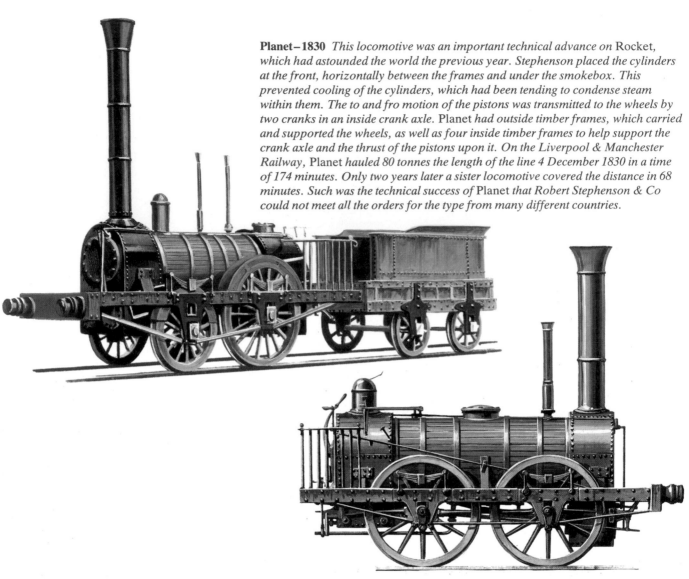

Planet – 1830 *This locomotive was an important technical advance on* Rocket, *which had astounded the world the previous year. Stephenson placed the cylinders at the front, horizontally between the frames and under the smokebox. This prevented cooling of the cylinders, which had been tending to condense steam within them. The to and fro motion of the pistons was transmitted to the wheels by two cranks in an inside crank axle.* Planet *had outside timber frames, which carried and supported the wheels, as well as four inside timber frames to help support the crank axle and the thrust of the pistons upon it. On the Liverpool & Manchester Railway,* Planet *hauled 80 tonnes the length of the line 4 December 1830 in a time of 174 minutes. Only two years later a sister locomotive covered the distance in 68 minutes. Such was the technical success of* Planet *that Robert Stephenson & Co could not meet all the orders for the type from many different countries.*

Samson *Built in 1832 by Robert Stephenson & Co for the Loire Railway in France (an amalgamation of the St Etienne-Lyons and the Andrézieux-Roanne lines). Sandwich timber frames were used, the timber reinforced both inside and outside by metal plates, and in general it was the first locomotive to adopt all the basic construction principles that were still used for locomotives more than a century later. It was built right up to the maximum axle load permitted at the time, 10 tonnes between the two axles.*

Austria *This was the locomotive that inaugurated the Kaiser Ferdinands Nordbahn in 1838, the first railway in Austria. Built by Stephenson in 1837, it was a Planet type of the improved Mercury series, in which in the timber frames were metal-plated (as in* Samson *and* Patentee*). The type was not a success in Austria and speedily displayed all the construction faults that the locomotives had shown in Great Britain. After a Planet type suffered a broken axle at speed in France in 1842, causing an accident that killed 55 passengers, an Imperial Chancellery decree banned the use of two-axle locomotives in the Austrian Empire.* Austria *was withdrawn altogether in 1846 and broken up in 1852.*

Planet was the progenitor of the modern locomotive nevertheless, for it had all the fundamental construction features that would be found in locomotives built over a century later, during the last and most brilliant period of steam. *Planet* was given robust outside frames built entirely of timber, a tubular boiler and a blast pipe. The crank axle was supported by no less than six frame-mounted bearings and it was driven directly from the pistons in the cylinders. Although it was an advanced overall concept for the period, however, *Planet* was not supported by adequate design of component parts or

Saxonia *Designed by Professor Andreas Schubert of Dresden, this locomotive was built by the Maschinenfabrik Ubigau and was one of the first to be built in Germany. It was the first German-built locomotive on the Leipzig-Dresden Railway in Saxony, which up to that time had imported engines from England and had had one from America. In 1841* Saxonia *had the rear carrying axle removed, but the experiment was not a success.*

Bury Liverpool–1830

The Bury Locomotive

Although his first locomotive could not take part in the Rainhill trials of 1829 as it was completed too late, Bury was one of the leading locomotive engineers of his day. His designs were distinguished by a upright, circular-section firebox, surmounted by a domed top. The lower part was a D-section, with the rounded part lying towards the tender. Bury used inside bar frames, all metal with no timber, and his machines were notably light and elegant. He was a strong advocate of two-axle locomotives and all his designs had either 2-2-0 or 0-4-0 wheel arrangement. As he was in charge of the motive power of the London & Birmingham Railway he

was able to put his theories into practice on that line for a number of years.

Liverpool was one of his most interesting designs. Intended for freight service it had the largest driving wheels seen up to that time, 6ft in diameter (1829mm). The other type shown here was a passenger single-driver, built for the London & Birmingham in 1837. Bury locomotives were well-designed and well-built, but they were too small and had insufficient power to cope with steadily increasing train weights. It was not unusual to see three or even four locomotives used on one train.

Bury locomotive–1837

Hercules *Built by Robert Stephenson and delivered to a line built by his father George (the Stanhope & Tyne) in 1833. The design reproduced the good features of* Samson, *with a rear carrying axle for the first time – in effect a freight version of* Patentee. *It was a large locomotive with 4ft 6in (1370mm) driving wheels and a weight in working order of about 14 tonnes. It was the prototype of a large family of locomotives that gave good service in British coalfields.*

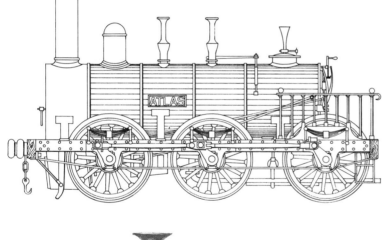

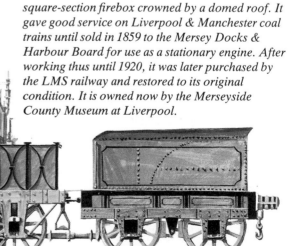

details, still less by sound workmanship and skilled assembly.

It was unfortunate that Robert Stephenson & Co's works at Newcastle lacked a firm and competent technical head at the time, and the owners, father and son, George and Robert Stephenson, were fully engaged in planning and constructing new railways and in designing new motive power and rolling stock. They had no time to supervise their own workshops and to insist that the quality of the work done in them matched their design concepts. In fact, this construction situation broadly typified the period between 1830 and 1840 everywhere, and it certainly did not help the reputation of the steam locomotive for mechanical reliability.

Atlas *This locomotive was built by Stephenson in 1834 for the Leicester & Swannington Railway and was derived from the* Hercules *of the previous year, save that there were three driving axles to augment adhesion and haulage capacity. It was one of the first outside-frame 0-6-0s with all axles sprung, and had a large boiler with a high-capacity firebox between the second and third axles. To allow the locomotive to run through curves of a small radius the middle pair of wheels were flangeless, a feature taken from Stephenson's new Patentee type. Atlas created a new locomotive type, much appreciated for freight working throughout Great Britain for many years afterwards. Indeed this sort of locomotive was built in large numbers up to 1890.*

Lion *Built in 1838 by Todd, Kitson & Laird with the 0-4-2 wheel arrangement, this locomotive had a square-section firebox crowned by a domed roof. It gave good service on Liverpool & Manchester coal trains until sold in 1859 to the Mersey Docks & Harbour Board for use as a stationary engine. After working thus until 1920, it was later purchased by the LMS railway and restored to its original condition. It is owned now by the Merseyside County Museum at Liverpool.*

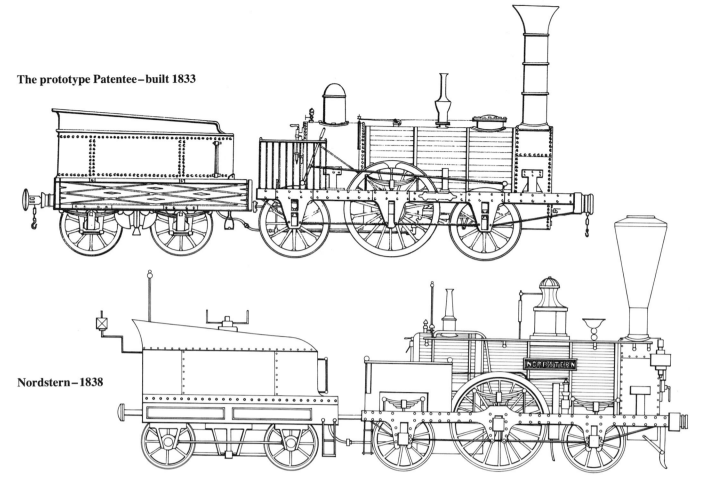

The prototype Patentee – built 1833

Nordstern – 1838

The Patentee

The Planet type locomotives were recognised as revolutionary machines in their day, although in service various defects in the design were soon recognised. Principal among them was the short wheelbase with the firebox outside it at the rear. This arrangement caused the locomotive to pitch continually when running, with consequent risk of derailment.

In October 1833, Stephenson took out a patent for a three-axle locomotive (a single-driver with carrying wheels front and rear). The arrangement not only corrected the previous design fault but allowed a larger boiler to be fitted. Thus was born the Patentee, one of the most famous locomotive types, not only because of its technical innovations but above all because of its widespread use in many other European countries.

Among the innovations used on it (which were patented – hence *Patentee*, the name of the first locomotive of the type) were a steam counterpressure brake, the abolition of flanges on the driving wheels, metal plating on both sides of the timber frames to increase rigidity and strength, and plate metal axlebox brackets or guards for all three axles. The cylinders were

placed inside and under the smokebox as in the previous type. The Patentee type was, in short, the Planet type with an extra carrying axle at the rear.

During the decade 1835–1845, the Patentee type was adopted by nearly all the locomotive builders of Great Britain, although each of them tried to retain their own design variations. As well as Robert Stephenson & Co itself, Sharp, Roberts & Co, Mather Dixon, Hawthorn, Rothwell and other works all built the Patentee type in large numbers. Other countries in Europe built Patentees in quantity as well, particularly France and Germany, while many British-built locomotives of this kind were used all over the continent.

Among the more important were *Nordstern* in Austria, built by Rennie in London in 1838

An Alais-Beaucaire Patentee – 1839

and arranged for wood-firing, with a large spark-arresting chimney. This was one of the largest and heaviest of the Patentee type, with $80lb/in^2$ boiler pressure ($5.6kg/cm^2$), a heating surface of $535ft^2$ ($49.7m^2$), driving wheel diameter 6ft (1829mm), and a weight in working order of 14.5 tonnes. A Patentee type built by Robert Stephenson & Co ran on the Alais-Beaucaire railway in France and two Patentees, *Snelheid* and *Arend*, were the first locomotives to run in Holland in 1839. From the same builder, but slightly smaller, came *Adler*, the first passenger locomotive to run in Germany, which inaugurated the pioneer Nuremburg-Fürth Railway on 26 October 1835, carried the Stephenson works number 118 and cost, it is recorded, 13,930 florins. Its driver on the opening day was an Englishman named Wilson.

The first locomotive built in Belgium was a Patentee, appropriately named *Le Belge*. The original design came from Robert Stephenson & Co, which firm licensed manufacturers in other countries to build Patentees. The driving wheel diameter of *Le Belge* was 5ft (1524mm), it

developed 40hp and had a maximum speed of 37¼mph (60km/h). A Patentee was also the first locomotive in Italy. The Kingdom of Naples inaugurated 5 miles (8km) of railway between Naples and Portici on 8 October 1839 and used a Patentee built by Longridge & Starbuck of Newcastle. This locomotive was named *Bayard*, after the promoter and builder of the line, Armand Bayard. It developed 65hp, weighed 13 tonnes in working order, and could run at 31mph (50km/h) with a seven-coach train weighing 46 tonnes. Another well-known Patentee was *Der Münchener*, built in Munich by a famous pioneer of the German railway industry, Joseph Anton Ritter von Maffei.

In Russia yet another Patentee built by Stephenson was the first locomotive to run there, on a St Petersburg-Pavlovsk railway in April 1838. The line was 6ft (1829mm) gauge,

Le Belge – 1835

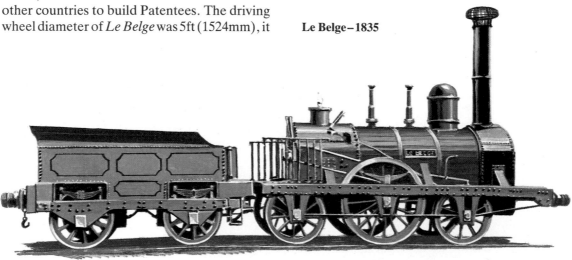

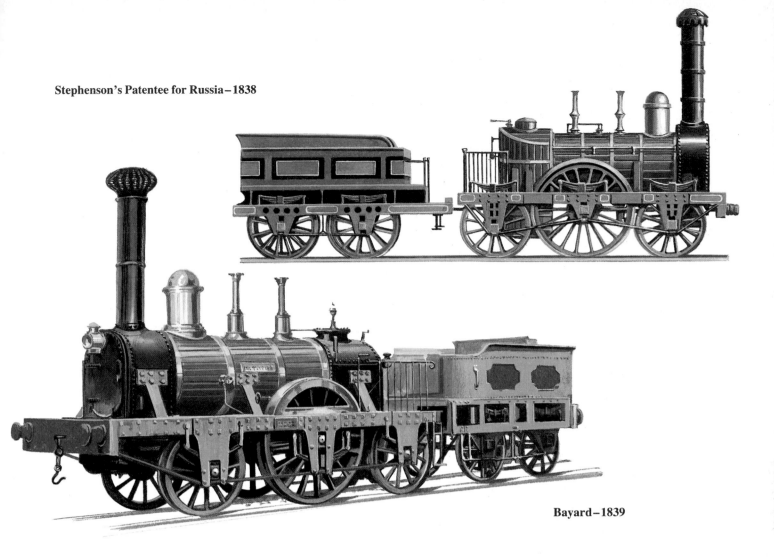

Stephenson's Patentee for Russia – 1838

Bayard – 1839

considerably wider than the standard 4ft 8½in (1435mm) gauge used elsewhere in Europe. This Russian railway was built by a Czech, Franz Anton von Gerstner, who to test quality and performance, ordered locomotives from three different British builders, Stephenson, Tayleur and Hackworth.

A Patentee was used by a Frenchman, Clapeyron, to conduct experiments which resulted in another advance in the design of the

steam locomotive. On the *Gironde*, a Patentee built in France by Le Creusot for the Paris-Versailles (Rive Droite) railway, he made alterations to the valve gear so that the admission of steam to the cylinder was cut off once the piston had completed 70 per cent of its stroke. For the remainder of the stroke the steam expanding in the cylinder did the work and the consumption of boiler steam was thus reduced.

Gironde – 1840

Der Münchner – 1841

Sharp type *This was simply a Patentee in which the frame was curved over the driving axle. It had been found that the depth of the axle-guards of a normal Patentee was such that they tended to work loose from the frame in service. The Sharp type allowed the guards to be shortened to avoid this trouble. Because of the frame curve, the Sharp was considered more pleasing in appearance than the usual locomotive and the one shown here, built for the Northern Railway of France in 1838, was particularly elegant.*

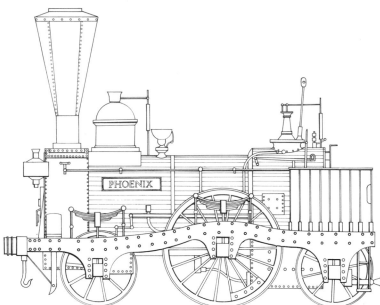

Phoenix *Sharp, Roberts built this locomotive in 1841 for the Kaiser Ferdinands Nordbahn. It was a wood burner and of the typical Sharp design that improved on that of the Patentee. Driving wheels were 5ft 6¾in (1700mm) diameter and the weight in working order was over 15 tonnes. The Austrian feature of a boiler filler cup behind the dome will be noted.*

Badenia *Emil Kessler built Badenia at Karlsruhe in 1841 as a copy of six 2-2-2 locomotives supplied by Sharp to the Baden Railway in 1839. The Patentee design was followed in general for the 5ft 3in gauge (1600mm) used briefly by this railway. Badenia had cylinders under the smokebox, a grate area of 10ft² (0.93m²), a heating surface of 457ft² (42.5m²) and a weight in working order of 16.2 tonnes. The locomotive could attain 28mph (45km/h).*

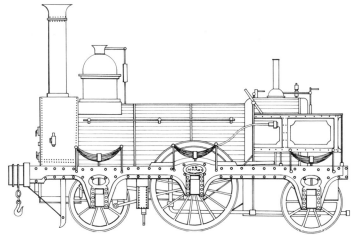

Sharp *In England these locomotives were commonly nicknamed 'Sharpies'. This one was built for the Sheffield & Manchester Railway in 1843, and the characteristic curvature of the frame is less in evidence than usual. The rudimentary plate shield for the footplate is an improvement over the usual railing, while the squared seating for the dome is a characteristic 'Sharpie' feature.*

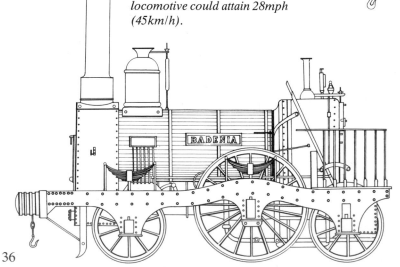

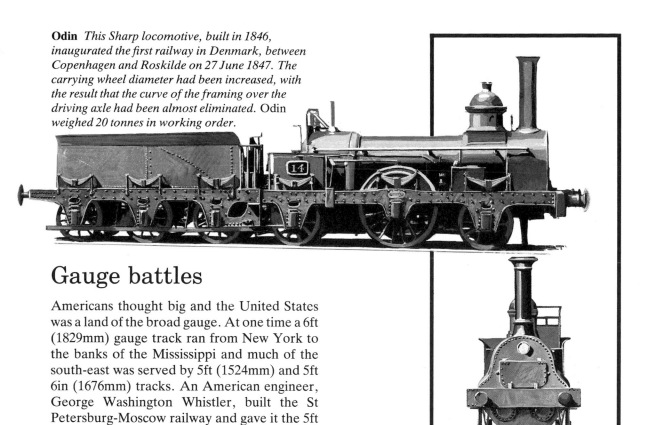

Odin *This Sharp locomotive, built in 1846, inaugurated the first railway in Denmark, between Copenhagen and Roskilde on 27 June 1847. The carrying wheel diameter had been increased, with the result that the curve of the framing over the driving axle had been almost eliminated. Odin weighed 20 tonnes in working order.*

Gauge battles

Americans thought big and the United States was a land of the broad gauge. At one time a 6ft (1829mm) gauge track ran from New York to the banks of the Mississippi and much of the south-east was served by 5ft (1524mm) and 5ft 6in (1676mm) tracks. An American engineer, George Washington Whistler, built the St Petersburg-Moscow railway and gave it the 5ft (1524mm) gauge still used by the vast Soviet Railways system. In the United States, however, broad gauge had vanished by 1887, as it did in Great Britain.

When the Great Western Railway was authorised to build a railway from London to Bristol on 31 August 1835, its engineer Isambard Kingdom Brunel proposed a gauge of 7ft 0¼in (2141mm), the widest ever used, which caused a lively episode in British railway history. Brunel maintained that the standard gauge then in use did not allow a firebox sufficiently large to give the highest rate of steam production, nor was a low centre of gravity possible for the rolling stock, both attributes being necessary to reach the highest speeds according to the thinking of the day. Therefore the GWR used the broad gauge, Brunel making sure that the line was as straight as practicable and that all curves were of the largest possible radius.

It was a decision that greatly disturbed railway circles, and there was even more criticism when Daniel Gooch, a young man of twenty-one in 1837, was put in charge of GWR locomotives. Gooch discarded the first inefficient locomotives and had two Patentees modified for the broad gauge by Robert Stephenson & Co. These had originally been intended for the 5ft 6in (1676mm) gauge New Orleans Railroad and were named *North Star* and *Morning Star*. Their performance was impressive. In 1838, *North Star* hauled a 46-tonne passenger train at an average speed of 38mph (62km/h), reaching a top speed of 45mph (72km/h).

Encouraged by the prestige of such results the Great Western expanded its routes, thus coming into collision with standard gauge towards the north and stirring up public debate. By June 1845 Parliament had to take a hand, setting up a Royal Commission to go into the question and to make recommendations. It was a battle fought not only by politicians, financiers and large landowners but by the engineers. On the one hand were Gooch and his friends, who backed the broad gauge as the only means of increasing locomotive power and speed; on the other hand were those–the majority–who maintained that the same aims could be attained on the standard gauge. In 1845 Great Britain had 1900 route miles (3062km) of standard gauge as against only 274 miles (442km) of broad gauge, which was a considerable factor in the argument.

North Star *Intended originally for the New Orleans Railroad in the United States, this locomotive was rebuilt for the 7ft 0¼in (2141mm) gauge of the Great Western, on which its performance supported the claims of Brunel.* North Star *was a Patentee, modified for the broad gauge, and hauled about 50 tonnes at a maximum speed of 45mph (72km/h). Along with* Morning Star, *it showed that most previous broad gauge locomotive designs were quite unsatisfactory, and further enhanced the reputation for flexibility and efficiency of the Patentee type. They had driving wheels as large as 7ft (2134mm) diameter and weighed 21 tonnes in working order.*

Iron Duke *Designed by Daniel Gooch and built in the Great Western's own works at Swindon in 1847. The possibility of a larger firebox and thus greater steam production was an advantage claimed by the broad gauge.* Iron Duke *had metal-plated outside teak frames, with three more frames inside between the cylinders and the firebox. The new 4-2-2 wheel arrangement assured stable running, but called for curves of ample radius.*

Lord of the Isles *This locomotive repeated the design of* Iron Duke *in general, and was built in 1851. It gave 30 years service running express trains. There were 29 in the class and, when the broad gauge was finally abolished on 20 May 1892, 23 were still in service.*

To support his ideas, Gooch had another large Patentee built, in only thirteen weeks, which, in June 1846, covered the 77.3 miles (124.4km) from London to Swindon at an average speed of 59½mph (96km/h). This was followed by a 4-2-2 type, the Firefly class, which included such well-known names as *Iron Duke* and *Lord of the Isles*. Even today, these are considered to be among the finest examples of steam power and engineering elegance, and they demonstrated amply what could be accomplished on the broad gauge.

Broad gauge nevertheless lost the battle, despite its supporters alleging falsification of the figures in their disgruntlement. The Royal Commission report stated that the full value of the railway system could be obtained only if all were of standard gauge, adding that the broad gauge was more costly to build. The last broad gauge Great Western train ran in May 1892.

Long boiler locomotives

On the Planet and Patentee types it had been observed that much of the heat in the firebox was not being used effectively. Furthermore it appeared that, because of the larger firebox and boiler made possible on the broad gauge of Brunel, more steam was produced for the locomotive. Robert Stephenson designed a boiler with longer tubes running through the barrel, which also entailed a longer barrel. To this lengthened barrel he added a square-section firebox, with a domed roof in which steam was collected for the cylinders, instead of in a dome on the barrel. In addition, his new design abandoned outside frames and relied on

Sézanne *Built in 1847 by Alfred Hallette for the Montereau-Troyes line, this locomotive was used in 1868 for a trial of oil-firing in place of coal. Sézanne had a weight in working order in excess of 20 tonnes and an 8.4 tonne adhesive weight. Maximum speed was 37¼mph (60km/h). It has survived until today because it was regarded as a reserve locomotive for over 50 years. It is now in the Mulhouse French Railway Museum, completely restored to original condition.*

Great A *Among the more outstanding long boiler locomotives was Robert Stephenson & Co's design for the London & North Western Railway. Two carrying axles in front were on a long wheelbase, while the driving axle was at the rear. Although its appearance was pleasing,* Great A *aroused much discussion, for it had 7ft (2134mm) driving wheels, the largest ever fitted to a long boiler locomotive. Some of the general type remained in service in Egypt until the early 1900s.*

L'Aigle *Built by Robert Stephenson & Co in 1846 for the Avignon-Marseilles Railway (later incorporated into the Paris, Lyons & Mediterranean). All characteristics of the long boiler type can be seen, with horizontal cylinders at one end balanced by the square domed firebox at the other, and the long boiler barrel for good steaming. The locomotive is now in the Mulhouse Railway Museum.*

Tarasque *Belonging to a class of long boiler locomotives built by Le Benet for the Avignon-Marseilles Railway in 1846, with the wheel arrangement changed from 2-2-2 to 4-2-0 to avoid the pitching and hunting motions characteristic of the type, just as had been done by Stephenson for the* Great A. *As a result of the change* Tarasque *had an adhesive weight of 12 tonnes in place of 10 tonnes, while the wheelbase was increased from 10ft 3in (3150mm) to 13ft 2in (4050mm) to give improved running.*

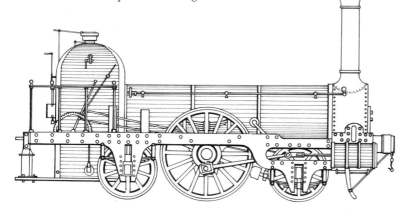

Nord No 17–50 *Designed by Clapeyron and built for the Northern Railway of France in 1846, this locomotive followed the Stephenson long boiler design, save that a stout outside frame was reintroduced for the bearings of the carrying axles and for the cylinders. The locomotives were unsteady when running and, to effect a cure, the back carrying axle was later placed to the rear of the firebox, increasing the wheelbase from 10ft 3in (3150mm) to 13ft 2in (4050mm). The idea was successful.*

inside frames only.

The long boiler called for an increase in the wheelbase to carry it, but this could not be provided because the locomotive's length would then exceed the length of the turntables then in use. So Stephenson reverted to the old Planet design and mounted the firebox at the rear of the frames, outside the wheelbase. This was a design compromise, but the long boiler locomotives were popular, although more so in Europe generally than in Great Britain.

Robert Stephenson & Co granted licences to other manufacturers to enable them to build the new long boiler design. French licensees objected that manufacturing high quality crank axles for inside cylinders was beyond their resources, so Stephenson revised the design, using outside cylinders to meet their objection. With the cylinders and connecting rods outside, more easily fabricated outside cranks were possible and the inside crank axle disappeared.

Despite all this, the greater steaming capacity of the long boiler could not be fully used because of a pitching motion at speed, induced by the overhanging firebox at one end and overhanging cylinders and smokebox at the other. Stephenson tried to get over this difficulty in 1845, by building the *Great A* with a 4-2-0 extended wheelbase. Comparative trials with a broad gauge Firefly class locomotive of the same wheel arrangement showed that the *Great A* could not match its rival, and the extended wheel arrangement did not entirely eliminate the pitching motion.

Ernst August *The long boiler locomotive in Germany followed the evolutionary path of the type in England and other European countries. To replace Planet and Patentee locomotives, many railways in the German states of the time adopted the long boiler from Stephenson and other British builders.* Ernst August *was German-built and the first product of Georg Egestorff of Linden, a suburb of Hanover. His firm was the predecessor of Hanomag.* Ernst August *went into service on the Hanover Railway in 1846, and its design showed several differences from the British prototypes. Among them were the inclined cylinders, a dome on the first ring of the boiler, and a traditional firebox instead of a square-section box with a domed roof.*

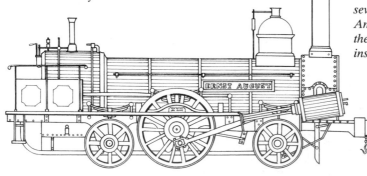

Centre Railway *The Centre Railway, later part of the Paris-Orleans Railway, put this locomotive type into service between 1846 and 1847, some built by Schneider and others built in the company's own Ivry works. They were of the classic long boiler type, save that the wheel arrangement was 2-4-0 with the coupled wheels of 5ft 3in (1600mm) diameter. The locomotives were used for both passenger and mixed traffic trains on various routes and they reached 31mph (50km/h) when hauling 180 tonnes. One of the class hauled a 51 wagon train of 340 tonnes in 1847. The last of them was withdrawn from traffic in 1878.*

Glück Auf *This was one of the first German 2-4-0s, built by Richard Hartmann of Chemnitz in 1848, and delivered to the Saxony-Bavaria Railway. It had 4ft 11in (1500mm) driving wheels and weighed 24 tonnes in working order. While otherwise a classical long boiler design, the firebox was no longer square in cross-section and carried a large dome.*

Paris-Orleans No 157 *The first locomotive designed by Camille Polonceau, built in 1850. Polonceau proposed to replace the mixed locomotive stock of the railway, and this 2-4-0 was one of his standard classes. A long boiler was retained, but with the firebox continuing its shell, and with inside cylinders. The outside frame was of the sandwich type (iron and timber) and there were two internal frames. Valves were outside the cylinders to aid maintenance.*

Baden Railway *The four-coupled locomotive could handle passenger and mixed traffic trains, but something more powerful was needed for freight and mountain work. A six-coupled long boiler design was attempted in Germany, and eight were built for the Baden Railway by Emil Kessler of Karlsruhe in 1845. The locomotive shown here hauled a 472 tonne train at a maximum speed of 16¾mph (27km/h) when on trial.*

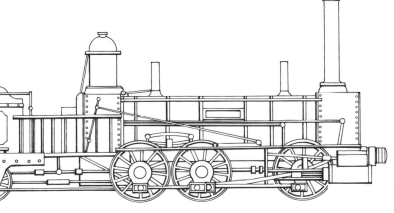

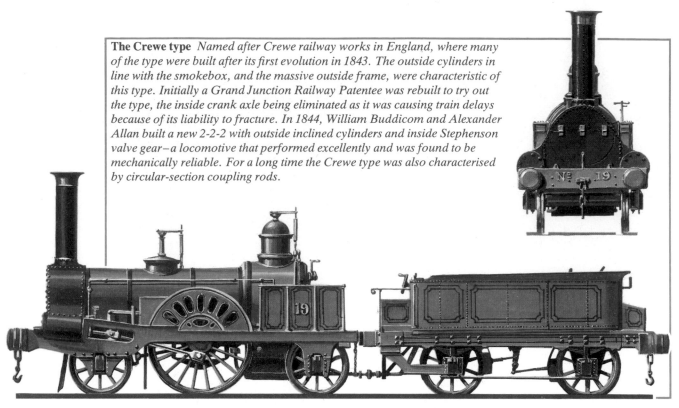

The Crewe type *Named after Crewe railway works in England, where many of the type were built after its first evolution in 1843. The outside cylinders in line with the smokebox, and the massive outside frame, were characteristic of this type. Initially a Grand Junction Railway Patentee was rebuilt to try out the type, the inside crank axle being eliminated as it was causing train delays because of its liability to fracture. In 1844, William Buddicom and Alexander Allan built a new 2-2-2 with outside inclined cylinders and inside Stephenson valve gear – a locomotive that performed excellently and was found to be mechanically reliable. For a long time the Crewe type was also characterised by circular-section coupling rods.*

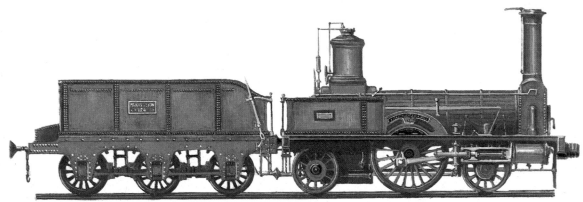

Lyons Railway *Designed by Alexis Barrault and built by the French firm of Cail in 1847, this locomotive was the prototype of a class that ran for many years on the Lyons Railway and its successor the PLM. Derived from the Stephenson long boiler type, it had improved running stability because the rear axle was placed behind the firebox, the wheelbase being thus increased. Nicknamed Perraches, the locomotives hauled passenger trains of up to nine coaches – 60 tonnes weight – at up to 37¼mph (60km/h).*

Saint Pierre *William Buddicom introduced the Crewe type to France, designing locomotives known to the French as Buddicoms. Buddicoms had outside inclined cylinders, a stout double frame, and a deep firebox placed between the second and third axles.* Saint Pierre *was built at Rouen in 1844, and is now on show at the Mulhouse French Railways Museum.*

The European Norris

William Norris, as we have seen already, was an engineer noted for producing locomotives of advanced design and for being a pioneer of standard interchangeable locomotive components to facilitate construction and maintenance. He was also a sound businessman who sold his locomotives outside the United States, in both Canada and Europe. In the Old World the first Norris locomotive imported was the *Philadelphia*, landed at Trieste in January 1838. This had been ordered by Schönerer, of the Vienna-Raab Railway (now known as Györ), and by 1844 the Austrians had ordered another nine locomotives from Norris, with a request for another four that year. William and his brother Octavius were interested in this European market and travelled from the United States in 1844 to open a new works on the northern side of Vienna, which started production in 1846. Initially this seemed to open up a wide prospect of profitable operations, but what was not foreseen was the rapid rise of the European locomotive industry. The great success of Norris-type locomotives induced many European builders to try their hand with designs based on (or more or less based on) the Norris. The Norris brothers had left it too late, and their Vienna works built no more than half-a-dozen

Jenny Lind *David Joy designed this locomotive, which was built by E B Wilson & Co in 1847 for the London Brighton & South Coast Railway. It was one of the many variations of Stephenson's basic Patentee design. Although double-framed like a Patentee, the outside frame bore the carrying wheel axleboxes only, and the driving wheel axleboxes were supported by the inside frame. Stephenson's valve gear was fitted and for the first time boiler pressure rose as high as 120lb/in^2 (8.45kg/cm^2). Jenny Lind ran well above 50mph (80km/h) during its first trials and showed a stability in running that was unknown up to that time. This was due to the length of the wheelbase and the transverse play given to the leading axle. Many more of this general type were built over a period of 40 years.*

Berlin-Potsdam *One of the first railways in Europe to import the Norris 4-2-0 locomotive from Philadelphia. They were of the classic Norris type with a Bury firebox, inclined cylinders fixed to the smokebox, and with a short-wheelbase bogie. Results on straight and level German railways were not as good as they had been on the American 'roads with their frequent gradients. The Norris designs were found to be unstable at the higher speeds needed, and ended their days as workshop stationary engines.*

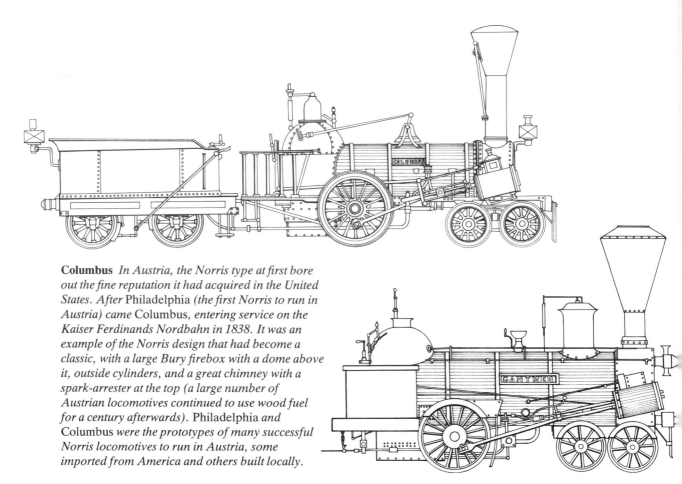

Columbus *In Austria, the Norris type at first bore out the fine reputation it had acquired in the United States. After* Philadelphia *(the first Norris to run in Austria) came* Columbus, *entering service on the Kaiser Ferdinands Nordbahn in 1838. It was an example of the Norris design that had become a classic, with a large Bury firebox with a dome above it, outside cylinders, and a great chimney with a spark-arrester at the top (a large number of Austrian locomotives continued to use wood fuel for a century afterwards).* Philadelphia *and* Columbus *were the prototypes of many successful Norris locomotives to run in Austria, some imported from America and others built locally.*

Ganymed *Wenzel Günther, formerly of the Wien-Raab Railway, built this locomotive at his works in Wiener Neustadt in 1846, established four years before.* Ganymed, *and other Norris type locomotives built subsequently, followed the basic Norris design, but variations were made to adapt the locomotives to conditions on Austrian railways at that time.* Ganymed *was larger than the American prototype, with 4ft 1½in (1260mm) driving wheels, a boiler pressure of 77lb/in² (5.4kg/cm²) and a large dome on the front ring of the boiler barrel. The bogie had leaf springs for each axle and the weight in working order was 17.6 tonnes, of which 10.4 tonnes was adhesive weight.*

Koloss *Built by Günther for the Kaiser Ferdinands Nordbahn in 1844, this locomotive was the first Austrian 2-4-0. It was developed from the Norris type but differed considerably. Coupled axles were provided on the lengthy wheelbase of 11ft 7in (3530mm) to provide maximum adhesive weight: at 17.4 tonnes, this figure was considered to be very high. It was divided equally, with 8.7 tonnes on each driving axle.* Koloss *had the first Austrian six-wheel tender, with a design that seemed to make it an integral part of the locomotive itself.*

Wurtemburg Railway *This locomotive was built by Emil Kessler in 1846 and was based in general on three Norris 4-4-0s supplied to the Wurtemburg Railway between 1844 and 1845. There were major differences from the original, however, the German builder fitting a square-section long-boiler firebox, while the cylinders were mounted horizontally. Stephenson's valve gear and slide valves were installed, while the coupled axles had compensated springing with the compensation lever anchored to the frames.*

locomotives for the Kaiser Ferdinands Nordbahn and the Austrian Northern State Railway.

There were technical reasons for the European railways turning against the pure Norris type, exemplified by the *Philadelphia*. The firebox overhanging the wheelbase led to the familiar pitching motion at speed, and the Austrians decided that this was accentuated at times by the design of the leading bogie. Numerous Norris type locomotives were built in Austria and Germany with the bogie replaced by a single leading axle.

In Austria there were many works which copied the Norris type. John Haswell built his first Norris 4-2-0 in 1841, named *Wien* in honour of the city in which his works were situated. Wenzel Günther started his operations in Wiener Neustadt in 1842 by building a Norris 4-2-0, although in his case he altered and re-designed some of the American details. George Sigl also started his works in 1842 by building a Norris 4-2-0. The Norris brothers' Vienna works were actually alongside those of Sigl, who

took the Norris establishment over after the brothers' unhappy Austrian experience closed their operation there. The Sigl and Günther works came together later on, in 1867.

In Belgium, the American influence was much felt in locomotive design. Cockerill of Seraing (a suburb of Liège) built some 36 Norris 4-2-0s during the years 1844–1847 and 37 4-4-0s, also of Norris-based design, during the years 1844–1853. Norris practice in locomotive building had little effect in France, however: Koechlin of Mulhouse was the sole builder to produce Norris 4-2-0s, producing eight during 1844–1845 for the Austrian Northern State Railway. Even these few were much modified from the true Norris, with horizontal cylinders instead of inclined, and an enormous cylindrical-section vertical firebox.

Where the Norris locomotive type had its greatest effect was in Germany. William Norris exported 21 of the 4-2-0 type there during the years 1839–1841, of which two (*Prussia* and *America*) were for the Berlin-Potsdam Rail-

Royal Neapolitan Railroads *William Norris of Philadelphia built one 4-2-0 for this line in 1843 and eight 4-4-0s in 1846 (works Nos 351–358). The 4-4-0 is shown here as it ran on the Roman Railroads 30 years after building, with added cab and other modifications. It differed from previous Norris 4-4-0s in its extended wheelbase and in carrying the Bury firebox between the driving wheels. The piston and coupling rods were unusually long, the boiler had 126 tubes and the boiler pressure was 86lb/in² (6kg/cm²). Eighteen modified Norris 4-4-0s from European builders also ran on other Italian railways.*

Borsig *Around 1840, enthusiasm for the Norris type was being shown by almost the entire European locomotive industry apart from that of Britain and France. British locomotive practice had previously held a monopoly in Germany, but the Norris type appeared to be an important advance. When August Borsig built his first locomotive in the Berlin district of Moabit he took his design from Philadelphia practice, although Borsig had a longer boiler than the Norris prototype, with a carrying axle at the rear. This greatly reduced the pitching motion otherwise caused by the firebox overhanging the wheelbase. On 21 July 1844 Borsig had a triumphant first trial run on the railway to Jüterborg, taking ten minutes less than a British locomotive which was run for comparison.*

Beuth *Built by Borsig for the Berlin-Anhalt Railway in 1843, this locomotive had a cleaner appearance than others derived from the Norris type. The bogie was abandoned and a return made to the 2-2-2 wheel arrangement. Borsig double slide valves were a technical feature that had some influence on later development.*

Drache *The first locomotive built by Henschel of Cassel in 1848, and one of the first in which the characteristics of the various design schools were combined. The boiler, for example, derived from the British long boiler type and the square Stephenson firebox was fitted, but the short wheelbase bogie and the 4-4-0 wheel arrangement came from Norris practice. The coupling rods were built up from two metal bars. Although well-designed and well-built, Henschel designs had no great success at first, and it was not until 1860 that their 50th locomotive was completed.* Drache *went to the North Hesse Railway.*

way, and 15 of the rest for the Berlin-Frankfurt Railway. Furthermore, the 4-4-0 version enjoyed initial success on the Wurtemburg, Hanover and Hesse railways, but from the end of 1840, European manufacturers took over the supply of Norris type locomotives to German railways. Emil Kessler of Karlsruhe (later Maschinenfabrik Esslingen) built them for the Wurtemburg Railway until 1853, while the Belgian builder

Cockerill supplied both 4-2-0 and 4-4-0 locomotives of the Norris type. The later famous names Borsig and Henschel, both started by building the Norris type, although in each case with design variations of their own. Norris locomotives were received with reluctance in Great Britain, although the Birmingham & Gloucester Railway acquired 17 4-2-0s starting in March 1839, all built in Philadelphia. They came in time to be regarded as too small and not up to hauling heavy trains for long distances. In the country where the steam locomotive was born, a foreign product was bound to be looked at with some hostility, but it is fair to say that much of the criticism arose because the locomotive's boiler pressure was reduced from 75lb/in^2 (5.2kg/cm^2) to 60lb/in^2 (4.2kg/cm^2) in England for safety reasons. This meant that the full power of the Norris design could not be used to demonstrate its superiority over others.

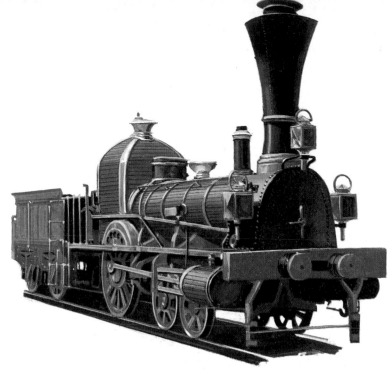

Steinbrück *Built by Haswell of Vienna for the Austrian Southern State Railway in 1848, this was a modified Norris type from four years previously, and was to be supplied to various Austrian and Hungarian railways until 1857. The Steinbrück type was known popularly as Kleine Gloggnitzer, for the original locomotives ran on the Vienna to Gloggnitz Railway. It was a 4-4-0 with 14½in by 23in cylinders (368mm by 579mm), driving wheels 4ft 7¾in in diameter (1420mm) and had a weight in working order of 23 tonnes, 15 tonnes of which was adhesive weight. On the Mürzzuschlag-Laibach (now known as Ljubljana) section, these locomotives could haul passenger trains of up to 135 tonnes and freights up to 290 tonnes over the 1 in 130 (0.77 per cent) ruling gradient. Steinbrück was sold to the Graz-Köflach Railway in 1860, where it was renamed Söding and worked until 1878. Today it is in the Vienna Railway Museum.*

Limmat *The first locomotive to run in Switzerland, built by Kessler in 1847. It was basically a Norris 4-2-0 prototype much modified, evident in the horizontal cylinders mounted ahead of the bogie and in the British-type long boiler and firebox. The cylinders, boiler and firebox are lagged in polished mahogany. Bought for about 35 000 francs, it ran on the Zurich-Baden Railway and was in service until 1882, receiving a new boiler in 1866. A full-scale reproduction is shown in the Lucerne Transport Museum.*

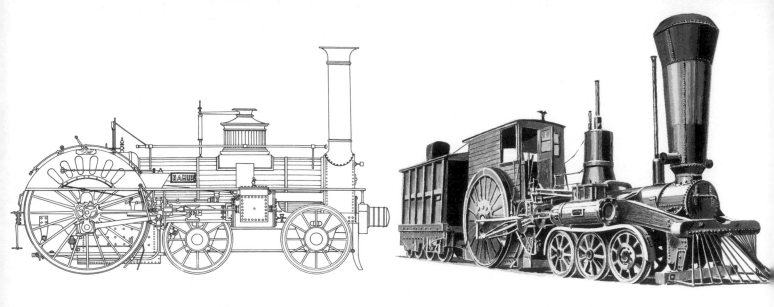

Namur *Built 1845 by Tulk & Ley of Whitehaven and designed by Thomas Crampton. Design innovations were the 4-2-0 wheel arrangement with the carrying axles on a long wheelbase, the driving wheels at the extreme rear, the outside cylinders mounted between the two carrying axles, and the deep firebox just ahead of the enormous driving wheels.*

John Stevens *William Norris built eight Cramptons for the Camden & Amboy Railroad in 1848. The designer was John Stevens, who provided 8ft 2¾in (2480mm) driving wheels and a three-axle bogie to carry the boiler barrel. The cylinders were very long, 37½in by 13in (965mm by 330mm), and mounted outside the frame with complicated valve gear. The boiler firedoor was under the driving wheel axle, with a correspondingly low platform for the fireman, while the driver's cab was high up above the boiler.*

The Crampton type

Express locomotive design in the middle of the last century had two main objectives, firstly to provide as large a diameter driving wheel as practicable, and secondly to keep the centre of gravity as low as possible. One result was the Crampton type, revolutionary in its day, in which a pair of enormous driving wheels was placed to the rear of the firebox, and the boiler was carried by two or three leading pairs of wheels. Thomas Russell Crampton, who had worked with Gooch on the Great Western, was the designer of a locomotive in which a deep firebox was carried between the second and third axles and, to avoid connecting rods of excessive length, the cylinders were brought to the rear and mounted between the first and second axles. Crampton was successful in persuading a British concern building the Namur-Liège Railway to order two prototype locomotives in 1845. However, there were

various difficulties in completing the railway, so the locomotives went on loan to the London & North Western Railway for a time. The LNWR was in competition with the Great Western Railway and the advent of *Namur* (renamed *London* while in England) created technical rivalry between the two, which was regarded as a sporting contest by the greatly interested general public. *London* took 12 coaches from London to Wolverton at an average speed of 58½mph (94km/h) with a top speed of 65mph (105km/h). Soon afterwards the Great Western extended one of their new 4-2-0 Firefly class and the speed record returned to the broad gauge. Crampton's reply was *Liverpool*, with a greater heating surface and higher boiler pressure than its rivals, although of increased weight. Records of the time claim that *Liverpool* reached 77½mph (126km/h), but the LNWR main line was not as favourable for sustained speed as that

Liverpool *The prototype of a second generation of Cramptons, built in 1848. To increase heating surface, the boiler contained 300 tubes, and an extra carrying axle was added to support the boiler barrel without increasing the wheelbase by much.*

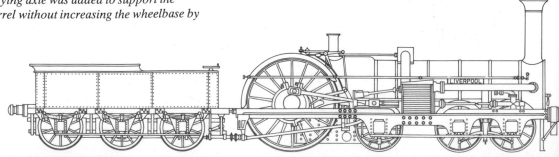

Le Continent *Built by Cail under licence from Crampton in 1852, this locomotive was the most fully developed of the Crampton type. The first true express locomotive in France, helped by great 7ft 6½in (2300mm) driving wheels, it had double frames, with the cylinders mounted halfway along them. The pipes carrying the steam from the boiler to the valves can be seen, as well as the exhaust pipe to the chimney. The Eastern Railway used* Le Continent *on Paris-Strasbourg expresses, and it ran until 1914. Today it is in the Mulhouse French Railway Museum.*

of the Great Western, so that the trains of the latter could run at a higher average speed.

Cramptons had their greatest success in France, aided by some design modifications to improve performance. They ran on the Northern and Eastern Railways, as well as on the Paris, Lyons & Mediterranean Railway. Germany, too, took up the Crampton, and many were built by Woehlert, Maffei and Kessler, among others, epitomising one of the most exciting periods of express locomotive design. Poor track limited Crampton success in the United States and only thirteen were built there.

Nord Crampton *Built by Cail in 1859, this locomotive belonged to the Northern Railway series, 165–170. Unlike other Cramptons, it had Walschaert's valve gear instead of Stephenson's. Altogether 127 Cramptons were built in France, and they gave excellent service on express trains. On 30 July 1853, Napoleon III authorised the Crampton locomotives on the Northern Railway to run up to 74½mph (120km/h), although they could achieve 87mph (140km/h) or more, thanks to their excellent stability and good steam circuit.*

Die Pfalz *A German Crampton built by Maffei in 1853 for the Palatinate Railway. The Munich builder introduced numerous variations to the basic Crampton design, notably the cylinders outside the double frames and the outside valve gear, which improved the accessibility of both for maintenance. The width of the locomotive was considerably increased, however, and the appeerence was not improved.*

Railway fever

By 1850 the new age of steam was at the height of its vigour. Even those who had smiled at first and prophesied decline and failure were forced to recognise this. In fact, what could be called railway fever was a feature of the last half of the 19th century, starting in Britain. The fever gripped America too, where the adventurous and vigorous pioneers seized upon the railway as their banner and as a powerful tool for use in colonising the immense continent. In Europe it swept across the broad fields of France, ran through the forests of Germany, reached the fjords of Scandinavia, started across the far steppes of Russia and travelled the length of the Italian peninsula.

The prospective gains were so great that they led – within a few, hectic years – to the greatest peaceful revolution in the history of humanity. There is a vast literature on the subject, telling the story of the changes the railways brought to so many people. Scientific and technical men were laying the foundations of what would become a new age of industrial civilisation, an age more dazzling, if more controversial, than any of the past.

The rapid expansion of railways geographically, and the vast effort needed, threw up many problems not forseen by the early promoters of lines or the designers of the first rolling stock. For example, mid-19th century passenger traffic along major routes could be carried in a

Matarò *Spain's first railway, from Barcelona to Matarò, was opened in 1848 and this locomotive was built for it by Jones & Potts of Warrington in England. In effect it was a Crewe type 2-2-2 with outside frames and inclined cylinders. Overall length was 39ft 4in (12000mm) and the tractive effort exerted was 3110lbf (1410kgf). Without the tender, the weight in working order was 26 tonnes. A full-scale reproduction was built for the centenary of the railway.*

few trains daily. They did not need many coaches and included a van for mails and luggage. On the other hand, freight traffic called for the most powerful locomotives possible, not only for long coal trains but for those loaded with every conceivable form of merchandise. And these had to compete with waterways, which were in use all over Europe and in America. However, because of the obvious

L'Elephant *Tayleur & Co built the original locomotive in England in 1835, under licence from Robert Stephenson & Co, and it hauled some of the first trains when the first railway in Belgium, between Brussels and Malines, opened that year. Originally an 0-4-2, an 1849 rebuild converted it to a 2-4-0, with a larger boiler for greater steam production. In its new form, it developed 100hp and weighed 20 tonnes in working order.*

Chiabrera *One of twelve locomotives built between 1853 and 1860 by Cockerill of Seraing for the Piedmont State Railways, this was a modification of the Norris type which had reached Europe a decade before. The Chiabrera had a short-wheelbase bogie, inclined cylinders with Stephenson's valve gear, and modest-sized driving wheels 4ft 1½in (1260mm) in diameter. It developed 220hp and could run at a maximum speed of 40mph (65km/h). Weight in working order was 27.3 tonnes, of which 21.2 tonnes was adhesive.*

L'Auroch *When Camille Polonceau was made responsible for the Paris-Orleans Railway's motive power from 1 August 1848, his first objective was the replacement of the existing locomotives with those that followed latest practice. Among the outstanding designs that appeared was this freight 0-6-0, of which 34 examples were built between 1854 and 1856. It had outside plate frames to which the inside cylinder casting was bolted, and a firebox between the second and third axles. In a later version the firebox was beyond the last axle. The locomotives ran for many years and even in 1930 there were still 30 in traffic.*

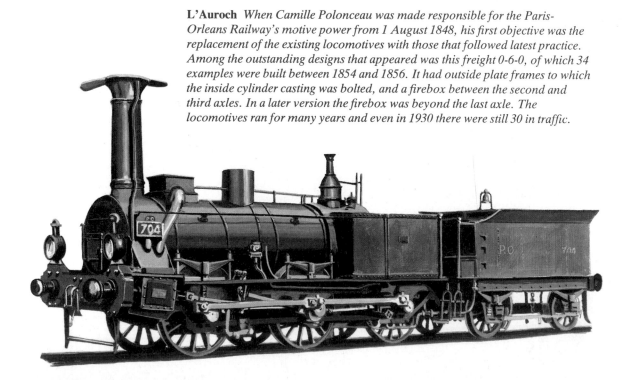

Bloomers *Designed by J E MacConnell in 1854 for the southern division of the London & North Western Railway, these locomotives were among the first to depart from the low centre of gravity theory held until that time. The boiler was mounted high, leaving space beneath for the inside cranks of the driving axle. Splashers covered much of the 7ft (2134mm) driving wheels, giving rise to the nickname Bloomer for the class, after an American lady, Mrs Bloomer, who was advocating rational female dress and trousers for women at that time.*

GNR No 215 *Built by R & W Hawthorn for the Great Northern Railway, this locomotive was designed by Archibald Sturrock in the hope of running from London to Edinburgh in eight hours. In this it was not a success proving too large and heavy and showing a tendency to become derailed. An unusual Crampton feature was the rigid wheelbase of the two leading axles, the rear leading wheels and the driving wheels being flangeless. Its weight in working order was 37.5 tonnes and it ran until 1870.*

Bristol & Exeter Railway *James Pearson designed splendid 4-2-4 tank locomotives for this broad gauge line in 1853. They had exceptional features, such as the unusual wheel arrangement, the enormous 9ft (2740mm) driving wheels, and the position of the cylinders – under the smokebox as usual, but partially emerging on either side. The locomotives were replaced in 1868 by four that were almost identical (illustrated here) with flangeless driving wheels and a weight in working order of 50.8 tonnes, of which 18.8 tonnes were on the driving wheels.*

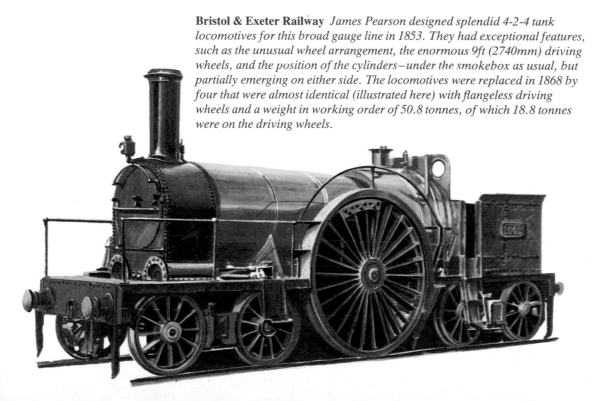

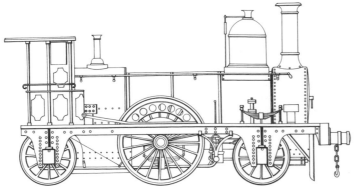

Lüneburg *Basing his design on the British Jenny Lind class, Georg Egestorff produced this locomotive for the Brunswick Railway, and thirteen were built between 1853 and 1867. As in the British design of the year before there were deep axleguards for the carrying wheels and the driving axle was in axle boxes mounted on the inside frames only. The firebox was between the second and third axles and the large dome was on the first ring of the boiler. These were the first express locomotives for the Berlin-Cologne line.*

advantages of steam railway transport, competition between rail and water was brief. The steam locomotive became a specialised machine adapted to the various needs. Design and construction became more standardised, which in turn allowed manufacturers to refine construction methods, with the result that a locomotive was not only a fast and economical machine, but also safe and reliable in service.

After the success of the Patentee type throughout Europe, the good service given by the Norris type in America, Austria and Germany and the more controversial results from Crampton locomotives, the stage was set

Corsair *After long resistance to the idea of a leading bogie – adopted by the Americans some time before – Europeans were converted at last for passenger locomotives on winding routes. One of the first successful examples was Corsair of 1849, designed by Daniel Gooch for the broad-gauge South Devon Railway, which was later part of the Great Western. A 4-4-0 tank with the frame resting on a spherical bogie bearing, Corsair was fitted with a sledge brake sliding on the rails, instead of brake blocks working against the wheel treads. Another railway technology innovation.*

Heidelberg *Esslingen Works built this locomotive in 1854 for express trains of the Wurtemburg Railway. It amalgamated features of both the Crampton type and the European Norris designs. It had a leading bogie, horizontal cylinders, large driving wheels 5ft 9¾in (1840mm) in diameter, a firebox between the driving axles, and a boiler pressure of 100lb/in^2 (7kg/cm^2). From about 1850 a rudimentary cab protected crews in Continental Europe.*

for the evolution of more standard construction but one which would still enable any desired speed and tractive effort to be obtained. By concentrating on proven methods the optimum results could be obtained. Until then the various locomotive builders had followed their own thinking in producing designs for any particular kind of traffic, which made poor use of experience gained and dissipated energy. After 1850, major constructional principles were established to guide the various locomotive designers, principles that could be either followed in their entirety or improved upon. This was particularly valuable between 1850 and 1870, when numerous building works were set up in countries which until then had imported locomotives for their railways. In Europe this happened in Italy, Spain, Switzerland, Hungary and in parts of the Austrian empire, as well as in some German states.

The period between 1850 and 1870 was the time, too, when men sought to improve locomotive thermal efficiency, enlarging grate areas and thus firebox heating surface so much that

Toess *Built in 1854 by Maffei, Munich, for the North Eastern Railway, this was one of the first locomotives to run in Switzerland, Maffei having supplied the very first in 1847. The Toess type continued for over a decade, some coming from Escher, Wyss of Zürich. Toess itself was of the European Norris type with 5ft 5½in (1670mm) driving wheels, a maximum speed of 31mph (50km/h) and a weight in working order of 43.7 tonnes with its tender, of which 14.2 tonnes was on the driving wheels.*

Kufstein *This was another machine characteristic of the 1850s, built by Maffei, Munich, for the Bavarian Railway in 1854. During this decade German locomotives began to acquire a distinctive national appearence after twenty years of following foreign designs. The Kufstein had a large grate for the period of 11.8ft² (1.1m²) area and a boiler pressure of 100lb/in² (7kg/cm²). It had an adhesive weight of 9.5 tonnes and a total weight in working order of 23 tonnes.*

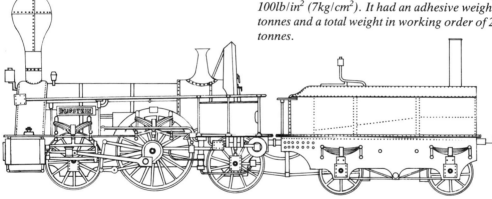

Dx Goods *This class of locomotives was designed by John Ramsbottom for the English London & North Western Railway and entered service between 1855 and 1872. The type is shown here after being reboilered and it had a long life, the last not disappearing until 1930. The versatility of the locomotives, their robustness and the simplicity of their construction made the class a great success. No less than 943 were built, a record number for any British steam locomotive class.*

Sampierdarena *Built by Ansaldo of Genoa in 1854 for the Genoa-Voltri section of the Piedmont State Railways, Sampierdarena was claimed to be the first locomotive built entirely in Italy. Count Cavour of Piedmont, who as Prime Minister encouraged railway building, persuaded Giovanni Ansaldo to found his locomotive works. Sampierdarena followed a classic British 0-4-2 design, with an inside frame and the firebox between the second and third axles. It developed 417hp, had a 114lb/in^2 (8kg/cm^2) boiler pressure, 5ft 3in (1600mm) driving wheels, and 21 tonnes adhesive weight out of a 27.8 tonnes weight in working order. During trials Sampierdarena attained 40mph (65km/h).*

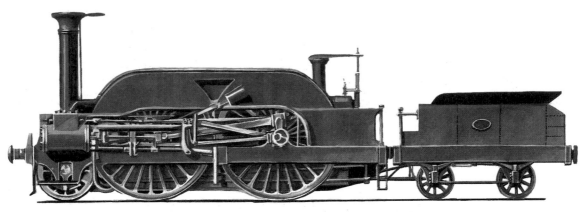

L'Aigle *A locomotive sensation of the Paris Exhibition of 1855 because of its enormous driving wheels, which at 9ft 3½in diameter (2840mm) were the largest coupled driving wheels to be used on the standard gauge. The locomotive was designed by Blavier and Larpent, engineers of the Western Railway, and was built by Gouin at Batignolles in Paris. The design had bizarre features, such as the double boiler running both above and below the coupled axles and a piston stroke of as much as 31½in (800mm). After a series of unsuccessful trials on the Western of France, L'Aigle disappeared from history.*

Raigmore *Designed by William Barclay, a nephew of Alexander Allan, who together with Buddicom evolved the Crewe type locomotive, it is evident that Raigmore was a typical Crewe type design. Four of the locomotives were built by Hawthorn of Leith for the Inverness & Nairn Railway in 1855. Crewe type characteristics were the lack of a dome (although two safety valves were provided), the shape of the outside frames, and outside cylinders inclined against the smokebox. This little class ran all types of train until they were rebuilt entirely in 1869.*

Express *Built by Kitson in England for the East Indian Railway, the second railway built in India and running from Calcutta to Raneegani. This was all of 135 miles (218km) and was opened in 1855. The railway used 2-2-2 tanks like Express (shown here) for their Calcutta suburban services. The first of the neat design was built in 1856. Driving wheel diameter was 6ft (1829mm), adhesive weight 10 tonnes, boiler pressure 120lb/in^2 (8.4kg/cm^2) and tractive effort 3970lbf (1800kgf).*

Victor Emmanuel Company *This class of locomotive was built by Gouin in 1858 for the Culoz-Turin route, which included the not-yet-opened Mont Cenis tunnel. Some of the class went to the Paris, Lyons & Mediterranean Railway when territory north of the tunnel passed from Piedmont into French hands after the war of 1861. The type had a grate area of 13ft^2 (1.21m^2) and a boiler pressure of 129lb/in^2 (9kg/cm^2). Cylinders were inside and the driving wheels were 5ft (1680mm) in diameter. Maximum speed was 46½mph (75km/h) and the weight in working order was 27.3 tonnes, of which 19.2 tonnes was adhesive.*

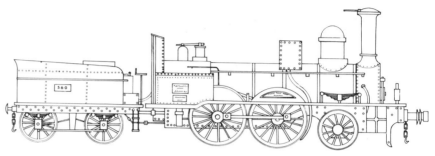

PLM Mammoth – 1856

The Mammoth type

To cope with heavier freight trains, railways in France put an 0-6-0 type named Mammoth into service from 1846, based on a successful British design. Outstanding Mammoths were Paris, Lyons & Mediterranean (PLM) Nos 1224–1243, built at their Nîmes shops in 1856 and which did not disappear until 1926. They had cylinders 17in in diameter (430mm) by 25¼in in stroke (640mm), inside frames, 129lb/in^2 (9kg/cm^2) boiler pressure, 43½mph (70km/h) maximum speed and a six-wheel tender. Mammoths were very popular in France and in some other European countries. The first Mammoth in Italy ran in 1849 and 91 were in service by 1875. The Madrid-Saragossa-Alicante Railway (MZA) in Spain took the Mammoth as one of its standard classes, and had 47 built between 1857 and 1858, by Wilson and Kitson in England and by Cail in France. These Mammoths had 17¼in by 23½in (440mm by 600mm) cylinders, 4ft 8¼in (1430mm) driving wheels and, including the tender, a weight in working order of 49.3 tonnes. One of this type was in traffic for 107 years; just one has been preserved.

MZA Mammoth – 1857

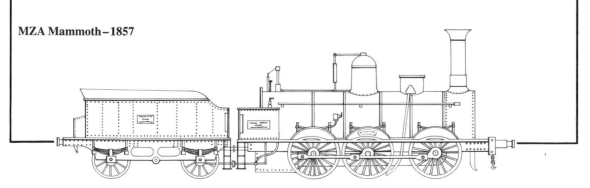

Paris-Orleans Nos 720–791 *Derived from the freight locomotives of 1854 (see page 52), this type was built by Camille Polonceau for the Paris-Orleans between 1855 and 1858. The principal modification was the shorter wheelbase to allow running through curves of lesser radius and to aid working on steeply-graded lines. This involved placing the firebox outside it at the rear in the old manner. The locomotives hauled 250 tonnes up a long gradient at Etampes at 18½mph (30km/h).*

coal instead of coke could be used as a fuel. Long and deep fireboxes appeared, running above the last driving axle and contained between the frames, those of the Belpaire type being rectangular at the top. It was realised too that a low centre of gravity was not entirely necessary to ensure running stability, and designers raised the whole boiler upwards, which allowed for firebox grates that spread the whole width of the locomotive above both wheels and frames.

Others sought better thermal efficiency by valve gear improvements, among them Egide Walschaert, who patented his valve gear in 1844, and his German rival Heusinger, who made some small improvements to the same valve gear that he had conceived independently in 1849. How to cut off the boiler steam supply to the cylinders during the piston's stroke was investigated as well. Variation of cut-off according to the horsepower and speed lessened steam con-

Prairie rangers

During the years in which schools of locomotive engineering were being consolidated in Europe, railway fever also gripped America. The rail system expanded rapidly during the 1850s, reported distances opened to traffic covering a five-year period were: 10850 miles (17500km) during 1851, 13320 miles (21500km) during 1852, 15500 miles (25000km) during 1853, 18900 miles (31500km) during 1854 and 21750 miles

(35000km) during 1855. Terrain and technical difficulties were great in many parts of the United States and the dream of crossing the continent was still a dream during the period from 1850 to 1860. The universally used locomotive was the American type 4-4-0 (see page 26) of which many thousands had already been built. One of the most famous of these was *General*, built by the Rogers Locomotive Works of Paterson, New Jersey in 1855 for the Western & Atlantic Railroad. Rogers was a great innovator and

General – 1855

Allan type *The origin of the Crewe type has been described already and the Allan type was an improved version of the next generation. Built at Crewe in February 1855, it belonged to a class of 2-4-0 that mounted a large firebox between the driving axles. The massive outside frames will be noted, along with the characteristic inclined cylinder position alongside the smokebox. The circular section coupling and connecting rods, used until then on many Crewe-built locomotives, were replaced by a more usual rectangular section. The locomotive ran on the London & North Western Railway.*

Chillon *Built by the Karlsruhe Works in 1857 for the Western Railway, Chillon represented a second generation of Swiss passenger locomotives. It was a long boiler 2-4-0, with horizontal cylinders and firebox outside the wheelbase at either end. Driving wheel diameter was 5ft 6in (1680mm), boiler pressure 114lb/in² (8kg/cm²), maximum speed 43½mph (70km/h) and with tender it weighed 40 tonnes, out of which 18 tonnes was adhesive weight.*

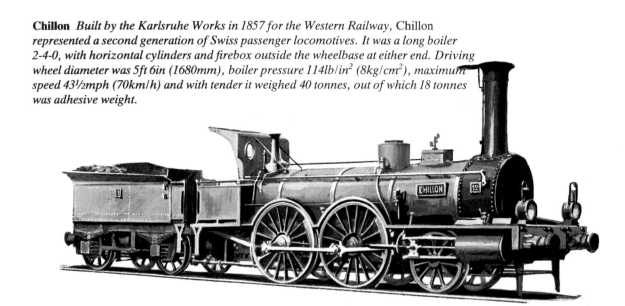

believed strongly in outside cylinders. In the Civil War between 1861 and 1865, *General* took part in the Andrews' raid. Lieutenant Andrews captured it and ran it with his Unionist army men along the Atlanta-Chattanooga linc to intercept Confederate supply trains. *General* ran out of fuel after 87 miles (140km) and was overtaken by Lieutenant Fuller, who had been chasing in a Confederate train hauled by another 4-4-0 named *Texas*.

William Mason followed the ideas of Rogers in regard to cylinder position and built *Phantom* for the Toledo & Illinois Railroad in 1857. Its cylinders were 15in by 22in (381mm by 559mm) and the driving wheels were 5ft 6in (1676mm) diameter.

Phantom – 1857

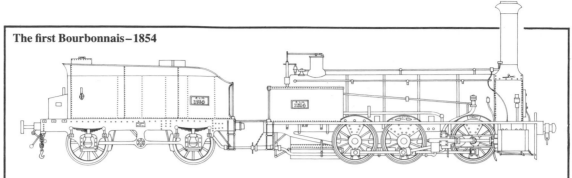

The first Bourbonnais–1854

The Bourbonnais type

By 1854 the inside cylinder 0-6-0 Mammoth type was outclassed for French freight and mixed trains of ever-increasing weight. Cail and Koechlin built fifty of a new type of 0-6-0 locomotive for the Bourbonnais Railway from 1854 onwards, and the type was prized throughout Europe in the decades that followed. The Paris, Lyons & Mediterranean Railway (PLM) alone acquired 1054 of them.

The first Bourbonnais locomotives had horizontal outside cylinders 17½in by 25½in (450mm by 650mm) and 4ft 3in (1300mm) driving wheels. The firebox was outside the wheelbase, Stephenson valve gear was fitted and the vertical

slide valves took steam from a Crampton type regulator. Later locomotives had a sandbox on top of the boiler. The Bourbonnais locomotives of the PLM could haul 1228 tonnes on the level, 508 tonnes up a 1 in 200 (0.5 per cent) gradient and 306 tonnes up a 1 in 100 (1.0 per cent) gradient.

A more advanced Bourbonnais locomotive was built for the Western Railway of Switzerland by Cail in 1858. In general it followed the French design, save that the grate area was enlarged to 15ft² (1.4m²) and the boiler pressure rose to 129lb/in² (9kg/cm²). Weight in working order was 32.3 tonnes.

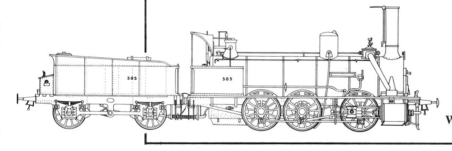

Western Railway of Switzerland–1858

Gotha *In Germany the British-inspired long boiler was fitted to locomotives long after it had been superseded elsewhere and, although well-built, such machines looked somewhat archaic even when new. Gotha, built by Borsig for the Thuringia Railway in 1855, was an outside-cylinder 2-4-0 whose features have been noted before, except for the boiler with its square-section firebox and a dome above the curved firebox top. The sheet metal cab, which was evolving at the time, can be seen.*

Einkorn *The Wurtemburg Railway standardised on Norris 4-4-0s for many years. The Class E passenger locomotives went into traffic in 1859 and the design still showed traces of the American prototype. Class E included* Einkorn, *built by Esslingen with some interesting features. The coupled wheelbase was extended to allow a large firebox between the axles, although the bogie wheelbase seems to have been made as short as possible. A great dome surmounts the boiler, together with a sandbox and a Crampton-type regulator.*

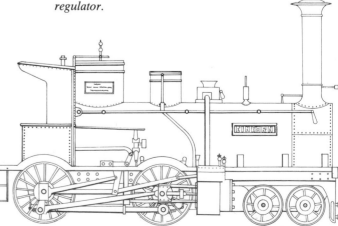

sumption considerably and contributed to the ability of a locomotive to take heavy trains long distances.

Greater steam production was sought by increasing the diameter of the boiler barrel, thus allowing an increase in the number of boiler tubes, which increased the heating surface. Working pressures were raised and frequently exceeded 143lb/in^2 (10kg/cm^2). To cope with this, more advanced safety valves were designed, such as Ramsbottom's, dating from the late 1850s, followed by Ashton's, the Lethuillier-Pinel type in France and Richardson's, the latter particularly favoured in Scandinavian countries. Putting water from the tender into the boiler under pressure produced pumping problems, and mechanical devices to try to overcome them. At last a Frenchman, Giffard,

Zürich *This single-driver was delivered by Borsig to the Leipzig-Dresden Railway in 1858 – a locomotive type looking back to the Patentee of 25 years before, but incorporating a long boiler. Weight in working order was 27.8 tonnes and adhesive weight 11.6 tonnes. In due course, from 1 January 1875, the Leipzig-Dresden was amalgamated with other railways to form the Saxon State Railway.*

Prins August *The first locomotive to run in Sweden, built by Beyer, Peacock of Manchester in 1856. It was an outside cylinder 2-4-0 with 5ft 6in (1676mm) driving wheels, a grate area of 15ft^2 (1.38m^2) and a 100lb/in^2 (7kg/cm^2) boiler pressure. Adhesive weight was 18.3 tonnes and the weight in working order, including the tender, was 38 tonnes. The maximum speed was 37½mph (60km/h) and the locomotive is preserved in the Gävle Railway Museum.*

Tarragona, Barcelona & France *This railway had an inside-cylinder 4-4-0 built by Slaughter, Gruning & Co in England, the first of a type that became widespread in Great Britain and in many other countries. Built in 1859, its widely-spaced driving axles gave room for a long grate; the valve gear was inside. The front bogie had outside frames with large longitudinal leaf springs. The class remained in service for over half a century, the last being withdrawn in 1911.*

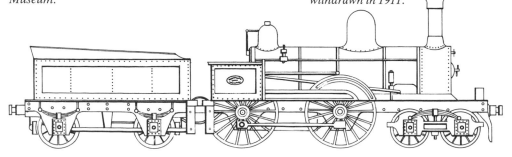

Olten *Swiss railways not unnaturally felt the need for steep gradient locomotives of high adhesive weight. They adopted a revolutionary type that had proved itself in the Austrian Alps, evolved by the Austrian engineer Engerth (see page 80). The* Olten *was a modified Engerth type, built by Esslingen for the Swiss Central Railway in 1854. The six-wheel truck at the rear, carrying the coal bunker, was articulated to the main frame and so arranged that part of its weight increased the adhesion of the rear pair of driving wheels. The articulation also allowed short radius curves to be traversed.*

Nembo *Built for Lombardy-Venetian Railroads in 1857, this was one of a widely-used family of British single-driver machines. Ten were produced by Beyer, Peacock of Manchester, a firm noted for handsome well-built locomotives. Of normal construction, the boiler pressure was 100lb/in² (7kg/cm²), driving wheel diameter 6ft 2in (1880mm) and it could develop 210hp. The* Nembo *(in English, Cloud) could run up to 43½mph (70km/h). Adhesive weight was 13.2 tonnes, the highest that the track could take.*

Lady of the Lake *One of the Problem class from John Ramsbottom, designed on the instructions of the directors of the London & North Western Railway, who wished for a locomotive that was cheap to build and to operate.* Lady of the Lake *was built at Crewe in 1862 and dispensed with the outside frame of the Crewe type. A* Problem *ran from Holyhead to Stafford (130 miles/210km) at an average speed of about 54mph (87km/h), the non-stop run being made possible by Ramsbottom's invention of the water trough to allow water to be picked up at speed.*

Atalanta *Joseph Beattie was a locomotive technology pioneer. He fitted large fireboxes, adapted to burn coal rather than coke. His leading axles floated on springs under the slide bars. Above all, he pioneered boiler feedwater preheating. Atalanta was one of 62 London & South Western Railway locomotives with all these features incorporated, 2-4-0s that entered service from London to Salisbury and Bournemouth between 1859 and 1860. Exhaust steam gave up its heat to feedwater in the two vertical tubes in front of the chimney.*

Caledonian Railway *An enlarged Crewe type 2-2-2 designed by Benjamin Connor for the Caledonian Railway, and built in their St Rollox shops in Glasgow in 1859. The massive outside frame was retained as well as the cylinder position alongside the smokebox, although the latter could be mounted horizontally because of the great 8ft 2in (2489mm) driving wheels. The machines were renowned for their sound construction and fine running over lines with many gradients. They were on expresses until 1885 and the last was broken up only in 1901.*

Delaware, Lackawanna & Western *This fine American type 4-4-0 was built by Danforth, Cooke & Co of Paterson, New Jersey, for the 6ft gauge (1829mm) Delaware, Lackawanna & Western Railroad in 1858. It was a coal burner with a large wagon top firebox and coned last boiler ring. Cylinders were 17in by 22in (432mm by 559mm) and each had a separate blast pipe. Driving wheel diameter was 5ft 6in (1676mm).*

Kopernicus *A handsome example of a German single-driver locomotive, built by Esslingen Works for the Hesse Railway in 1860. Driving wheel diameter was 5ft 6in (1680mm) and boiler pressure 103lb/in² (7kg/cm²). The horizontal cylinders were notable, as was the firebox in the normal position between the rear axles. Adhesive weight was 11.5 tonnes and weight in working order 25 tonnes.*

invented the steam injector in 1859. In this, a jet of steam entrains the water, the latter cooling the steam just sufficiently to allow its pressure to rise above that of the steam in the boiler. Exhaust steam was recycled by condensation in the water supply as well, to save heat, and later for the planned preheating of feed water. The feed water heating experiments made then were not, however, used widely until the end of the century.

The handling of exhaust steam from the cylinders was also studied and numerous improvements were made, American engineers tending to favour a separate exhaust from each of the two cylinders. Where wood was used as a fuel in Europe, there was much research into suitable spark-arresting apparatus, for these were not only a discomfort to the passengers, but were a fire hazard to the train and its

(continued on page 70)

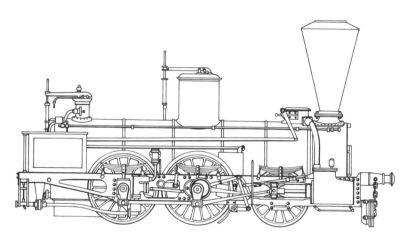

Austrian Südbahn *German and Austrian firms built a mixed-traffic 2-4-0 for this line from 1859. The locomotive design is attributed to the Englishman Joseph Hall, who had worked for builders in Bavaria and then in Austria since 1839. Outside frames were used, with the cylinders and all the motion outside the frame members. The firebox was included in the boiler shell and the latter carried a Crampton type regulator. This locomotive type was used by many Austrian and Hungarian railways.*

Südbahn freight locomotive *Hall's design was used for 0-6-0 freight locomotives as well, and the Südbahn had a total of 219 of them, while the type was also built for other many railways. The example illustrated was sold second-hand to the Graz-Köflach Railway later, and it remained in service until 1965, having been built in 1860! Indeed, one of the class is still available for special trains. The short wheelbase allowed the connecting rod to drive the rear axle. The cab and air brake apparatus are modern additions.*

Romont *The Lausanne-Freiburg-Berne Railway had some remarkable locomotives specially built to cope with a short, 1 in 83 (1.2 per cent) gradient in its branch between Romont and Bulle. Esslingen Works built twelve 4-4-0 saddle tanks in 1862. They had 1117ft² (103.8m²) heating surface, cylinders 16in by 24in (410mm by 612mm), driving wheels of 4ft 5½in (1370mm) diameter and a weight in working order of 41 tonnes, of which 27 tonnes was adhesive. The locomotives were 33ft 3in long over buffers (10120mm), could reach 37¼mph (60km/h) and could haul 500 tonnes on the relatively level sections of the railway or 350 tonnes on the branch with the gradient. Romont stayed in service until 1905.*

Paris-Orleans Nos 236–250 *Fifteen single-drivers were built for the Paris-Orleans in 1862, designed by Victor Fourquenot who was recognised as one of the most brilliant locomotive engineers of his day. They had Gooch outside valve gear, and a great dome over the firebox. The diameter of the smokebox was greater than that of the boiler barrel. Although small, the locomotives were used on the Paris-Bordeaux mail train, averaging 37¼mph (60km/h) inclusive of 17 stops. Lacking adhesion, the locomotives were generally confined to level lines and they vanished about 1900.*

Kuessaburg *Another Hall 2-4-0, a type that was long admired in Germany. This locomotive was built by the Karlsruhe Works for the Baden State Railway in 1862. The outside springs for all axles were very typical of this sort of 2-4-0, as was the Crampton type regulator on top of the boiler.*

Byciclette *A nickname given to a suburban type 2-4-0 tank of the Western Railway of France. Cail built 134 of them over 30 years from 1855 to 1884. Used on local trains or for shunting, most of them were to be found in the Paris region. Bunkers and water tanks ran the whole length of the inside-cylinder locomotive, which had a grate area of 11.3ft^2 (1.04m^2) and, originally, a boiler pressure of 121lb/in^2 (8.5kg/cm^2). The Byciclettes had 5ft 5in (1660mm) driving wheels, weighed 37 tonnes in working order, and had a maximum speed of 37¼mph (60km/h).*

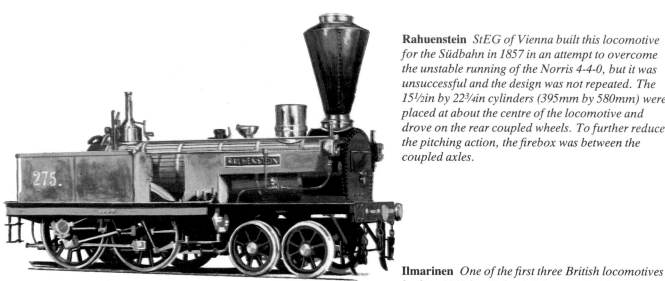

Rahuenstein *StEG of Vienna built this locomotive for the Südbahn in 1857 in an attempt to overcome the unstable running of the Norris 4-4-0, but it was unsuccessful and the design was not repeated. The 15½in by 22¾in cylinders (395mm by 580mm) were placed at about the centre of the locomotive and drove on the rear coupled wheels. To further reduce the pitching action, the firebox was between the coupled axles.*

Ilmarinen *One of the first three British locomotives built in 1860 for Finland, it inaugurated the Helsinki-Hämeenlinna railway. The design was a cross between the American 4-4-0 and the British Allan type 2-4-0, the outside frames and inclined cylinders alongside the smokebox being typical of the latter. Driving wheels were 5ft (1524mm) diameter, boiler pressure 121lb/in^2 (8.5kg/cm^2) and weight in working order 29 tonnes, of which 17.8 tonnes was adhesive. The locomotive was taken out of service in 1911.*

Caroline *The oldest surviving locomotive to have run in Norway, this 2-4-0 was one of a pair built by Robert Stephenson & Co in 1861, with 4ft 8in (1422mm) driving wheels and outside cylinders 12in by 20in (306mm by 508mm). For many years it worked from Oslo to the Swedish border, until sold for industrial use in 1919.* Caroline *was bought back by the Norwegian State Railway in 1954 and restored for the railway's centenary.*

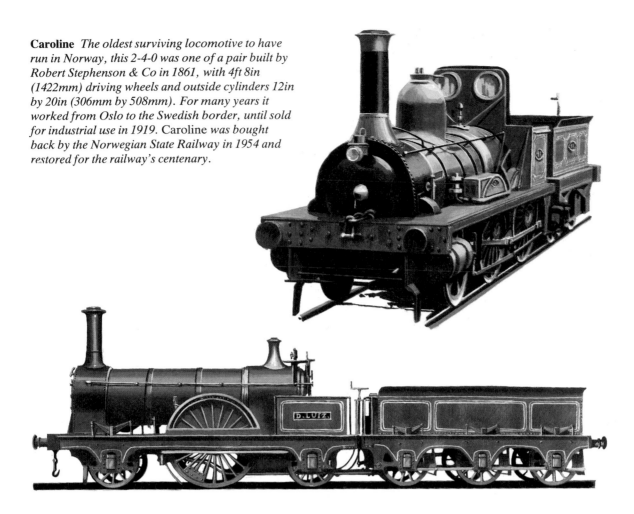

Dom Luiz *Beyer, Peacock, Manchester, built one of their handsome single-driver locomotives for the South Eastern Railway in Portugal in 1862. Except for the domeless boiler, it followed the Jenny Lind type, with driving axle bearings in the inside frames only. The* Dom Luiz *was in traffic for over 70 years and today has been accurately restored to original condition.*

Great North of Scotland Railway *These locomotives ran on this railway from 1862, when the first was built by Robert Stephenson & Co, until after the line was absorbed by the London & North Eastern Railway in 1923. The last was taken out of traffic in 1932. W. Cowan produced the design at a time when the outside cylinder 4-4-0 was little known in Great Britain. Driving wheel diameter was 5ft 1in (1550mm) and an old-fashioned feature was the dome over the firebox.*

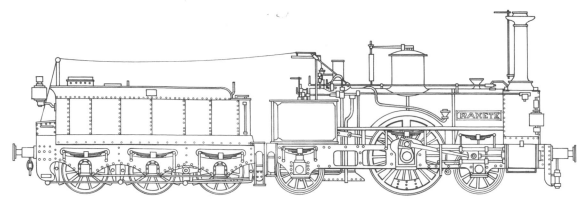

Rakete II *A typical Austrian 2-2-2 locomotive of the period was built by G. Sigl of Vienna for the Kaiser Ferdinands Nordbahn in 1862. The double plate frames had apertures for lightness, and the cylinders and motion were placed outside in the Hall manner. Driving wheel diameter was 6ft 6in (1980mm), boiler pressure 77lb/in² (5.4kg/cm²) and the heating surface 1140ft² (106m²). The cylindrical dome was an Austrian feature of the day. With a six-wheel, high-capacity tender, Rackete II was 46ft 7in (14,200mm) long over buffers, and the height from the rail to the top of the chimney was 15ft 5in (4700mm).*

Munin *Beyer, Peacock of Manchester delivered the first eight examples of this express locomotive to Sweden in 1864. As always with its locomotives, this firm produced light and elegant lines, for it pioneered British ideas in the production of handsome locomotives. Driving wheel diameter was 6ft 1½in, it had inside cylinders and Allan's valve gear, adhesive weight was 12 tonnes and the weight in working order was 25 tonnes. Munin could attain 56mph (90km/h) maximum speed; it was broken up in 1908.*

Rigi *One of six freight 0-4-6 locomotives built for the Zürich-Zug-Lucerne Railway, this one was made by Esslingen in 1863. Because of the great overhang of the locomotive at the rear, some of its weight was carried on a tender axle and Beugniot articulation (which had had some success on mountain locomotives–see pages 81 and 84) was adopted. Rigi's cylinders were 17in by 27in (431mm by 686mm), grate area 15ft² (1.4m²), heating surface 1140ft² (106m²) and driving wheel diameter 4ft 5½in (1370mm). The coupled wheelbase was 8ft (2440mm), which allowed short radius curves to be tackled, adhesive weight was 26 tonnes, total weight in working order 52 tonnes and maximum speed 25mph (40km/h). Rigi was taken out of service in 1878.*

Belgian State Railway Class 28 *Alfred Belpaire, as locomotive engineer of the Belgian State, experimented with coal-burning fireboxes for four years before fitting them to new locomotives from 1864. His improved grate was long, to increase area and firebox volume above it, and it could burn small coal instead of coke. His fireboxes had rectangular tops, of the type which have carried his name ever since, and he and engineers elsewhere (Kirtley and Beattie in England for example) made a considerable advance in locomotive technology by making coal-burning possible. Class 28 was an outside frame 0-6-0, with driving wheels 4ft 9in (1450mm) in diameter and a weight in working order of 33 tonnes. A total of 262 Class 28 locomotives were built between 1864 and 1883. The last of them ran until 1931.*

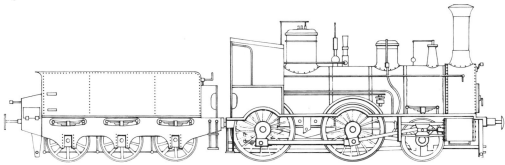

Hertha *Esslingen Works built this locomotive for the Zealand Railways in Denmark in 1863. There were 18 in the class built between 1863 and 1871. The design followed that of German 2-4-0s of the period, with outside cylinders, 5ft 4½in driving wheels (1640mm), and 129lb/in² (9kg/cm²) boiler pressure. Weight in working order was 30.7 tonnes (adhesive weight 19.1 tonnes) and they were able to exceed their laid down 62mph (100km/h) maximum speed.*

The Italian Bourbonnais *The French Bourbonnais type (see page 60) arrived in Italy in 1861. It became very popular and in the end there were 729 in Italy, comprising 11 very similar classes, working on all major railways. The Adriatic System (RA) locomotive illustrated was one of 62 built by Koechlin of Mulhouse, Grafenstaden, and the Italian Pietrarsa Works at Naples between 1864 and 1879. Cylinders were 17¾in by 25½in (450mm by 650mm), grate area 14.5ft² (1.35m²), heating surface 1363ft² (126.6m²) and boiler pressure 129lb/in² (9kg/cm²). Fully loaded the tender weighed 20.9 tonnes. The locomotives developed 410hp at 18½mph (30km/h) and maximum speed was 31mph (50km/h).*

surroundings. The massive chimneys carried by many locomotives of the period, especially in eastern areas of Europe, were brought about by the inverted cones and baffles fitted inside them–to the detriment of free escape for the exhaust in many cases.

From around 1860 the steam locomotive took on the general basic form it was to have for 100 years, losing the sometimes unsightly improvisations of development and becoming a harmonious symbol of power and speed. European designers sought a handsome outline to an ever-increasing degree, transforming a heavy and snorting monster into an elegant machine. British engineers were in the lead here, blending fine lines and mechanical might admirably. The same could not be said for most German locomotives of the time, where appearence was too often sacrificed to utility; nor could it be claimed for Austrian and Hungarian designs, although the locomotives of these two countries did achieve striking personalities of their own. In France outward appearance was given little importance, although this did not prevent the building of such elegant types as the Bourbonnais, which were to become celebrated in most European countries. The Americans were almost literally in a world of their own. Enthusiasm for the new steam locomotive led to what would now be regarded as over decoration.

Cudworth *These 2-2-2 locomotives worked the Continental Mail Express from London to Admiralty Pier, Dover for 20 years, as well as other expresses, at speeds of up to 60mph (96.5km/h). Designed by J. I. Cudworth, and built at the Ashford Works of the South Eastern Railway in 1865, they revived the old but tried Patentee type outside frames. The driving wheels were 7ft (2134mm) in diameter, boiler pressure was 135lb/in^2 (9.4kg/cm^2), adhesive weight 12.5 tonnes and weight in working order 33 tonnes.*

Victorian Government Railways *Class B of this railway was a 2-4-0, built from 1862 onwards, that both in design and construction was among the best locomotives to run in Australia. Beyer, Peacock & Co and R. & W. Hawthorn built the first 26 in England between 1852 and 1864, and followed with six more in 1872. Two were built in Australia by the Phoenix Foundry of Ballarat in 1880. The outside frame, inside cylinder design was typical of British locomotives of the 1860s, which led to the coining of the type name Old English. The original spark-arresting chimney was replaced in time by the normal cast iron cylindrical type.*

Metropolitan Railway *This was the first standard locomotive class built for the underground railways of London, which were expanding fast in 1864. The design was originated by Sir John Fowler, but detail work was done by the builder, Beyer, Peacock of Manchester. Technical details were of interest: 4-4-0 tank with a short-wheelbase bogie, outside inclined cylinders alongside the smokebox and inside Allan's valve gear. The boiler had 164 tubes and the pressure was 135lb/in^2 (9.4kg/cm^2). Condensing apparatus was fitted to these tank locomotives, exhaust steam being directed into the side tanks for condensation to avoid steam clouds in the tunnels. The adhesion weight was 31 tonnes and weight in working order 42 tonnes. Between 1864 and 1886, Beyer, Peacock supplied 120 of these locomotives to the two London underground railways.*

State Railways Co., Holland *Beyer, Peacock & Co of Manchester was the main supplier of locomotives to this Dutch company for more than 50 years. This 2-4-0 was one of 33 delivered in 1865, which were prized for their clean and handsome appearance. They had inside cylinders and valve gear, with the firebox placed between the driving wheels in the traditional British fashion. Driving wheel diameter was 5ft 6in (1676mm) and a simple screen gave some protection to the enginemen. The first delivery was followed by another in 1872 and the class had great influence on Dutch locomotive practice, which for a long time thereafter followed British ideas.*

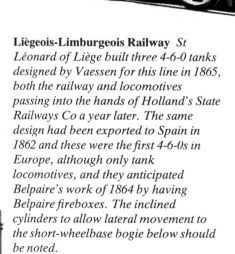

Liègeois-Limburgeois Railway *St Léonard of Liège built three 4-6-0 tanks designed by Vaessen for this line in 1865, both the railway and locomotives passing into the hands of Holland's State Railways Co a year later. The same design had been exported to Spain in 1862 and these were the first 4-6-0s in Europe, although only tank locomotives, and they anticipated Belpaire's work of 1864 by having Belpaire fireboxes. The inclined cylinders to allow lateral movement to the short-wheelbase bogie below should be noted.*

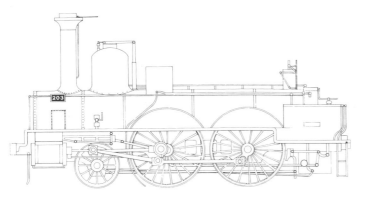

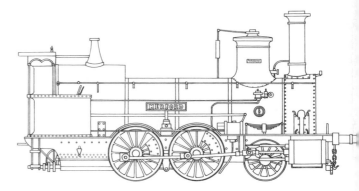

Paris-Orleans Nos 201-212 *These 2-4-0 express locomotives were built to Victor Fourquenot's design in 1864 and were the prototypes of a successful family that totalled about 400 in France. Fourquenot took the old long boiler type, but gave the coupled axles compensated springing, with a large spring each side, and provided leading carrying axlebox lateral play by letting the boxes slide in inclined planes. The short and deep Ten-Brinck firebox was outside the wheelbase. The Paris-Orleans had 94 of these locomotives and they were built also for the Paris, Lyons & Mediterranean and the State railways.*

Herford *Built by Haswell of Vienna for the Cologne-Minden Railway, this 2-4-0 retained the Stephenson square firebox, though its top was rounded. For the first time a boiler was made of steel rather than iron plates, although the use of steel for this purpose did not become general practise until after the turn of the century. An ineffective mechanism was supposed to prevent scale formation inside the boiler. Chemical additives for scale prevention came only 50 or more years later.*

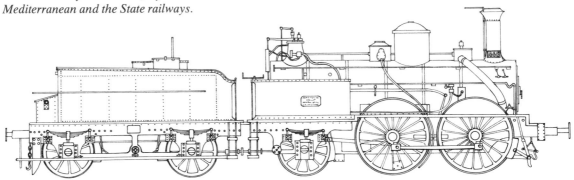

Northern of France Nos 2451-2551 *The British locomotive builder Sharp held that 0-4-2 wheel arrangement locomotives were better than 2-4-0s for weight distribution, adhesion and general stability. The argument was accepted by the Paris, Lyons & Mediterranean and Northern Railways, the the latter introducing this locomotive class, with inside cylinders and 5ft 10½in (1800mm) driving wheels, in 1867. Adhesion weight was 23 tonnes and weight in working order 32.4 tonnes. As mixed traffic locomotives, they worked fish trains from Channel ports to Paris.*

New South Wales Government Railway *This important Australian system put 13 locomotives built by Beyer, Peacock & Co into service between 1865 and 1870. Later known as Class 23, the design included outside inclined cylinders mounted above the carrying axle and measuring 18½in by 24in (457mm by 610mm). The first three of the locomotives had 5ft 9in (1750mm) driving wheels, but the rest were 5ft 6in (1676mm) to increase tractive effort. After working main line passenger and mail trains for 25 years the class was relegated to branch lines.*

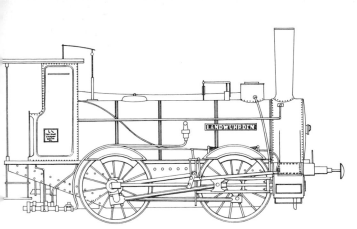

Landwührden *Georg Krauss built his first locomotive in Munich in 1867 and it won a gold medal at the Paris World Exhibition of that year. As a simple 0-4-0 with a domeless boiler, it had 143lb/in^2 (10kg/cm^2) boiler pressure, 5ft (1520mm) driving wheels, and a weight in working order of 27 tonnes. The type worked on the Oldenburg State Railway until about 1900.*

Ardennes type *The Bourbonnais locomotives built for the Eastern Railway of France had a slightly longer wheelbase and had the cylinders placed well forwards to counterbalance the weight of the firebox at the other end. They were known as the Ardennes type, after the area in which they first worked. Introduced in 1867, the type was built until 1884, by which time the Eastern had a total of 346.*

Finnish Class A3 *A class built in 1869 by Dübs of Glasgow for the Riihimäki to St Petersburg railway. The design was a development of Class A1 (see page 66), in which the grate area went up to 13.3ft^2 (1.24m^2), heating surface was reduced to 879.4ft^2 (81.7m^2), and driving wheel diameter increased to 5ft 7in (1700mm). Inside Stephenson's valve gear was fitted.*

East Indian Railway *The most prosperous of the eight railway systems on the Indian peninsula during the last century, the East Indian was a great user of the 0-6-0 type, to the point where they still had over 1000 of them in traffic in 1930. The locomotive shown was built by Neilson & Co, Glasgow, in 1867. With inside cylinders and valve gear, it had 120lb/in^2 (8.4kg/cm^2) boiler pressure, driving wheels 5ft (1524mm) in diameter, and a weight in working order of 34 tonnes. On the level, this locomotive could haul 470 tonnes.*

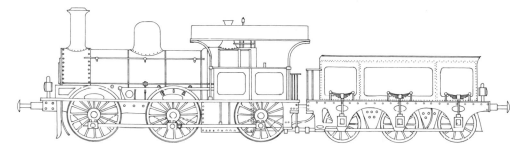

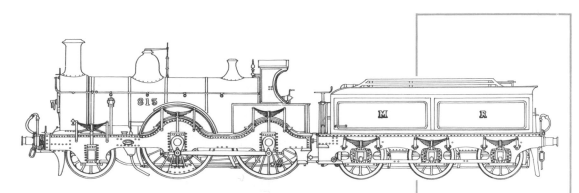

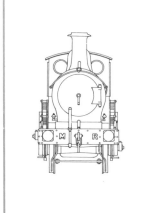

Kirtley 800 class *Matthew Kirtley designed this express locomotive in 1870, and his Midland Railway had 48 of them built by Neilson & Co of Glasgow and in its own Derby Works. British locomotive practice was spreading across the world and these locomotives were considered to be fine technical examples, both of classic British design and for their excellent performance. On the rails they had good stability, excellent steam production and high speed. They were outside frame locomotives, with inside cylinders 18in by 24in (457mm by 610mm) and inside Stephenson's valve gear. The boiler had 223 tubes, the total heating surface was 1225ft² (11.4m²), driving wheels were 6ft 8in (2030mm) diameter, and weight in working order about 40 tonnes. The locomotives were well-known to the public and very popular with the enginemen, who appreciated their good riding and swift reaction to demands made upon them. The last in traffic was old 827, going for scrap in July 1936.*

Great Northern 8ft singles *When Patrick Stirling designed and built a 4-2-2 express locomotive in 1870, hardly anyone appreciated that it was a remarkable product. It embodied all the best locomotive practice of the day, and during tests and trials came to be recognised as a fundamental step forward in locomotive design. Stirling took the classic single-driver locomotive and added a long-wheelbase bogie at the front, while the rear carrying wheel supported a large firebox. Outside cylinders avoided mounting the boiler high to clear the cranks of an inside crank axle, for low centre of gravity was still thought desirable. The result was an efficient and fast locomotive with excellent stability and of a very handsome appearance on 8ft (2438mm) drivers. In all, 53 of the type were built, and they hauled trains daily from London to York at an average speed of 54 mph (87 km/h) including stops. These 8ft singles opened the era of the leading bogie, until then neglected in Great Britain. The first 8ft single, No 1, is today preserved at the National Railway Museum, York.*

The tank locomotive

Ventnor (Isle of Wight Railway) – 1868

During railway development in the various European countries, various motive power problems were encountered, some of which had features in common that suggested using the same solution in each country. For instance, the main lines radiating from large cities had to be connected by short lengths of railway, and at the same time other short lines were built into the suburbs to bring workers to the city. Also main lines often had branches that led to remote and formerly isolated districts, branches that seemed unlikely ever to produce heavy traffic. On both suburban and branch lines locomotives would not be called upon to run great distances so that the coal and water supplies in the tender could be low. The same thing applied to shunting locomotives, and it was realised that the tender could be abolished and the coal and water carried on the locomotive itself. This had the extra advantage that it could be designed to run in either direction, and that the time wasting

operation of putting it on a turntable at the end of each journey could thus be avoided. So the tank locomotive was developed and was very successful in all European countries, as well as elsewhere. In the United States, however, they were little used, even for shunting, because of the greater distances involved, and the sort of trains that were commonly run.

The tank locomotive tended to be an all-purpose, mixed traffic locomotive for almost any sort of train, which could also be used as a pilot for heavy trains in need of assistance, and which was therefore seen everywhere, tirelessly working on shunting duties. Here are two British examples, the *Jura* of the London, Chatham & Dover Railway, built by Neilson & Co in 1866, and the *Ventnor* built by Beyer, Peacock for the Isle of Wight Railway, which with six similar locomotives, worked all trains of that line from 1864 until it was absorbed into the Southern Railway in 1923.

Jura (London, Chatham & Dover Railway) – 1866

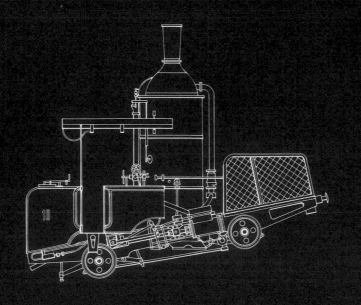

Conquering the Mountains

By the mid-nineteenth century, the hard work of the pioneers had carried the railway across the plains and, indeed, across ground that was far from level. Nevertheless the lines terminated at the steeper slopes of major mountain ranges and it seemed for a while that these obstacles would be insurmountable. To examine how railways began to evolve techniques to cross these natural barriers, we must return to 1850.

The attack on the mountains was pioneered in Austria. Karl von Ghega (born plain Carlo Ghega in Venice) was a champion of railways at the Imperial Court of Vienna. He persuaded the Hapsburg authorities to agree to a railway across the Semmering pass in the Austrian Alps, part of a route from Vienna to the seaport of Trieste. Work started in 1848 on a series of viaducts and tunnels more ambitious than anything previously undertaken and on a colossal scale. It was planned so that no gradient would exceed 1 in 40 (2.5 per cent), although no locomotive at the time could tackle such a gradient, and certainly not those of the length of the Semmering line. The Austrians therefore organised a competition to find the best mountain freight locomotive, a competition comparable to the Rainhill trials of 1829, and in its way just as important.

The conditions of the Semmering contest called for tractive efforts, speeds, capacity for gradient climbing, boiler pressures and braking systems that were then on the frontiers of technology and engineering. A prize of 20000 ducats was offered for the locomotive that best met the competition's terms and there were second, third and fourth prizes of 10000, 9000 and 8000 ducats respectively. The date set for the running trials was 31 July 1851, and there were four entries (and so a prize for everyone), ranging from the traditional to the frankly experimental. First prize went to a traditional design, *Bavaria*, built by Maffei of Munich, but only because the time allocated to the trials was short, which prevented two new articulated designs from showing their full potential. In the event, these three, and the fourth, *Vindobona*, were found to be too prone to failure to be used in regular service, but the Semmering trials did show the world that mountains could be mastered.

In 1852, the inclines were at last conquered when the chief engineer of the Semmering railway, Engerth, designed an articulated loco-

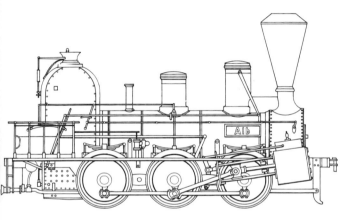

Alb *Designed by Joseph Trick of Esslingen Works, Alb was claimed as one of the first mountain locomotives in the world. It worked on the Stuttgart-Ulm line in Wurtemburg, and was an 0-6-0 with inclined outside cylinders and a boiler with a Stephenson square firebox. There was an innovation in the suspension, as probably for the first time all three axles were compensated, the compensating levers supporting the locomotive at two points on each side. Many components were of cast iron, including the wheels, which were 4ft (1220mm) in diameter. In the Swabian Jura, Alb hauled 120 tonnes up the Geislingen gradient, partly at 1 in 45 (2.2 per cent), on 1 November 1848. Nevertheless, locomotives of the class put too great a stress on the track and the front coupling rods were removed to convert them to 2-4-0s.*

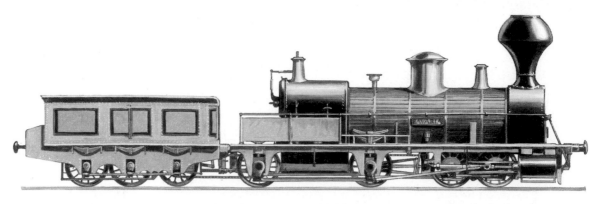

Bavaria *This locomotive, built by Maffei of Munich, won the Semmering trials in 1851. In a fresh approach to an eight-coupled design, the axles were divided into two outside-coupled groups, the two groups being linked by a chain drive, just as had been used by Stephenson on the Killingworth locomotive 38 years before. The first axle of the tender was also converted into a driven axle by another chain drive. In service there was constant trouble because the chain drives were too weak, but in the trials the design, though complicated, did allow* Bavaria *to win by hauling 132 tonnes up 1 in 40 (2.5 per cent) at better than 11 mph (18 km/h).*

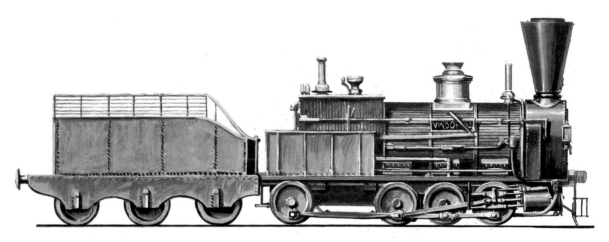

Vindobona *The most traditional of the four Semmering contestants in 1851, but also the most disappointing. Originally built by Haswell of Vienna as an 0-6-0, it proved to be too heavy, and an additional driving axle was added behind the firebox. The boiler was semi-oval in section and contained as many as 286 tubes, while the firebox overhanging at the end was square in section with a flat top that anticipated the work of Belpaire, although Hackworth had actually pioneered flat tops in the 1830s. The long wheelbase stressed the track severely, and for the trials the first pair of wheels was uncoupled. Loss of adhesion and much wheel slip was the result.*

Seraing *This was the entry of the Belgian firm of Cockerill for the Semmering trials. The authorship of the articulated 0-4-4-0 design was claimed by J F Laussemann, and it anticipated the patents of Robert Fairlie a dozen years later. To increase heating surface without overlong tubes, the firebox was placed at the centre of the locomotive with two identical boiler barrels on either side, which were above inside-cylinder, four-wheel bogies. The fireman rode on one side of the firebox and the driver on the other. Such an articulated locomotive was not, however, original, having been anticipated by Horatio Allen (see page 20).*

The Seraing *was a tank locomotive, but in order to take part in the trials a tender for water and fuel had to be added, for the weight was outside the rules if supplies were carried upon the locomotive itself. On trials, fuel consumption was too high and it gained third prize only.*

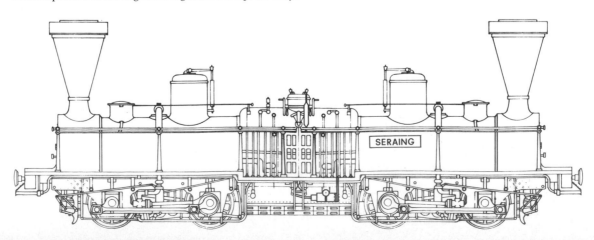

Mastodons of the Giovi

About the same time as the Semmering trials were held, the final section of the Piedmont State Railways' route from the capital Turin to the major seaport of Genoa was being planned. This involved going through the Apennines at the Giovi pass, with a 2 mile 50yd summit tunnel (3.26km), and with a long 1 in 28½ (3.5 per cent) gradient leading up to it from the sea. Germaneo Sommeiller (later the engineer of the Mont Cenis tunnel) decided to master the gradient with Cockerill-designed back-to-back 0-4-0 saddle tanks, controlled by one locomotive crew.

Twenty of these locomotives (ten pairs) were delivered for the railways' opening in 1853, half from Cockerill and the rest from Robert Stephenson & Co. The driving wheels were 3ft 6in (1070mm) in diameter, weight in working order 28 tonnes, and each developed 191hp (382hp for a pair). One pair of wheels on each locomotive had a hand brake. The maximum speed was 22 mph (35 km/h) and they could work a 150 tonne train up the gradients from Pontedecimo to Busalla at an average speed of 13½ mph (22 km/h).

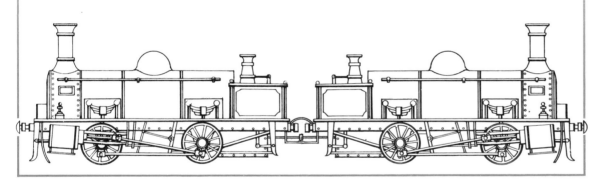

Wiener Neustadt *One of the four Semmering contestants was this original design built by Günther of Wiener Neustadt. The frame carried a great elliptical-section boiler with a saddle tank above, broken halfway by a square-section dome. The locomotive was an 0-4-4-0, the outside cylinders of each of the four-wheel bogies being at the inner ends, in a manner anticipating the Georg Meyer articulated locomotives of 20 years later (see page 103). The* Wiener Neustadt *was a tank locomotive, but during the trials its fuel supplies proved insufficient. Nevertheless it won second prize and the trials committee recommended its purchase, provided that the space for fuel was augmented. Because of the unusual design, this locomotive aroused the most interest.*

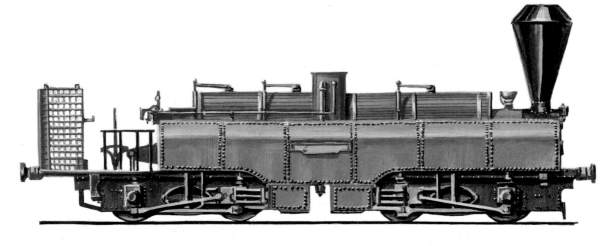

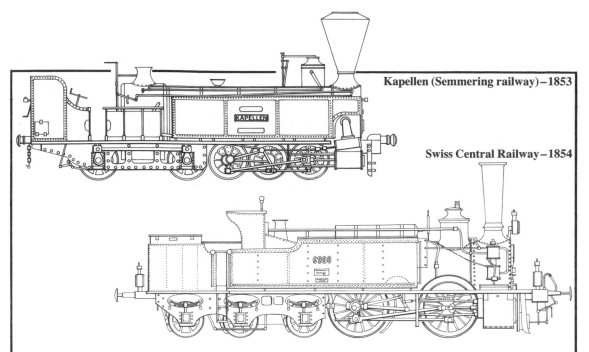

Kapellen (Semmering railway) – 1853

Swiss Central Railway – 1854

Engerth locomotives

The four locomotives that took part in the Semmering trials were disappointing. Apart from not performing very well, they showed up the weaknesses of coupling axles by chain drives and how expensive the complications of articulation could be. It was the Austrian Wilhelm Engerth who solved the Semmering motive power problem. He took out a patent in December 1852 for an articulated locomotive in which the first axle of the tender was driven by a gear train from the coupled axles of the locomotive, the two axles of the tender being coupled in turn. The first axle of the tender was under the boiler and two arms of the tender frame extended either side of the firebox to articulate the tender to the locomotive by a bearing ahead of the firebox. Part of the tender's weight rested on the locomotive through this bearing to increase adhesion of the locomotive itself.

The first 0-6-4 Engerth locomotive was tried on the Semmering in November 1853 and was a great success, both in tractive effort and in fuel economy. First batches of the Engerths totalling 26 locomotives were built by Esslingen Works in Germany and Cockerill in Belgium. The *Kapellen* was one of this class and had 3ft 6in (1070mm) driving wheels, a boiler pressure of 106lb/in^2 (7.4kg/cm^2), grate area of 13.75ft^2 (1.28m^2) and a heating surface of 1512ft^2 (140.5m^2).

In practice the gear train was found to be a nuisance, so it was removed and the tender's wheels were uncoupled. So was born the modified Engerth type, whose sole advantages were a shorter total wheelbase than usual and increased locomotive adhesion because part of the tender's weight was supported. The Swiss had 110 modified Engerth locomotives in all, both 0-4-6 and 0-6-4 (see page 62), some of which had inside cylinders and the last of which ran until 1905. Between 1854 and 1858 the Esslingen Works provided 26 mixed traffic 0-4-6 locomotives that could haul 220 tonnes up a 1 in 100 gradient (1.0 per cent) and which had a maximum speed of 37 mph (60 km/h). The modified Engerth was used in quantity in both Hungary and France, while the Northern of France put an 0-4-6 inside cylinder class as well as an 0-8-4 freight class into service in 1856. This last was built by Schneider and it could haul a 40-wagon train (450 tonnes) up a 1 in 200 gradient (0.5 per cent). The Eastern Railway of France had similar 0-8-4 freight locomotives, but found that they derailed too often, and from 1860 rebuilt then into ordinary 0-8-0s. This fate awaited most modified Engerths in France and Austria, but not in Hungary or Switzerland.

Northern Railway of France – 1856

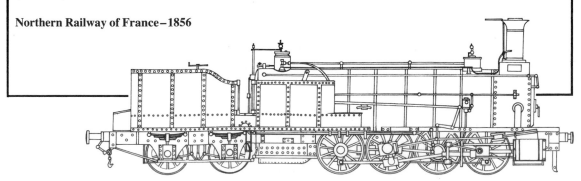

La Rampe *Edouard Beugniot, chief engineer of the Koechlin works at Mulhouse, designed a locomotive in which the tender supported part of the locomotive's weight instead of the reverse, as in the modified Engerth. The leading tender axle had four axle boxes, two external belonging to the tender, and two internal supporting an extension of the locomotive's frames.* La Rampe *was built in 1859 for the Paris, Lyons & Mediterranean, an 0-8-6 with a Beugniot bar for the two leading axles which allowed them to traverse ¾in (20mm) in relation to each other to aid running through curves. It had inside cylinders, 3ft 11in (1200mm) driving wheels and a weight in working order of about 71 tonnes, of which 47 tonnes was adhesive.*

motive. On this two trucks were driven by the pistons, connected together by gear wheels with an 0-6-4 wheel arrangement. Within four years the gear wheels were being removed as they gave trouble, and from 1861 the locomotives were rebuilt to orthodox tender locomotive design, some to the 0-8-0 wheel arrangement which became the classic mountain type until beyond the end of the century. Engerth's articulation transferred part of the tender truck's weight to the locomotive to help adhesion. Another innovator, Edouard Beugniot, devised similar articulation in which the tender supported part of the locomotive's weight, so that it was just as successful in the mountains as the modified Engerth. Like the latter, the Beugniots were eventually rebuilt to the ortho-

dox 0-8-0 pattern. The long boiler 0-8-0 was a development of the Bourbonnais type and came into use at about the time of Engerth's locomotives.

As far as the track itself was concerned, new techniques were used for building tunnels, viaducts and steeply graded railways. For really severe gradients, Blenkinsop's rack locomotive was revived at the end of the 1860s, and rack railways eventually reached the very tops of mountains where no other wheeled vehicle could run. The first trans-Alpine tunnel opened in 1871, the Mont Cenis (known to the French and Italians as the Fréjus), which allowed the Indian Mail to run from France the whole length of Italy to the port of Brindisi. The St Gotthard

(continued on page 86)

Petiet *Jules Petiet, locomotive engineer of the Northern of France, designed a well-tank locomotive of high performance and unusual layout in 1862. It had a single driving axle at each end, both driven from a forward pair of cylinders. Between the driving wheels there were six smaller-diameter carrying wheels. The great firebox spread over the carrying wheels and had a grate area of 28ft² (2.61m²). The barrel of the boiler was surmounted by a large water preheater, and gases from the firebox passed through the boiler tubes before turning through 180 degrees to pass through the preheater tubes to a chimney at the rear. The locomotive's wheelbase was too long to pass through curves easily and stressed the track; nor did it steam very well. Petiet also built 0-8-0 and 0-6-6-0 well-tanks with the same sort of boiler, all destined for mountain work, but none performed satisfactorily.*

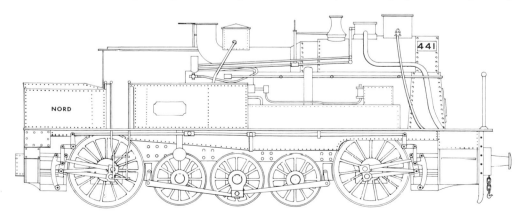

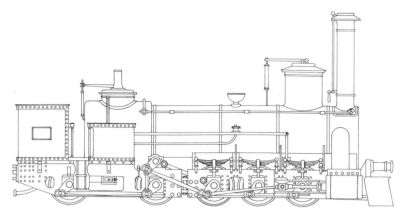

Steyerdorf *Pius Fink, in collaboration with Engerth, improved on the Engerth type in 1862 by driving the tender coupled axles through coupling rods instead of by gears. A jackshaft driven from the last of the driving wheels was mounted directly above the first tender axle, to which it was coupled. The articulated tender axles were coupled also. Steyerdorf and three sisters worked on an Austrian State Railway Co's line from Jaszenova to Oravica and Anina in south-east Hungary. They had no particular success and were soon displaced by 0-8-0s and 0-8-0 tanks.*

Cantal class *The Paris-Orleans' Murat-Aurillac line in the Massif Central called for high-adhesion tank locomotives to work the 1 in 33 (3 per cent) gradients over the Lioran pass. Victor Fourquenot designed the first five-coupled locomotive in Europe for the task, giving it a large firebox with two firedoors. A double frame was provided for the two rear axles, while these and the two front ones had lateral displacements of about $^1/_4$in or $^3/_4$in (7 or 17mm). A curious feature was the sandbox arranged around the chimney. The Cantal class could haul 150 tonne trains at 12$^1/_2$ mph (20 km/h) over the Lioran pass, but they were not a success. Their 60 tonnes weight in working order was thought to be excessive, and they were often subject to hot boxes. They were relegated to banking duties until withdrawn from traffic in 1924.*

Barcelona-Saragossa-Pamplona *This sharply graded railway (later incorporated into the Northern of Spain) had some 0-8-0 locomotives in 1865 that were to be in traffic for around a century. The first 12 were built by the Avonside Engine Co of Bristol, and another eight were added in 1877 from Schneider in France. Cylinders were 20in by 24in (506mm by 610mm) and outside; Stephenson's valve gear was inside, driving wheel diameter was 4ft 3in (1290mm) and, including the tender, the weight in working order was about 75 tonnes. The locomotives were built for the gauge that is general in Spain, two Spanish yards (1674mm) – near enough 5ft 6in.*

Fairlie locomotives

Chimbote-Huallanca Railway – 1873

Class R, New Zealand – 1877

Railways were reaching out into the less-populated regions of Europe, as well as into under-developed countries and colonial territories. The lines linking centres of population had to be built cheaply and often quickly, so that they tended to be full of curves and usually steeply graded. Robert Fairlie, using as his starting point the *Seraing* locomotive of the Semmering trials, patented an articulated locomotive in 1863 and 1864 with two four-wheel bogies, of which each pair of axles were driven from separate sets of cylinders at either end of the locomotive. *Little Wonder*, an 0-4-4-0 tank locomotive built for the 600mm gauge (1ft 11½in) Festiniog Railway in Wales, attracted great attention from engineers because of its adaptability to the winding railway and its remarkable tractive effort, which took trains up continuous gradients of 1 in 83 (1.2 per cent).

Fairlie locomotives became popular in South America, Mexico, Sweden, Russia, New Zealand, Australia and in any place where time and capital were so lacking that curves and gradients could not be avoided. Fairlies had a large central firebox, from which two boiler barrels stretched out in either direction, with two- or three-axle identically driven bogies under them. The Festiniog had a Fairlie built in their Boston Lodge workshops in 1885, almost identical to *Little Wonder* of 1869, while the Chimbote-Huallanca Railway in Peru had a much larger 0-6-6-0 from the Avonside Engine Co in 1872, named *Escalador de Montes* (Scaler of Mountains). Single Fairlies were also popular in New Zealand for passenger trains, and one worked until 1945. These had a single boiler barrel and driven bogie, while a bunker and cab were supported by an undriven bogie at the other end. Classes R and S were delivered to New Zealand from 1877.

Festiniog Railway – 1885

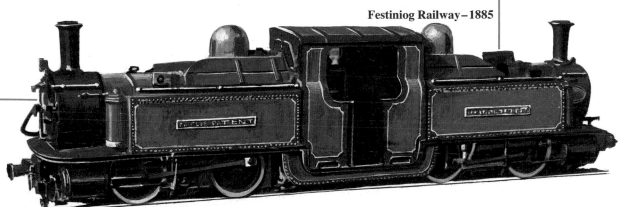

Ludwig's Hesse Railway *The first German eight-coupled locomotive was built by Esslingen Works for this railway in 1869. As was usual in Austria and Germany at this date, double frames were used, in this case with outside valve gear. The locomotive had a heating surface of 1798ft^2 (167m^2), a 129lb/in^2 (9kg/cm^2) boiler pressure, 3ft 7in (1090mm) driving wheels and a weight in working order of about 45 tonnes.*

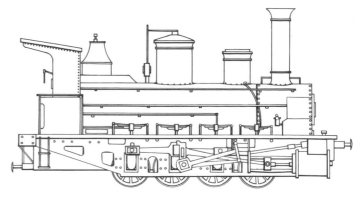

Porrettana line *This Beugniot articulated 0-8-6 was built by Koechlin for the Porrettana route between Bologna and Florence in 1862. As one result of the Italian war of independence, this locomotive and a sister spent the first three years of their lives working on the Austrian Südbahn out of Trieste, before reaching the Porrettana.*

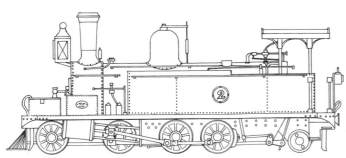

Tarragona, Barcelona & France *This railway (later incorporated into the Madrid, Saragossa & Alicante) had five 0-8-0 locomotives from Sharp, Stewart in 1878, which were followed by batches of four in both 1879 and 1880. They were very British in appearance, even to the massive sandboxes above each cylinder, and lasted almost until the end of the steam locomotive in Spain. Cylinders were 20in by 26in (508mm by 660mm) and driving wheels 4ft 6½in (1390mm) diameter.*

Cape Government Railway *This 3ft 6in gauge (1067mm) railway in South Africa was worked in three divisions – Cape Western, Cape Midland and Cape Eastern – until a through rail connection was completed between the divisional headquarters at Cape Town, Port Elizabeth and East London. Robert Stephenson & Co built six 2-6-2 tank locomotives in 1874, with cylinders 15in by 20in (381mm by 508mm), 3ft 2in (970mm) driving wheels and a weight in working order of about 29 tonnes.*

Swiss Central Railway – 1871

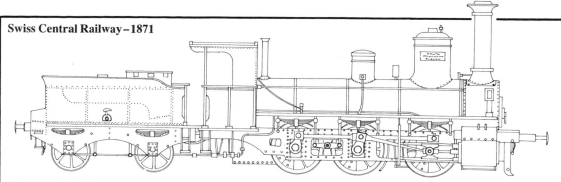

In the Swiss Alps

Not unnaturally, the railway met major terrain difficulties in the Swiss Confederation. Civil engineers had to extend their skills to the limit to pierce the mountain ranges and devise means to get round the precipices. Difficult weather also impeded the running of trains in the winter. Tunnels, daring bridges and, in places, unavoidable gradients, stand as monuments to the hard work and skill of all who took part in the battle against nature's forces. Swiss locomotives of the time avoided carrying wheels, all their weight having to be used for adhesion, at first 0-4-0s, then 0-6-0s and 0-8-0s. Of the 0-4-0 wheel arrangement were four well tanks, built locally in 1874 by SLM Winterthur for the short Gotthard Railway. These had a grate area of 11.8ft^2 (1.1m^2), an 867ft^2 (80.5m^2) heating surface, a boiler pressure of 143lb/in^2 (10kg/cm^2) and 4ft 4in driving wheels. Weight in working order was 29 tonnes and they could attain 31mph (50km/h). Ten years later after the opening of the Gotthard tunnel (which, anticipating history, the Italians called the People's Road), the Gotthard Railway received 31 locomotives from Maffei of Munich during 1882–1890, all with the 0-8-0 wheel

arrangement, a weight in working order of 53 tonnes, maximum speed of 28mph (45km/h) and developing 600hp. Two or three of them handled trains on the Gotthard gradients for 30 years, and after electrification some of them had another career on the Hungarian State Railways. The Swiss Central Railway had some outside frame 0-6-0s from Esslingen Works, of the almost standard central European type of that time. Cylinders were 16½in by 24¾in (421mm by 632mm), driving wheels 4ft 1½in (1260mm) and weight in working order 35.6 tonnes.

Gotthard Railway – 1872

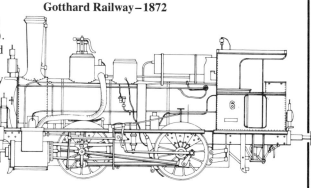

Gotthard Railway – 1882

Paris, Lyons & Mediterranean *Following on the success of the 0-8-0 long boiler locomotives of the Paris-Orleans Railway, the PLM took up the type from 1868 onwards. By widening the frames at the rear, it was possible to fit in a wider firebox with a grate area of 22.35ft² (2.08m²). At first the boiler pressure was 129lb/in² (9kg/cm²), but later this went up to 143lb/in² (10kg/cm²) and then 157lb/in² (11kg/cm²). Wheel diameter was 4ft 1½in (1260mm) and weight in working order about 52 tonnes. The type was highly successful on heavy freight trains as well as on mountain lines with much curvature. For example, they worked from Grenoble to Veyne and from Veyne to Briançon, as well as up the 1 in 33 gradients (3.0 per cent) leading to the Mont Cenis tunnel. One locomotive at each end of a train could work 400 tonnes at 11mph (18km/h) up a 1 in 40 (2.5 per cent) gradient. In all there were 134 of the type on the PLM and they lasted to within a few years of the end of steam.*

tunnel was opened in 1882, but the Simplon tunnel did not follow until 1905. In Italy itself the Genoa-Turin route over the Giovi pass was completed in 1854 and other trans-Apennine routes followed: Bologna-Florence in 1864 and Rome-Ancona in 1866.

Other countries in central Europe dealt with great mountain obstacles when building both international and internal routes, but a coherent rail network was gradually achieved. In some parts of Europe, however, mountains did not present difficulties and rail development was swift, as in the British Isles, which by 1880 had 15562 miles (25049km) of railway route, while Belgium could boast a denser rail network in relation to the country's size than any other – a position it has maintained to the present day. The ending of the Civil War in the United States gave a fresh impulse to railway building, as will be seen in the next chapter. This was highlighted in 1869 by the completion of one of the boldest ventures ever undertaken by man, a railway route from the Atlantic to the Pacific.

During two decades, from 1850 to 1870, railways expanded to reach the most distant corners of the world. They arrived in the Indian peninsula to lap the foothills of the Himalayan mountains, they came to Central and to South America in the shadow of the Andes, and they started up in Australia and in New Zealand.

Darjeeling Himalayan Railway *This 51 miles (82km), 2ft 6in gauge (762mm), railway was opened from Silguri on the Indian plain to the hill station of Darjeeling in 1881. The vertical height climbed was 6100ft (1920m) with curves of 144yd radius (130m) and a ruling gradient of 1 in 30 (3.3 per cent). Sharp, Stewart in Britain built eight 0-4-0 tanks for the line, with a very short wheelbase and considerable overhangs front and rear. These were rebuilt into saddle-tank locomotives from 1886. The first four had 2ft (610mm) driving wheels, augmented to 2ft 2in (660mm) for subsequent locomotives. The original weight in working order was 11 tonnes and the load that could be hauled up the 1 in 30 (3.3 per cent) gradient was originally put at 18 tonnes, latterly raised to 27–28 tonnes.*

Rack locomotives return

In 1812, John Blenkinsop held that adhesion alone would not allow a locomotive to haul a train, and hence provided his *Prince Royal* with rack rail traction (see page 10). Fifty years later Nicolas Riggenbach of Basle in Switzerland revived the rack rail (now put in the centre of the track) for locomotive mountain climbing. His ideas and experiments brought him a patent dated 12 August 1863, but it gained no immediate application on a railway. The earliest mountain rack railway (cog railway in the United States) was built by Silvester Marsh in 1869. Marsh's first locomotive, nicknamed *Old Peppersass*, had a vertical boiler, a chain drive to the pinion to engage the rack, and climbed the 6289ft (1917m) Mount Washington in New Hampshire on a 3¾-mile railway (6km) with gradients up to 1 in 5 (20 per cent). The same year, on 9 June, Lucerne canton authorised Europe's first rack railway up the Rigi mountain from Vitznau. The Rigi Railway was 4¼ miles long (7km) and rose 3290ft (1003m). It opened to traffic in 1871. Riggenbach suggested that a normal railway on a 1 in 40 gradient (2.5 per cent) would have to be 43 miles (70km) long to link Vitznau with the Rigi summit, and that the cost would be prohibitive. So, in 1870, the first three rack locomotives were built in the Swiss Central's works at Olten. They had a near vertical boiler to prevent water uncovering the tubeplate on gradients, a boiler pressure of 129lb/in^2 (9kg/cm^2) and developed 170hp each. The pistons drove the rack pinion directly and the maximum speed was not more than 5½mph (9km/h).

Riggenbach rack railways were built in various parts of the world, together with others with improved rack rails following the Abt, Strub and Locher systems. Edouard Locher built the steepest rack railway in the world, up Mount Pilatus in Switzerland with gradients up to nearly 1 in 2 (50 per cent). For such a steep gradient a horizontal rack rail was provided with teeth on both sides and the locomotive had a pair of pinions. The locomotive was incorporated into a railcar built by SLM Winterthur in 1886, with a boiler across the frame to prevent water uncovering the firebox top. The car could carry 64 passengers and the weight in working order was 12 tonnes.

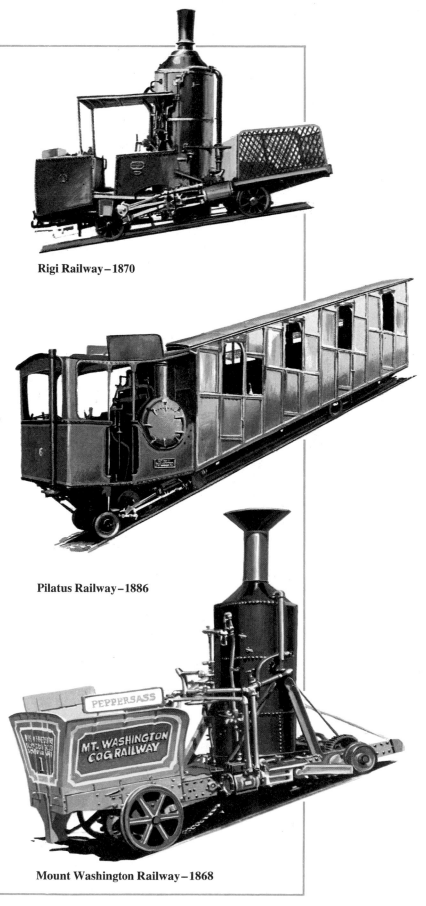

Rigi Railway – 1870

Pilatus Railway – 1886

Mount Washington Railway – 1868

Western Epic

The march to the American west started just as the first railway track was laid on the eastern seaboard. Covered wagons rather than trains conveyed the first pioneers, the wagons going as far as the Pacific coast long before the first trains ventured across the mountains westwards. By 1850, however, rails had crossed the Allegheny mountains and spread over areas of the western plains in Ohio and Illinois. The decade that followed saw railroads pushed west to the Mississippi river and across the state of Iowa to the Missouri. The Civil War in the first half of the 1860s saw a considerable advance in railway technique and some expansion of the system, even if the advance westwards was slowed by long and bloody fighting. Railways played their part in the war, not only carrying stores, troops, munitions, wounded and refugees, but also, on occasion, actual fighting troops.

Technical locomotive improvements were concentrated on the American 4-4-0, already celebrated in the United States and which was to be the basic locomotive type until the end of the 19th century (see pages 26 and 58). Swan-neck frame longer wheelbase bogies appeared, introduced by the locomotive builder Rogers, and the wagon top boiler was evolved, in which the top of the firebox had a greater diameter than that of the boiler barrel, and a coned boiler ring made the connection. After 1860, coal came into general use as a fuel instead of wood as the

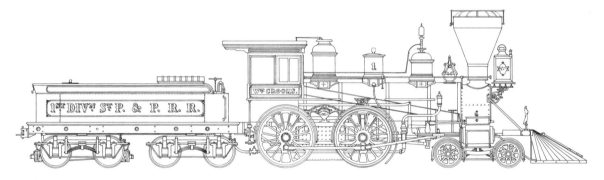

William Crooks *This was the first locomotive to run in Minnesota, in September 1861. Of the classic American type, it was built by the New Jersey Locomotive & Machine Co, Paterson, for the St Paul & Pacific Railroad. Cylinders were 12in by 22in (305mm by 559mm), driving wheels 5ft 3in (1600mm) diameter, boiler pressure 110lb/in² (7.5kg/cm²) and weight in working order 46.3 tonnes. It hauled the first passenger train over the 10 miles (16km) between St Paul and St Anthony. Saved from breaking up, it is preserved in original condition by the Burlington Northern Railroad.*

cost of the latter went up, accelerated by the demands of war. Coal had a higher thermal value, and it was burnt in steel rather than copper fireboxes from the 1860s. In 1856, in Great Britain, Henry Bessemer had invented a furnace to provide cheap steel in quantity, so production was no longer a problem.

The great ambition in the United States was to build a rail route from the Atlantic coast to the Pacific Ocean, although many scoffed at the idea as an unrealisable dream. Theodore

Pennsylvania *Designed by James Millholland, this 0-12-0 tank was the first twelve-coupler in the world. Intended for banking coal trains between Delaware and Schuykill, it was a Camel locomotive as devised by Ross Winans (see page 27). The long and narrow firebox had the advantage that the grate area was enlarged, but it was difficult to fire adequately and restricted boiler barrel length.* Pennsylvania *went into service on the Philadelphia & Reading in 1863. The driving wheels were 3ft 7in (1090mm) diameter, grate area 31ft^2 (2.9m^2), heating surface 1399ft^2 (130m^2) and weight in working order 50 tonnes, an exceptional figure at that time. A peculiarity of the locomotive was that there was no coal bunker, for the brief journeys made allowed firing at each end of the gradient.*

Consolidation *The tendency to build heavy locomotives to work freight over steeply-graded lines was exemplified in 1866 when Baldwin delivered the first 2-8-0 in the world to the Lehigh Valley Railroad. The wheel arrangement was known as the Consolidation type after the name of the locomotive, and it became extremely popular. The designer was Alexander Mitchell and it had 20in by 24in cylinders (508mm by 610mm), a grate area of 25ft^2 (2.31m^2), driving wheels 4ft in diameter (1220mm) and a weight in working order of 39 tonnes. With the advent of the Consolidation type a high adhesion locomotive with a reasonable maximum speed became available, two requirements of importance in developing freight traffic over the expanding American railway network.*

Dehone Judah tried to interest Congress in a transcontinental line in 1859, but found the time not yet ripe. He returned to California to found the Central Pacific Railroad Co, despite financial and legal difficulties of every sort. With the enthusiasm and determination of a true pioneer he was soon back in Washington to campaign for his cause. He was rewarded when President Lincoln signed the Pacific Railroad Act on 1 July 1862. This authorised the Central Pacific to build a railroad from San Francisco to the Californian border, or farther eastwards if the Union Pacific Railroad had not by that time reached the border. The latter railroad had been authorised by the same Act to start eastwards from the Missouri. The first Central Pacific sleepers were laid in California at Sacramento on 8 July 1863, but progress was slow, delayed by money problems aggravated by lack of aid from Washington, where the Government was by then financing the Civil War. Labour shortages were made good by sending across the Pacific for Chinese to work on contract. Attracted by the high pay offered for the colossal task of helping to bridge a continent they came by the thousand, and it is estimated that the Central Pacific employed as many as 10 000 altogether.

From the east, the Union Pacific was commenced on 19 October 1865, its starting point being the town of Omaha on the Missouri. The

America *This locomotive aroused the greatest interest at the Paris Universal Exhibition of 1867. While of no great interest technically, it did represent the American type then in use throughout the United States. Nevertheless, the builder, Grant Locomotive Works, Paterson, New Jersey, had gone to the trouble of nickel-plating the boiler barrel and various other components, and the cab was a masterpiece of the cabinet maker's art. It won a gold medal at the exhibition, after which it went to the Chicago, Rock Island & Pacific Railroad, bringing the first train of that line into Council Bluffs (opposite Omaha) in May 1869, and from 1871 being used on Chicago-Omaha mail trains.*

Seminole *Another historic American type. Built by the Rogers Locomotive & Machine Co, Paterson, New Jersey in April 1867, it went to the Union Pacific and was typical of the decorated and colourful locomotive liveries of the period. Cylinders were 16in by 22in (406mm by 559mm), driving wheels 4ft 6in diameter (1370mm), boiler pressure 130lb/in² (8.6kg/cm²), weight in working order 27 tonnes and it developed 500hp. As with others of the American type it worked either passenger or freight trains.*

Pride of the Prairie *No 119 of the Union Pacific Railroad was an American type coal-burner with bar frames and separate blast pipes for each cylinder. At this time coal was taking over from wood as a fuel as the latter was becoming too costly. No 119 was built by the Rogers Locomotive and Machine Co and touched cowcatchers with* Jupiter *of the Central Pacific at Promontory Point, Utah, on 10 May 1869 to mark the successful completion of the first transcontinental railway from the Atlantic to the Pacific.*

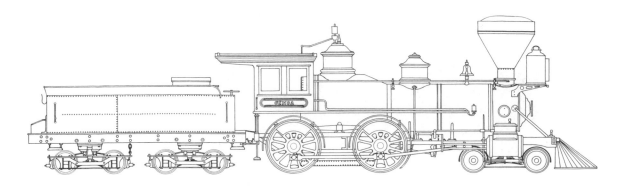

Genoa *One of the numerous American type locomotives built by Baldwin that went to the Virginia & Truckee Railroad in 1872. The design had all the standard features, although Genoa was one of the diminishing band of wood-burners. The great coned chimney with an internal spark deflector was a feature that vanished almost entirely between 1870 and 1880, and its going marked the end of the pioneering age of the American railroad. At this time the American type was claimed as cheap to build costing, together with the tender, $8000 to $9000, compared with a similar British locomotive which might cost $11 000.*

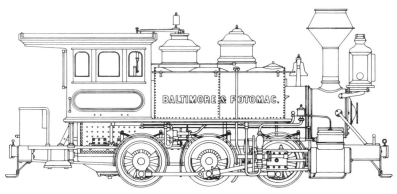

Baltimore & Potomac *This short line was a subsidiary of the great Pennsylvania Railroad and gave the latter access to railroads south of Washington without using the tracks of rival companies. This 0-6-0 saddle tank is a typical American shunting locomotive or 'yard goat'. The saddle tank was popular on American shunting locomotives for many years, but not the limited coal space this one had. In the later years of steam shunting, locomotive tenders with adequate bunkers were provided to keep them hard at work in the yard for as long as possible.*

workers came from all parts–Boston Irish, immigrants from Europe and (later) many demobilised soldiers from both Union and Confederate armies. They lived together in tension and violence, gradually inured to the taxing conditions of work and the possibility of attack by Indians. Head-of-rail towns appeared overnight for the workers to live in and for their recreation. Some survive today, while others vanished as their buildings were dismantled and carried forward in sections to a fresh site as the railway advanced. Reporters described the towns as Hell on Wheels, and recorded how the Union Pacific Irish were pitting themselves against the Central Pacific Chinese in a merciless race to build as much route for their respective companies as possible. Rivers were spanned, hillsides excavated, mountains carved through (with the newly-invented dynamite) and great trestle viaducts erected. In the rush not a little of the work was poorly executed, and had to be re-done as soon as the railroad was opened. The Union Pacific was at North Platte, Nebraska, in November 1866; by February 1867 it had reached Julesburg, Colorado, and in

Countess of Dufferin *This locomotive is preserved in the Sir William Whyte Park at Winnipeg as a symbol of the part played by the railway in binding together the provinces of Canada. Built for the Northern Pacific Railroad in the United States by the Baldwin Locomotive Works in 1872, it was sold some years later to the contractor James Whitehead, who was then pushing the new Canadian Pacific Railway across the wastes of Manitoba, and from 1881 it became No 1 of the Canadian Pacific. It was sold again in 1897 to a British Columbia lumber firm, and bought back in 1910 by the Canadian Pacific to become a monument to their railway.*

San Juan *During the 1870s William Mason designed the Mason Bogies, which in conception were the same as the British Fairlie type and, like them, were built with both double and single boiler barrels. San Juan was built in 1878 and was one of a class of 18 for the Denver, South Park & Pacific Railroad. This was a 3ft gauge (914mm) line in the Rocky Mountains that ran to the silver mines of Leadville and on to Gunnison. The wheel arrangement was 2-6-6, a leading axle being provided to aid running through sharp curves.*

Uncle Dick *Built in 1878 this was the largest and most powerful locomotive in the United States in its day. It was built for banking on a temporary line through the Raton pass on the New Mexico border, later part of the Atchison, Topeka & Santa Fe main line. After the opening of the final line and tunnel, Uncle Dick went on to shunting work until withdrawn in 1921. A 2-8-0 saddle tank with 20in by 26in cylinders (508mm by 660mm), 3ft 6in driving wheels (1067mm), a boiler pressure of 145lb/in² (10.2kg/cm²) and weight in working order of 65 tonnes, it had a tractive effort of 22 200lbf (10 100kgf).*

Philadelphia & Reading *In 1880 the Baldwin Locomotive Works built its 5,000th locomotive, one of a type little known in the United States, a 4-2-2. Otherwise entirely American in design, it had the wheel arrangement used in Europe for high speed trains. Joseph E Wootten was the engineer of the Philadelphia & Reading Railroad for which the locomotive was built, and he designed the boiler with its wide firebox extending out above the carrying wheels, the first Wootten firebox. Intended for burning anthracite, this firebox had a grate area of no less than 54ft² (5m²). Driving wheels were 6ft 6in in diameter (1980mm) and weight in working order was 38.6 tonnes. During trials the locomotive attained 90mph (145km/h), but the poor track in the United States at that time could not take the high axle load necessary for a single driver's adhesion, and the locomotive was sold to the Eames Vacuum Brake Co, finishing its brief days in Britain, demonstrating the vacuum brake to railways there.*

El Gobernador *From 1882, it seemed that there was a race to build the world's largest locomotive. It began with* Champion, *the Lehigh Valley's 4-8-0, which exceeded in size and power the first Consolidation, and it continued with the Central Pacific's 4-8-0s from their Sacramento shops, heavier than* Champion *by about 10 tonnes. Then Sacramento produced* El Gobernador *in 1884, a huge 4-10-0 locomotive, designed by A J Stevens and intended for banking duties on Sierra Nevada gradients, with 4ft 9in driving wheels (1450mm) and a weight in working order of 67 tonnes. Only one was built because the long wheelbase was ill-suited to mountain curves, although Stevens' six- and eight-couple locomotives gave excellent service on the Central Pacific for many years.*

New York, Philadelphia & Norfolk Railroad *This railroad was a subsidiary of the Pennsylvania Railroad, with which it was subsequently merged. No 7 was identical with Class D8ᵃ of the Pennsylvania and was a highly developed version of the American type. Baldwin built it in 1884, with 18in by 24in cylinders (457mm by 610mm), a boiler pressure of 140lb/in² (9.8kg/cm²), driving wheels 6ft 2in in diameter (1570mm) and a weight in working order of 38.6 tonnes. Sparks, even from coal firing, continued to give trouble, and from this time the smokebox was extended in front of the chimney to contain an internal spark-arrester.*

November of the same year it was at Cheyenne, Wyoming. The final meeting of the rival railroads was at Promontory Point, Utah, on 10 May 1869. There *Jupiter* of the Central Pacific and *Pride of the Prairie* (No 119 Union Pacific) ceremonially crept towards each other until their cowcatchers touched and their drivers opened bottles of champagne. A transcontinental service was started a few days later.

The American type 4-4-0 was gradually progressing technically during these years, and its development was reflected in its outward appearance. The centre of gravity rose steadily, driving wheel diameters increased, boilers became larger and were adapted for coal burning, and maximum speeds went up. It showed its worth until the turn of the century,

but from the 1870s it was challenged by others. It is estimated that in 1860 the American type made up 80 per cent of the locomotives built, but ten years later the figure had fallen to 60 per cent. In 1885 it was 50 per cent, in 1890, 15 per cent and there were virtually none by 1900. More sophisticated locomotives were being designed for specific traffics to replace the 4-4-0, such as the Mogul (2-6-0), Consolidation (2-8-0), Ten-Wheeler (4-6-0) and the Atlantic (4-4-2) types. Progress led during the 1880s to the building of the largest and heaviest locomotives yet seen. This was made possible by the spread of steel rails, stronger and more resistant to the hammering they had to take than the previous iron rails, and another result of Bessemer's cheap steel. The first steel rails in

Pennsylvania Railroad *Built at the Pennsylvania Railroad's Altoona shops in October 1885, this locomotive was the first of the Class R Consolidation 2-8-0s. Although derived from the Lehigh Valley's* Consolidation, *the boiler was pitched much higher, so that in this respect the design anticipated those common a decade later. There were 111 of the R class (later H3 class) and some had Belpaire fireboxes, which were a feature of many later Pennsylvania locomotives. Cylinders were 20in by 24in (508mm by 610mm), boiler pressure 140/in^2 (9.8kg/cm^2) and weight in working order was 52 tonnes, of which 45.6 tonnes was adhesive.*

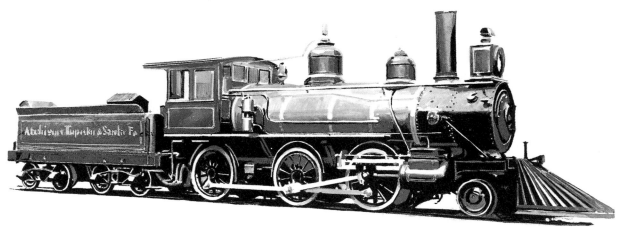

Atchison, Topeka & Santa Fe *The Mogul type 2-6-0 was very popular in the United States until the end of the 1880s, not only for fast freight trains, but also for mixed traffic duty, although in the 1870s the type had caused little interest, as six-coupled wheels were not yet regarded as necessary. This type was acquired by almost all railroads for the most varied of duties, and it was exported all over the world, not least to the countries of Central and South America. Such exports went on for many years.*

Denver & Rio Grande Buena Vista *was a typical western States Ten-Wheeler 4-6-0, a type that gained in popularity during the 1880s. The Denver & Rio Grande Railroad ran through the Rocky Mountains, and had long gradients and winding tracks through largely uninhabited and otherwise inaccessible regions. Locomotives had to be simple, with good steam production and with coupled wheels of relatively small diameter to deal with the conditions. This Baldwin was built in 1887 with 18in by 24in cylinders (457mm by 610mm), 4ft 6in (1370mm) driving wheels and a weight in working order of 44 tonnes. An extended smokebox with internal spark arrester had replaced the large spark arresting chimney of former years.*

the United States were imported from Great Britain in 1863 and local production soon followed. The first really large locomotive was *Champion* of the Lehigh Valley in 1882. It was simply a Consolidation with the front carrying axle replaced by a bogie, the new type being called the Mastodon. Other 4-8-0s appeared and the Central Pacific capped them all in 1884 by building a 4-10-0, *El Gobernador*, in its Sacramento workshops.

The building of larger and larger locomotives did not necessarily lead to better and better performance. On the contrary, some types were bitter disappointments and a great deal of money was wasted. All the same, this period of activity and experiment was the prelude to a new age of the locomotive that led to the heyday of steam in the splendour of its maturity.

Pennsylvania & New York Railroad *The limit placed on maximum axle load by the poor track of many United States' railways meant that adhesive weight and hence locomotive power could be increased only by adding coupled axles, despite the design and construction changes involved. Baldwin built this 4-8-0 in 1887 especially to keep within strict axle load limitations, taking account of the desire of the customer for a 2-8-0 of the period. A bogie in place of the leading axle had to be provided to help spread the total weight of about 51 tonnes along the track, rather than to aid running through curves, which was unnecessary because of the low operating speed. The locomotive had 20in by 24½in cylinders (508mm by 670mm), 4ft 2½in driving wheels (1280mm) and a boiler pressure of 130lb/in² (9.2kg/cm²).*

Colorado Midland Railway *This locomotive was one of 12 4-6-0s built by the Schenectady Locomotive Works for the Colorado Midland in 1887, a road which brought the standard gauge into the heart of the Colorado Rocky Mountains. It was of the Ten-Wheeler type that was beginning to supplant the American type. This had the advantage that driving wheels from 4ft 4in (1320mm) to 6ft 6in (1980mm) could be fitted as required. The Colorado Midland locomotives had 4ft 9in driving wheels (1450mm), weighed 53 tonnes in working order, and had a tractive effort of about 15 200lbf (6900kgf). Because of financial difficulties, the Colorado Midland soon had to close down much of its route and retained only the Colorado Springs to Cripple Creek section, this line closing finally in 1940.*

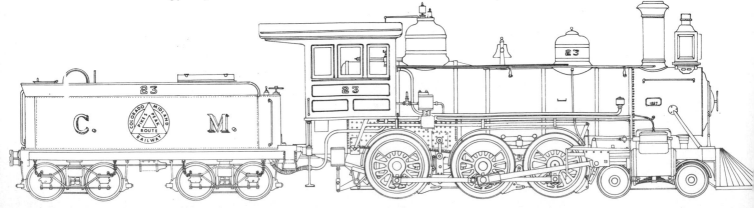

Compound *It is questionable if this was the first American Pacific type locomotive, for the design started as a 4-6-0 (then at the height of its popularity) and the trailing axle was added at the last moment. Compound was built in 1889 for the Chicago, Milwaukee & St Paul Railway by the Schenectady Locomotive Works, and made a contribution to the short history of the compound locomotive in the United States. It was a two-cylinder compound design with a right-hand high-pressure cylinder 21¾in (553mm) in diameter and a left-hand low pressure 31in (787mm) in diameter, both having a stroke of 26in (660mm). As an express locomotive it had 6ft 6in driving wheels (1980mm), a boiler pressure of 200lb/in² (14kg/cm²) and a weight in working order of 66 tonnes, of which 40.8 tonnes were adhesive.*

Philadelphia & Reading *This railroad long held to the Camel design of Ross Winans and James Millholland, continuing to use the boiler-mounted cab on updated designs. The locomotive shown was a 2-8-0 with a Wootten firebox for anthracite burning, built for the Philadelphia & Reading by the Baldwin Locomotive Works in 1890. The general features of Winans' prototype were followed, with the driver in the cab astride the boiler barrel, and the fireman standing on the tender, protected by a large roof. The fireman not only fired through a firedoor in the usual manner, but also fed two mechanical hoppers which placed coal on the grate in parts remote from the firedoor.*

Empire State Express *The 1890s saw great rivalry between the New York & Hudson River and the Pennsylvania Railroads for New York-Chicago traffic. In 1893 the New York & Hudson River took delivery of No 999, designed by William Buchanan and bearing on its tender the name of the train it hauled, the Empire State Express. Large driving wheels were a conspicuous feature of the locomotive, 7ft 3in (2210mm) diameter, although the illustration shows the locomotive as rebuilt with smaller driving wheels. Cylinders were 19in by 24in (483mm by 610mm) and boiler pressure 180lb/in² (12.6kg/cm²). There is a claim that the 999 reached 112.5mph (180km/h) over a single mile at Batavia on 10 May 1893, while running five miles at an average speed of 102.8mph (166km/h). There is doubt about this claim however, as two separate clocks gave the timing, but it was given great publicity.*

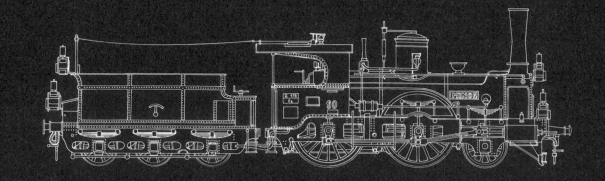

Twenty Years of Progress

By 1870 it could be said that almost everywhere the railway had passed all possible tests, and had left behind its chaotic – if fascinating – pioneering stage. Railways had entered into communal social life to the full and were accepted by everyone.

A great deal of ground had been covered and much progress made in a bare half-century. With pride and satisfaction, people saw with amazement how radically Man's lot for countless generations to come had been altered during those few years, although it must be said that consternation had sometimes been mixed with the pride. During the next 20 years the spirit of initiative and adventure that had marked the coming of steam became more vigorous than ever. Confidence and daring could now be based more soundly on past achievement, and there was fresh awareness of what could be done within the foreseeable future. Nevertheless there was conflict over which of the varying paths were to be followed. Different ways of building locomotives – all of them technically superior if their backers were to be believed – added an element of confusion, despite the accumulation of practical experience pointing to the solution of most theoretical problems. A universally-accepted locomotive technology had yet to emerge and the diversity of approaches was encouraged by the growing wealth of industrial countries. As examples, the

Great Southern & Western Railway *These mixed-traffic 5ft 3in gauge (1600mm) locomotives belonged to the largest class to run in Ireland. There were 111 of them, designed by A MacDonnell and almost all built at the Inchicore, Dublin, railway works. The first of the type appeared in 1866 and building went on until 1903, successive batches being modernised slightly externally. The class was of the traditional British simple inside-cylinder design, and was not dissimilar to the Dx Goods class built at Crewe (see page 56). Almost half the class still existed as late as 1959 and No 184 is still in traffic, belonging to the Railway Preservation Society of Ireland and hauling special trains from time to time.*

method of building locomotive frames and the positioning of cylinders were still controversial matters and, while some held that rigid-wheelbase single-drivers were sufficient to handle fast passenger trains, others anticipated the future and provided a leading bogie. The period is one of the most interesting in the steam locomotive's story from the historian's point of view, so numerous were the types produced and the ideas tried. It was not until 1890 that fundamental design theory could be said to be settled, for what was decided then lasted until the end of steam.

It should not be forgotten that during the first 50 years of the railway both trains and track were often costly, largely because of errors that

(continued on page 105)

Pythagoras *No 31 was one of a class of locomotives built between 1870 and 1871 for the passenger trains of the Austrian North Western Railway. A 4-4-0 that represented the best locomotive practice of the day in the Hapsburg domains, it had a long boiler with the firebox inside the wheelbase, and outside frames with the Hall arrangement of outside cranks. Outside Stephenson's valve gear was fitted. The locomotives worked the Vienna-Prague route, taking 100 tonne trains at a 26mph (42km/h) average speed over a ruling gradient of 1 in 100 (1.0 per cent).*

Metz *The most modern European locomotive at the beginning of the 1870s, its elegant appearance was contributed to by the long boiler and the carrying wheels widely separated from the 6ft 6in (1980mm) driving wheels towards the rear. The deep firebox was between the two driving axles and had a grate area of $16.9ft^2$ ($1.57m^2$). Outside cylinders were beyond the wheelbase and inside Stephenson's valve gear was applied. The Cologne-Minden Railway had 30 of this class, 12 built by Borsig between 1871 and 1872 and 18 by Hartmann in 1873 and 1874. These long-wheelbase locomotives were designed for the Berlin-Cologne expresses and took ten coaches at over $43\frac{1}{2}$mph (70km/h) maximum speed.*

No 1 Japan *In 1872 the first locomotive ran in the Land of the Rising Sun, on a $17\frac{3}{4}$ miles (28.8km) railway from Tokyo to Yokohama. No 1 was built in 1871 by the Vulcan Foundry, but the class of ten was completed by similar locomotives from the Yorkshire Engine Co, Avonside Engine Co, Sharp, Stewart and Dübs & Co. They were 2-4-0 tanks, with a weight in working order of 19 tonnes originally, later raised to 25 tonnes, with horizontal outside cylinders and inside Stephenson's valve gear. On arrival in Japan, none of them had cabs, but this was such an obvious inconvenience that they were fitted forthwith.*

Humboldt *This 0-6-0 outside-frame locomotive was one of an almost standard design of the period. The importance of* Humboldt *is that it was the first locomotive built by Floridsdorf in 1871, a works which gained great renown later. The class worked freight trains on the Austrian North Western Railway. Cylinders were 17in by 24¾in (435mm by 632mm), boiler pressure 143lb/in² (10kg/cm²), grate area 18.4ft² (1.71m²), heating surface 1450ft² (135m²) and driving wheels 3ft 10½in diameter (1180m).*

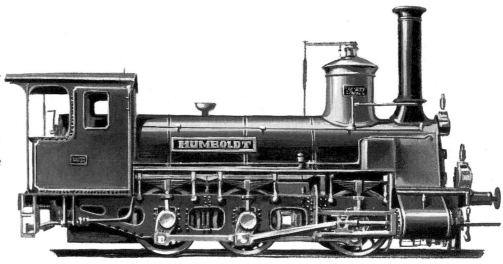

No 224 NBR *When put into service in 1871 this locomotive was an important innovation, the first inside cylinder express passenger 4-4-0 in Great Britain. The designer was Thomas Wheatley of the North British Railway (NBR), who provided inside cylinders, frames and valve gear for his 4-4-0, to create a general type popular in Britain for many years afterwards. No 224, rather large and heavy for express work, was the locomotive involved in the Tay Bridge disaster of 28 December 1879, when the bridge collapsed in a gale while a train carrying 78 passengers was crossing. The whole train fell into the river and there were no survivors, but the locomotive was retrieved a few weeks later and remained in traffic until 1919.*

901 class NER *The most powerful class of British express passenger locomotive in its day, it was designed by Edward Fletcher and the first of the class of 55 went into traffic in 1872. Among the trains that they hauled was the Flying Scotsman over the North Eastern Railway (NER) part of its journey from London to Edinburgh. Fletcher was not a great locomotive designer by chance, for he had worked alongside George Stephenson in designing* Rocket *for the Rainhill trials of 1829. His locomotives were simple, robust and trustworthy, if lacking something in elegance. The 901 class had inside cylinders, originally 17in by 24in (432mm by 610mm), 7ft (2134mm) driving wheels, and weighed about 40 tonnes in working order. With the aid of these locomotives the London-Edinburgh time was reduced to nine hours, an average speed of 43½mph (70km/h). One of the class, hauling eight coaches from York to Newcastle, averaged the excellent speed for the day of 59mph (95km/h).*

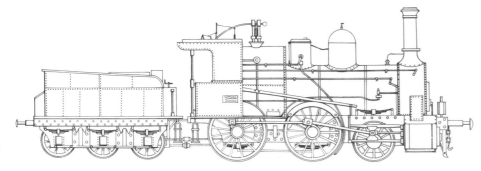

Wörth *Built by Hartmann in 1872 for the Saxon State Railway, this locomotive was the first of a type later popular in Germany. It was a passenger 2-4-0 with outside cylinders and inside Stephenson's valve gear. The large firebox between the coupled wheels was raised high above the boiler barrel, and the smokebox had a greater diameter than the boiler.*

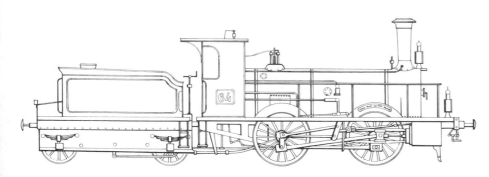

Swiss North Eastern *A popular type in Switzerland at this period was the mixed traffic 0-4-0 locomotive. This one was built by Schwartzkopf, Berlin, with some features of interest. Grate area was 16.1ft² (1.5m²), heating surface 943ft² (87.6m²), boiler pressure 171lb/in² (12kg/cm²), wheelbase 8ft 2½in (2500mm) and length over buffers 24ft 5in (7440mm). Weight in working order was 24.5 tonnes and the maximum speed was 40mph (65km/h). It was in service until 1890.*

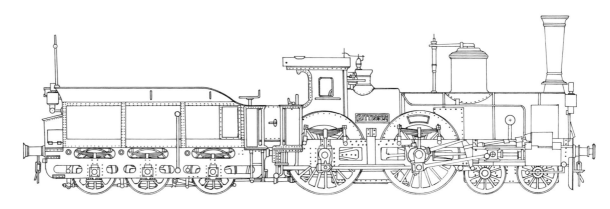

Rittinger *In 1873, the Sigl works in Vienna built this 4-4-0 express locomotive with double frames, Hall cranks and a leading bogie at their own expense. Rittinger was shown at the Paris Exhibition that year as a prototype express passenger locomotive of the future. The Austrian North Western Railway acquired it on return from Paris. With 16¼in by 23¾in cylinders (411mm by 632mm), it could attain 50mph (80km/h). The firebox was between the coupled axles, while the bogie was pushed to the rear to even out the load on all axles.*

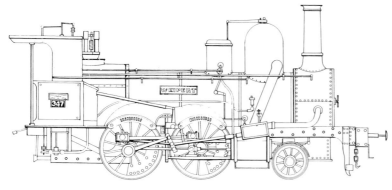

Weipert *Another 2-4-0 locomotive built by Hartmann for the Saxon State Railway in 1872. The leading axle could move laterally on the Novotny principle to follow curves. To accommodate this movement the cylinders were pushed to the rear, just ahead of the front drivers, and hence the connecting rods drove on the rear axle. Allan's valve gear was also mounted on this rear axle. The outside steam pipes to and from the cylinders may be noted.*

L'Avenir *Designed by Georg Meyer and built by Cail in 1868, this locomotive revived the design of* Wiener Neustadt *(see page 79) with two independent driven bogies and with the cylinders of both at the inner ends. The boiler supported on the bogies was built of steel, and frequent fracturing of this contributed to the locomotive's lack of success. It was in fact an experiment, aided by money from the State Railway of France, and was tried out on the Northern Railway of France, the Paris-Orleans, the Grand Luxembourg Railway in Belgium and in Switzerland, before sale to the Charentes Railway. The name, L'Avenir, (Future), showed that it was intended to be a locomotive of the future, although it did not attract the interest that was its due. Its 600hp and capacity for climbing gradients on curves was never appreciated, and it was broken up in 1886.*

A4 class *The Baldwin Locomotive Works built nine American type 4-4-0s in 1872–73 for the Hyvinkää-Hanko Railway in Finland. The locomotives worked the main line between Helsinki and St Petersburg and their appearance showed their American origin very clearly. They had 15in by 20in cylinders (381mm by 508mm), a grate area of 13ft^2 (1.2m^2), a heating surface of 730ft^2 (67.1m^2) and a boiler pressure of 120lb/in^2 (8.4kg/cm^2). The weight in working order of the A4 class was 30 tonnes, of which 18.2 tonnes was adhesive, and they were wood burners. Despite their small size, they worked on passenger trains for over thirty years and the last of them was withdrawn in 1918.*

Terriers *Terrier was the nickname given to this class of 50 locomotives because of the rapid to and fro movement when they were working, which seemed to echo the vitality of a terrier. They were built for the London, Brighton & South Coast Railway between 1872 and 1880 and were originally intended for London suburban services, although later they worked traffic on branch lines all over the system. When they came into the hands of the Southern Railway after 1922, some of them were sent to the Isle of Wight. Their weight in working order was 24.6 tonnes and their tractive effort 7395lbf (3355kgf).*

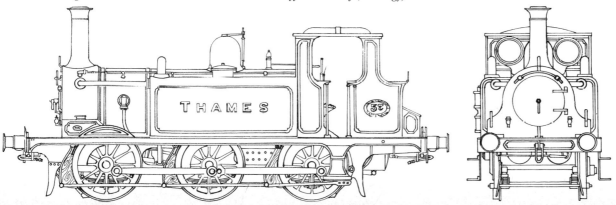

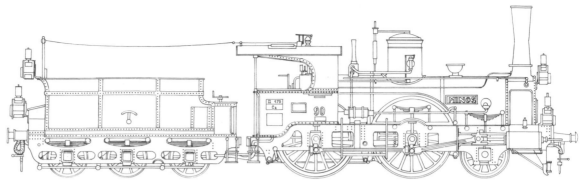

Minos *The Kaiser Ferdinands Nordbahn in Austria had a 2-2-2 built by Floridsdorf in 1873, rebuilt as shown ten years later to increase its power. The new wheel arrangement was 2-4-0, cylinders were 15in by 24³⁄₄in (382mm by 632mm), the large driving wheels were 6ft 5³⁄₄in in diameter (1960mm) and the boiler pressure was 143lb/in² (10kg/cm²). After rebuilding, the adhesive weight rose to 27 tonnes out of a weight in working order of 39 tonnes. Minos ran on the Vienna-Brünn (now Brno) service for many years, until withdrawn in 1913.*

Urban *The name of the designer Urban became the nickname of this class, supplied to the Belgian Grand Central Railway by St Léonard and Couillet from 1866 to 1877. They were well-built machines with an excellent performance, fast yet compact 2-4-0s with low-pitched boilers and Belpaire fireboxes deep between the coupled axles. The length less the tender was only 23ft 3in (8.5m). Cylinders were mounted between the leading pair of wheels and the first pair of 6ft 10¹⁄₂in (2100mm) driving wheels, and the weight in working order was about 37 tonnes. The class continued to work after the Belgian Grand Central was taken over by the Belgian State Railway on 1 January 1897, in particular on Brussels-Antwerp trains.*

Andaluces *Hartmann built 23 of Andaluces' class between 1877 and 1901 for the Andalusian Railway and two more came from a St Petersburg builder, among the very few steam locomotives exported from Russia before 1914. They were a heavy mixed traffic type, with cylinders 17³⁄₄in by 25¹⁄₂in (450mm by 650mm), inside Stephenson's valve gear and driving wheels 4ft 3in (1300mm) in diameter. They ran for a great many years in the provinces of Cadiz, Cordoba, Algeciras and Utrera, and even today old drivers on the Spanish National System will say that they were the best steam locomotives to run in Spain.*

l to be put right later. There was no way to progress other than by trial and error because of lack of experience, and the track in particular led to much trouble from lack of rigidity when sleepers were either laid direct on the ground or on more or less yielding ballast. From the 1860s, the availability of stronger steel rails in place of iron was a great step forward, and it was found that they must be of at least 70lb/yd (35kg/m) weight and preferably more. Improved fastening of the rail to the sleeper was devised to replace the simple spike with its head over the foot of the rail. Track ballasting became imperative, both for effective drainage and to supply a certain amount of flexibility as the train (continued on page 110)

Glasgow & South Western Railway *James Stirling, brother of the more famous Patrick (who produced the 8ft singles – see page 74), designed 4-4-0s for this railway. The first appeared in 1873 and was the prototype for a class of 22 built over the next four years. An innovation was the steam-actuated reversing gear. Following his brother, James Stirling did not provide a dome on the boilers. This class worked Glasgow-Carlisle expresses.*

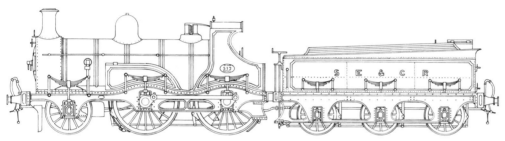

London, Chatham & Dover Railway *This company put four locomotives into service in 1873 designed by William Martley and bearing the names* Europe, Asia, Africa *and* America. *Two more were added in 1876. They were 2-4-0s in the inside cylinder, outside frame, British tradition, with external springs above each axle, polished brass domes and a carefully-matched tender. The first four were built by Sharp, Stewart & Co, while the last two came from the company's own shops at Longhedge in London. They were soon recognised as fast engines giving an excellent performance, becoming known as the Mail Engines to the public. They ran the mail from London to Dover at an average speed of 45mph (72.5km/h). The London, Chatham & Dover was merged into the South Eastern & Chatham Railway in 1899.*

Livingstone *Designed by Anton Elbel, this locomotive and* Focault *were built by Floridsdorf in 1874. Based on Rittinger's design of the year before, the type soon displaced 2-4-0s on all major Austrian railways. Livingstone was a 4-4-0 with a long-wheelbase bogie with outside frames above, although the outside frame was abolished for the rest of the machine. The firebox was between the driving axles, and the cylinders were mounted so far back as to be almost in the centre. With a twelve-coach train of 96 tonnes,* Livingstone *could travel at 37$\frac{1}{4}$mph (60km/h) up 1 in 100 (1.0 per cent) gradients. It developed 515hp and its maximum speed was 50mph (80km/h).*

The compound locomotive

The competition between the various locomotive designers to use combustion heat effectively led to the building of very sophisticated boilers. With over 100 tubes in the boiler barrel and ever-larger fireboxes, boiler pressures had by 1870 reached $143lb/in^2$ ($10kg/cm^2$), and not infrequently $171lb/in^2$ ($12kg/cm^2$). At that date compound stationary and marine engines were already in use, and in 1873 a Swiss engineer, Anatole Mallet, experimented with a compound locomotive, following unsuccessful experiments in England and the United States. In a compound locomotive steam is made to work twice over, with consequent fuel savings. In the first high pressure cylinder or cylinders the steam is only partially expanded. This expansion is completed and the residual energy extracted in a low pressure cylinder or cylinders. The temperature gradient within each cylinder is reduced considerably and thus condensation losses are minimised. The high and low pressure cylinders have to be arranged to do about the same amount of work and the low pressure cylinders are

normally of a greater diameter as steam at low pressures occupies a greater volume. Mallet obtained a patent on 10 October 1874, and three little compound locomotives were built by Schneider for the Bayonne-Biarritz Railway, which was opened in 1876. One of these was *Anglet*, on which Mallet perfected his ideas. The locomotives were 0-4-2 tanks, with high pressure cylinders 9½in by 17¾in (240mm by 450mm) and low pressure ones 15¾in by 17¾in (400mm by 450mm), each locomotive being a two-cylinder compound. Boiler pressure was $171lb/in^2$ ($12kg/cm^2$) and driving wheel diameter 3ft 11in (1200mm). While hauling double-deck passenger coaches weighing 50 tonnes over 1 in 67 (1.5 per cent) gradients they had maximum speed of 25mph (40km/h) and showed a 25 per cent fuel saving. Compound locomotives had their complications and defects, but they were accepted very quickly in the years to come.

Ardross *One of Class F of the Highland Railway and designed by David Jones in 1874. The design was the last derived from the Crewe type of Alexander Allan (see page 42), with the typical cylinder mounting and outside frames. The locomotives of the class were long-wheelbase 4-4-0s with a reasonable 42 tonne weight in working order. Driving wheel diameter was 6ft 3in (1905mm), boiler pressure $140lb/in^2$ ($9.8kg/cm^2$) and tractive effort $10880lbf$ ($4950kgf$). They were built in small batches until 1901.*

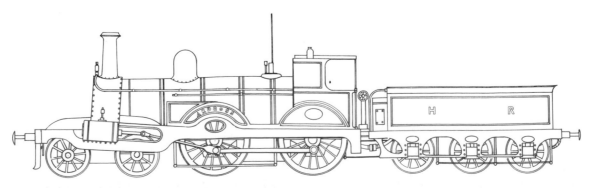

Gylfe *Built for the Jutland Railway by Esslingen Works in 1875, this was one of a class of 12 0-4-2 locomotives, a wheel arrangement popular in Germany at that time. With cylinders were 16in by 22in (406mm by 559mm), boiler pressure 129lb/in² (9kg/cm²), driving wheels 5ft 4½in diameter (1640mm) and adhesive weight 24 tonnes, it could attain 55¾mph (90km/h) and could haul a passenger train on the level at an average speed of 43½mph (70km/h).*

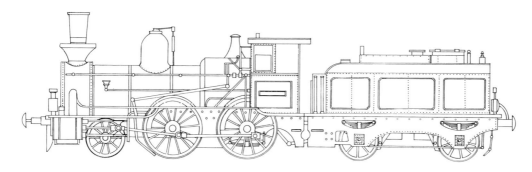

Sträken *The Swedish State Railways had this 2-4-0 locomotive built by Borsig in 1874 for Stockholm-Gothenburg passenger trains. It had cylinders mounted ahead of the driving wheels, Allan's valve gear, 5ft 1¾in (1570mm) driving wheels, and a 143lb/in² (10kg/cm²) boiler pressure. Adhesive weight was 21.1 tonnes and maximum speed 46½mph (75km/h). A type of spark arrester specially favoured in Sweden was mounted at the base of the chimney, in which an internal baffle returned glowing fragments to the smokebox. In all 53 of the class were built and one is preserved at the Gävle Railway Museum.*

Webb's Precursor *One of several classes of 2-4-0 designed by Francis W Webb for the London & North Western Railway, one or two of which were highly successful. They were all painted black with polished brass nameplates (as was customary on that line) and lined out in red and white. Originally there were two versions, one with 5ft 6in (1676mm) driving wheels as illustrated, and one with 6ft 7½in (2019mm) driving wheels, both first built in 1874. The former class was intended for the more heavily graded parts of the main line between Crewe and Carlisle.*

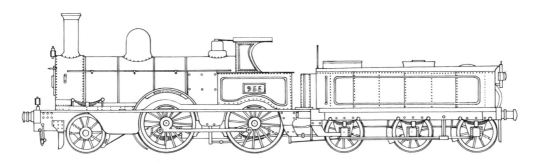

Paris-Orleans 265–390 *To run heavier and faster express trains, Victor Fourquenot built the first examples of a 2-4-2 express locomotive for the Paris-Orleans in 1876. The class totalled 126 eventually, and was developed from 2-4-0s Nos 201-212, a successful design which greatly influenced French locomotive practice (see page 72). The new class was provided with a rear carrying axle, both to correct the pitching motion noticed with the 2-4-0s at high speeds, and to carry the weight of the firebox. Locomotive power was increased by raising the boiler pressure to 129lb/in² (9kg/cm²) and later to 143lb/in² (10kg/cm²). They were considered to be handsome locomotives and they had the boiler, cylinders, dome and sandboxes finished in brass. For many years the class handled the Paris-Bordeaux expresses, covering the 359 miles (578km) at an average speed of 46½mph (75km/h) while hauling 160 tonnes. Another group of 2-4-2s brought the grand total on the line up to 162, of which 115 were still in service in 1938. One of the class is preserved in the Mulhouse Railway Museum.*

Outrance *The original design, nicknamed Outrance (Utmost) because of its strength and adaptability, was first delivered to the Northern Railway of France in 1877 by the Société Alsacienne of Belfort. The type was derived from British practice and consisted of 2-4-0s, although most of them were rebuilt from 1890 as shown in the picture, with a leading bogie. The double frames were typical of British practice in 1877, and when a bogie was provided it, too, had outside frames. A Belpaire firebox was fitted, and a Crampton type regulator with outside steam pipes to the inside cylinders. Maximum speed was 62mph (100km/h) with a bogie and one reached 78½mph (127km/h) on trial in 1890.*

New South Wales Government Railway *These Class 79 locomotives first entered service in Australia in 1877. Built by Beyer, Peacock & Co at Manchester (34 locomotives) and Dübs & Co at Glasgow (26 locomotives) the design was based on that for 4-4-0 tanks for the Metropolitan Railway (see page 71), although for Australia a large six-wheel tender was added. The bogie pin was placed in a bracket to the rear, just ahead of the driving wheels. This class 79 was intended to replace Class 23 (see page 72) and it will be seen that it repeated many features of the latter. One Class 79 locomotive is preserved in working order.*

Prussian P2 class *A numerous class of locomotives on the Royal Prussian Union Railway from the end of the 1870s, and the first standard locomotive class of the railway. The intention was to eliminate the very diverse collection designs that it had inherited from its constituent railways. Class P2 was a mixed traffic locomotive and 242 of them were built by many different German firms from 1877 to 1885. They had 16½in by 23½in cylinders (420mm by 600mm), a boiler pressure of 143lb/in² (10kg/cm²), driving wheels 5ft 8in diameter (1730mm) and a weight in working order of 36.7 tonnes, of which 24.5 tonnes was adhesive. They could haul a 339 tonne freight train up a 1 in 50 gradient (2.0 per cent) at 25mph (40km/h) or a 93 tonne passenger train at 50mph (80km/h).*

Waverley class *Dugald Drummond designed this handsome locomotive in 1876 for the North British Railway. Drummond had worked with Stroudley, and had absorbed the latter's ideas on locomotive simplicity and elegance (see page 112). This class was the first of Drummond's 4-4-0s and served as a prototype for other 4-4-0s that he designed later, as he moved first to the Caledonian Railway and then to the London & South Western Railway. The Waverley class, or Class 476, had inside cylinders 18in by 26in (457mm by 660mm), 6ft 6in (1980mm) driving wheels and a weight in working order of 44 tonnes. Among the innovations were the coupling rods 9ft (2742mm) long, a length that surprised locomotive engineers of the day. The 12 locomotives of the class worked Edinburgh-Carlisle expresses.*

Jungfrau class *A class of five locomotives built by SLM Winterthur for the Swiss Central Railway in 1878. The 2-6-0 tank wheel arrangement was little known in Europe at the time. The cylinders were 16½in by 23½in (420mm by 600mm), driving wheels 4ft 2in diameter (1280mm), grate area was 17.2ft² (1.6m²), heating surface 1162ft² (108m²) and boiler pressure 143lb/in² (10kg/cm²). As was customary in Switzerland at the time, the Crampton regulator was fitted. Weight in working order was 52.1 tonnes, of which 41.4 tonnes was adhesive, the locomotives had a maximum speed of 34mph (55km/h) and they developed 370hp.*

ran over it. Taken together, these developments allowed greater maximum axle loads and thus heavier and faster locomotives, which were urgently needed to eliminate costly double or even triple heading of trains.

The more powerful locomotives were also needed due to the increasing weight of rolling stock which, during the course of a few years, grew from the four-wheel coach to the six-wheel one, and then to the eight-wheel bogie coach. Even when introduced, this had a tare weight of as much as 20 tonnes, and similar changes took place in the freight stock. However, when locomotives, rolling stock and track had all been improved the original infrastructure became insufficient. Bridges and embankments had to be reinforced, water supply and coaling installations improved and longer turntables built, not to mention the lengthening of loops and sidings to accommodate longer trains. In Great Britain the non-availability of long turntables limited the wheelbase of locomotives and hampered their designers for years.

(continued on page 114)

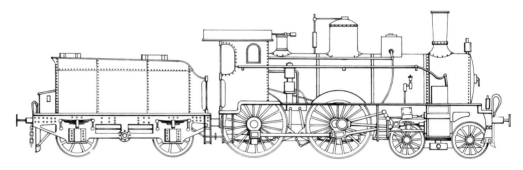

Adriatic System Class 150 *Railways were grouped into three systems in Italy in 1885, the Adriatic, the Mediterranean and the Sicilian Systems. The Adriatic inherited this 4-4-0 express locomotive class from the old Roman Railroads, 72 of them being built between 1881 and 1886 by German and Italian builders. Cylinders were 17in by 24in (432mm by 610mm), boiler pressure 143lb/in² (10kg/cm²), driving wheel diameter 6ft 0¾in (1850mm) and Stephenson's valve gear was fitted. They developed 500hp at 37¼mph (60km/h) and the tractive effort was 10 300lbf (4680kgf).*

Paris, Lyons & Mediterranean *One of the finest locomotive designs of its day was this 2-4-2 of the PLM. Built from 1876 and derived from the Fourquenot locomotives on the Paris-Orleans, they had Belpaire fireboxes and outside Gooch's valve gear. Driving wheel diameter was 6ft 10½in (2100mm), boiler pressure 129lb/in² (9kg/cm²) and weight in working order 49.7 tonnes, of which 27.1 tonnes was adhesive. Their long and low appearance made the class readily recognisable and they were popular with the public. Batches built totalled 400, some from the PLM's own workshops and 40 from Sharp, Stewart in Britain. In particular they worked expresses on the Paris-Lyons-Marseilles main line.*

Prussian T3 class *The most numerous class of tank locomotive in Germany. From 1878 a first batch of 400 was built, but later the class reached 1300 without counting those built for private railways, industry and for export. Primarily a shunting locomotive, the T3 class was an 0-6-0 well tank with 13¾in by 21½in cylinders (350mm by 550mm), 3ft 7¼in driving wheels (1100mm) and outside Walschaert's valve gear (Heusinger in Germany). Axle load was about 11 tonnes. The locomotives were extremely robust and versatile; as well as working branch lines, they were seen in German yards for many decades.*

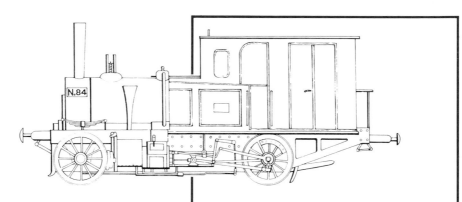

Valkyrian *One of five Class Cb locomotives that entered service on the Swedish State Railways in 1886. They were 4-4-0s with a Belpaire firebox and outside cylinders 16½in by 22in (419mm by 559mm) with Allan's valve gear. The bogie wheels were large at 3ft 7¼in (1100mm) compared with the 6ft 2in (1880mm) driving wheels. Boiler pressure was 143lb/in² (10kg/cm²) and the weight in working order 40.5 tonnes, of which 25.5 was adhesive. The tender weighed 21.5 tonnes when loaded with 1830 gallons of water (8.3m³) and 3 tonnes of coal. The maximum speed was supposed to be 56mph (90km/h), but the locomotives proved to be so unstable that they were rebuilt to Class Cc between 1903 and 1905.*

Prussian compound *August von Borries took up Mallet's compound locomotive and in 1880 Schichau built a pair of two-cylinder compounds for branch lines in the Hanover division of the Royal Prussian Union Railway. They were 2-2-0 tank locomotives to a design just becoming fashionable, with a luggage van at the rear of the frame. Trials confirmed the value of compounding in saving fuel, even if it led to a more complicated locomotive and needed a more skilled crew. Von Borries became a leading German exponent of compounding in later years, and the two-cylinder compounds of his design bore his name.*

Stroudley locomotives

Class G – 1881.

William Stroudley spent many of the last years of his life as locomotive engineer of the London, Brighton & South Coast Railway, and designed for them some of the most celebrated British locomotive classes. Among others, he designed the Terrier class 0-6-0 tank (see page 103) and Class G, one of the last British 2-2-2 locomotives, and considered to be a peak of good construction and performance. In all, 24 Class G were built at Brighton in 1881 and 1882. They followed traditional British practice with inside cylinders 17in by 24in (432mm by 610mm) and 6ft 6in driving wheels (1980mm). They were used on London to Portsmouth expresses and were not withdrawn until 1908.

Stroudley then developed from the G class another class of express locomotive, which attracted the attention of all European engineers. The new Gladstone, 36 of which were built from 1882 to 1891, was an 0-4-2 with driving wheels as large as the G class, 6ft 6in (1980mm), with a boiler pressure of $140lb/in^2$ ($9.8kg/cm^2$) and a weight in working order of 38 tonnes. They were good riding, powerful locomotives for express work, despite the unusual wheel arrangement for the task. Their performance dispersed scepticism of the front coupling when they entered service. The class had some members in service until 1932 and *Gladstone* is now in the National Railway Museum, York.

Gladstone class – 1882.

Class K NZGR *The New Zealand Government Railways was anxious to try out the much-praised locomotives of the United States on its own track, and it ordered two Class K locomotives from the Rogers Locomotive Co in 1877. The new locomotives were a success when compared with British types, and six more were ordered in 1878. The 2-4-2 design was then new in America and was known later as the Columbia type. Class K handled passenger trains between Christchurch and Dunedin. On New Zealand main lines their maximum speed was restricted at first to 32mph (51km/h), but they could reach 62mph (100km/h) quite easily.*

Southend *The pioneer of one of the most popular tank locomotive wheel arrangements in Great Britain, the 4-4-2, although in this case with outside cylinders. Designed by William Adams for the London, Tilbury & Southend Railway and built by Sharp, Stewart in 1880, the weight in working order was 56.1 tonnes and the maximum axle load was 16 tonnes. There were 36 locomotives in the class altogether and a few stayed in service until 1935.*

State Railway Co Holland *Beyer, Peacock built this fine 2-4-0 for the company in 1880, and by 1895 had supplied 176 of them, including one arranged as a two-cylinder compound. Trials showed them to be so competent that they became the standard locomotive for both passenger and freight trains on the line. They had Belpaire fireboxes, cylinders 18in by 26in (457mm by 660mm) and driving wheels 7ft (2134mm) diameter. No 326 of the class is preserved at Utrecht Railway Museum.*

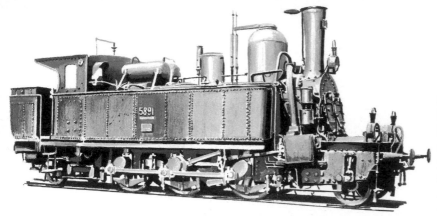

Swiss Central Railway *This was one of the most powerful tank locomotives in Switzerland until the end of the century. The first five were built at the Olten works of the Swiss Central from 1882 to 1884 and it is claimed that they were the first European 2-6-2 tank class. Cylinders were 17¾in by 23½in (450mm by 600mm) and driving wheel diameter was 4ft 11½in (1510mm). Interestingly it was an outside frame design, otherwise almost unknown on the Swiss standard gauge, although commonplace in neighbouring Germany and Austria. The weight in working order was 65.7 tonnes with an adhesive weight of 43.5 tonnes. They could develop 800hp and the maximum speed was 46½mph (75km/h).*

As locomotives increased in weight, power and speed, they needed some better form of brake than the traditional hand one, operating brake blocks on one or two pairs of wheels, not only to stop the new trains, but to reassure public opinion, which had been disturbed by serious accidents in both Europe and North America.

It was in the 1860s in the United States that both vacuum and air brakes were developed. The former was the simplest and least expensive, but the working pressure could not, of course, be greater than one atmosphere and was usually about 12lb/in² (0.84kg/cm²). On the other hand, the air brake usually worked at 60lb/in² (4.2kg/cm²), and was devised by George Westinghouse in 1869. A steam pump on the locomotive compressed the air, which was stored in cylinders, not only on the locomotive but on all the vehicles of the train, connected by flexible brake pipes. Compressed air applied brake blocks to all the wheels when

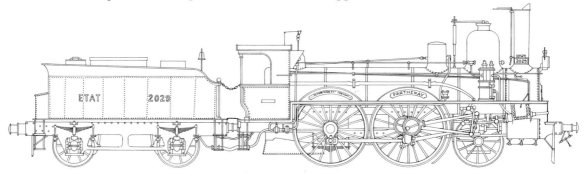

Parthenay *Needing a passenger locomotive for their more steeply graded main lines, the State Railway of France introduced Nos 2011-2068. These were 2-4-0s based on some locomotives acquired when the Vendée Railway was taken over in May 1878. The new ones were built by Schneider and Fives-Lille from 1880, and were clearly influenced by the work of Fourquenot, as were many other French passenger locomotive designs. Wheels were grouped in the centre, and cylinders and firebox overhung at either end. The grate area was 14.35ft² (1.33m²) and the heating surface 1280ft² (119m²). On the 1 in 66 Rivarennes gradient (1.6 per cent) the locomotives could haul a 75 tonne train at 27mph (44km/h) and they ran Paris-Bordeaux 200 tonne expresses at an average speed of 56mph (90km/h).*

Meridionali Railroads *This line, merged into the Adriatic System in 1885, had its first 4-4-0 type from Borsig in 1882 and 1883. There were 18 of them with 17¾in by 23½in cylinders (450mm by 600mm), driving wheels 6ft 0¾in (1850mm) and boiler pressure 143lb/in² (10kg/cm²). They developed 500hp at 37¼mph (60km/h) and the tractive effort was 11 000lbf (5000kgf). The class had inside Stephenson's valve gear and the maximum speed was 52½mph (85km/h). The type was well adapted for the level lines of the Po valley and those running along the Adriatic coast.*

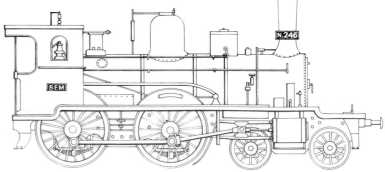

Prussian T0 class *This curious little tank locomotive of the Royal Prussian Union Railway ran on Hanover division branch lines. It was built by Henschel in 1883 and revived the 2-2-0 wheel arrangement, with outside cylinders near the locomotive centre and 3ft 8½in (1130mm) driving wheels under the cab. Boiler pressure was 171lb/in² (12kg/cm²), grate area 8.6ft² (0.8m²) and heating surface 371ft² (34.5m²). One of the smallest Prussian locomotives, its weight in working order was 20 tonnes, of which 10.6 tonnes was adhesive.*

Austro-Hungarian State Railway Co *This company put the first of Class I into service in 1882 and it totalled 40 by 1891. The class was a 2-4-2, and in effect it was a copy of the Paris-Orleans 2-4-2s in France. The grate area was 24.7ft² (2.3m²), heating surface 1540ft² (143m²), boiler pressure 129lb/in² (9kg/cm²) and driving wheel diameter 5ft 10¾in (1800mm). Of the 50 tonnes weight in working order, 26.7 tonnes was adhesive. The double dome was an Austrian feature of the day, steam being collected in one dome and conveyed to the regulator in the forward dome by external steam pipe. These locomotives ran up to 56mph (90km/h) on Vienna-Budapest expresses.*

Natal Government Railways *This locomotive belonged to a class built for a 3ft 6in gauge line (1067mm) in South Africa from 1882. By 1885 it totalled 37 locomotives, built by Kitson & Co and Robert Stephenson & Co. It was a small 4-6-2 tank with outside cylinders within the footplating, and inside Stephenson's valve gear. Weight in working order was 29.1 tonnes and tractive effort was 13 650lbf (6275kgf).*

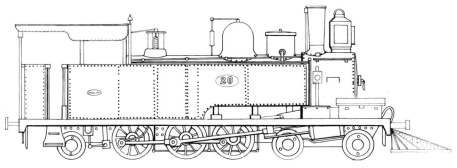

Dean Goods *The Great Western Railway in Britain not only considered itself the most prestigious passenger carrier of the age, but it also prided itself on its freight service. To support the latter, William Dean designed this 0-6-0 type in 1883, which was so successful in traffic that the total built was eventually 280. Some of them were still in service after the Second World War. During the First World War many ran on War Department duties in France and the Middle East, and in the Second World War 108 of them served at home and overseas, on occasions after capture by the Germans. One of the class is preserved in the Great Western Railway Museum at Swindon.*

Western of France *This locomotive was of the enlarged Bourbonnais type favoured by several French railways. It was built for the Western Railway in 1883, a line incorporated from 1909 in the State Railway. The type was a long boiler 0-6-0 with outside Gooch's valve gear, a dome incorporating the Crampton regulator, and with outside steam pipes to the cylinders. The driving wheel diameter was 4ft 8½in (1440mm) and the maximum speed 37¼mph (60km/h). The class remained in traffic for many years, and in 1909 all 341 built for the Western Railway were still running. Ten had been rebuilt to compounds, and the last few were withdrawn only in 1964. Each of these had run over one million miles (1.65 million kilometres) at that time.*

the driver used his brake control. Westinghouse developed his ideas further in 1872 and made the brakes automatic, so that they were applied automatically should any part of the system lose air pressure. Thus, if a train broke in half, the rupturing of the brake connections applied the brake to both halves. Vacuum and air braking were taken up by the world's railways, although it was not until the 1890s that they became general on passenger trains and they were even later on freight. Nowadays, the air brake has almost ousted the vacuum on railways, although the latter has yet to vanish entirely.

A question that divided European locomotive designers during the 1870–1890 period was the use of a leading bogie, although it was in general use in America. Designers in Austria, Britain, France and Germany discounted its ability to guide a locomotive through curves and questioned its stability, asserting that it led to rolling and might even lead to derailment. This attitude could be traced back to the faulty weight distribution and hence instability of the earlier Norris bogie locomotives, but the 4-4-0 wheel arrangement was so undeniably suitable

Webb Coal Tank *This 0-6-2 tank was designed by Francis W Webb for the London & North Western Railway in 1881 and built at Crewe. It had inside cylinders 17in by 24in (432mm by 610mm), driving wheels 4ft 5½in diameter (1360mm) and a 140lb/in² boiler pressure (9.8kg/cm²). By 1897 there were 300 of this class, which had a weight in working order of 43.8 tonnes and a tractive effort of 14 030lbf (6360kgf).*

Class N NZGR *Following on the excellent results given by Class K (see page 113), the New Zealand Government Railways ordered the first Prairie type 2-6-2 from Baldwin in 1885. They did very well on the Christchurch-Dunedin route. Cylinders were 15in by 20in (381mm by 508mm), driving wheels 4ft 1in (1245mm) and boiler pressure 135lb/in² (9.4kg/cm²). Weight in working order was 45½ tonnes and tractive effort was 30 per cent greater than that of Class K. With passenger trains, up to 62mph (100km/h) was attained and 700 tonne freight trains were hauled at up to 25mph (40km/h).*

Victoria Government Railways *This Class A was one of the most famous locomotive types running in Australia during the last century. Ten of the 4-4-0s were built by Beyer, Peacock, Manchester, in 1884, to a design for New South Wales but adapted for the 5ft 3in (1600mm) gauge of Victoria. They worked the route from Melbourne to Albury (on the way to Sydney) and were very fast machines. Speed together with elegance earned them the nickname Peacock Highflyers. The Class A became Old A after 15 with slightly larger dimensions were built in Australia by Phoenix Foundry as the New A class.*

Prussian Class S1 *With this class the 2-4-0 wheel arrangement reached its apogee in Germany. A total of 261 were built between 1885 and 1895, to a design prepared by the Magdeburg division of the Royal Prussian Union Railway. A large firebox was provided with a grate area of 22.2ft² (2.07m²) and the cylinders were 16½in by 23½in (420mm by 600mm), while the driving wheel diameter was 6ft 6in (1980mm). Weight in working order was 41.3 tonnes, of which 27.6 tonnes was used for adhesion. These powerful and fast locomotives worked Berlin-Hanover expresses of 170 tonnes at speeds up to 52½mph (85km/h).*

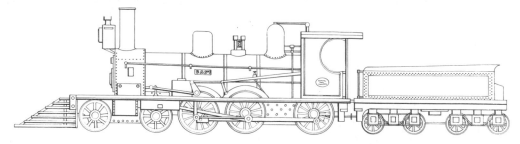

Central Argentine Railway *Neilson of Glasgow built 16 of this 4-6-0 type for Argentina between 1884 and 1885, at a time when very similar locomotives were going to India, both countries using the 5ft 6in (1676mm) gauge. Later the design was the basis for David Jones' 4-6-0 for the Highland Railway, the first British home 4-6-0. The driving wheel diameter was 4ft 6in (1370mm), boiler pressure 150lb/in² (10.5kg/cm²) and weight in working order 45.7 tonnes, of which 34.2 tonnes was adhesive.*

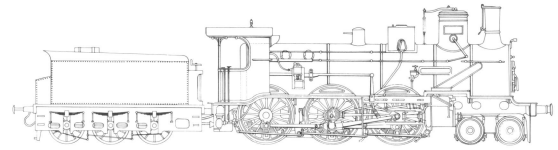

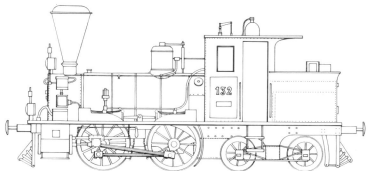

F1 class *SLM Winterthur built this first example of a dozen locomotives for the Finnish Railways in 1885. The design was based on the Forneys built for United States' elevated urban railways, while Sweden and Denmark also used Forney-based locomotives. Forneys were outside cylinder 0-4-4 tanks, arranged so that they could run through sharp curves. The Finnish locomotives had a grate area of 9.65ft² (0.9m²), a heating surface of 430ft² (40m²) and could attain a maximum speed of 37mph (60km/h). They remained in service until 1935, and had a tractive effort of 6730lbf (3300kgf).*

Vittorio Emanuele II *The Turin works of the Upper Italy Railways designed and built this locomotive under the direction of Cesare Frescot in 1884. The first 4-6-0 tender locomotive in Europe, it was named after the reigning King of Italy, Victor Emmanuel II. The Giovi pass relief line was then being built on an almost continuous gradient of 1 in 62 (1.6 per cent) and a locomotive with high adhesion and a high steaming rate was needed to work it. An innovation was a combustion chamber within the boiler adjoining the firebox, although the short-wheelbase bogie appears to be old fashioned. Outside Gooch's valve gear was fitted and the boiler pressure was 143lb/in² (10kg/cm²), which was raised later to 157lb/in² (11kg/cm²). It developed 630hp and could take a 130 tonne passenger train up the Giovi relief line gradient at 25mph (40km/h). Maximum speed was 50mph (80km/h). Between 1887 and 1896 the Mediterranean System (successor to the Upper Italy) had 54 more of the class built by Miani & Silvestri of Milan, Ansaldo of Genoa and by Maffei in Germany.*

Austrian North Western Railway *StEG in Vienna delivered a class of 0-6-0 tanks to this railway in 1884, which were improved versions of Classes Xa and Xb of 1881–1882, and were known as Class Xc. Their cylinders were 13½in by 19½in (342mm by 500mm), driving wheels were 3ft 3½in diameter (1010mm), boiler pressure was 143lb/in² (10kg/cm²) and weight in working order 36.5 tonnes. They were followed by the nearly similar Xd and Xe classes built by both StEG and Floridsdorf. In all, 51 of these classes were built between 1881 and 1901 and some were still in Austrian service in 1960, the last disappearing in 1964.*

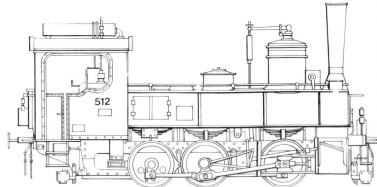

Swiss Central Railway *This locomotive was one of a class of five built at the Swiss Central's Olten works during 1885–1887 and another two were completed in 1890. The locomotives were 2-6-0s, a wheel arrangement not used in Switzerland until then. The first four had firebox roofs raised high above the boiler barrel, together with Crampton regulators and outside steam pipes, as was usual on Olten locomotives of the day. They were well adapted to hauling heavy trains and had a maximum speed of 34mph (55km/h). All were withdrawn by 1916.*

for high speed trains that it had to be adopted. In Great Britain, Thomas Wheatley introduced the 4-4-0 in 1871, followed by Kirtley, Drummond, Sacré, Connor, Adams and Johnson, so that the pattern was accepted by the turn of the century. In Austria *Rittinger* pioneered the 4-4-0 concept and was followed by Swiss and Italian designs. France, however, waited until nearly 1890 before adopting this wheel arrangement and the Germans were even later.

Steam locomotives are not complicated pieces of machinery. Indeed, they are very simple and the underlying thermodynamic principles were well-understood by 1850. But it was not until the last 25 years of the 19th century that there was an active search to increase locomotive efficiency. The compound locomotive developed by the Swiss Anatole Mallet in 1873 (first tried 1876), revolutionised the use of boiler steam, although all the claims made for increased power and lower fuel consumption were not realised at first: as well as being more complicated and costly to build, the compound called for a certain amount of skill from the driver and in the hands of unskilled crews the full potential of the type could not be realised.

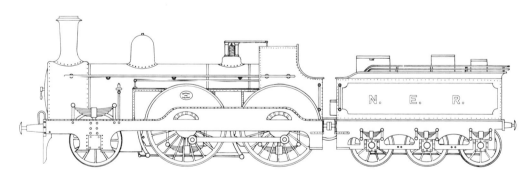

North Eastern Railway *By 1885 this railway was in great need of locomotives to work night expresses over the 123½ miles (199km) from Newcastle to Edinburgh. In that year a locomotive was built, nominally by Wilson Worsdell, the locomotive superintendant who had just arrived. The class was nicknamed Tennant after the presumed designer. They were built at the railway's Darlington works and had cylinders 18in by 24in (457mm by 610mm), driving wheels 7ft 1in (2159mm) diameter and a boiler pressure of 140lb/in^2 (9.8kg/cm^2). Weight in working order was 42.1 tonnes, while the bogie tender when fully-loaded reached 31 tonnes. The Tennants had a wheelbase of 20ft 6½in (6725mm), which was long for a locomotive to run on a curving line, but they reached 62mph (100km/h) frequently, and were capable of 77½mph (125km/h).*

Also, some compound designs were misconceived and disappointing (those of Francis Webb in Britain for example), and not a few footplate men were opposed to anything new and were obstructive in consequence. Certainly, compound locomotives could be likened to racehorses that needed constant care and attention from the driver; it was necessary to train special footplate crews, able to cope with the mysteries of double expansion. After the advent of de Glehn's four-cylinder compound in 1885 the situation improved, both mechanically

Spinners *By 1887 the single-driver express locomotive was considered to be obsolete. Nevertheless, Samuel Johnson of the Midland Railway designed a 4-2-2 type in that year. The single driver then took on a new life thanks to the advent of steam sanding gear, which delivered an assured supply of sand beneath the driving wheels to increase adhesion. The locomotives were nicknamed Spinners and 102 were built at Derby up to 1900. They had 18in by 26in cylinders (457mm by 660mm), driving wheels 7ft 4in (2230mm) and a 160lb/in² (11.2kg/cm²) boiler pressure. Later locomotives had 7ft 6in (2286mm) drivers and 18½in by 26in (470mm by 660mm) cylinders. The Spinners were very fast and could attain 93mph (150km/h) and maintain average speeds of 62mph (100km/h). One of the locomotives won a gold medal at the Paris Exhibition of 1889.*

De Glehn Compound *Alfred de Glehn of the Société Alsacienne (an Englishman despite his name) designed this four-cylinder compound for the Northern Railway of France in 1885. Originally a 2-2-2-0 with two pairs of uncoupled driving wheels and with the high pressure cylinders outside and the low pressure inside, in 1892 Gaston Bousquet of the Northern Railway rebuilt the locomotive into a 4-2-2-0 with a leading bogie as shown in the picture. Northern No 701 was a sensation at the time, with excellent performance. Grate area was 24.5ft² (2.27m²), heating surface 1085ft² (101m²), HP cylinders 13in by 24in (330mm by 610mm), LP cylinders 18in by 24in (460mm by 610mm), driving wheels 6ft 11½in (2110mm) diameter and boiler pressure 157lb/in² (11kg/cm²). Axle load was 14.3 tonnes, Walschaert's valve gear was fitted and the maximum speed was 59mph (95km/h).*

Paris-Orleans Nos 1801–31 *This design by Victor Fourquenot for the Paris-Orleans was intended as a mountain passenger locomotive. It was a 2-6-0 with Gooch's valve gear, cylinders 18¾in by 23½in (480mm by 600mm), a boiler pressure of 143lb/in² (10kg/cm²) and a weight in working order of 51.5 tonnes, of which 39.1 tonnes was adhesive. The first locomotive of the class was delivered on 27 June 1885, and they were used on the route from Clermont Ferrand to Tulle that had 1 in 40 (2.5 per cent) gradients. With 125 tonnes the class could run at 25mph (40km/h) up these gradients.*

Belgian State Class 12 *A characteristic if bizzare locomotive of the Belgian State Railway designed by L R Masui in 1888. It was an outside-framed, inside-cylindered, 2-4-2 of heavy aspect, and though having a large Belpaire firebox, the class was recognised to be underboilered. The famous square-section chimney of Masui was applied, although later locomotives of the class had his* tronconique *chimney of large diameter, tapering towards the top. Grate area was no less than 50.5ft² (4.71m²), it could develop 850hp, and on trial 68mph (110km/h) was attained. In 1921 there were 24 still in service, but they were withdrawn a year later.*

Caledonian Railway *A well-known British single-driver designed by Dugald Drummond and built by Neilson & Co for the Caledonian in 1886, this was a 4-2-2 with 18in by 26in (457mm by 660mm) cylinders and a boiler pressure of 150lb/in² (105kg/cm²). Instead of steam-operated sanding gear, air was used, for the air brake was just coming into general use and compressed air was available. Taking part in a railway race in 1888, the locomotive ran the 101 miles (163km) from Carlisle to Edinburgh at an average speed of 62mph (100km/h).*

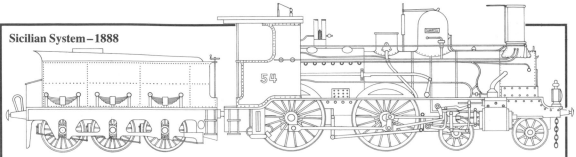

Sicilian System – 1888

Italian locomotive designs

After the political and administrative consolidation of the Italian peninsula that followed the unification of the country under the crown of Savoy, the railways were adapted to the fresh national outlook and overall planning. One of the tasks was to give adequate rail service from the north to the south of the country, as well as bringing railways to hitherto unserved areas. In this great endeavour the engineers were the leaders, and in locomotive construction there was a special commitment. Little by little Italian railways were able to free themselves of dependence on foreign builders, a dependence that had been their lot since railways came to Italy 40 years before. The Turin design office of the Mediterranean System (started 1872) and the Florence locomotive research department of the Adriatic System, led by engineers Frescot and Riva respectively, produced sound locomotive designs expressly for Italian conditions, which included track that left much to be desired. The Italian-designed locomotive began to take on a distinctive appearance, although the two design

centres each developed their own style (see page 118 for a Turin design). Among the express locomotives, the two which stood out were 4-4-0s, one for the Mediterranean System of 1889 and the other for the Adriatic System of 1890. The Mediterranean had 31 4-4-0s numbered from 1701 upwards, built between 1889 and 1890. The system named all its locomotives and the 1701 class carried those of operatic heroines, 1721 shown here being *Giuditta* (Judith). They had 6ft 10½in (2100mm) driving wheels, a 171lb/in^2 (12kg/cm^2) boiler pressure, had a 62mph (100km/h) maximum speed, and developed 600hp. They weighed 49.8 tonnes in working order, had an axle load of 15.9 tonnes and could haul 160 tonnes on the level at 50mph (80km/h). The Adriatic 4-4-0 was used on the Indian Mail, taking it from the Mont Cenis tunnel to the port of Brindisi in the south during its two day journey by train, which was followed by an 18-day ship voyage to Bombay. There were 36 of this class of Adriatic 4-4-0, 24 of them built by Breda in Milan and 12 by Ansaldo, Genoa, in 1890 to 1901. Driving wheels were 6ft 3½in (1920mm), boiler pressure 171lb/in^2 (12kg/cm^2), maximum designed speed was 62mph (100km/h) and 650hp was developed. Weight in working order was 48.3 tonnes (29.5 tonnes adhesive) and the tractive effort was 14, 450lbf (6570kgf). The class had six-wheel tenders carrying 5480 gallons of water (12m^3) and 4 tonnes of coal. The Sicilian System also had 4-4-0s. StEG of Vienna built seven in 1888, and Breda added another 11 in 1895. Cylinders were 16½in by 23½in (420mm by 600mm), boiler pressure 143lb/in^2 (10kg/cm^2), driving wheel diameter 5ft 10¾in (1800mm) and they developed 520hp at 37¼mph (60km/h). When the Italian State Railways was formed in 1905, these three 4-4-0 types became the 560, 552 and 500 classes respectively.

Mediterranean System 4-4-0 – 1889

Adriatic System 4-4-0 – 1890

Jubilees *This 0-4-2 locomotive type was built first at the Nine Elms, London works of the London & South Western Railway in 1887, the year of Queen Victoria's first Jubilee. Thus the new locomotives became known as the Jubilees. The designer was William Adams, who set out to provide his railway with a mixed traffic locomotive, in which he was highly successful: 90 of the class were built and, while the first of them was taken out of traffic in 1928, the last did not disappear until over 20 years later. As well as being built at Nine Elms, Neilson & Co supplied 40 of the class in 1892 and 1893. It was a Jubilee that hauled Queen Victoria's funeral train on the Gosport-Fareham section of the journey on 2 February 1901.*

Düsseldorf *Class BX were the first compound locomotives of the Bavarian State Railway, and incidentally the last German 2-4-0 express locomotive design. The class totalled 14, built from 1890 to 1891, with a grate area of $21ft^2$ ($1.95m^2$), $1063ft^2$ ($99m^2$) heating surface, $171lb/in^2$ ($12kg/cm^2$) boiler pressure and 6ft 1½in (1870mm) driving wheels. They were von Borries two-cylinder compounds with an HP cylinder 17in by 24in (430mm by 610mm) and an LP cylinder 24in by 24in (610mm by 610mm). Walschaert's (Heusinger in Germany) valve gear was fitted.*

A massive casing carrying the steam pipe between the two cylinders ran across the boiler, surmounted by a sandbox. An important innovation was the Krauss-Helmholtz bogie. The front pair of driving wheels could slide laterally in the main frames, and they were connected to the leading carrying wheels by a bogie frame, this revolving on a bogie pin towards its rear. By this means the carrying wheels could move radially 1¼in (31mm) and the driving wheels could move laterally 1in (25mm).

Thyland Railway *As in Finland (see page 118) the Forney locomotive type had some success in Denmark. This section of the State Railway had a dozen, of which six were built by the Esslingen Works in 1882 and 1883. The general design followed that of the American locomotives introduced by Matthias N Forney, with the coal and water supples carried over the bogie at the rear so that their gradual consumption would not affect adhesive weight. The Danish locomotives had 12in by 16in cylinders (305mm by 406mm), 3ft 6¾in (1090mm) driving wheels, a boiler pressure of $143lb/in^2$ ($10kg/cm^2$) and a weight in working order of 23.3 tonnes with 11.7 tonnes maximum axle load. The coupled wheelbase was only 5ft 3in (1600mm), to aid running through sharp curves, and the maximum speed was 28mph (45km/h).*

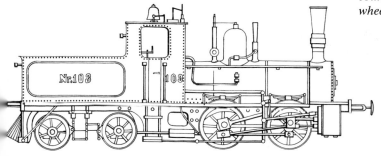

123

and for the locomotive crew, and de Glehn's work was the basis of the later success of the compound in France. Compounding had many critics and gave rise to bitter debates, but its introduction stimulated engineers who were against the idea to improve traditional locomotives. The articulated locomotives that Anatole Mallet first designed in the mid-1880s were another great advance and were widely used all over the world, especially for very large locomotives in the United States.

PLM C1 class *This locomotive was one of the milestones of French locomotive history. As the first compound on the Paris, Lyons & Mediterranean Railway it had considerable influence on practice afterwards, and was a version of the 2-4-2 simple express locomotives of the day. It was built at the PLM's Paris works in 1888. While the two driving axles were coupled, the forward axle was driven from the inside HP cylinders and the rear axle from the outside LP cylinders. The steel Belpaire firebox and boiler had, for the first time, a pressure as high as 214lb/in² (15kg/cm²). Walschaert's valve gear was fitted and the driving wheel diameter was 6ft 6½in (2000mm). Weight in working order was 53.5 tonnes, of which 29.6 tonnes was adhesive. During trials on the Paris-Laroche section it developed 705hp at 44mph (71km/h) up a slight gradient with a 240 tonne train. It was found that four cylinders in the place of the two of a simple locomotive made C1 run more smoothly, and there was less stress on the track. It stayed in service on the Paris-Dijon main line for many years, until moved to Nîmes in 1914 to haul local trains.*

Lancashire & Yorkshire Railway *The first example of this 2-4-2 tank class was built at the Horwich works of the railway in 1889, the prototype of a class of 330. John Aspinall was the designer and it had 18in by 26in cylinders (457mm by 660mm), 5ft 7⅞in driving wheels (1720mm), a boiler pressure of 160lb/in² (11.2kg/cm²) and a weight in working order of 56.8 tonnes including 1340 gallons of water (6090m³). Tractive effort was 14900lbf (6780kgf). Average speeds of 37¼mph (60km/h) at the head of ten-coach trains full of passengers were remarkable considering the size of the locomotive and the hilly nature of the routes. The last of the class was withdrawn in 1954 and is preserved today by the Standard Gauge Steam Trust.*

Teutonic class *Francis W Webb together with T Wilson Worsdell were the pioneers of the compound locomotive in Great Britain. Webb on the London & North Western Railway built his prototype compound in 1882, appropriately named* Experiment. *Results were not too satisfactory, but after many tests and modifications and working on other locomotives, Webb designed the ten Teutonic class locomotives, built at Crewe in 1890.* Teutonic *was similar to but larger than* Experiment *and was a 2-2-2-0 with two pairs of uncoupled driving wheels. It was a three-cylinder compound with two outside HP cylinders 14in in diameter (356mm) and a single LP cylinder of 30in (762mm) diameter. The piston of the latter was connected to the forward driving wheels, while the HP pistons drove the rear drivers. Thus the locomotive was a double single-driver, and the designer hoped to combine the advantages of singles with those of coupled locomotives. The Teutonics were fast and regularly hauled expresses at over 62mph (100km/h) representing another British step forward in railway practice. All the class were withdrawn in 1903.*

North Eastern Railway *This railway attracted attention in 1888 when a single driver 4-2-2 was put into service. At first sight like Johnson's Midland 4-2-2s, the North Eastern locomotive was in fact very different, being a von Borries two-cylinder compound. The designer was T Wilson Worsdell, who found that compounding was still viewed with some doubt in Britain. In the first 11 locomotives of Class J, built between 1889 and 1890, the HP cylinder was 18in (457mm) in diameter and the LP 26in (660mm) both necessarily having a stroke of 24in (610mm). Driving wheel diameter was 7ft 1¼in (2166mm) and boiler pressure 175lb/in² (12.3kg/cm²). In a second batch of ten locomotives built in 1889 and 1890, the HP cylinder was enlarged to 20in (508mm) diameter and the LP cylinder to 28in (711mm), while driving wheel diameter went up to 7ft 7¼in (2370mm). Weight in working order was 43.17 tonnes for the first batch and 47.5 tonnes for the second. Technically they were interesting locomotives and were appreciated by the crews. Nevertheless all were rebuilt into simple locomotives after four or five years, and were finally withdrawn between 1918 and 1920.*

Dutch Rhenish Railway *These celebrated locomotives were introduced into Holland in 1889 and gained the nickname Rhine Bogies. There were 59 in the class, the first batch being built by Sharp, Stewart in Britain. They were typical British inside cylinder 4-4-0s with all the latest refinements, and had 6ft 7½in (2020mm) driving wheels and a 147lb/in² (10.3kg/cm²) boiler pressure. For many years the class handled Dutch expresses with great competence.*

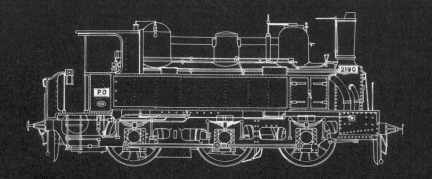

The Golden Age

At the start of the 1890s men were scenting the fresh air of a new century. The political order and social equilibrium that marked the 20 years after the Franco-Prussian War of 1870 to 1871 allowed the major powers of Europe to concentrate on rapid economic advance and to expand their commercial and industrial supremacy across the world. The United States, after the battering of the bloody Civil War, was likewise on the move towards becoming a first class and giant industrial nation, turning to advantage the spirit of the pioneers who had by then almost completed the conquest of the vast territories of the West. In this time of ambition and initiative, the railway played a leading role, for it was the communication frame that supported the rapidly expanding commerce and industry. The steam locomotive was long past the pioneering and evolutionary stage, and represented the driving force behind the commercial achievement of the 19th century.

Development of railways had been extraordinary to the point where, in the 1880s, some 15 500 miles (25 000km) of new route were being opened to traffic each year. The United States

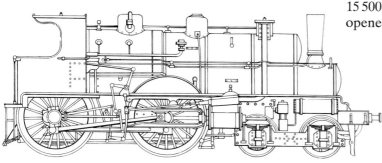

Flaman boilers *French engineers were sceptical about the advantages of the leading bogie, although the acceleration of express trains was posing problems of stability that needed a quick solution. The Eastern Railway's engineers were converted to the bogie only in 1890, but they still followed the design principles of the old Crampton locomotives that had given such good service on their lines (see page 49), putting the rear driving wheel behind the firebox. They also put a leading bogie at the front end and fitted a Flaman boiler with two barrels, one above the other. The lower barrel was full of smoke tubes, while the upper, which was connected to it, held water and acted as a steam chamber. A low centre of gravity was obtained without overhanging weights at either end of the wheelbase. During 1890–1894 the railway had Nos 801–840 of this 4-4-0 type.*

was in the lead with new track, followed by India, France, Germany, Canada and Italy, although such growth could not be maintained and was not to be repeated again. Trains ran through mountain ranges, passing under the peaks in lengthy tunnels excavated at great risk. Great rivers were a barrier no longer because of fresh bridge construction techniques, including that of the suspension bridge. Previously inaccessible territories heard the sound of locomotives of ever-increasing power and efficiency, although the locomotives themselves faced more difficulties than ever before as the trains they hauled grew heavier and demands for speed increased.

Compound locomotives, which came to be adopted as the norm during the 1880s, aroused great hope of increasing the amount of steam produced for each pound of coal burnt. They were not, however, universally welcomed.

The Mallet

The St Gotthard tunnel railway had become a major international route by 1890, and its curving gradients made it a severe test of steam locomotive ability. Anatole Mallet, after his first compound locomotive designs (see page 106), put forward the idea of an articulated locomotive with a rear group of driving wheels driven by high pressure steam, and the forward group driven from low pressure cylinders. A flexible pipe conveyed steam from HP to LP cylinders. Mallet patented this idea in June 1884, and in 1889 a little 0-4-4-0 tank Mallet compound was shown at the Paris Universal Exhibition. In a practical demonstration this succeeded in hauling a load of 10 tonnes up a gradient of 1 in 14.3 (7 per cent) to the surprise of everyone. This was the starting point for major new designs that in time developed into the largest and most powerful locomotives in the world.

Swiss railways were quick to recognise the work of their countryman Mallet, both for local lines with exceptional gradients, and for mountain main lines with much curvature and which needed locomotives that were both powerful and flexible. The Gotthard Railway was the first to put a Mallet articulated locomotive into service in Switzerland, an 0-6-6-0 tank built by Maffei, Munich, in 1890. It weighed 87 tonnes in working order with an axle load of 14.5 tonnes on each axle. The HP cylinders were of 15¾in (400mm) diameter, the LP 22¾in (580mm), while the stroke of all of them was 25¼in (640mm) and the boiler pressure 171lb/in² (12kg/cm²). Driving wheel diameter was 4ft 0½in (1230mm) and the distance between the last axle of the front group of wheels and the first axle of the second group was 8ft 10in (2700mm), a remarkable dimension for a mountain locomotive. This first Swiss Mallet could haul 200 tonnes at 11mph (18km/h) on a gradient of 1 in 37 (2.6 per cent). However, it remained the sole example of its design, as unfortunately the boiler could not produce sufficient steam to meet the full requirements of the cylinders.

Class B6, Japan *A popular locomotive type in Japan that illustrated the early influence of Britain on the rapidly-spreading 3ft 6in gauge (1067mm) railway system. Dübs & Co of Glasgow sent the first of this 0-6-2 tank type to Japan in 1890. The type was also built by Sharp, Stewart, by the North British Locomotive Co, and by the Kobe works in Japan. In all, 530 of the type were built in Great Britain alone. Cylinders were 16in by 24in (406mm by 610mm), driving wheels 4ft 1¼in (1250mm) diameter and boiler pressure 180lb/in² (12.6kg/cm²). Weight in working order was 51.2 tonnes, of which 38.2 tonnes was adhesive.*

Taking each country in turn, the bulk of British engineers were against the compound, only F W Webb and T Wilson Worsdell supporting the system. Germany was in two camps, Prussian engineers accepting compound locomotives with reservations and the Bavarians decidedly in favour. France and Austria both took up the compound boldly, the Swiss and the Belgians had their doubts, and in Italy on the whole opinion was against them. These were, of course, the feelings of the majority, for in every one of the countries some engineers at least favoured the compound. After the work of Wilhelm Schmidt in Prussia, the superheated locomotive arrived at the end of the century, and was at first regarded as an alternative to the compound in using steam efficiently.

Swiss 2-6-0 *SLM Winterthur built 15 of this advanced two-cylinder compound type between 1890 and 1901. They were 2-6-0s that on the level could haul trains of up to 900 tonnes weight. They had cylinders 17¾in and 25¼in by 25½in (450mm and 640mm by 650mm) and driving wheels 5ft 2½in (1590mm) diameter. Small four-wheel tenders were fitted with a capacity of 4 tonnes of coal and 2110 gallons of water (9.6m³).*

Wigmore Castle *At the very end of the Great Western Railway's broad gauge period (see page 37) eight convertable 2-2-2s were built for it in 1891, the first of which was given the name Wigmore Castle in 1893. Meanwhile 22 standard gauge 2-2-2s of the same design were built in 1891 and 1892 and, on the abolition of the broad gauge in 1892, the eight convertibles were changed to standard gauge. As 2-2-2s the class was unsteady at speed, and from 1893 to 1894 they were rebuilt as 4-2-2s. More of these were built up to 1899, when the class totalled 80. It was one of the most elegant and efficient single-driver locomotive designs ever seen, and brought the reign of the single-driver to a triumphant conclusion. Dimensions were orthodox, cylinders 19in by 24in (483mm by 610mm), 7ft 8½in driving wheels (2350mm), boiler pressure 160lb/in² (11.2kg/cm²) and a maximum axle load of 18 tonnes. The last of these single-drivers disappeared in 1915.*

PLM Nos B111–400 *This class was in origin a rebuild of the celebrated Paris, Lyons & Mediterranean 2-4-2s of 1876 (see page 110). The company experimented successfully with leading bogies to give greater stability at high speeds during 1889–1890, and as a result rebuilt four of the 2-4-2s to 4-4-0s at its Paris works in 1891: between 1891 and 1898 there were 96 of these 4-4-0 rebuilds. A major feature of the rebuilds was the placing of the firebox between the pairs of driving wheels, to allow which the boiler barrel was shortened. The original cylinders were retained, but springing had to be modified considerably and a substantial cab was fitted. As rebuilt, the maximum speed went up to 71½mph (115km/h) instead of 56mph (90km/h) because of the greater stability offered by the leading bogie. In later years the class showed that it could reach 74½mph (120km/h) on slight down gradients.*

Belgian State Class 6 *From 1885 the Belgian State Railway tried a few prototype 2-6-0 locomotives with varying fortune. Eventually 32 locomotives of Class 6 were built between 1889 and 1891 for service on the old, steeply-graded Grand Luxembourg main line. These outside frame locomotives had exceptionally large fireboxes, extending the full width of the loading gauge. The grate area was 72ft² (6.7m²). The locomotives were not successful, as the boiler could not supply sufficient steam to give a satisfactory performance, and the firebox was expensive to maintain. After alterations from 1906 onwards, the Class 6 bis proved to be a little better, but all the locomotives were withdrawn in 1921.*

Class XIII ÖNWB *During the 1890s, engineers in the Hapsburg domains abandoned the outside locomotive frame. This 0-6-0 long boiler design for the Austrian North Western Railway (ÖNWB) is characteristic of the period and was built for heavy freight work in 1891, with a maximum speed of 28mph (45km/h). Cylinders were 18½in by 24¾in (470mm by 632mm) and the driving wheel diameter was 3ft 10¾in (1190mm). To allow the locomotive to run long distances, a large tender was added carrying 7.3 tonnes of coal and 2380 gallons of water (10.8m³). The ÖNWB had 18 of the class between 1891 and 1896.*

Greater Britain *This was the last 'double-single' design of F W Webb for the London & North Western Railway, and was perhaps the designer's greatest disappointment, save for the similar John Hick class, which had smaller driving wheels and were much worse. The Teutonic class (see page 125) was repeated in Greater Britain built in 1891, except that the latter had the 2-2-2-2 wheel arrangement. As before it was a three-cylinder compound with the HP cylinders outside for the rear driving axle, and a single LP cylinder inside for the front driving axle. The boiler was larger with a greater steam raising capacity than that of the* Teutonics, *and to avoid excessive tube length a combustion chamber was placed halfway in the boiler barrel. In practice the combustion gases were at too low a temperature to burn within this combustion chamber and it was useless. The locomotive could attain 74½mph (120km/h) on a good day, but all too often needed a pilot locomotive for heavy trains. The double-single driving wheel arrangement led to frequent slipping of the wheels and to other difficulties, and was abandoned after this locomotive and the rest of its class had been built. Thereafter Webb compound designs had coupled wheels.*

Novosibirsk-Tashkent Railway *This was one of the railways of the immense Russian Empire and it put this two-cylinder compound 2-6-0 into service from 1892. It was such a success that up to 1913 over 1000 of the class had been built for various railways. They were known as Class N after Czar Nicholas, and there were 13 sub-classes built to the special requirements of the railways that ordered them. The 4-4-0 type had been found to be inadequate for Russian conditions and became unpopular, too, following the derailment of two of them while hauling an Imperial train with the Czar aboard. A new locomotive design was ordered capable of hauling 400 tonne trains at 50mph (80km/h). Professor N L Shchukin designed the Class N, with the Belgian Alfred Belpaire acting as a consultant. The class had cylinders 21¼in and 29½in by 25½in (540mm and 749mm by 648mm), driving wheels 5ft 6¾in in diameter (1700mm) and a boiler pressure of 171lb/in² (12kg/cm²). Outside Joy's valve gear was fitted. The locomotives weighed 54.8 tonnes in working order with an axle load of 14.5 tonnes. For many years Class N was the most popular type in Russia for all sorts of work. Even in 1939 about half of them were still running, and it was only in the later 1950s that the last disappeared.*

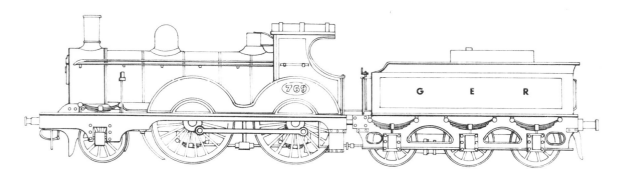

Great Eastern Railway *This locomotive belongs to the T19 class of this British railway, designed by James Holden, and 110 were built between 1886 and 1897. Cylinders were 18in by 24in (457mm by 610mm), driving wheels 7ft (2134mm) in diameter, and boiler pressure later 160lb/in² (11.2kg/cm²). Weight in working order was 42 tonnes. One of these locomotives was tried with oil firing in 1893 (named* Petrolea *for a time), using waste oil products of the Stratford works of the railway. A number of locomotives were oil-fired for a decade or more, until the waste oil ceased to be available.*

Jura-Simplon Railway *This was one of the most modern and neatest Swiss end-of-the-century locomotive designs. There were 30 in the class, built by SLM Winterthur between 1892 and 1896. They were two-cylinder compounds with the HP cylinder 17¾in (450mm) in diameter, the LP cylinder 26½in (670mm) and the stroke for both 25½in (650mm). Driving wheel diameter was 6ft (1830mm), boiler pressure 171lb/in² (12kg/cm²), grate area 21.7ft² (2m²) and heating surface 1388ft² (129m²). The maximum axle load was 14.9 tonnes, each locomotive could develop 670hp, and the maximum speed was 56mph (90km/h). A 180 tonne train could be hauled up a gradient of 1 in 100 (1.0 per cent) at 28mph (45km/h).*

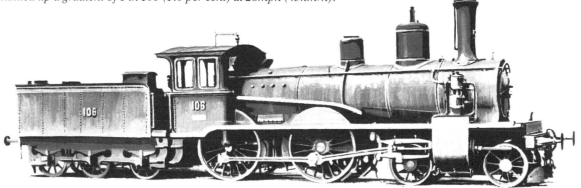

Prussian Class S3 *While in France compound locomotives were accepted only gradually, and in England there were vociferous critics, in Germany the pioneer August von Borries did not expect too much of them and followed two parallel paths when designing for the Royal Prussian Union Railway. He provided compound locomotives for long distance and high speed work, and simple locomotives for local trains in which frequent stops did not allow full advantage to be taken of compounding. Thus the compound Class S3 was designed for express trains and was highly successful. From 1893 no less than 1072 of them were built, while they were complemented by the simple Class P4 with smaller driving wheels for stopping trains, of which 1191 were built. The S3 class consisted of two-cylinder compounds with 18in and 26³⁄₄in by 23¹⁄₂in cylinders (460mm and 680mm by 600mm), driving wheels of 6ft 6in diameter (1980mm), grate area 24.4ft² (2.27m²), heating surface 1270ft² (11m²), and an axle load of 15.2 tonnes. On the level, 320 tonnes could be hauled at 46¹⁄₂mph (75km/h).*

New South Wales Government Railway *This 4-6-0 of Class P6 is considered to have been the most successful steam locomotive ever to run in Australia. When the first was built in 1891, it was an enormous advance on locomotives then running. Altogether there were 191 units in the class, 106 of them built by Beyer, Peacock, 20 by Baldwin, 45 by Clyde Engineering Co of Sydney, and the remaining 20 in the Everleigh works of the railway. Cylinders were 20in by 26in (508mm by 660mm), driving wheel diameter 5ft (1524mm) and weight in working order 66 tonnes. They were designed as mixed traffic locomotives, but in spite of their modest driving wheel diameter, they hauled expresses from Sydney to Newcastle and Albury at speeds of up to 70mph (113km/h). A tribute to the design was its selection – over 20 years after the first one was built – for working trains on the Australian transcontinental railway, from Port Augusta to Kalgoorlie.*

London & South Western Railway *William Adams designed this splendid 4-4-0 simple express locomotive in 1892. It was in open competition with the compounds of F W Webb, and indeed Adams went so far as to alter a 4-4-0 to a two-cylinder compound for a short period, though with no great success. Adams held that well-designed simple locomotives, with optimum use of the steam generated, would give as great an advance in efficiency and performance as compounding. The 7ft 9in (2360mm) wheelbase of the Adams bogie is of note. For a time these locomotives were the most powerful 4-4-0s in the country and indicated it by their graceful yet aggressive appearance. The one shown is the version with smaller driving wheels for the steeply-graded main line west of Salisbury.*

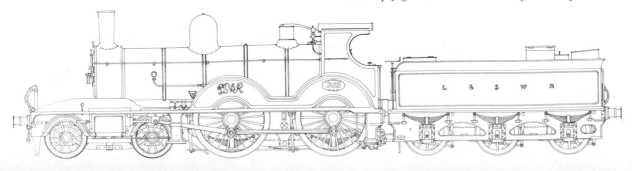

Philadelphia & Reading

The World Columbian Exposition

To celebrate the 400th anniversary of America's discovery, a great exhibition was organised at Chicago, known as the World Columbian Exposition. The railway industry was prominent among the exhibitors, and the London & North Western Railway of England showed their *Greater Britain* locomotive (see page 130). The latest American designs were also on display, together with prototype steam locomotives for the future. Even the compound locomotive, which was at the start of its brief American period, was exhibited with various wheel arrangements. Samuel Matthew Vauclain was the technical manager of the Baldwin Locomotive Works and his four-cylinder compound designs were prominent. The pair of high pressure and low pressure cylinders on one side of the locomotive, together with the valve, were included in a single iron casting, which was bolted to a similar casting on the other side of the locomotive. The two castings together made a saddle of the smokebox. This cylinder design was simple to build, facilitated inspection and maintenance, and became a standard for all sorts of American locomotives.

Two Vauclain compounds shown at Chicago were of particular interest, both of them with the 2-4-2 wheel arrangement. The first was a Baldwin prototype carrying the name *Columbia*, and the 2-4-2 became known as the Columbia type from then on. Cylinders were 13in HP and 22in LP by 26in stroke (330mm and 559mm by 660mm), driving wheels 7ft (2134mm) in diameter, and the boiler pressure 180lb/in^2 (12.6kg/cm^2). Weight in working order was 57 tonnes and the maximum axle load was 18 tonnes. The second locomotive was also a Vauclain compound, built for the Philadelphia & Reading Railroad with that line's preferred Wootten firebox and camelback cab position. Cylinders were 13in and 22in by 24in (330mm and 559mm by 610mm), driving wheels 6ft 6in (1980mm) diameter, boiler pressure 180lb/in^2 (12.6kg/cm^2) and grate area 76.5ft^2 (7.1m^2). Also at Chicago was a typical simple 4-6-0 built for the Great Northern Railway by the Brooks Locomotive Works of Dunkirk, New York, with a Belpaire firebox, cylinders 19in by 26in (483mm by 660mm), 6ft 1in driving wheels (1850mm) and a boiler pressure of 180lb/in^2 (12.6kg/cm^2). The class worked a transcontinental railway just south of the Canadian border.

Baldwin–Vauclain compound

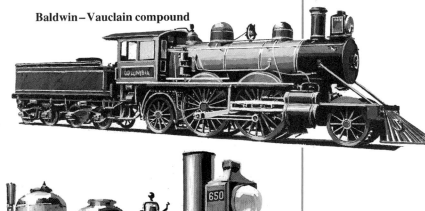

Great Northern Railway

133

Baden State Railway Class IVe—1894

De Glehn compounds

The four-cylinder de Glehn compound design awakened lively interest in Europe, and two railways with steeply-graded lines had de Glehn 4-6-0s little different from one another. They were among the first European locomotives with the 4-6-0 wheel arrangement, which was to be used widely later. The Société Alsacienne built the first Baden Class IVe in 1894 and the class eventually totalled 83. All three driving axles were coupled, and the HP outside cylinders were for the second driving axle, while the LP inside worked on the first one. Reciprocating masses were all but fully-balanced with this arrangement, which meant very smooth running. Cylinders were 13¾in HP and 21¾in LP by 25¼in stroke (350mm and 550mm by 640mm). Weight in working order was 58.8 tonnes and the maximum axle load was 13.9 tonnes. Up Black Forest 1 in 200 gradients (0.5 per cent) the class could haul 150 tonnes at 46½mph (75km/h). The second locomotive was built for the Gotthard Railway in Switzerland with cylinders 18in and 19¾in by 23½in (458mm and 498mm by 600mm), driving wheels 5ft 3¼in diameter (1610mm) and maximum axle load 16.3 tonnes.

Gotthard Railway 4-6-0 – 1894

Japan No 860 *This locomotive was the first to be built in Japan, at the Kobe works in 1893, after eight months work. Designed by Richard Francis Trevithick (nephew of the builder of the first steam locomotive) and by three Japanese engineers, it was a two-cylinder compound 2-4-2 tank locomotive, with a high pressure cylinder 15in (381mm) diameter, a low pressure 22½in diameter (572mm) and a stroke of 20in (508mm) for both. Driving wheel diameter was 4ft 5in (1346mm). No 860 went into traffic on the Kyoto-Osaka line and it is recorded that No 860 saved 15–20 per cent fuel when compared with similar imported but simple locomotives.*

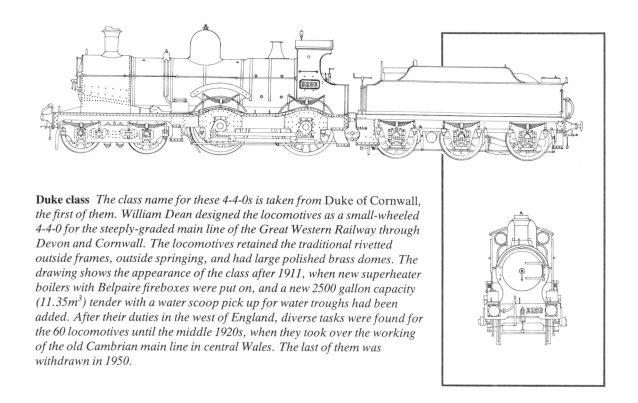

Duke class *The class name for these 4-4-0s is taken from* Duke of Cornwall, *the first of them. William Dean designed the locomotives as a small-wheeled 4-4-0 for the steeply-graded main line of the Great Western Railway through Devon and Cornwall. The locomotives retained the traditional rivetted outside frames, outside springing, and had large polished brass domes. The drawing shows the appearance of the class after 1911, when new superheater boilers with Belpaire fireboxes were put on, and a new 2500 gallon capacity (11.35m³) tender with a water scoop pick up for water troughs had been added. After their duties in the west of England, diverse tasks were found for the 60 locomotives until the middle 1920s, when they took over the working of the old Cambrian main line in central Wales. The last of them was withdrawn in 1950.*

Originally, boiler steam was superheated by circulating within tubes mounted among the hot gases in the smokebox. Schmidt then evolved the superheater that was to be accepted worldwide, with the steam tubes mounted inside enlarged flue tubes through the boiler barrel, an arrangement first used in a Belgian State Railway Class 35 inside-cylinder 4-6-0 in 1903. It was left to a Bavarian, Anton Hammel, to show that, by superheating a compound locomotive, efficiencies could be reached that had seemed unobtainable hitherto. However, it

was the work of Alfred de Glehn that was a major contribution to keeping compound locomotives in traffic. His four-cylinder arrangement provided for the work of the cylinders to be balanced to increase stability and regularity of effort. In the event, superheated de Glehn type compounds were to be the most efficient express steam locomotives in the world, although it was recognised that they were more costly to build than a simple locomotive and needed greater skill in handling.

In the United States the compound loco-

Vladicaucasus Railway *This heavy 4-6-0 type was typical on the 5ft (1524mm) gauge Russian railways after the turn of the century. Hanomag of Hanover built this one in 1896. It was a two-cylinder compound with 19¾in and 29in by 26in cylinders (502mm and 737mm by 660mm), driving wheels of 6ft 1in (1850mm) diameter and a heating surface of 1620ft² (151m²). Outside Joy's valve gear was fitted. The design features showing the German origin of the type are clear, although the railings around the outside of the footplating and the headlight are unmistakably Russian.*

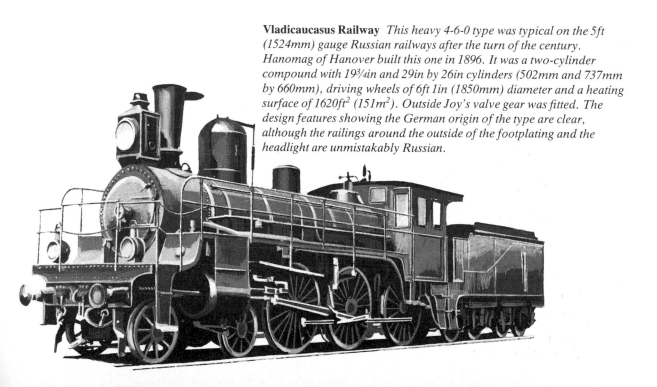

Grande C class PLM *First built at the Paris works of the Paris, Lyons & Mediterranean Railway in 1898, this Grande C class locomotive was a development of the compound C1 class 2-4-2 of 1888 (see page 124). The Grande C class locomotives were known popularly as the* coupe-vents *(windcutters), because of the pointed cab and smokebox door shape, which, together with the streamlining of the chimney and dome, made the locomotives recognisable immediately. The class were four-cylinder compound 4-4-0s, the outside HP cylinders 13½in by 24½in (340mm by 620mm) and the inside for the front coupled axle 21¼in by 24½in (540mm by 620mm). Driving wheel diameter was 6ft 7in (2000mm). Walschaert's valve gear was fitted for the outside cylinders and Gooch's valve gear for the inside. The boiler had a Belpaire firebox and a Crampton regulator.*

motive had only a brief period of popularity. That country had its own type, the Vauclain compound built mostly between 1895 and 1905, in which high and low pressure cylinders were mounted one above the other on each side, the piston rods of each pair being joined to a common crosshead and connecting rod. By the second decade of the century compound designs had become sporadic, for the railroads had found that their compounds were efficient at medium speeds only, where the optimum steaming rate of the boiler matched steam consumption. The greater flexibility of simple locomotives made them preferable for reaching the highest speeds, even if their overall coal consumption was greater. Compounding had one area of use thereafter, in the great Mallets built for the heaviest freight work. Mallet articulated locomotives enjoyed considerable popularity in the United States and many different designs were produced (see page 128). Compound Mallets were later abandoned in favour of four simple cylinders, and around

Dunalastair class *Designed by John McIntosh and built for the Caledonian Railway in 1896, Dunalastair was the prototype of a particularly successful family of inside cylinder 4-4-0 locomotives. The design was based on some Drummond 4-4-0s with 6ft 6in (1980mm) driving wheels but with a much larger diameter boiler – a boiler that was lengthened for locomotives built from 1897 on, and increased in diameter for locomotives built from 1904. The last of these was fitted with a superheater in 1910, which improved the performance still further when more were built, and one of these is illustrated. Most of the class had a bogie tender to carry 4½ tonnes of coal and 3575 gallons (16.23m³) of water.*

Japanese National Railways *These locomotives were built for various 3ft 6in gauge (1067mm) railways in Japan, and became the 5500 class of the Japanese National Railways when the lines were nationalised. Beyer, Peacock built the one shown in 1894 and it belonged to a recognisable type of British 4-4-0 (see page 109) with inclined outside cylinders and driving wheels of 4ft 7in diameter (1395mm). The weight in working order was 31.6 tonnes, 20 tonnes adhesive. The type was very popular and remained in service in Japan for 60 years or more.*

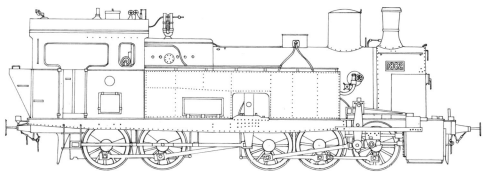

Prussian Class T15 *In March 1897 the Royal Prussian Union Railway took delivery of the first of this 0-6-4-0 Hagans articulated locomotive class. It was designed for mountain branch lines in Thuringia, which had curves down to 218yd radius (200m) and a ruling gradient of 1 in 33 (3.0 per cent). Christian Hagans had devised a locomotive that had six coupled wheels in front supported in the main frames, and a further four coupled wheels to the rear in a bogie. The rear coupled wheels were driven from the piston rods through a complicated system of levers and rods which allowed for the bogie movement. In effect a ten-coupled locomotive was obtained, suited for the duties envisaged. Despite the many complications, Hagans' creations were judged to be satisfactory and the railway had some 95 of them.*

Goldsmid *This was the name of the first of two B2 class locomotives designed by Robert Billington that were put into service on the London, Brighton & South Coast Railway in June 1895. The class was conceived as a replacement for the old Class G single-drivers on the London-Portsmouth route (see page 112), although in the event Class B2 showed no great advantage over the latter. In many ways an advanced design, the locomotive (nicknamed Grasshopper) was a 4-4-0 with 18in by 26in cylinders (457mm by 660mm), 6ft 9in (2056mm) driving wheels and a grate area of 18¼ft² (1.7m²). Unfortunately the boiler was not large enough to supply sufficient steam for heavy working, and the B2s were relegated to light passenger trains, such as those that ran from London to Brighton in one hour. Billington designed the Class B4 in 1901, and it was a considerable improvement over the B2.*

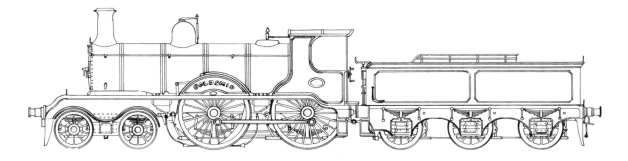

137

Adriatic System Class 270 *This 0-6-0 tank was designed by the Locomotive Research Office of the system at Florence, as a mountain branch passenger locomotive, as well as to haul local trains on the mountain main lines from Rome to Ancona and Rome to Pescara. They were effective little machines with cylinders 17in by 23in (430mm by 580mm), driving wheels 4ft 11½in diameter (1510mm) and a boiler pressure of 171lb/in² (12kg/cm²). Walschaert's valve gear was fitted and the weight in working order was 44 tonnes, with 1.2 tonnes of coal and 1100 gallons of water (5.0m³). They developed 400hp and the maximum speed was 40mph (65km/h). Between 1898 and 1909 a total of 207 were built, and there were others built for private railways. Builders were Ansaldo, Breda, Saronno Works and Mechanical Works, Milan, in Italy and Maffei in Germany. After the formation of the Italian State Railways in 1905 they became Class 851, and in later years they were to be seen shunting in yards all over Italy.*

Great Eastern Railway *This was the last single-driver for this railway, and ten were built in 1898 to a traditional design by James Holden. They were 4-2-2 outside-framed locomotives with inside cylinders and Stephenson's valve gear. Driving wheel diameter was 7ft (2134mm) and weight in working order was 50 tonnes, of which 18.3 tonnes rested on the driving wheels. The three-axle tender carried 2800 gallons of water (12.7m³) and 750 gallons of oil fuel (3.4m³), for the locomotives were arranged for oil-burning (see page 131). The class contributed to the last glory of the single-driver, but were soon found to be unsuitable for main line work.*

3100 were built between 1903 (when the Baltimore & Ohio Railroad had the first Mallet in the United States) and 1952 (when the last one was completed for the Norfolk & Western Railway). The first United States' Mallet was the world's largest steam locomotive at the time, and successive designs continued to hold the title thereafter.

Higher train and locomotive speeds in Great Britain were encouraged by another manifestation of the English love of sport, a kind of follow-up to the Rainhill trials of 1829. Various railway companies took part in a race to the north, using their ordinary service expresses between London and Aberdeen. The objective was to attain the highest average speed between the two cities, using either the east coast route or the west coast one. The prize was won by the west coast London & North Western Railway and its partner the Caledonian Railway. During the nights of 22 and 23 August 1895, the 540.2 miles (843km) were covered in 512 minutes, including three stops of two minutes each for a change of engines. The average speed over the entire distance was 63.5mph (102.5km/h) and the event made news even outside the British Isles. This was just a beginning, and railway races up to the period of the First World War became ever-harder fought. The constant quest for better locomotive performance and higher speed introduced the question of aerodynamic

Class 6 – 1893

Gölsdorf compounds

In 1893 an Austrian locomotive appeared which foreshadowed a great advance in design. Karl Gölsdorf, locomotive designer of the Austrian State Railway, introduced his Class 6 two-cylinder compound 4-4-0 that year and carried out many trials with it. The locomotive had a long-wheelbase leading bogie, with a bogie pin somewhat to the rear so that much of the front weight was taken on the bogie wheels. A high steaming capacity boiler was pitched high, so much so that critics feared that the whole thing might turn over on curves. They need not have worried, however, for the machine was found to be remarkably stable as well as fast, with a maximum speed of 81mph (130km/h). Driving wheel diameter was 6ft 10½in (2100mm) and it could develop 1200hp. On the Vienna-Karlsbad (now Karlovy Vary) route, Class 6 locomotives cut the running time from 12 to eight hours.

Gölsdorf designed a Class 60 two-cylinder compound 2-6-0, which was built for the Austrian State Railway from 1895. This had 4ft 1½in driving wheels (1258mm), a 185lb/in² (13kg/cm²) boiler pressure, and an adhesive weight of 43 tonnes. Class 170 followed in 1897, a 2-8-0 two-cylinder compound locomotive initially intended for the Arlberg pass route. Illustrated is a Class 270, a two-cylinder simple version of the compound, built from 1917, but the compound 2-8-0 had its firebox above the frames so that a large 41.9ft² (3.9m²) grate area was possible, while to aid running through curves the first and second driving axles had some transverse movement. The locomotives could develop 1400hp, had a weight in working order of 68 tonnes and a maximum axle load of 14.2 tonnes. On trial the first locomotive hauled 550 tonnes up a 1 in 100 (1.0 per cent) gradient, with continuous curvature, at an average speed of 16½mph (26.5km/h) and also reached a maximum speed of 52mph (84km/h). A total of 796 Class 170 locomotives was built from 1897 to 1919, and after the First World War they were running in half-a-dozen countries as a result of the peace treaties and war reparations.

Class 60 – 1895

Class 270 – 1917

Prussian Class P4 fitted with an experimental smokebox superheater during first trials.

Superheated steam trials

It had been realised for some time that increasing the temperature of steam entering cylinders would minimise heat losses due to condensation and therefore reduce cooling of the cylinder walls. In addition, high temperature steam has greater energy for its unit volume. It was a German, Wilhelm Schmidt, who took up the matter of superheated steam for locomotives, following up work already carried out by Hirn on stationary engines. From 1897 a series of experiments were made on the Royal Prussian Union Railway, using some 4-4-0 locomotives of both the compound S3 and simple P4 classes. Several different designs of superheater were tried, and finally a smokebox superheater was selected. Steam from the boiler was run through superheater tubes concentric with the smokebox walls on its way to the cylinders. Combustion

gases, after passing through the boiler tubes, were directed by baffles in the smokebox to flow over the superheater tubes before passing up the chimney. By this means steam was heated to 570°F (300°C) before reaching the cylinders. Excellent results were obtained from superheated locomotives, and indeed it was found with surprise that they were one quarter more powerful than their non-superheated sisters. Later Schmidt improved his superheater by running his tubes carrying boiler steam inside enlarged smoke tubes running through the boiler, thus clearing the smokebox of excessive clutter. This new arrangement was first used in a Belgian State locomotive in 1903, and it was in this form that the superheater became standard equipment for the railways of the world. Sometimes superheating is claimed as the only basic advance in technology made after George Stephenson's original locomotive.

Swedish State Class Cc *This was a successful 4-4-0 design for the Swedish State Railways, and 79 were built between 1892 and 1903. The design was an improvement on the Cb class (see page 111) with rather larger dimensions. Individual Class Cc locomotives were used for experiments from time to time. In 1914, one was converted to a two-cylinder Gölsdorf compound, and in 1917 another was equipped to burn powdered peat fuel (see illustration). Also in 1917, one was superheated.*

Swiss Central Railway *Powerful locomotives were needed for the line in the direction of the St Gotthard tunnel from Berne to Rothkreuz. Resort was made to a large-boilered Mallet compound 0-4-4-0 type, and SLM Winterthur built 12 of them between 1897 and 1900. The distance between the last axle of the leading group of driving wheels and the first axle of the following group was 6ft 2¾in (1900mm), a considerable figure for a locomotive working a route with limited radius curves. The class could develop 800hp and had a maximum speed of 34mph (55km/h). The tender could carry 6 tonnes of coal and 5670 gallons (12.5m³) of water.*

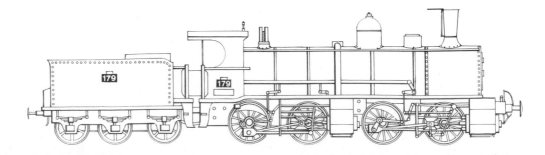

Klondykes *These 4-4-2 locomotives (the first outside-cylinder Atlantic type in Britain) were given the nickname Klondyke, for when the first was built in 1898 the Yukon gold rush was news. H A Ivatt designed the class for the Great Northern Railway of England, and the railway's works at Doncaster built 21 of them between 1898 and 1903. Cylinders were 18¾in by 24in (476mm by 610mm) and later 19in (483mm) diameter, the coupling rods drove on the rear pair of driving wheels and were 10ft (3281mm) long, and the grate area was 26.75ft² (2.48m²). They had long and useful lives, the last not being withdrawn until 1950, and one is preserved in the National Railway Museum at York. From 1902 the class was built with a larger boiler which, after superheating, made them outstanding locomotives.*

Palatinate Railway *This Class P 3¹ inside cylinder 4-4-2 was built by Krauss, Munich, in 1898. Double frames of different lengths were used so that the firebox could be wider, as it was supported by the outside frames only. Cylinders were 19¼in by 22½in (490mm by 570mm), driving wheel diameter 6ft 6in (1980mm) and the boiler pressure 186lb/in² (13kg/cm²). Weight in working order was 59.6 tonnes and adhesive weight 30 tonnes. Locomotives of the class worked express trains in the upper Rhine area, and it was one of the pioneer classes that started European engineers on the road to using the 4-4-2 in place of the 4-4-0 or 4-6-0.*

Bavarian State Class DXII *The Krauss-Helmholtz bogie performed very satisfactorily on the Class BX 2-4-0s (see page 123) and the Bavarian State Railway used it again to even greater effect on the Class DXII 2-4-4 tank locomotives intended for Munich suburban services. The weight of the coal supplies and much of that of the water was carried by the rear bogie, so the weight of the locomotive proper could be used for adhesion. Even so the Krauss-Helmholtz bogie, incorporating the front pair of driving wheels, was used to transfer part of the locomotive weight to the leading pair of wheels. Only the second driving axle was carried solely by the main frames. A total of 74 of these successful locomotives were built from 1898, and afterwards German engineers used the Krauss-Helmholtz bogie in many different designs.*

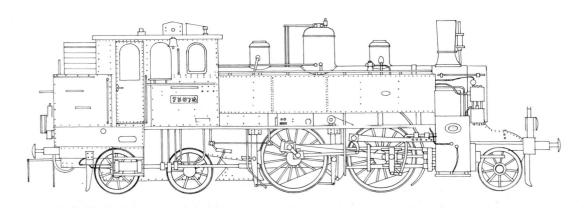

141

State Railways of France *This railway took delivery of some 4-4-0 express locomotives from the Baldwin Locomotive Works in 1899. The design was one of the last developments of the American type. The locomotives had bar frames and were supplied both as two-cylinder simples and as Vauclain four-cylinder compounds (as illustrated) with a pair of cylinders one above the other on either side, each pair supplied with steam by a single valve. The compound version could develop 943hp at 46½mph (75km/h). The locomotives were used satisfactorily on the difficult State Railways route from Paris to Bordeaux via Chartres and on other heavily-graded lines. They were withdrawn from traffic between 1928 and 1932.*

Illinois Central Railroad *Representing United States' locomotive practice at the end of the 19th century, this 4-8-0 when built was nearly the largest and heaviest locomotive in the world. No 640 was a product of the Brooks Locomotive Works, Dunkirk, New York, in 1899. The dimensions of the boiler had not been exceeded at that time and, exceptionally in America, a Belpaire firebox was provided with a 38ft² (3.49m²) grate area. Heating surface was 3500ft² (325m²), boiler pressure 195lb/in² (13.6kg/cm²), cylinders 23in by 30in (584mm by 762mm) and driving wheel diameter 4ft 8½in (1435mm). Weight in working order was 105 tonnes, of which 87.5 tonnes was adhesive, and tractive effort was 41 750lbf (18 950kgf). The maximum axle load was 22 tonnes, which confined the locomotive to track laid with heavy rail. The routes so equipped were then expanding in the United States.*

design for locomotives at the turn of the century. In the search for something that could travel consistently at 81 to 87mph (130 to 140km/h) smokeboxes, cabs and chimneys were streamlined, and one or two locomotives were designed boxed in completely. However, despite good results with the boxed in designs, after a few years it was decided that streamlining was too futuristic and it was abandoned until later.

Higher speeds and the greater weight of locomotives drove engineers everywhere to the use of a larger number of coupled wheels and thus more complex wheel arrangements. By the

end of the 19th century the Ten-wheeler (4-6-0) was prominent on the passenger trains of the United States and the old American type 4-4-0 was relegated to the past. The 4-6-0 gained general acceptance in Europe as well, but it was actually the generally poor track that drove the designers to the multi-axle locomotive, despite their reluctance to have more than two pairs of large driving wheels and to have rear carrying wheels in addition to those at the front. Advanced designers increased 4-6-0 driving wheel diameters and made a larger firebox possible on the 4-4-0 type by adding trailing

(continued on page 148)

Mediterranean System compound 4-6-0 *No 3101, almost at once renumbered 3061 and later Italian State Railways 656 class, was built in 1898 as a development of Europe's first 4-6-0 (see page 118). It was a two-cylinder compound with cylinders 19¾in and 28¾in by 25¼in (500mm and 730mm by 640mm) and with driving wheels 5ft 6in diameter (1675mm). Maximum speed was 50mph (80km/h). A total of 25 of the class were built, but from 1900 the class was superseded by a larger two-cylinder compound 4-6-0 with a long-wheelbase bogie, later the Italian State 660 class.*

Austrian State Railway Class 180 *This 0-10-0 two-cylinder Gölsdorf compound was built in 1901 for freight and mountain work. Cylinders were 22in and 32½in by 24¾in (560mm and 850mm by 632mm), driving wheel diameter 4ft 1½in (1260mm) and boiler pressure 200lb/in² (14kg/cm²). Weight in working order was 69 tonnes, maximum axle load 13.8 tonnes and maximum speed 31mph (50km/h). After the First World War many of the class went to Italy as war reparations and the illustration shows one of these as an Italian State 477 class.*

Adriatic System Class 500 *One of the most interesting locomotive designs of 1900, built in Italy. For No 3701 (almost at once renumbered 5001) the Locomotive Research Office at Florence abandoned the traditional boiler position and produced a 4-6-0 locomotive design with the cab and firebox at the front over the bogie and the cylinders at the rear. Enginemen nicknamed the locomotive* Mucca *(the Cow) and complained about coal dust whirling round the fully-enclosed cab. It was a four-cylinder Plancher compound, that is with the two HP cylinders (inside and out) on one side of the locomotive and the two LP cylinders on the other; dimensions 14¾in and 23in by 25¾in (370mm and 580mm by 650mm). Weight in working order was 69 tonnes, of which 43 tonnes was adhesive. Coal was carried in a bunker at the side of the boiler and the water tank tender had a capacity of 4400 gallons (18.9m³). The locomotive was a much-discussed exhibit at the Paris Universal Exhibition in 1900. The Western of France offered a dynamometer car trial, and between Paris and Evereux on 30 January 1901 critics were confounded: a ten-coach train of 130 tonnes was hauled at a maximum speed of 78mph (126km/h). A total of 43 of the 500 class were built between 1900 and 1906, and the last of them disappeared in the 1940s.*

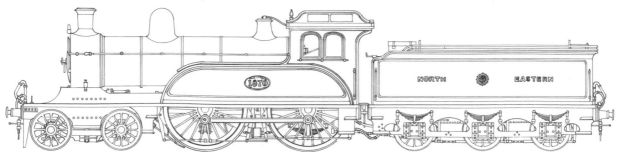

North Eastern Railway *In the 1890s this English railway was faced with rising passenger traffic and trains which were becoming progressively heavier. Higher speeds and greater safety resulted in an increase of travel and the railways had to provide more trains. More powerful and faster locomotives were needed and T Wilson Worsdell of the North Eastern designed a really high speed locomotive, two of which were built in the company's Gateshead works in 1896. They had cylinders 20in by 26in (508mm by 660mm), driving wheels 7ft 7¼in diameter (2315mm) and a boiler pressure of 175lb/in² (12.3kg/cm²). The design was an elegant and compact 4-4-0 with a weight in working order of 51.9 tonnes, of which 34.5 tonnes was adhesive weight. They, and sister locomotives with smaller driving wheels, were able to haul trains at average speeds in excess of 62mph (100km/h).*

Chicago & North Western Railway *When it became necessary to replace the old American type 4-4-0 with more powerful locomotives, this railroad was one of the first to adopt the 4-4-2 Atlantic type, shortly before the type appeared on the Atlantic Coast Line. This example was built by the Schenectady Locomotive Works in 1900, with cylinders 20in by 26in (508mm by 660mm), driving wheels 6ft 8in diameter (2030mm) and a boiler pressure of 200lb/in² (14kg/cm²). Compared with the Mogul 2-6-0 type, the Atlantic had the advantage that it was easy to provide a wide grate above the trailing carrying wheels and a more comfortable cab was also possible. The Atlantic type greatly contributed to railway evolution in the United States, first as a front-rank passenger locomotive, later for fast second line trains.*

Wurtemburg State Railway Class AD *Esslingen Works built this 4-4-0 locomotive for the Wurtemburg State in 1899. It was a typical German design of the period, save for the two domes connected by a steam duct, a feature taken from Austrian practice. The Class AD was a two-cylinder compound with cylinders 17¾in and 26½in by 22in (450mm and 670mm by 560mm). Although well-built and fast, as a 4-4-0 the class was already outmoded; 4-6-0, 4-4-2 and 2-6-0 wheel arrangements were taking over in Europe as larger and more modern locomotives were needed.*

State Railway Co Holland *British locomotive builders supplied most of the steam locomotives for Dutch railways. The State Railway Co had used a highly successful 2-4-0 design from Beyer, Peacock of Manchester (see page 113) and the same company supplied an equally successful 4-4-0 type from 1899. Like the 2-4-0s, the 4-4-0s had outside frames, inside cylinders, Belpaire fireboxes and six-wheel tenders, to which was added an outside frame bogie. The number built was 187, with cylinders 20in by 26in (508mm by 660mm), driving wheel diameter 7ft (2130mm), boiler pressure 157lb/in^2 (11kg/cm^2) and weight in working order 53 tonnes. Dimensions are given for the later superheated type.*

Danish State Railways *Class K 4-4-0 was one of the most popular for the level lines of Denmark at the turn of the century. Between 1894 and 1902 German manufacturers supplied all 100 of them, except that the first five were built by Neilson & Co in Scotland and another 20 by Breda in Italy in 1900. Many were superheated later (Class K-11) and in this form the cylinders were 17in by 24in (430mm by 610mm), boiler pressure was 171lb/in^2 (12kg/cm^2) and driving wheel diameter 6ft 1½in (1870mm). Heating surface was 757ft^2 (70.4m^2) with 202ft^2 (19m^2) superheater surface added. Outside Allan's valve gear was fitted. Weight in working order was 44.2 tonnes, adhesive weight 26.2 tonnes and maximum speed 62mph (100km/h). The pair of concave plates in front of the leading wheels acted as miniature snow ploughs.*

Paris-Orleans *This company introduced a locomotive type in 1899 with features not seen on the railway before. No 580 was a 4-4-2, the first French Atlantic type, with a double-dome boiler and a boiler pressure as high as 214lb/in^2 (15kg/cm^2). It was found to be fast and stable in trials and convinced Paris-Orleans engineers of the value of the leading bogie. On the Paris-Toulouse line in May 1900, No 580 took a 207 tonne train at average speeds of 50mph (80km/h) and reached a maximum speed of 68mph (110km/h). Another seven of these 4-4-2s were built in 1900, some of which were two-cylinder compounds. The latter had no great success as they were no more powerful and fuel consumption was only slightly reduced. All eight locomotives were taken out of traffic in 1928.*

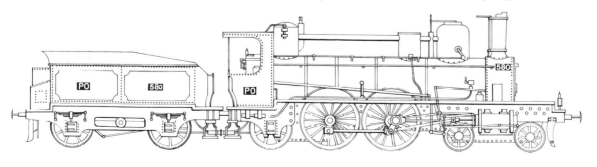

Precursor *To take the place of the unreliable compound express locomotives of F W Webb (see pages 125 and 130), a new engineer, George Whale, designed a simple 4-4-0 type for the London & North Western Railway. More powerful and with greater adaptability than its predecessors,* Precursor, *the first locomotive of the class, was built at the Crewe works of the LNWR in a few weeks and delivered in March 1904, followed by another five in April and June 1904. First trials quickly showed that the new class was very satisfactory and another 100 were ordered, being delivered in the short period of 76 weeks. The Precursor class took 400 tonne trains from London to Glasgow and Edinburgh at average speeds of 56mph (90km/h).*

Thun Lake Railway *This small Swiss railway worked a Berne-Interlaken route along the shores of Lake Thun. The 2-6-0 tank type was built by SLM Winterthur in 1903 for the local trains of the line. It had a grate area of 14.9ft^2 (1.4m^2), a heating surface of 101ft^2 (94m^2) and a weight in working order of 44 tonnes, of which 35.7 tonnes was adhesive. It carried one tonne of coal and 1540 gallons of water (7m^3). Maximum speed was 37¼mph (60km/h).*

New Zealand Government Railway Class Q *Needing locomotives more powerful than Class N (see page 117) and of a later type, this railway went to the Baldwin Locomotive Works for a new design. An additional requirement was an extensive grate to burn low-grade coal from workings near Dunedin. Baldwin produced a 4-6-2 design which has claims to have been the world's first Pacific type; delivery started in 1901. The grate was carried over the rear truck and could be given great width. The locomotive had a maximum axle load of 10.3 tonnes and a tractive effort of 17 250lbf (7825kgf).*

Northern of France – 1900

The French Atlantic

In the first few years of the 1900s, enthusiasm for the Atlantic type spread to France and there was competition between the various railways to put the most efficient and fastest machine into service with the 4-4-2 wheel arrangement. The Atlantic offered an advantage over other four-coupled types because a wide firebox and grate could be fitted over the rear carrying axle. At the 1900 Paris Universal Exhibition, the Northern Railway of France showed the first de Glehn-Bousquet four-cylinder compound Atlantic, built by Société Alsacienne. Cylinders were 15½in and 22in by 25¼in (390mm and 560mm by 640mm), grate area 30.1ft² (2.8m²), driving wheel diameter 6ft 8¼in (2040mm), boiler pressure 228lb/in² (16kg/cm²) and the locomotive could develop 1575hp. They were in the forefront of French locomotive practice and took passenger trains from Calais to Paris in 2 hour 50 minutes, inclusive of a 5 minute stop at Amiens. This was an overall average speed of 67mph (108km/h), quite exceptional for the time.

The high reputation gained by the Northern Railway Atlantics induced the Paris-Orleans to acquire larger locomotives in 1903, later fitted with superheaters. Cylinders were 14¼in and 23½in by 25¼in (360mm and 600mm by 640mm) and the grate area went up to 33.3ft² (3.1m²). Boiler pressure and driving wheel diameter remained the same at 228lb/in² (16kg/cm²) and 6ft 8¼in (2040mm). On the Paris-Bordeaux line these locomotives could achieve average speeds of 62mph (100km/h). The Paris, Lyons & Mediterranean Railway followed with four-cylinder compound Atlantics in 1906 (Nos 2971–2990). Grate area was 32.25ft² (2.98m²), cylinders 13½in and 22in by 25¾in (340mm and 560mm by 650mm), driving wheel diameter 6ft 6½in (2000mm), boiler pressure 228lb/in² (16kg/cm²) and weight in working order 69.7 tonnes, with 34.1 tonnes available for adhesion. They covered the distance from Paris to Lyons in 5 hours 15 minutes at an average speed of 60.5mph (97.5km/h) and could run up to 87mph (140km/h).

Paris-Orleans – 1903

Paris, Lyons & Mediterranean – 1906

Finnish Class Hk *The Finnish State Railways acquired their locomotives in the United States at the end of the 19th century. A fresh 4-6-0 design was built by Baldwin in 1898 and 1900, and by the Richmond Locomotive Works in the latter year – an overall total of 32 being completed. These small-size Finnish locomotives had the typical appearance of the American Ten-Wheeler type and could run at up to 52½mph (85km/h). Cylinders were 16in by 24in (406mm by 610mm), driving wheels 5ft 2in (1570mm) diameter and the boiler pressure was 171lb/ft² (12kg/cm²). Tractive effort was 12 730lbf (5775kgf) and weight in working order 44.5 tonnes, with a maximum axle load of 10.5 tonnes. They worked on the St Petersburg to Helsinki route and elsewhere.*

ÖNWB Class XVIb *The popularity of the Atlantic type and of compounding was noted in Austria. The Austrian North Western Railway (ÖNWB) introduced the Class XVIb for their Vienna-Prague expresses in 1901, a two-cylinder compound 4-4-2 Atlantic. The design had 6ft 3½in (1920mm) driving wheels, a weight in working order of 61.5 tonnes and a maximum axle load of 14 tonnes. The large six-wheel tender carried 4 tonnes of coal and 3430 gallons of water (15.5m³). The class hauled passenger trains over the saw-toothed profile from Vienna via Zellerndorf to Znaim (now Znojno) and covered the 62½ miles in 95 minutes, during which they reached a maximum speed of 56mph (90km/h). The long-wheelbase bogie was well-adapted to cope with reverse curvature and the Austrian feature of a double dome connected by a steam pipe was intended to reduce the carry-over of boiler water to the cylinders to a minimum.*

carrying wheels. Thus the Atlantic type (4-4-2) was evolved which, in both the United States and in Europe, served well as a high speed express locomotive. The Atlantic found its way to most countries in Europe and it was especially popular in France and Britain, where some very large designs were to be found. The Atlantic paved the way for the Pacific type (4-6-2) in which all the latest refinement of locomotive design could be accommodated readily. The origin of the Pacific is obscure and still a matter of discussion among railway historians. Some hold that the Class Q, built by Baldwin for the New Zealand Government Railways, was the first Pacific design, while others point to earlier locomotives which undoubtedly had the 4-6-2 wheel arrangement, whatever the reason may have been for its adoption (see page 97). At any rate, for many years it was rare to see an express train that was not being hauled by a Pacific in most European countries, and often in those outside Europe as well. A group of German engineers described the Pacific as the 'finest locomotive in the world', and it came to Europe on the Paris-Orleans Railway in 1907 in the form of de Glehn compound No 4501. But its advantages were already apparent to the Germans and just afterwards Anton Hammel produced handsome designs for Bavarian State Railway. Britain on the other hand was indifferent to the idea until the 1920s, and only George Churchward on the Great Western Railway produced a single Pacific locomotive, *The Great Bear*, in 1908. Other countries such as Italy

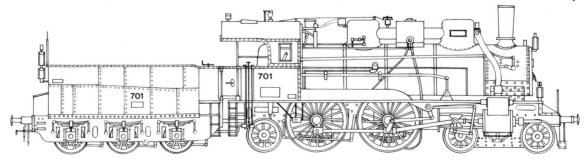

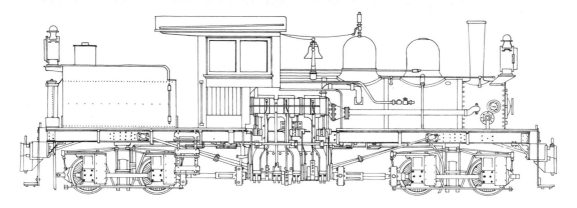

Shay locomotives *At the end of 1881, an American named Ephraim Shay took out a patent for an articulated locomotive that could work the rough and temporary track of lumber companies extracting timber from the vast forests of the United States. The locomotives necessarily ran at low speed because of their design and they were confined to industrial use. A typical Shay built in 1902 is shown. Three simple cylinders were mounted vertically at the centre of the locomotive, nearly always on the right. Their pistons drove a horizontal articulated shaft running from the first to the last pair of wheels, and all axles of the two bogies were driven through gearing. Shay locomotives were built by the Lima Locomotive Works (Ohio) and in all 2761 Shays were built up to 1945.*

Mediterranean System *The first 4-8-0 design in Europe was built for traffic up the Giovi pass behind Genoa, towards that port's hinterland (see pages 79 and 118). The Locomotive Design Office at Turin was responsible for the 4-8-0, of which 40 were built between 1902 and 1906. They were two-cylinder compounds with a large Wootten firebox, cylinders were 21¼in and 31½in by 26¾in (540mm and 800mm by 680mm), driving wheels 4ft 7in (1400mm) diameter and boiler pressure 171lb/in² (12kg/cm²). The class developed 900hp at 28mph (45km/h) and the maximum speed was 37mph (60km/h). For various reasons the class was not very successful.*

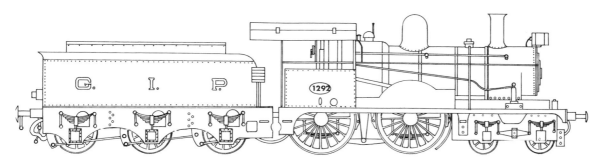

Great Indian Peninsula Railway *This Indian railway had some 4-4-0 express locomotives from the Vulcan Foundry in England in 1904 that were fine examples of their type. They had inside cylinders and motion, the former 18½in by 26in (470mm by 660mm), driving wheels were 6ft 7in (2009mm) diameter and adhesive weight was 29.7 tonnes. On the level lines they worked trains up to 300 tonnes in weight, and they had a tractive effort of 13 100lbf (5960kgf).*

Baden State Class VIb *Maffei built this 2-6-2 tank for the Baden State Railway in 1900. The cylinders were 17¼in by 24¾in (435mm by 630mm), driving wheel diameter 4ft 9in (1480mm), boiler pressure 186lb/in² (13kg/cm²), grate area 19.7ft² (1.83m²) and heating surface 1280ft² (116m²). The Austrian and south German feature of a double dome connected by a steam pipe will be noted.*

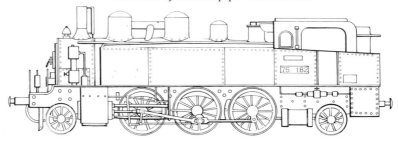

Metropolitan Railway *After London's underground railway routes had been electrified in 1905, a number of the old steam locomotives of the class built from 1864 (see page 71) were equipped with cabs and retained for repair trains and for emergencies. The condensing gear for use in tunnels was still retained, the example shown demonstrating the extent to which modernisation was carried out for the new duty. The last locomotive was withdrawn in 1936 and one of them is preserved in the London Transport Museum.*

Prussian Class S9 *Among the early trial electric motor coaches in Germany were some that reached extremely high speeds on test. In reply a mechanical engineer's conference was organised in 1902 to make proposals for a steam locomotive that could haul 180 tonnes at a constant 74½mph (120km/h) and reach a maximum speed of 93mph (150km/h). A Henschel engineer called Kuhn produced the winning design, proposing a three-cylinder locomotive entirely streamlined, including the tender, and with a wedge-shaped cab placed ahead of the smokebox. A 4-4-4 was built by Henschel to this design in 1904. The wheel arrangement was as unusual in Europe as it was in the United States, where it originated. During its trials there was difficulty in maintaining the designed boiler presure, but it did on one occasion attain 90mph (145km/h). Results were good in general but they scarcely justified the trouble of streamlining. The locomotive was in traffic until 1918.*

showed caution too, as their track could not support such large machines.

The Pacific type had a triumph in the United States, where such locomotives to many different designs totalled some 7000. Their extreme flexibility made them suitable not only for express trains, but also for fast freight work. Pacifics were built for all the major railroads, which competed with each other to put the fastest and most powerful locomotive into service. It is as well to emphasise that the primary reason for greater and greater investment in new and improved locomotives was this competition–the imperative need to offer the best possible service in the shortest possible time. Competition was especially marked between the various cities on the east coast of America, where the battle was all the fiercer because several railroads had routes between the same major centres and were in direct rivalry. This kind of thing was not so marked in Europe, for even in those countries that did not have a state railway system, care was taken to allocate areas to specific companies in an endeavour to cut down the wasteful expenditure inherent in such competition. The Pacific type had a long life in the United States, although before many years had passed the Hudson type (4-6-4) outclassed it on the heaviest trains and the Pacifics were left to do the donkey work.

GWR City class – 1903

Great Western developments

During the early 1900s the Great Western Railway (GWR) made a leap ahead in locomotive practice, especially in express locomotives, for which duty the single-driver was still then widely used. A fresh approach in passenger locomotive design had been seen in the Duke class of 1895 (see page 135), which was developed into the Bulldog class and which then appeared for express passenger duties as the Badmington and Atbara classes, with a final evolution to the City class in 1903. The City class boilers were domeless and had Belpaire fireboxes, the work of a new mechanical engineer G J Churchward. The boiler barrel was coned to meet the top of the Belpaire firebox, rather in the manner of the American wagon-top boiler. Outside frames were retained, cylinders were 18in by 26in (457mm by 660mm) and the driving wheels were 6ft 8½in diameter (2040mm). The City class leapt to fame on 9 May 1904, when *City of Truro* (illustrated here) was claimed to have run at just over 100mph (160km/h) and without doubt achieved just under that speed. The locomotive was working an ocean mail train up from Plymouth and it was running down the

Whiteball bank at the time. Just before building the Cities, G J Churchward had put a prototype 4-6-0 into service that was quite different from anything that had gone before. It had two outside cylinders, a Belpaire firebox and 6ft 8½in (2040mm) driving wheels. This was the first of 52 Saint class locomotives which, like the Cities, were superheated later with beneficial results. Saint class locomotives were tried against three de Glehn 4-4-2 compounds that Churchward had obtained from Société Alsacienne of Belfort (see page 147). One was of the Northern of France type built in 1902, and two more were of the Paris-Orleans type, all suitably adapted for the lesser British loading gauge. In order to make a comparison on the same basis, a Saint class locomotive was converted for a time to the 4-4-2 wheel arrangement, although the compounds were of course four-cylinder and the Saint a two-cylinder simple. The results of the comparitive trials surprised many. Churchward did not accept compounding, but on the other hand he did appreciate the advantages of four cylinders and thereafter large Great Western express passenger locomotives were built as four-cylinder simples (see page 155).

GWR Saint class – 1902

GWR de Glehn compound – 1903

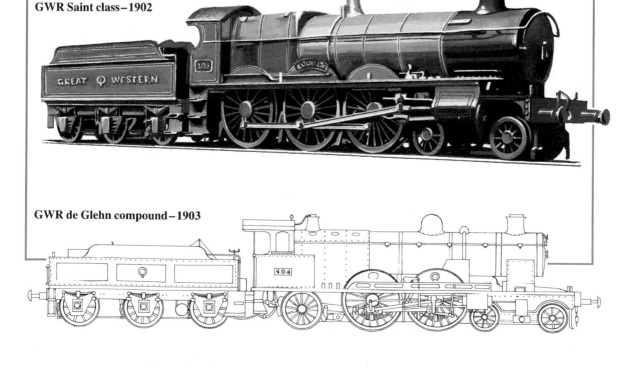

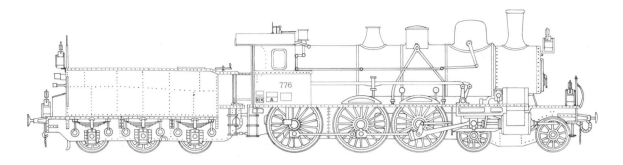

ÖNWB Class XIX *The Austrian North Western put four 4-6-0s into service in 1904, designed by Beutel and built by StEG of Vienna. They were large four-cylinder compound locomotives with the LP cylinders outside and all four cylinders connected to the front coupled axle. Cylinders were 13¾in and 23½in by 25½in (350mm and 600mm by 650mm), driving wheel diameter was 5ft 9½in (1770mm), boiler pressure 193lb/in² (13.5kg/cm²), grate area 33.4ft² (3.1m²) and heating surface 2140ft² (198.6m²). Weight in working order was 63.9 tonnes. The class developed 1050hp at 28mph (45km/h) and the maximum speed was 50mph (80km/h). They looked very impressive and the design, although distinctively Austrian, was quite different from the contemporary Gölsdorf compounds. Unfortunately they were not a great success on Vienna-Prague expresses, and were withdrawn from traffic in 1932.*

Belgian State Class 18 *During the 1890s the Belgian State Railway had no adequate express locomotives. A de Glehn compound 4-4-0 hired from France had been tried and rejected as too complicated. Then five Dunalastair class 4-4-0s (see page 136) were built in Britain in 1898 and 40 more came from Belgian builders between 1899 and 1900. These were Class 17 and the 140 Class 18 locomotives (see illustration) built from 1902 to 1905 had a larger grate area. The last five of these were superheated as Class 18S and another 15 were built as Class 18 bis with a larger superheated boiler. No less than 891 Caledonian-type 0-6-0s were acquired in addition, as well as 36 Caledonian-type mixed traffic 4-6-0s.*

Madrid-Saragossa-Alicante (MZA) *Henschel built this fine de Glehn compound 4-6-0 type for the MZA in 1905, followed by others from Henschel, Maffei and Hanomag from 1907 to 1911 to a class total of 73. The Belpaire firebox had a grate area of 29ft² (2.7m²) and boiler pressure was 200lb/in² (14kg/cm²). Walschaert's valve gear was fitted, cylinders were 13¾in and 21¾in by 25½in (350mm and 550mm by 650mm) and driving wheel diameter was 5ft 8¾in (1750mm). The locomotives gave excellent service over the gradients and curves of MZA main lines, and also after the major private railway companies had been merged into the Spanish National Railways System in 1941.*

During these years the locomotive was refined still further and became more complicated. From around the turn of the century, multi-cylinder designs became common, a pair of cylinders being replaced by three or four. On multi-cylinder locomotives the reciprocating parts could be balanced more readily and, taken together, the cylinders had greater volume so that tractive effort could be distributed over a greater number of wheels much more easily. As a result of all this, locomotives became more costly to build and maintain, and the motion machinery was not only more intricate but also heavier, especially when slide valves were used. Four-cylinder locomotives first appeared with compounding, but soon four-cylinder simple expansion designs, using superheated steam, arrived on the scene. These were popular in particular in Great Britain in the early years of the 20th century. The four-cylinder simple was also used in Belgium, where J B Flamme built excellent locomotives, and German designers produced them as well, but it was in Germany that the three-cylinder superheated simple expansion locomotive was developed in the second decade of the century. The Prussian three-cylinder machines were remarkably versatile and powerful, notably the $S10^2$ class (4-6-0), P10 (2-8-2) and the G12 (2-10-0), and they were the forerunners of a number of other three-cylinder designs.

For freight the period 1890 to 1920 saw the spread of the articulated locomotive, very often huge machines and in a great diversity of types. The already renowned Mallet was joined by another articulated type, the Garratt. These (continued on page 156)

Baltimore & Ohio Railroad *At the St Louis World Fair in 1904 many United States locomotive manufacturers showed their best and latest products. Among them was the largest and most powerful locomotive in the world and the first Mallet compound locomotive in the United States. It was the result of a wish expressed by J H Muhlfield of the Baltimore & Ohio for a machine that could haul the maximum number of wagons over Allegheny Mountain gradients. This 0-6-6-0 was built on the same lines as European Mallets, except that it was much larger. The HP cylinders for the rear group of driving wheels were 20in by 32in (508mm by 813mm) and the LP cylinders at the front were 32in by 32in (813mm by 813mm). Boiler pressure was 235lb/in^2 (16.5kg/cm^2). During trials it was found that the locomotive's running stability was none too good, but this did not matter overmuch as it was used as a banking locomotive up the steepest gradients were speeds were low. The design was an appropriate forerunner of the Mallet type in the United States, which later included the largest and most powerful steam locomotives ever built.*

Gotthard Railway *Two or three locomotives had to be used by this line on gradients leading up to the Gotthard tunnel (see page 134). Anton Hammel of Maffei designed a four-cylinder compound 2-8-0 of high tractive effort and eight of them were built in 1906. They had bar frames, a large firebox mounted above the wheels and originally 488ft^2 (45m^2) of the heating surface was devoted to a Clench steam drier, later replaced by a smoke flue superheater. Cylinders were 15^1/2in and 25in by 25^1/4in (395mm and 635mm by 640mm), the locomotives could develop 1500hp and their maximum speed was 40mph (65km/h).*

Bavarian State No 3201 *Anton Hammel tried his hand at a high-speed locomotive and Maffei built this 4-4-4 for the Bavarian State Railway in 1906. It was a four-cylinder compound with all four cylinders connected to the front driving axle and with bar frames. Cylinders were 16¼in and 24in by 25¼in (410mm and 610mm by 640mm). A wide grate had an area of 50.5ft² (4.7m²) and a smoke flue superheater was provided. Heating surface was 2340ft² (214.5m²) with the addition of 403ft² (37.5m²) superheating surface, boiler pressure was 200lb/in² (14kg/cm²) and the driving wheels were 7ft 2½in (2200mm) diameter. The maximum axle load was 16 tonnes. On 2 June 1907 the locomotive attained 96mph (155km/h) with a 150 tonne train between Munich, and Augsburg and shortly afterwards took a 150 tonne train from Munich to Nuremburg at an average speed of 74½mph (120km/h). Such speeds had no practical significance as the signal spacing did not allow sufficient braking distance for the train to pull up.*

Prussian Class P8 *This mixed traffic 4-6-0 design was built from 1906, and eventually no less than 3956 were built for Germany and for export. The class had smoke flue superheaters which gave remarkable results. Cylinders were 23¼in by 24¾in (590mm by 630mm), driving wheel diameter was 5ft 8¾in (1750mm), heating surface 1648ft² (150.2m²), to which was added 537ft² (49.88m²) superheating surface, and the weight in working order was 69.5 tonnes. During trials in August 1906 all were astonished at the performance. It could haul 450 tonnes up a 1 in 100 gradient (1.0 per cent) at 31mph (50km/h) and it developed nearly 2000hp at 46½mph (75km/h), an output which until that time had been regarded as impossible. The Class P8 was a universal locomotive in Germany for many years, and in 1980 the last few were still running in eastern Europe.*

GWR Star class *It has been noted already that the Great Western Railway took four-cylinder simple design from de Glehn compounds (see page 151). George Churchward designed the four-cylinder simple Star class 4-6-0, the first of which appeared in 1907 and was at once a great success. Cylinders were 15in by 26in (381mm by 660mm) with inside Walschaert's valve gear and derived motion for the outside valves. Just as with the de Glehn compound, the inside cylinders were connected to the first pair of driving wheels and those outside to the second pair. No 4003* Lode Star *is preserved at the Great Western Railway Museum, Swindon.*

Italian State Railways

The unification of three major railways into the Italian State Railways in 1905 was the occasion for the design of twelve standard locomotive classes to handle all traffic. One of these was a powerful mountain locomotive class that had been lacking in Italy hitherto. Florence Locomotive Research Office designed the 0-10-0 four-cylinder Plancher compound Class 470, which was built in 1907 by Maffei, Munich, and from 1908 to 1911 by Mechanical Works, Milan, and by Breda, to a class total of 143. Cylinders were 14¾in and 24in by 25½in (375mm and 610mm by 650mm), driving wheels 4ft 5½in (1360mm) diameter and boiler pressure 228lb/in^2 (16kg/cm^2). A water tank tender with guard's compartment could be coupled to either end. The locomotives weighed 74.8 tonnes in working order (carrying 1.6 tonnes of coal), and could develop 1000hp at 31mph (50km/h). Later, 129 of the class were superheated to Class 471, many of which were converted to orthodox tender locomotives at the same time.

The first Italian superheated design was the 2-6-0 Class 640 (with inside cylinders and outside Walschaert's valve gear and piston valves) and 169 were built from 1907 to 1911. Boiler pressure

Class 640 – 1907

was 171lb/in^2 (12kg/cm^2) and driving wheel diameter 6ft 0¾in (1850mm). Weight in working order was 54 tonnes, maximum axle load 14.7 tonnes, maximum speed 62mph (100km/h) and they could develop 800hp at 46½mph (75km/h). The first locomotives of the class were built by Schwartzkopff, Berlin, and went into service on the Milan-Turin route. The few remaining Class 640 locomotives were still running branch lines in the same area in 1980.

Class 470 – 1907

Danish State Railway Class P *The Atlantic came to Denmark later than to the rest of Europe, but the four-cylinder compound 4-4-2 Class P was among the most advanced of the type when introduced in 1907. These were built by Hanomag in Germany and more were built by Schwartzkopf of Berlin in 1910. Cylinders were 13½in and 22½in by 23½in (340mm and 570mm by 600mm), driving wheels 6ft 6in diameter (1980mm) and boiler pressure 186lb/in² (13kg/cm²). Weight in working order was 69 tonnes, maximum axle load 16½ tonnes and maximum speed 62mph (100km/h).*

had characteristic driven bogies far apart at either end, joined by frame girders which supported the boiler. The Garratt became popular almost everywhere, except in the United States which never used them. There was a revival, too, of the Meyer with its two sets of cylinders on the bogies, back-to-back in the centre of the locomotive, which facilitated pipe arrangements from the boiler to the cylinders and from the latter to the chimney. In 1914 came the Mallet Triplex type in the United States. These had three driving units, one of them under the tender, each unit having two cylinders. They were briefly popular until the flexible steam tubes leading to and from the cylinders were found to be too expensive to maintain. So there were no more Triplexes, a pity perhaps for they were handsome machines. However, in the United States, colossal Mallet types were built for one purpose, the haulage of enormous freight trains over mountain gradients, with one locomotive at the head and another pushing at the rear. Great tractive effort was developed, for such trains could weigh up to 15 000 tonnes and be 1¼ miles (about 2km) long, but naturally

(continued on page 162)

The first Garratt

Herbert William Garratt had accumulated considerable experience on the railways of Africa, South America and Australia before returning to Great Britain. There he put forward the idea of an articulated locomotive to be as powerful as a Mallet and with the same possibility of multiple driven axles, but which would be more flexible when working mountain lines with limited radius curves. Garratt patented his idea in 1909, took it to Beyer, Peacock & Co and together they worked out a locomotive design. The driven bogies were positioned at either end of the locomotive, each with two cylinders mounted upon them. The boiler and cab were carried on a girder frame slung between the bogies, with articulated steam pipes to serve the cylinders. Water tanks were placed over each bogie with a coal bunker at one end. Not being constrained by the wheels, the firebox could be given any dimensions desired.

Unlike later Garratts, the first two Beyer-

Garratts of 1909 were both compounds and had their cylinders at the inner ends of the bogies. They were built for a 2ft (610mm) gauge line in Tasmania where sharp curves and reverse curves had restricted the power of locomotives hitherto. Cylinders were 11in and 17in by 16in (279mm and 432mm by 406mm), boiler pressure 195lb/in² (13.7kg/cm²), driving wheel diameter 2ft 7½in (800mm) and weight in working order 34 tonnes. Because of curvature, the bogie wheelbase was only 4ft (1220mm). The two locomotives worked until 1930 and one of them returned to Great Britain in 1947. It can be found now in the National Railway Museum at York.

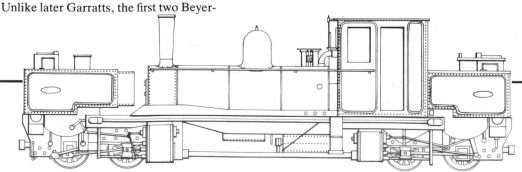

Holland Iron Railway Co *This 4-4-0 was the first superheated locomotive to run in Holland and it was built at Werkspoor's works in 1907. With Stephenson's valve gear for the inside cylinders, its cylinder dimensions were 19¾in by 26in (500mm by 660mm), boiler pressure 150lb/in² (10.5kg/cm²) and driving wheel diameter 6ft 7in (2010mm). Although built in Holland, the appearance of the locomotive shows its British ancestry very clearly, and indeed the design was based on a British-built original. To the characteristic inside-cylinder 4-4-0 with a polished brass dome, the German invention of the superheater was added.*

Swiss Federal Railways *Perhaps one of the handsomest locomotive types from Switzerland was this 4-6-0 built by SLM Winterthur from 1907 to 1915, to a class total of 71. They were four-cylinder compounds with cylinders 16¾in and 24¾in by 26in (425mm and 630mm by 660mm), driving wheels 5ft 10in (1780mm) diameter, boiler pressure 200lb/in² (14kg/cm²), grate area 30.1ft² (2.8m²) and maximum axle load 15.2 tonnes. Fast and powerful, they competed for years with the spreading use of the electric locomotive on the busiest routes. The last were taken out of service in 1946 and sold to the Netherlands State Railways to make good war losses.*

Moscow-Kursk Class Shch *The Moscow-Kursk Railway was one of the principal lines of imperial Russia and the Class Shch 2-8-0 went into service on it in 1907. The class letters were in honour of Professor N L Shchukin, who designed the locomotive in collaboration with A S Raevsky. About 2200 of the class were built and, as with other locomotive classes in Russia, Class Shch was built both as a simple and as a two-cylinder compound. In addition, individual locomotives were altered or rebuilt in many guises during their lives. The railing round the footplating, characteristic of Russian practice, may be noted.*

First European Pacific PO Nos 4501–4570 – 1907

PO Nos 5301–5490 – 1911

Paris-Orleans developments

It was the Paris-Orleans Railway which introduced the 4-6-2 Pacific type into Europe. The design was prepared in collaboration with the builder, Société Alsacienne, and it was a superheated de Glehn compound enlargement of the Paris-Orleans Atlantic type of 1903 (see page 147). The first 70 Pacifics were built between 1907 and 1909 with cylinders 15½in and 25¼in by 25¾in (390mm and 640mm by 650mm), grate area 46.2ft^2 (4.3m^2), boiler pressure 228lb/in^2 (16kg/cm^2) and driving wheel diameter 6ft 0¾in (1850mm). Weight in working order was 90 tonnes. They were powerful locomotives of good adhesion, able to accelerate passenger trains of 350–400 tonnes quickly and smoothly. They worked the lines from Paris to Bordeaux, Le Mans and Toulouse. Another Paris-Orleans design was built from 1911, principally for the gradients of the Massif Central. This was a superheated 2-8-2 tank with Zara trucks front and rear. The Zara truck was designed in Italy in 1900 and fitted to many Italian State classes, notably Class 640 (see page 155). The truck combined a carrying wheel and a driving axle in a bogie frame, so that considerable lateral movement was given to the carrying axle. The Paris-Orleans 2-8-2 tanks had cylinders 23½in by 25¾in (600mm by 650mm), driving wheels 4ft 7in (1400mm) diameter, boiler pressure 171lb/in^2 (12kg/cm^2), a heating surface of 1785ft^2 (166.22m^2) and a superheater heating surface of 442ft^2 (41m^2).

Austrian State Railway – Class 310 *From 1908, Floridsdorf Works built a 2-6-4 express locomotive for the Austrian State, designated Class 310. Karl Gölsdorf had developed a four-cylinder compound locomotive especially suited to express train work because of more effective balancing of the reciprocating masses. Track in Austria restricted the maximum axle load, while low grade fuel called for a large grate area – two factors which led to the adoption of a four-wheel bogie at the rear to carry a large firebox. To help in running through curves with driving wheels as large as 7ft 0¼in diameter (2140mm), a leading Krauss-Helmholtz bogie was provided. Class 310 could develop 1800hp, could run at 62mph (100km/h) on the Vienna-Salzburg route, and took expresses from Vienna to Prague in 5 hours 25 minutes.*

Bavarian State Pacific *The 1908 Munich Regional Exhibition saw the first appearance of this 4-6-2 Pacific locomotive, which it was realised even at the time would go down in history, for it was the apex of Anton Hammel's lifetime work with locomotives. Built by Maffei, the Pacific was a superheated four-cylinder compound. Grate area was 49ft² (4.52m²) and heating surface 2355ft² (218.4m²), to which was added 538ft² (50m²) superheating surface. Cylinders were, HP inside 16¾in by 24in (425mm by 610mm) and LP outside 25¾in by 26½in (650mm by 670mm), all connected to the second driving axle. The locomotive had bar frames, a boiler pressure of 214lb/in² (15kg/cm²) and driving wheels 6ft 1½in (1870mm) diameter. Weight in working order was 88 tonnes and maximum axle load 16 tonnes. It was an exceedingly handsome locomotive with all components designed appropriately, and finished off with a coned smokebox door and wedge-shaped cab front. It was a masterpiece that even today is considered to have been one of the world's best steam locomotives. It developed 1750hp at 43½mph (70km/h) and was very fast, despite the modest driving wheel diameter, hauling 650 tonnes at 74½mph (120km/h) which in 1908 was very impressive indeed.*

Little River Railroad Co *One of the smallest Mallet compounds built in the United States. It was a Baldwin 1909 design for a 9¾ miles (14km) lumber railway in the Smoky Mountains, Tennessee. Wheel arrangement was 2-4-4-2 with cylinders 15in and 23in by 22in (381mm and 584mm by 559mm) and with 4ft diameter (1220mm) driving wheels. Weight in working order was 64.5 tonnes and the distance between the axles of the two sets of driving wheels was 5ft 3¾in (1620mm). For various reasons the Little River Railroad found it to be unsatisfactory and it was sold subsequently to a lumber 'road in Washington.*

Northern of France *The compound Atlantics of this railway were very satisfactory (see page 147), but they lacked adhesive weight for accelerating heavy loads. This led to the building of a superheated 4-6-0 de Glehn-Bousquet compound type in 1908, derived from the Atlantic. These had an impressive performance and could take 100 tonne express trains up 1 in 200 gradients (0.5 per cent) at 74½mph (120km/h). The locomotives ran for many years and the illustration shows one in a later, modernised form. The last disappeared in 1968.*

George the Fifth Class *These locomotives, designed by C J Bowen Cooke, were a superheated version of the Precursor class (see page 146), with altered cylinder dimensions and valve vents. The class was able to haul 450 tonne expresses from London to Crewe at an average speed of 59mph (95km/h) and were well-adapted to this heavy service. A total of 90 George the Fifths were built at Crewe between 1910 and 1916, and the one shown, built in 1911, was the 5000th Crewe-built locomotive, named* Coronation *in honour of King George's crowning.*

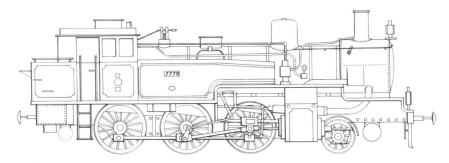

Prussian Class T12 *German cities were served by local railways for passenger and freight trains, both of which called for tank locomotives of some power. Such locomotives were among the least publicised machines of large railways, but for all that could not be less efficient. An example of such motive power was the superheated simple 2-6-0 tank of the Royal Prussian Union Railway T12 class, which became common on German local lines and in the yards from 1902. Henschel and other firms built some 1000 of the class. Cylinders were 21¼in by 25in (540mm by 630mm), driving wheel diameter 4ft 11in (1500mm), boiler pressure 171lb/in² (12kg/cm²), grate area 18.4ft² (1.73m²), heating surface 1110ft² (103.36m²) and superheater heating surface 317ft² (29.5m²). They were large locomotives with a weight in working order of 62.9 tonnes and 16 tonnes axle load. Maximum speed in either direction was 40mph (65km/h) and the tractive effort was 27 300lbf (12 395kgf). The coal bunker at the rear was not built high so that the driver had a good view when running backwards.*

Wurtemburg State Railway Class C *This four-cylinder compound 4-6-2 Pacific class earned technical approbation in Wurtemburg when it appeared in 1909, although differing from the Bavarian Pacific (see page 159). The locomotives were nicknamed Beautiful Wurtemburgers, which perhaps sounds better in German, had bar frames and cylinders 16½in and 24½in by 24in (420mm and 620mm by 612mm). Boiler pressure was 214lb/in² (15kg/cm²), driving wheel diameter 5ft 10¾in (1800mm), grate area 42ft² (3.9m²), heating surface 2240ft² (208m²) and superheater heating surface 572ft² (53m²). Weight in working order was 87 tonnes and they could develop 1900hp. Neither as fast or as powerful as the Bavarian locomotives, they could take 350 tonnes at 37mph (60km/h) up a 1 in 100 (1.0 per cent) gradient. Esslingen Works built 51 of Class C between 1909 and 1921, and a few were still in service in 1950.*

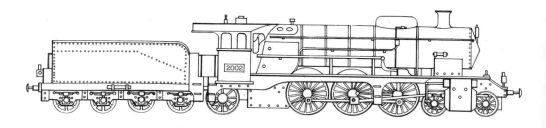

Baltimore & Ohio Class A3 *With the re-laying of long stretches of American railways with heavier rail, it became possible to build locomotives with a greater axle load. Thus 4-4-2 Atlantic locomotives could be designed with adequate adhesive weight, even if on two axles only, at the same time fitting in a large firebox over the trailing carrying axle. Because of these factors Baldwin built 26 Atlantic locomotives for the Baltimore & Ohio Railroad in 1910, the Class A3. Cylinders were 22in by 26in (559mm by 660mm), grate area 56ft² (5.2m²), heating surface 2345ft² (218.3m²), driving wheel diameter 6ft 8in (2020mm) and boiler pressure 205lb/in² (14.4kg/cm²). The weight in working order was 86 tonnes and the tractive effort 24250lbf (11000kgf). Even if they were not superheated, they were good orthodox locomotives, although they had a brief career on first-rate trains as the Pacific type soon outshone them.*

South & South Eastern State Railways *Henschel of Kassel in Germany built six of these inside-cylinder 4-6-0s for this 5ft 5½in (1665mm) gauge Portuguese railway in 1910. Boiler pressure was 200lb/in² (14kg/cm²), grate area 31.2ft² (2.9m²) and driving wheel diameter 5ft 0½in (1540mm). Portugal also had private railways, and all state and private lines were amalgamated into the Portuguese Railways Co from 11 May 1927.*

Saxon State Railway Class ITv *Georg Meyer was ahead of his time in 1872 when he built L'Avenir (see page 103) and the general indifference that he met then was only broken on the standard gauge in Europe when the Saxon State had compound 0-4-4-0 Meyer locomotives from Hartmann, Chemnitz, in 1910. The general arrangement with double driven bogies followed that of* Wiener Neustadt *many years before (see page 79), with the leading bogie driven by the HP cylinders 14¾in by 25in (360mm by 630mm) and the rear bogie by the LP cylinders 22½in by 25in (570mm by 630mm). Flexible steam pipes served the cylinders for boiler steam and exhaust. A coal bunker was at the rear and water tanks ran along the boiler sides. The class worked trains of up to 200 tonnes on 1 in 40 (2.5 per cent) gradients in the Ore Mountains south-west of Dresden for many years. The last was withdrawn from service in 1966 and one is now in the Dresden Transport Museum.*

State Railway Co, Holland *This four-cylinder simple 4-6-0 was perhaps the best express locomotive to run in Holland. Between 1910 and 1928 Beyer, Peacock, Werkspoor and German firms built 128 of them, and the class played a vital part in keeping the railways going in two world wars. Cylinders were 15¾in by 26in (400mm by 660mm), driving wheels 6ft 0¾in (1850mm) diameter and the boiler pressure was 171lb/in² (12kg/cm²). Walschaert's valve gear was fitted inside and a Belpaire firebox with a grate area of 30.1ft² (2.8m²). Weight in working order was 72 tonnes and tractive effort 22 650lbf (10 300kgf). No 3737 of the class, built by Werkspoor, is preserved in the Utrecht Railway Museum.*

Belgian State Class 10 *An exciting stage of Belgian locomotive history was the so-called Flamme period (1904–1914), due to the successful innovations of J B Flamme the chief engineer. He held that superheated four-cylinder simple locomotives would show the greatest efficiency, and proved it by building the Class 10 Pacific 4-6-2, among the most powerful of their type in the decade 1910–1920. Built in Belgium from 1910, the class had a short boiler barrel with the cylinders and bogie pushed out ahead of it. The class developed 2250hp and had a large heating surface, 2498ft² (232m²), to which was added 817ft² (76m²) of superheating surface. The class hauled heavy expresses on the Brussels-Liège and Brussels-Luxembourg lines, with which they could exceed 74½mph (100km/h) with ease.*

speed was low. It was not until the 1939–1940 period that United States' Mallets assumed the mixed traffic characteristics that were to make them some of the most extraordinary locomotives in the world.

The first 20 years of the 20th century saw great effort put into improving the efficiency of the steam locomotive through a variety of new devices and accessories. Among these was the feedwater heater, the idea being to warm the water from the tender by the heat remaining in the exhaust steam before it went into the boiler. Inventors had a field day with many different feedwater heaters.

More fundamentally, oil began to displace coal as fuel in areas where it was plentiful, just as coal had displaced wood in the past. Oil firing spread in the 1920s, particularly in the United States, for it offered not only fuel economy, but also enabled one man to fire automatically the grate areas of powerful locomotives. These huge grates were a problem to fire satisfactorily with coal, even when mechanical stokers were used. Meanwhile a challenger to the supremacy of steam had come on the stage – electric traction. Werner von Siemens had demonstrated the world's first practical electric locomotive at the Berlin Trades Exhibition in 1879, although few foresaw then that electricity would be a rival to steam. Nevertheless, the potential challenge to steam was there and the first tentative efforts at main line electrification

Bodensee-Toggenburg Railway *This private Swiss railway had a 34 mile (55km) route along the shores of Lake Constance. Maffei built it nine superheated 2-6-2 tank locomotives in 1910. Cylinders were 21¼in by 23½in (540mm by 600mm), driving wheels 5ft 0½in (1540mm) diameter, and the boiler pressure was 171lb/in² (12kg/cm²). Weight in working order was 74.8 tonnes and the maximum axle load 15.8 tonnes. Side tanks carried 2200 gallons of water (10m³) and the rear bunker 3 tonnes of coal.*

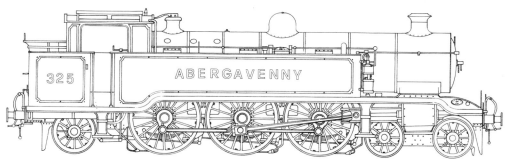

London Brighton & South Coast Railway *The relatively short main lines of this railway allowed express trains to be worked by large tank locomotives. After building 4-4-2 inside-cylinder tanks, D E Marsh built two superheated 4-6-2 tank outside cylinder locomotives,* Abergavenny *in 1910 with Stephenson's valve gear, and* Bessborough *in 1912 with Walschaert's valve gear. Cylinders were 21in by 26in (533mm by 660mm), driving wheels 6ft 7½in (2018mm) diameter, boiler pressure 170lb/in² (11.9kg/cm²) and heating surface 1586ft² (147.35m²), to which was added 365ft² (33.17m²) superheating surface. The locomotives could run at speeds in excess of 81mph (130km/h) and they worked expresses from London to Brighton (including the Southern Belle, made up of cream*

and umber Pullman cars), London to Portsmouth and London to Eastbourne until the start of electrification in 1932, although they were in traffic for some 15 years after that.

Prussian Class S10 *Among engineers of the Royal Prussian Union Railway there was a division between those who supported the compound locomotive and those who held that the advent of superheating had made compounding unnecessary. A superheated four-cylinder simple 4-6-0 was built by Schwartzkopff of Berlin, in 1910, the S10 class, and developed in general from Class P8 (see page 154). The S10 class was fast but from the start there was trouble with valve events and fractures of the valve gear radius rod, as well as excessive steam consumption. Hence the design was altered to a three-cylinder simple and 120 of these were built, known as the S10² class. The S10² class could haul 650 tonnes at 56mph (90km/h) and developed more than 2000hp.*

Swiss Federal Railways *In the second decade of the 1900s this railway had started electrification of its main lines, although steam locomotive building continued for a number of years to meet increasingly heavy traffic. The decision was taken to electrify the Gotthard route in 1912, and simultaneously a new steam locomotive class was introduced to handle the ever-heavier trains running over the route until electrification was completed. A superheated 2-10-0 was built by SLM Winterthur, the first two four-cylinder simples and 30 others four-cylinder compounds. The compound variety had cylinders 18½in and 27¼in by 25¼in (470mm and 690mm by 640mm), driving wheels 4ft 4¼in (1330mm) diameter, a grate area of 39.8ft² (3.7m²), heating surface 2270ft² (211.3m²), superheater heating surface 576ft² (54.5m²) and a boiler pressure of 214lb/in² (15.0kg/cm²). Adhesive weight was 75 tonnes and thus the maximum axle load was 15 tonnes. The class could develop 1350hp and haul a 300 tonne train up a gradient of 1 in 40 (2.5 per cent) at 15½mph (25km/h). Not infrequently three or four of these locomotives could be seen struggling up to the Gotthard tunnel with a massive freight train.*

were made in the United States in 1895, in Switzerland in 1899 and in Germany and Italy in 1901. Even so, electrification was not yet regarded as an alternative to steam but rather as a solution to special problems, such as the working of long tunnels or steep gradients. Just the same, this was the beginning of the long battle between the two forms of traction, which may have started gently enough but which then, as often as not, became a matter of political argument that embroiled many sections of public opinion. The steam locomotive had become part of the lives of almost everyone and all felt that they had a right to be heard.

Smyrna-Cassaba Railway *This was a relatively short line inland from Smyrna (now Izmir) in Turkey. Like other railways in Turkey this one had 0-6-0 tank locomotives from Maffei of Munich for short workings and for shunting. This one was the first of many and it was built in 1912. They were simple and robust machines with cylinders 16¾in by 25in (430mm by 630mm), driving wheels 4ft 1in (1250mm) diameter and a boiler pressure of 171lb/in² (12kg/cm²). They were handy little machines and the Turkish State Railways still had the last few of them in service in 1980.*

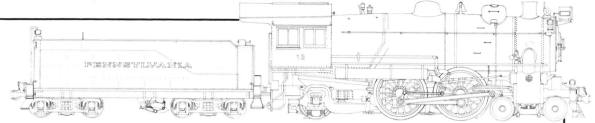

Pennsylvania Railroad Class E6–1910

United States' locomotives

Track and other works were improved substantially in the United States during the early 1900s so that locomotive builders were able to design ever-heavier and more powerful locomotives, accentuating a division between American practice and that of Europe which had started in the 1890s. There was, too, a pioneering spirit among the American designers and a desire always to do better than the next man in pushing the art of locomotive building to the limit. It might be added as well that trade unions were already insisting on the overmanning of trains, so to save wages the railways were driven to run the infrequent and excessively heavy trains so characteristic of North America. The appearance of the Baltimore & Ohio's Atlantics in 1910 (see page 161) spurred on the Pennsylvania Railroad to build their superheated 4-4-2 Class E6 in the same year. This had a Belpaire firebox with a grate area of 54.8ft² (5.1m²) and a large diameter boiler with pressure at 205lb/in² (14.6kg/cm²). Cylinders were 23½in by 26in (597mm by 660mm), driving wheel diameter 6ft 8in (2034mm) and weight in working order 109 tonnes, with a maximum axle load of no less than 30 tonnes. The Class E6 could develop 2500hp

and haul an eight coach load of about 600 tonnes at speeds up to 90mph (145km/h).

The Pacific 4-6-2 type was already being built for slower and heavier trains and the first for the faster work was the 1912 Class K3 of the New York Central Railroad, again spurred on by competition. Class K3 derived from two earlier classes built between 1903 and 1910 and had cylinders 23½in by 26in (597mm by 660mm), driving wheels 6ft 6½in (2000mm) diameter, boiler pressure 200lb/in² (14kg/cm²), heating surface 3420ft² (318.43m²) and superheating surface 832ft² (77.37m²). Weight in working order was 134 tonnes and the maximum axle load 29.4 tonnes. A total of 281 of Class K3 were built, and their best-known work was to take the Twentieth Century Limited of about 700 tonnes from New York to Chicago in 18 hours, an average speed of 53mph (86km/h). However, in contrast to the giant express locomotives, there was a need still for small branch line locomotives. Such was the 2-6-0 built by the Canadian Locomotive Co in 1910 for the Grand Trunk Railway, a couple of years before 1913, when the line was absorbed into the Canadian National Railways. The process of combining railroads into larger and larger units was in full swing in North America.

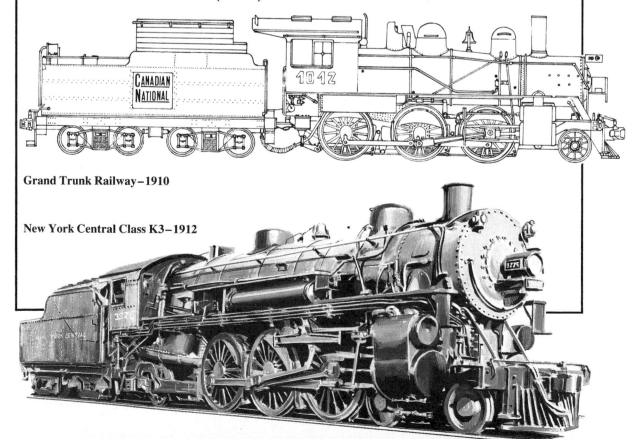

Grand Trunk Railway–1910

New York Central Class K3–1912

Soviet Railways Class S *This 2-6-2 locomotive class originated in a ministerial decree of March 1908 intended to ensure replacement of old motive power. The first of Class S were built by the Sormovo works at Nijni Novgorod (now Gorky) in 1911, and by 1918 at least 900 were in traffic. The class had a Krauss-Helmholtz truck at the front end and a bissel truck at the rear. Among the S class were a few built for the standard gauge in 1913, rather than the Russian 5ft (1524mm) gauge. These worked on the Warsaw-Vienna Railway in what is now Poland, and were known as Class Sv. Class S was an important passenger locomotive all over western Russia for more than thirty years and a few were still working there in 1980. The locomotive illustrated is arranged for oil firing, used since the mid-nineteenth century for those Russian railways in the vicinity of oilfields.*

Italian State Class 685 *This was a superheated simple four-cylinder 2-6-2 with a leading Zara truck. The first was built in 1912 and the class was derived from the Plancher compound Class 680, with the addition of the superheater. Cylinders were 16½in by 25½in (420mm by 650mm) and driving wheels 6ft 0¾in (1850mm) diameter. Including rebuilds from compounds, the 685 class totalled 390, and some of them had Caprotti poppet valve gear, five of which were rebuilt with Franco-Crosti boilers in 1940. At the start of 1980 at least one was still in traffic, and a Caprotti compound rebuild is in the Museum of Science and Technology, Milan.*

Prussian Class G8¹ *The Royal Prussian Union Railway standardised its locomotive classes and sought a universal heavy freight 0-8-0 locomotive to haul 1500 tonnes or more. Class G8 was built from 1902, the first from Schichau of Elbing (now Elblag), and this was variously modified until Class G8¹ was evolved from 1912. This became one of the most widely used freight locomotives in the world. Cylinders were 23½in by 26in (600mm by 660mm), driving wheels 4ft 5in (1350mm) diameter and boiler pressure 200lb/in² (14kg/cm²). Heating surface was 1569ft² (144.43m²) and superheater heating surface 547ft² (51.88m²), while the weight in working order was 68 tonnes and the maximum axle load 17 tonnes. Class G8¹ could haul 810 tonnes at 12½mph (20km/h) up a gradient of 1 in 100 (1.0 per cent). Between 1912 and 1923 no less than 5297 of the class were built, including those exported to other railways.*

Prussian Class T18 *Class T18 was a superheated 4-6-4 tank locomotive derived from the celebrated P8 class (see page 154) and the first was built by Vulkan Works, Stettin (now Szczecin), in 1912. The rear bogie carried part of the firebox, the cab and the 4½ tonnes of coal in the rear bunker. The total wheelbase was 38ft 5in (11700mm). Grate area was 25.8ft^2 (2.4m^2), heating surface 1415ft^2 (131.39m^2) and superheating surface 441ft^2 (40.9m^2). As well as for heavy suburban work Class T18 was used for short distance express trains, notably Stettin to Berlin. Construction continued after the formation of the German State Railway in 1920, and the class total was 460.*

Bavarian State Railway *This is one of the few large Mallet compound tank classes built for use in Europe. The Bavarian State desired a locomotive to work 500 tonnes or more up the 1 in 40 (2.5 per cent) gradients of the Upper Franconia branch lines, without the necessity for a banking locomotive. A superheated 0-8-8-0 was built by Maffei in 1913, and by 1923 there were 25 of them of two distinct classes, although sharing main dimensions. Cylinders were 20½in and 31½in by 25¼in (520mm and 800mm by 640mm), boiler pressure 214lb/in^2 (15kg/cm^2) and driving wheel diameter 4ft (1216mm). These locomotives could haul more than 650 tonnes up a 1 in 40 (2.5 per cent) gradient at 12½mph (20km/h) or a passenger train at 31mph (50km/h).*

Southern Pacific *One of the hardest sections of this railroad was that between Sacramento, California, and Sparks, Nevada. The 140 mile line (226km) rises up to 7042ft (2147m) above sea level with continuous curvature, gradients in excess of 1 in 50 (2.0 per cent), and 39 tunnels. Consolidation 2-8-0s were replaced by some Mallets in 1909, but these were not popular with the enginemen as the cabs filled with smoke in the tunnels and, with cabs at the rear, the great length of the boiler frequently cut off the view of the line ahead when running through curves. For these reasons a Mallet design, running backwards with the cab in front was proposed, a design that was facilitated by the adoption of oil firing. The 2-8-8-2 Class Mc2 Mallet compounds were built by Baldwin from 1910, and had cylinders 26in and 40in by 30in (660mm and 1016mm by 762mm). With one of these locomotives at the head of a train and with two banking locomotives, a freight train of about 100 wagons and weighing 4500 tonnes could be worked from Sacramento to Sparks in 10 hours. One Class Mc2 Mallet could handle a twelve-coach passenger train.*

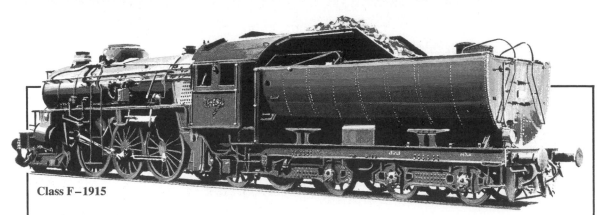

Class F – 1915

Swedish designs

Swedish State Railways introduced two interesting fresh designs in 1914–1915. Class J was an inside-cylinder superheated 2-6-4 tank with cylinders 16½in by 23in (420mm by 580mm), driving wheels 4ft 3¼in (1300mm) diameter and

Class J – 1914

boiler pressure 171lb/in^2 (12kg/cm^2). Weight in working order was 62 tonnes, adhesive weight 33 tonnes and maximum speed 46½mph (75km/h). Two Swedish firms, Motola Verkstad and Nydquist & Holm, built 45 of the class between 1914 and 1918. The second design was a major express superheated four-cylinder compound Pacific 4-6-2 locomotive. The Nydquist & Holm design for this Class F was accepted and they built eleven of them in 1915. They had plate frames and an outside-frame bogie. Cylinders were 16½in and 25in by 26in (420mm and 630mm by 660mm), all of them connected to the second driving axle, driving wheels 6ft 2in (1880mm) diameter and boiler pressure 186lb/in^2 (13kg/cm^2). Grate area was 38.5ft^2 (3.6m^2), heating surface 2038ft^2 (189.3m^2) and superheating surface 732ft^2 (68m^2). Weight in working order was 88 tonnes, maximum axle load 16 tonnes, and maximum speed 62mph (100km/h). Because of the spread of electrification, the class was sold to the Danish State Railways in 1937, where they were known as Class E.

State Railway Co, Holland *This 4-6-4 inside-cylinder superheated tank class was built by Beyer, Peacock & Co of Manchester for the State Railway Co in 1913. A total of 26 were built to handle short distance express trains. The boiler had a Belpaire firebox, cylinders were 20in by 26in (508mm by 660mm), driving wheel diameter 6ft 0¾in (1850mm) and weight in working order 92 tonnes. The idea of a tank locomotive for express trains was in the air at this time, for example in Germany where Class T18 was the best-known (see page 167) and in Britain and Switzerland (see page 163). French and Danish designs came later, while Italy had had an express passenger 4-6-4 tank in 1905, and later had a mountain 2-8-2 tank (see page 181).*

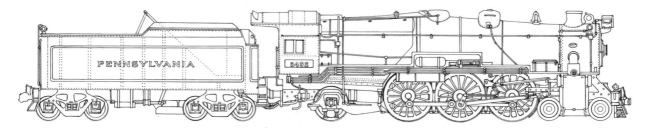

Pennsylvania Railroad Class K4 *The United States built many locomotives of the 4-6-2 Pacific type. Among the best were the Wabash Railroad Class J1 (see below) and the New York Central Class K3 (see page 165), but the most celebrated of all was the Pennsylvania's Class K4, first built in 1914 and derived from the Class E6 Atlantic (see page 165). Class K4 was one of the great successes of American locomotive building, and because of the soundness of the original design, they remained in service for over thirty years. In all 425 were built, 75 by Baldwin and the rest by other locomotive firms or the Pennsylvania's own works at Altoona. They were two-cylinder superheated simples with cylinders 27in by 28in (686mm by 711mm), driving wheel diameter 6ft 8in (2030mm) and 205lb/in² (14.3kg/cm²) boiler pressure. Walschaert's valve gear was fitted, and weight in working order was 138 tonnes with a maximum axle load of 30.2 tonnes. Tractive effort was 44 300lbf (20 100kgf) and on trial the first K4 developed 3200hp. The locomotives worked passenger trains over Allegheny mountain grades between Altoona and Pittsburgh, or across level plain country just as needed.*

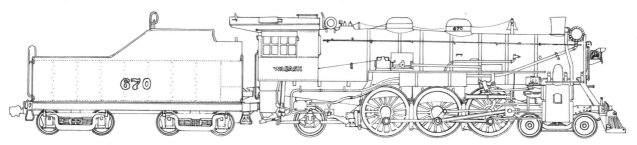

Wabash Railroad *This road had 16 Pacifics in 1912, ten built by the American Locomotive Co and six by Baldwin. Although overshadowed by the New York Central Class K3 Pacifics of the same year, this Class J1 was in the front rank of American 4-6-2s. Cylinders were 24in by 26in (610mm by 660mm), grate area 62.4ft² (5.8m²), heating surface 4470ft² (415m²) and driving wheel diameter 6ft 2in (1880mm). Compared with Class K3, the Wabash Pacifics had lesser dimensions, nor were they superheated. Nevertheless they could perform work of the highest level on such celebrated trains as the Cannonball, Banner Blue and Detroit Limited. Like most American locomotive designs of the period the driver's cab was mounted high, indeed above the height of the driving wheels.*

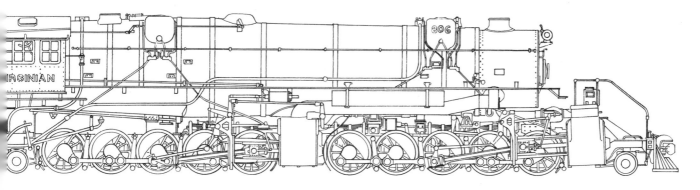

Virginian Railway *This road served the West Virginian coalfield and its most difficult section was between Elsmore and Clark's Gap, 18 miles (29km) of single track with gradients up to 1 in 47½ (2.1 per cent), up which it was desired to work the maximum number of loaded wagons. After experience with Mallet locomotives, the Virginian had ten 2-10-10-2 Mallet compounds built by the American Locomotive Co in 1913. They were gigantic locomotives with cylinders 30in and 40in by 32in (762mm and 1217mm by 813mm) and driving wheels 4ft 8in (1420mm) diameter. Boiler pressure was 214lb/in² (15kg/cm²), heating surface 8660ft² (800.4mm²), superheating surface 2062ft² (192.2m²) and grate area 109.5ft² (10.1m²). Such monsters could not travel fast and on their usual banking service they did not exceed 15½mph (25km/h), a speed limit enforced also by the inertia forces generated by the massive LP pistons and motion.*

State Railways France *From 1913 Société Alsacienne, Schneider and Fives-Lille supplied this line with 70 large-boilered and superheated 2-8-0s, and during the First World War, Nasmyth, Wilson and the North British Locomotive Co in Britain built another 200 from 1916 to 1918. Cylinders were 23¼ by 25½in (590mm by 650mm), driving wheel diameter 4ft 9in (1450mm), boiler pressure 171lb/in² (12kg/cm²), weight in working order 76 tonnes and maximum axle load 16.5 tonnes. Tractive effort was 34950lbf (15880kgf) and 1400hp could be developed. The leading coupled axle and the carrying axle were combined in a Zara truck, the coupling rods working on the second coupled axle. Later many of the class had feedwater heaters added. As a general heavy freight locomotive design the class was particularly useful during the First World War, and one of their duties was hauling rail-mounted artillery of the largest calibre.*

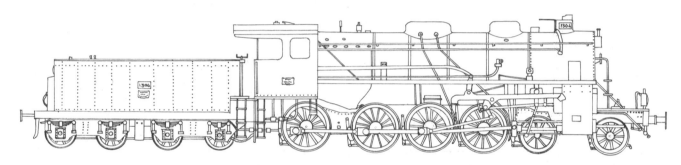

Madrid-Saragossa-Alicante *One of the earliest compound locomotives to run in Spain was this superheated mixed traffic 4-8-0. It was four-cylinder with cylinders 16½in and 25½in by 25¼in (420mm and 650mm by 640mm), driving wheels 5ft 3in (1600mm) diameter and weight in working order 88 tonnes. Seven were built by Hanomag in Hanover in 1914, another 25 by the American Locomotive Co in 1916, and a final one from Hanomag in 1920. The class gave long and hard service over the steeply-graded main lines of the Madrid-Saragossa-Alicante and on the Spanish National afterwards.*

Hungarian State Railways Class 324 *No less than 895 of this two-cylinder superheated 2-6-2 class were built from 1909 to 1923, together with another 20 in 1942 for the Slovakian Railways. The first 355 were built as von Borries compounds, superheated later and afterwards rebuilt to simple. Cylinders of the compounds were 18¼in and 19¼in by 25½in (460mm and 490mm by 650mm), driving wheel diameter 4ft 8½in (1440mm), grate area 33.3ft² (3.1m²), heating surface 2310ft² (214m²) and boiler pressure 214lb/in² (15kg/cm²). Weight in working order was 58.1 tonnes and 1100hp could be developed. A simple locomotive is shown here, as built with a Brotan boiler, the firebox of which was composed of water tubes surrounded by firebrick walls.*

Italian State Railways Class 880 *After a first 12 of this 2-6-0 tank class built by Breda in 1915, the same firm supplied another 48 in 1922. In addition, 26 were rebuilt from an earlier non-superheated Class 875. The locomotives were intended for suburban and branch line traffic and the superheater fitted was an innovation for such small locomotives. The class had Walschaert's valve gear, cylinders 17¾in by 23in (450mm by 580mm) and driving wheels 4ft 11½in (1510mm) diameter. Boiler pressure was 171lb/in² (12kg/cm²), for the Italian State in common with some other railways was reluctant to increase pressures because of the greater maintenance costs this brought. Class 880 developed 500hp at 37mph (60km/h), weight in working order was 50.9 tonnes and maximum speed 46½mph (75km/h). A number of the class were still in traffic in 1980.*

Chicago, Burlington & Quincy Railroad *The main lines of this company extended west from Chicago into the states of Iowa, Nebraska and Wyoming and south-west to Colorado and Texas. The railroad introduced a new 4-6-2 Pacific type with Class S3, ten of which were built by the Baldwin Locomotive Works in 1915. The class was a two-cylinder simple with cylinders 27in by 28in (686mm by 711mm), driving wheels 6ft 2in (1880mm) diameter, a boiler pressure of 180lb/in² (12.6kg/cm²) and a 59.2ft² (5.5m²) grate area. The Pacific type was adopted very rapidly during the second decade of the 20th century by many American railroads, firstly because it was demonstrably the best type for increasingly heavy express trains, and secondly because the type was extremely versatile. On many railroads, when the locomotives were not working express trains, they could handle locals and fast freight equally well, and such characteristics made the type attractive to lesser railroads as well as the major ones. It is estimated that, from the first New York Central Pacific of 1903, about 7000 of the type were built for American roads and a good number of these were used solely for branch lines and fast freight.*

Erie Triplex Mallet – 1914

America specialises

During the years of the First World War, American railways went ahead of those in Europe in designing heavy locomotives suited to special traffics and in technical research to refine details. The American locomotive industry specialised from about 1910, after many years of seeking a universal locomotive (first the American type then the Ten-Wheeler), and a whole range of high-output locomotive types were evolved directed at specific traffics. The Pacific type was an exception to this specialisation, not because it was intended to be, but because of the type's natural adaptability. Just the same, these were the years in which increasingly specialised locomotive types appeared, although in contrast locomotive components became more and more standardised before assembly and auxiliary apparatus was standardised for all uses.

These two pages show the diversity of types built during this period. There is a 2-8-8-0 Mallet compound, of which 86 were built for the Baltimore & Ohio Railroad from 1916 to 1920.

Cylinders were 28in and 41in by 32in (635mm and 1041mm by 813mm), driving wheels 4ft 10in (1474mm) diameter, boiler pressure 210lb/in^2 (14.7kg/cm^2), grate area 88.2ft^2 (8.2m^2), heating surface 5819ft^2 (541m^2) and superheating surface 1415ft^2 (132m^2). This huge machine weighed 220 tonnes in working order, of which 208 tonnes was adhesive weight. The class was used for hauling trains over the mountain lines and for banking purposes on the same routes with the heaviest trains. The Vanderbilt tender with a cylindrical water tank will be noted.

An even larger locomotive was the Triplex Mallet compound for the Erie Railroad, a 2-8-8-8-2 tank with the HP cylinders for the driving wheel set at the centre, and two sets of LP cylinders for the driving wheel sets at each end – all cylinders were 36in by 32in (914mm by 813mm). Unfortunately, even its great boiler could not supply the demands of the cylinders, and there was difficulty in keeping the flexible joint connections to the cylinders steam tight. Baldwin built three Triplexes between 1914 and 1916, which had a weight in working order of 390 tonnes each. They were used for banking on the 1 in 66 (1.5 per cent) Susquehanna incline in the

St Louis & South Western Railroad – 1916

Baltimore & Ohio Mallet – 1916

Union Pacific Santa Fe–1917

Louisville & Nashville Mikado–1917

Scranton coalfield of Pennsylvania. A couple of Triplexes were also built to the same design for the Virginian Railway in 1916.

The St Louis & South Western Railroad had some traditional Ten-Wheelers built by Baldwin in 1916, almost the last of the American 4-6-0s. The two cylinders were 22in by 28in (559mm by 711mm), driving wheels 5ft 8½in (1750mm) diameter and the boiler pressure was 200lb/in² (14kg/cm²). For a 4-6-0, the grate area was exceptional at 49.4ft² (4.6m²), the heating surface was 2470ft² (229.9m²) and superheating surface 537ft² (49.9m²). Weight in working order was 95 tonnes and maximum axle load 25 tonnes. The class was used for short distance express trains.

Specialised freight locomotives of interest included the 2-10-2 Santa Fe type and the 2-8-2 Mikado type. The 2-10-2 was built for the Union Pacific Railroad by Baldwin from 1917 for heavy trains on more or less level routes. Cylinders were 29½in by 30in (749mm by 762mm), driving

wheels 5ft 3in (1600mm) diameter, weight in working order 167.1 tonnes and adhesive weight 129.9 tonnes. This type caused difficulties at first, lacking stability on curves and making for excessive rail wear, but solutions to these problems were found and its higher speed and greater handiness made the class preferable to the Mallets used previously, even if the tractive effort was lower. The first 2-8-2 Mikado type ran on the Louisville & Nashville Railroad and illustrated is a version built in the company's workshops between 1917 and 1918. Cylinders were 27½in by 30in (698mm by 762mm), driving wheel diameter 5ft (1524mm) and boiler pressure 185lb/in² (13kg/cm²). Maximum axle load was 29 tonnes. The class was not capable of high speed but it handled long mineral trains from Indiana and Tennessee to the ports of Mobile and New Orleans with great effectiveness. Other batches of 2-8-2 locomotives for the road came later, the last being built by Baldwin in 1929.

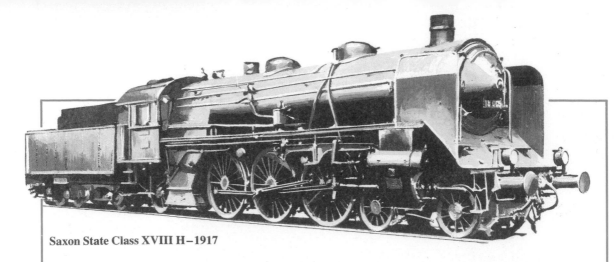

Saxon State Class XVIII H–1917

German Pacifics

During 1917 and 1918 two Pacific classes went into service that were prototypes for standard 4-6-2s built later for the German State Railway in the 1920s. Hartmann built five 4-6-2 Class XVIII H for the Saxon State Railway in 1917, three-cylinder simples after the Prussian S10^2 design (see page 163). Cylinders were 19¾in by 25in (500mm by 630mm), all connected to the second coupled axle, driving wheel diameter was 6ft 2½in (1900mm), boiler pressure 200lb/in^2 (14kg/cm^2), grate area 48.4ft^2 (4.5m^2), heating surface 2318ft^2 (215m^2) and superheating surface 775ft^2 (72m^2). Weight in working order was 93 tonnes and 1700hp could be developed. The bogie tender carried 7 tonnes of coal and 6825 gallons of water (31m^3) and loaded weighed 62 tonnes. Maximum speed was 74½mph (120km/h) and the class could haul 500 tonne passenger

trains at a continuous speed of 62mph (100km/h)

The Baden State Railway had an even more powerful 4-6-2, Class IVh, 20 of which were built by Maffei in 1918. They were four-cylinder compounds with HP cylinders inside for the first driving axle 17⅜in by 26⅞in (440mm by 680mm) and LP cylinders for the second axle 26⅞in by 26⅞in (680mm by 680mm). Driving wheel diameter was 6ft 10½in (2100mm), grate area 53.8ft^2 (5m^2), heating surface 2380ft^2 (221m^2) and superheating surface 882ft^2 (82m^2). Weight in working order was 97 tonnes and maximum axle load reached 18 tonnes. Maximum speed was 87mph (140km/h) and 1950hp could be developed. In the early years of the German State these two classes, together with the Prussian S10^2 class, were the backbone of the express locomotive stock.

Baden State Railway Class IVh–1918

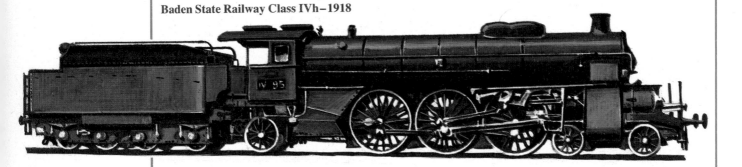

Japanese National Railways Class C51 *This 3ft 6in (1067mm) gauge system used 4-6-2 Pacifics from 1919, built by Kisha Seizo Kaisha, Mitsubishi, and in the railway's own workshops. They greatly improved the passenger service offered. With dashing looks, the 4-6-2s were superheated two-cylinder simples with cylinders 21in by 26in (530mm by 660mm), boiler pressure 186lb/in^2 (13kg/cm^2), grate area 26.85ft^2 (2.5m^2), heating surface 1818ft^2 (169m^2) and superheating surface 441ft^2 (41m^2). Driving wheel diameter was 5ft 8½in (1750mm) and Walschaert's valve gear was provided. Class C51 could run at 62mph (100km/h) with heavy passenger trains.*

Prussian Class G12 *This three-cylinder superheated 2-10-0 was designed after the various German railways sought a standard heavy freight locomotive in order to reduce the many classes in service in 1916. Henschel built the first in 1917, and as well as for Prussia, the class was built for the railways of Saxony, Baden, Wurtemburg and Alsace-Lorraine. By 1924 there were 1519 of them. Cylinders were 22½in by 26in (570mm by 660mm), driving wheel diameter 4ft 7in (1400mm), grate area 34.9ft² (3.25m²), heating surface 2095ft² (194.96m²) and superheating surface 735ft² (68.42m²). Weight in working order was 95.7 tonnes, maximum axle load 16.4 tonnes and they could develop 1540hp. Maximum speed was 40mph (65km/h) and they could haul 1010 tonnes up a 1 in 100 gradient (1.0 per cent) at 37mph (60km/h). Some of the class were still working in the German Democratic Republic in 1980.*

Italian State Class 735 *This superheated 2-8-0 was based on the Italian State Railways' 740 class (see pages 181 and 209). The Americans were given the order because Italian industry was too busy turning out munitions for the First World War. The American Locomotive Co asked for permission to alter detail in the interests of fast production, and the result was a purely American design. The first 100 Class 735s were built in 1917 (only 93 were delivered as seven were lost when a ship transporting them sank) and another 300 were added in 1919, some by Montreal Locomotive Works. Cylinders were 21¼in by 27½in (540mm by 700mm), driving wheels 4ft 6in (1370mm) diameter, grate area 30.1ft² (2.8m²), heating surface 1642ft² (152.6m²) and superheating surface 458ft² (42.68m²). Weight in working order was 63.7 tonnes and the maximum axle load 13.9 tonnes, a figure which allowed the locomotives to work anywhere in Italy. At 31mph (45km/h) the locomotives developed 980hp. A standard Italian bogie tender was fitted (differing in small details through being built in America) with capacity for 6 tonnes of coal and 4842 gallons of water (22m³). Class 735 gave excellent service for both sides during the Second World War and were popular with engine crews, who at first nicknamed them Wilsons after the United States' president.*

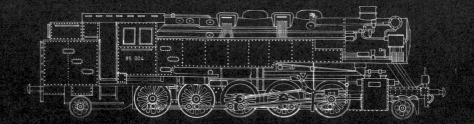

Between the Wars

The 21 years between the end of the First World War and the start of the Second were of decisive importance for railway traction throughout the world; great efforts were made to keep the steam locomotive in its pre-eminent position by exploring all possible technical improvements. Few realised that steam was on the wane in the 1920s and 1930s, except in countries lacking their own coal and oil supplies, like Switzerland and Italy. In those two countries, and to a less extent in other countries, political and economic pressures caused extensive railway electrification to be undertaken. Another rival to steam was diesel traction, Ackroyd Stuart's first crude diesel-mechanical locomotive having been tried out at Hull in England in 1894. The first diesel-electric railcar was built in Sweden in 1912 and the same country produced the first diesel-electric locomotive in 1917, a unit scarcely distinguishable from a railcar. In 1924 several countries put diesel locomotive prototypes on trial, and in the same year Sweden made the first diesel locomotive export to Tunisia. From then

Great Northern Railway (GNR) *Herbert Nigel Gresley designed this 2-6-0 mixed traffic locomotive and ten went into service on this English railway in 1920. After the grouping of the GNR into the London & North Eastern Railway from 1923, the locomotives became Class K3 and another 183 of them were built (the illustration shows an LNER-built locomotive lettered GNR in error). The class was a superheated three-cylinder simple machine with outside Walschaert's valve gear and derived motion for the piston valve of the inside cylinder. This Gresley derived motion was later a feature of many of his large three-cylinder designs. The K3 class had a tractive effort of 30031lbf (13644kgf), a weight in working order of 73.7 tonnes and a maximum load of 20.3 tonnes. The locomotives worked secondary passenger trains and fast freights, on which latter they took up to 55 four-wheel wagons at 45mph (72km/h).*

on the diesel started its march towards a takeover, although initially used only for shunting locomotives and railcars. However, by 1939 in Italy, about two-thirds of the railway route mileage was served by at least one, and usually many more, diesel railcar daily passenger services.

Steam, electric and diesel traction existed side by side between the wars, often exchanging duties for operational reasons, which made for diversity and interest. The steam locomotive was still superior as a traffic machine and could tackle any task – electric and diesel traction were more specialised at the time. After a century or so, the steam locomotive still flourished because of a continuous and fertile process of improvement; its superiority was maintained by a flow of new inventions which improved its efficiency and performance. Indeed, since the time of the Rainhill trials in

(continued on page 186)

Finnish Class Hv2 *This light two-cylinder 4-6-0 was built for the Finnish State Railways in Germany, Schwartzkopff supplying 15 in 1919. Another 18 were built by the Finnish firm Lokomo of Tampere between 1922 and 1926. Cylinders were 20¼in by 23½in (510mm by 600mm), boiler pressure 171lb/in² (12kg/cm²), grate area 20.15ft² (2m²), heating surface 1185ft² (110m²) and superheating surface 333ft² (31m²). Driving wheel diameter was 5ft 8¾in (1750mm), weight in working order 57.1 tonnes and adhesive weight 38.4 tonnes. The six-wheel tender carried 5 tonnes of coal (or wood) and 3150 gallons of water (14.3m³). Some of the class were fitted with Knorr feedwater heaters during 1925. After many years of hard work the last of the class was withdrawn in 1969.*

Norwegian Trunk Railway *This railway had three two-cylinder simple 2-8-2 tank locomotives from Baldwin, Philadelphia, in 1918. They were of compact design with the high-pitched boilers then fashionable in the United States. The side water tanks had their fronts sloped downwards to help the driver's view when buffering up to a train, while the rear coal bunker was recessed at either side, again to allow the enginemen a better view. Cylinders were 22in by 23½in (560mm by 600mm), driving wheel diameter 4ft 5in (1350mm) and boiler pressure 171lb/in² (12kg/cm²).*

Belgian State Class 33 *Eight superheated four-cylinder compound 2-8-0s were built by Tubize for the Belgian State Railway in 1921. Cylinders were 16½in and 23½in by 26in (420mm and 600mm by 600mm), driving wheel diameter 5ft (1520mm), boiler pressure 228lb/cm² (16kg/cm²), grate area 34.4ft² (3.2m²), heating surface 1925ft² (179.3²) and superheating surface 645ft² (60m²). They could develop 1900hp and maximum speed was 50mph (80km/h). No more than eight of the class were built as the Belgian State turned to a cheaper two-cylinder simple design.*

Canadian Pacific Railway Class G3c *The 4-6-2 Pacific type locomotive was used extensively in Canada in the first half of the 20th century. Class G3c in particular gained a reputation as the most efficient and balanced design in the country, and it was the standard main line locomotive of the Canadian Pacific. The first was built by Montreal Locomotive Works in 1923 and it was immediately a success, both with the footplate crews and with the passengers. It was very flexible in service and had the power to handle heavy trains, often composed of coaches with six-wheel bogies. The class had two simple cylinders 25in by 30in (635mm by 762mm), a boiler pressure of 200lb/in² (14kg/cm²), driving wheels 6ft 3in (1905mm) diameter and a tractive effort of 42 400lbf (19250kgf). Class G3c was improved upon in successive batches and the last of these known as Class G3g, had a boiler pressure of 275lb/in² (19.25kg/cm²) and a tractive effort of 58300kgf (26500kgf). The class was compact for its wheel arrangement, with a wheelbase of 34ft 9in (10600mm) and a total length over couplers (including the tender) of 81ft 5in (24800mm).*

North Western Railway *This Indian railway had two-cylinder simple 2-8-0s built by the Vulcan Foundry in England in 1919. Many more with a superheater were built later and known as Class HG/S. The class was well-known on the Khyber Pass railway and some were still in service during 1980. Solidly British locomotives in design, they had cylinders 22in by 26in (559mm by 660mm), driving wheels 4ft 8½in (1435mm) diameter, a boiler pressure of 180lb/in² (12.6km/cm²) and a grate area of 42.9ft² (3m²). Maximum axle load was 16.5 tonnes and on the level the class could haul 1600 tonne freight trains. After the creation of Pakistan in 1948, the railway system comprised nearly all of the North Western Railway, and the old name was displaced by Pakistan Railways.*

Czechoslovakian State Railways *After the First World War, Czechoslovakia was carved out of the old Austro-Hungarian dual monarchy, and the new nation inherited a railway system that was disjointed and which suffered from a severe shortage of motive power. Class 365 was a fresh design to meet the shortage, a two-cylinder simple 2-6-2 derived from one of Karl Gölsdorf's compound designs and built by ČKD Prague from 1921. Cylinders were 22¼in by 26¾in (570mm by 680mm), boiler pressure 186lb/in² (13kg/cm²), driving wheel diameter 5ft 10in (1780mm), grate area 43ft² (4m²), heating surface 2782ft² (258.6m²) and superheating surface 478ft² (44.5m²). Maximum speed was 68mph (110km/h). A typically Austrian tender design was fitted, with a water tank filler lid that ran the whole length of it alongside and under the coal space. Other Austrian features included the cab design.*

Eastern of France 231.001–040 *The Eastern Railways was the only major railway not to order 4-6-2s before the First World War. When they were ordered, the railway chose 40 of the standard State Railways design, which were delivered from 1920 on for the heavy traffic of the Paris-Belfort route. These were four-cylinder de Glehn compounds (the illustration shows them in a modernised state as Class 231B of French National Railways) with cylinders 16½in and 25¼in by 25½in (420mm and 640mm by 650mm), driving wheels 6ft 4½in (1950mm) diameter and boiler pressure 289lb/in² (17kg/cm²). A Schmidt smoke flue superheater and Walschaert's valve gear were fitted, and 2300hp could be developed. Weight in working order was 97 tonnes with 55 tonne adhesive weight. The maximum speed was 74½mph (120km/h), and the locomotives ran the 98½ miles (159km) between Metz and Strasbourg in 1 hour 36 minutes at an average speed of just under 62mph (100km/h), while hauling a 420 tonne train.*

Northern of Spain *Among all the Spanish railways, the Northern had the greatest number of 2-8-0 locomotives. The first of this class appeared in 1909, but the greater number were built between 1920 and 1940. A 1921 version is illustrated here. In all, there were 436 of them, built by nine different firms, among which there were British, German and Belgian manufacturers as well as Spanish. With a Belpaire firebox the class had cylinders 24in by 25½in (610mm by 650mm), driving wheels 5ft 1¼in (1560mm) diameter and a weight in working order of 70.5 tonnes. During the Spanish Civil War (1936–1939) the class was used with enthusiasm by the combatants, and the locomotives became dispersed over many different railways. In common with the rest of the locomotive stock, many ended up in a bad state of repair, and it was primarily because of this that the Spanish National Railway System was formed in 1941.*

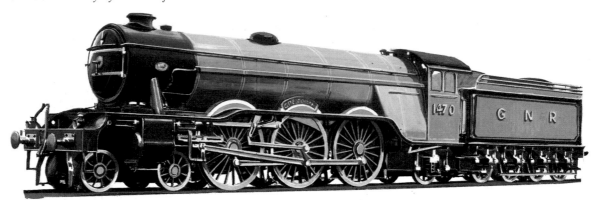

Great Northern Railway *The Doncaster plant of this English railway built two three-cylinder simple 4-6-2s in 1922, designed by H N Gresley. After the formation of the London & North Eastern Railway from 1 January 1923, these became Class A1 and another ten were built during 1923, the first of which was named* Flying Scotsman *after the well-known London to Edinburgh express train. The three cylinders were 20in by 26in (508mm by 660mm), driving wheel diameter was 6ft 8in (2030mm), boiler pressure 180lb/in^2 (12.6kg/cm^2), grate area 41.25ft^2 (3.81m^2), heating surface 2930ft^2 (272.01m^2) and superheating surface 525ft^2 (48.77m^2). Weight in working order was 94 tonnes and maximum axle load 20.3 tonnes. The locomotives could take a 650 tonne load at an average speed of 52¾mph northwards out of London. Many more of the class were built and some improvements made, the locomotives then being known as Class A3, and later the Class A1s were reclassified A10.* Flying Scotsman *has been preserved in working order and today hauls occasional special trains.*

Soviet Railways Class E *This superheated 0-10-0 belongs to the most numerous locomotive class in the world, for some 12,000 to 13,000 of Class E were built from 1921 to about 1950. At the end of the First World War and after the Russian Revolution, the railways badly needed locomotives and a simple standard design was evolved, the Class E 0-10-0. Russian builders were in no position to accept orders, so 500 were ordered from Sweden and 700 from Germany. From 1925, however, Russian builders began to produce Class E, with some improvements brought about by experience, and they were assisted by Hungarian and Czechoslovakian builders after the Second World War. Cylinders were 24¼in by 27½in (620mm by 700mm), driving wheel diameter 4ft 4in (1320mm), boiler pressure 171lb/in^2 (12kg/cm^2) and weight in working order 81.5 tonnes. The locomotives have been used for almost every sort of work throughout the Soviet Union.*

Italian State Class 940 *This locomotive was a tank version of the Italian State Railways' standard 2-8-0 Class 740 freight locomotive. Building railways across the Italian peninsula from coast to coast was difficult because of the Apennine mountains and in the age of steel bridges, before the advent of reinforced concrete, engineers found it necessary to build routes full of sharp curves and with many steep gradients. In particular the lines from Rome to Ancona and Rome to Pescara were tough problems for motive power, and the Locomotive Research and Design Office at Florence produced the Class 940 superheated, two-cylinder simple, 2-8-2 tank to overcome them. Cylinders were 21¼in by 27½ (540mm by 700mm), driving wheel diameter 4ft 6in (1370mm), boiler pressure 171lb/in² (12kg/cm²) and grate area 30.1ft² (2.8m²). The leading carrying axle and the first driving axle were joined in a Zara truck – or Italian bogie as the Italians prefer to call it. Fifty of Class 940 were built from 1921 to 1922 and the Italian State acquired three more when taking over a minor railway. The locomotives carried 3½ tonnes of coal and 2200 gallons of water (10m³). Weight in working order was 87.3 tonnes, of which 61.6 tonnes was adhesive, 980hp could be developed at 28mph (45km/h) and the maximum speed was 37mph (60km/h). No 940.001 is now in the Museum of Science and Technology at Milan, but a number of the class were still in traffic in 1980.*

Prussian Class P10 *This was the last Prussian design for express passenger trains, a three-cylinder simple 2-8-2 and first built by Borsig, Berlin, in 1922. It was claimed to be the first eight-coupled European express locomotive, forerunner of other classes made necessary by competition from the electric locomotive and by greater and greater passenger train loads. It reproduced the three-cylinder arrangement of the 4-6-0 S10² and 2-10-0 G12 classes, cylinders were 20¼in by 26in (520mm by 660mm), boiler pressure 200lb/in² (14kg/cm²) and driving wheel diameter 5ft 8¾in (1750mm). The boiler had a Belpaire firebox and to fit the locomotive for express work the leading carrying axle and the first driving axle were supported in a Krauss-Helmholtz bogie. The last carrying axle was well to the rear to allow space for a grate with the large area of 43ft² (4m²). Heating surface was 2555ft² (238m²) and superheating surface 830ft² (77.2m²). Weight in working order was 110.4 tonnes and maximum axle load just under 19 tonnes. A total of 260 Class P10 were built between 1922 and 1927 and they could haul 700 tonne passenger trains at speeds up to 74½mph (120km/h). Trains of 660 tonnes could be taken up a 1 in 100 gradient (1.0 per cent) at 25mph (40km/h).*

Roumanian State Class 231 – 1922

Central and eastern Europe

At the end of the First World War, the railways of central and eastern Europe were engaged in the building of new locomotive classes to supersede obsolescent types and to replace those in a bad state of repair. The Roumanian State Railways procured 4-6-2 locomotives from Maffei and Henschel in Germany in 1922, based on Maffei prototypes of 1913. All four cylinders were pushed well forward so that they could be connected to the front driving axle. Cylinders were 16½in by 25½in (420mm by 650mm), driving wheel diameter 6ft 1in (1855mm), boiler pressure 186lb/in^2 (13kg/cm^2), grate area 43ft^2 (4m^2), heating surface 2740ft^2 (254.5m^2) and

superheating surface 650ft^2 (60.5m^2). Weight in working order was 89 tonnes and maximum axle load 16 tonnes.

The Polish State Railways acquired five 4-6-0 prototypes of Class Ok22 from Chrzanow works in 1922, and another 185 were built from 1928 to 1934. In effect the design was the old Prussian P8 class with a higher-pitched boiler. Cylinders were 22¾in by 24¾in (575mm by 630mm), boiler pressure 171lb/in^2 (12kg/cm^2), driving wheel diameter 5ft 8¾in (1750mm) and grate area 43.4ft^2 (4.01m^2). For many years Class Ok22 worked alongside Class Ok1 (ex-Class P8 after acquisition by Poland) and a few of them were still in existence in 1980. Finally, an impressive superheated three-cylinder simple 4-6-2 express locomotive is shown, 43 of which were built for the Czechoslovakian State Railways by Škoda from 1925. These handsome Class 387.0 machines had 21¼in by 26¾in (525mm by 680mm) cylinders, all of which were connected to the second driving axle, driving wheels 6ft 4¾in (1950mm) diameter, heating surface of 2430ft^2 (226m^2) and superheating surface of 688ft^2 (64.4m^2). Weight in working order was 89.6 tonnes, of which 50.2 tonnes was adhesive, and maximum speed was 81mph (130km/h). Tractive effort was 35 050lbf (15 920kgf).

Polish State Class Ok22 – 1922

Czechoslovakian State Class 387.0 – 1925

GWR Castle Class *The 73 locomotives of the Star class built from 1907 to 1923 were the most advanced British express locomotive in their time (see page 155). When the Great Western Railway (GWR) decided to have something better, C B Collet, who had succeeded Churchward, improved the Stars to make the new Castle class. The first Castle went into traffic in August 1923 and the arrangement of its four cylinders followed that of the Stars, although they were of a larger diameter and the boiler was bigger. Cylinders were 16in by 26in (406mm by 660mm), driving wheel diameter 6ft 8½in (2046mm), boiler pressure 225lb/in² (15.75m²), heating surface 2018.7ft² (187.7m²) and superheating surface 262.62ft² (24.4m²). Weight in working order was 81.1 tonnes and maximum axle load 19.9 tonnes. In all 154 Castle class locomotives were built from 1923 to 1950 and others were rebuilt from earlier locomotives. They were fast and could put up average speeds of 81mph (130km/h) on the London-Bristol line. The first of the class,* Caerphilly Castle, *is now in the Science Museum, London, while another,* Pendennis Castle, *has been taken to the Hamersley Iron Ore Railways in north-western Australia, and is preserved in working order.*

Danish State Railways Class S *Two of these large 2-6-4 tanks were built by Borsig, Berlin, in 1924 and another 18 were made by Frichs in Denmark from 1927 to 1928. Cylinders were 17in by 26¼ (430mm by 670mm), driving wheels 5ft 9¼in (1730mm) diameter and weight in working order 97 tonnes, of which 50.1 tonnes was adhesive. The first two of the class were regarded as main line express locomotives, but for nearly all their lives the members of the class worked Copenhagen surburban services with great efficiency.*

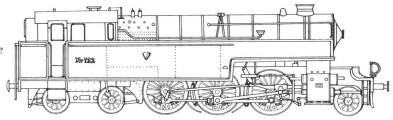

Eastern of France *To haul the increasingly-heavy expresses of the Eastern Railways at higher speeds, M F Duchatel designed this 4-8-2 locomotive, and a prototype was built at the Epernay works of the railway in 1925. It was a four-cylinder de Glehn compound with cylinders 17¾in and 26in by 28½in (450mm and 660mm by 720mm) and driving wheel diameter 6ft 4¾in (1950mm). A Belpaire firebox had a grate area of 47.7ft² (4.43m²), boiler pressure was 228lb/in² (16kg/cm²), heating surface 2335ft² (217.6m²) and superheating surface 996ft² (92.6kg/cm²). The prototype was given a long series of tests and trial runs which went on until 1929. The Eastern Railways then ordered another 40 of the class, while the State Railways had 49 of them. The prototype developed 2450hp and could haul 700 tonnes at average speeds of 62mph (100km/h) with maximum speeds of 74½mph (120km/h). Slight alterations to the rest of the class improved their performance.*

German State Class 01 *With the formation of the German State Railway on 1 April 1920, the new administration was faced with the problem of unifying more than 200 major classes of locomotives. It was decided that entirely new standard designs should be developed for use all over the country and that as far as possible components and auxiliary apparatus should be interchangeable between classes. As a start, two fresh 4-6-2 express locomotive designs were built in 1925, one being a two-cylinder simple and the other a four-cylinder compound. These were the 01 and 02 classes respectively and ten of each were built. In the event the compound did not show sufficient superiority over Class 01 to justify the higher construction and maintenance costs so that later all of Class 02 was rebuilt to Class 01. The latter had cylinders 25¾in by 26in (650mm by 660mm), a boiler pressure of 228lb/in² (16kg/cm²), and a 6ft 6½in driving wheel diameter (2000mm). Grate area was 48.4ft² (4.5m²), heating surface 2560ft² (238m²), superheating surface 1076ft² (100m²) and weight in working order was 109.8 tonnes. The class was powerful (1800hp could be developed) and they were very fast. Over the 178 miles (287km) between Berlin and Hamburg, a Class 01 took a 280 tonne train at an average speed of rather more than 74½mph (120km/h) and the class was known to run up to 95mph (154km/h). At the same time the locomotives were capable of hauling 800 tonnes at 62mph (100km/h) on the level.*

German State Class T18 *In the 1920s the Krupp firm was developing the Zoelly steam turbine and several countries tried out turbine locomotives. Germany was among the first. Maffei built a prototype locomotive, T18 class, for the German State Railway in 1926, with a high pressure boiler, 315lb/in² (22kg/cm²), and instead of boiler steam going to cylinders it was fed to a turbine mounted across the frames in front of the smokebox. The turbine drove a jackshaft through a gear train, and the jackshaft was in turn coupled to the driving wheels. A smaller turbine was used when the locomotive travelled backwards. The wheel arrangement was 4-6-2, the grate area 37.7ft² (3.5m²), heating surface 1700ft² (160m²) and superheating surface 548ft² (51m²). Driving wheels were 5ft 8¾in (1750mm) diameter and with the turbine running at 8800rev/min, 2000hp could be developed. Weight in working order was 104 tonnes and the maximum axle load 20 tonnes. During trials, the T18 locomotive showed excellent fuel savings compared with a conventional locomotive, but it was neither as powerful nor as fast and its construction was complicated and expensive. Nevertheless it worked on fast trains until destroyed during the Second World War.*

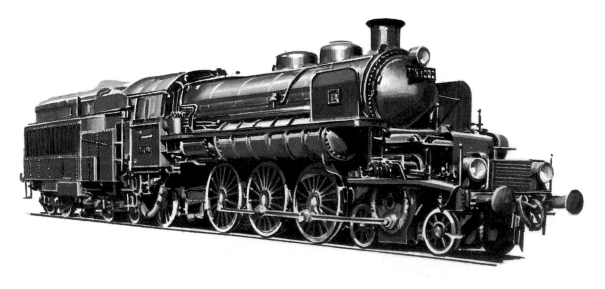

Northern of Spain *To take express trains from Madrid to the Atlantic coast the Northern introduced 4-8-2 locomotives at about the same time as the Eastern of France (see page 183). Hanomag built six four-cylinder de Glehn compounds and later Spanish firms built another 60. Cylinders were 18in and 27¾in by 26¾in (460mm and 700mm by 680mm), driving wheel diameter 5ft 8¾in (1750mm), boiler pressure 228lb/in² (16kg/cm²) and grate area 53.75ft² (5m²).*

Southern Railway *This United States' road had one of the handsomest 4-6-2 classes in the country. Class Ps-4 was derived from a government standard design and the first of 62 locomotives was built by the American Locomotive Co in 1923. The two cylinders were 27in by 28in (686mm by 711mm), driving wheels were 6ft 1in (1854mm) diameter, boiler pressure 205lb/in² (14.3kg/cm²) and grate area 70ft² (6.5m²). Valve gear fitted was either Walschaert's or Baker's and three different types of feedwater heater were used, Coffin, Elesco or Worthington. Weight in working order was 154 tonnes and the tractive effort 48 700lbf (22 100kgf). The class had an attractive livery of green and gold, and either four-axle or six-axle tenders were fitted, the latter having a capacity of 16 tonnes of coal and 11 650 gallons of water (53m²).*

Royal Scot Class *After the grouping of the railways in the United Kingdom, the new London, Midland & Scottish Railway inherited over 5000 locomotives. There was a great diversity of types and many were old, so there was an urgent need to standardise on a fresh locomotive stock. The North British Locomotive Co was commissioned to build a three-cylinder simple 4-6-0 express passenger class, and from 1927 the company produced 50 of them very rapidly. Another 20 were added to this Royal Scot class in 1930, and these 4-6-0s approached the performance standards of the GWR Castle class (see page 183).*

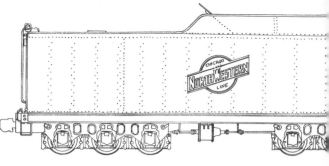

South African Railways and Harbours Class 15CA *The 4-8-2 wheel arrangement had a great success on the 3ft 6in (1067mm) gauge railways of South Africa from its first introduction on the old Natal Government Railway in 1909. Class 15CA was one of the best 4-8-2s, and it was introduced to work the 955 miles (1540km) between Cape Town and Johannesburg, a journey which before its arrival took 35 hours or more and was slowed by six locomotive changes. The first 23 of Class 15CA were built by the American Locomotive Co in 1926, Baldwin built another 10 in 1928, and Breda in Italy built 10 in 1929. Meanwhile the North British Locomotive Co in Great Britain built 47 between 1928 and 1930. The two cylinders were 23in by 28in (584mm by 711mm), driving wheel diameter 4ft 9in (1450mm), boiler pressure 200lb/in^2 (14kg/cm^2), grate area 48.4ft^2 (4.5m^2), heating surface 2755ft^2 (258m^2) and superheater surface 68.8ft^2 (64m^2). Weight in working order was 107.8 tonnes, maximum axle load 18.3 tonnes and tractive effort 44250lbf (20080kgf). With the aid of the Class 15CA locomotives, the Cape Town-Johannesburg time was cut to 29 hours by the Union Limited and the Union Express, and only one locomotive change was needed.*

1829, engineers had never relaxed their efforts toward improvement, although it is curious to see how the fundamentals established and perfected by 1840 were still in use 80 to 100 years later. Examples of this were the Stephenson's multi-tube boiler and Egide Walschaert's valve gear, the latter being used almost universally. Among its rivals were the new poppet valve gears, taken from internal combustion engine practice. Among these were the valves of Arturo Caprotti, first used on a locomotive in 1921, and those of Lentz, Renaud and others.

Locomotive design in Europe was affected by the political organisation of railways, which between the wars had developed towards state-run organisations. Even nominally private railway companies were heavily controlled by the state. In most European countries at the dawn of the railway age the industrial revolution had scarcely started, and the state was the only source of the large sums needed for railway building. Despite efforts here and there to put railways into private hands after they had been started by the state, governments found that, if they were to exercise adequate control for the benefit of their country, they had to take complete responsibility. Even where there was sufficient money in private hands, as in Great Britain, France, and increasingly in Germany,

(continued on page 191)

Turkish State Railways *This railway system for many years took most of its motive power from German sources. The 4-8-0 shown was one of 25 built by Henschel in 1926 and Krupp in 1934 for what amounted to mixed traffic use on the difficult line from Haydarpasa to Ankara. The design made use of experience gained with the Prussian P10 (see page 181) and with the P8 (see page 154). Cylinders were 25in by 26in (630mm by 660mm), driving wheel diameter was 5ft 5in (1650mm), boiler pressure 171lb/in^2 (12kg/cm^2) and grate area 32.25ft^2 (3m^2). Tractive effort was 35750lbf (16180kgf) and while the locomotives were excellent hill climbers they had a good turn of speed on the level. Except for the cow-catcher, appearance was pure German.*

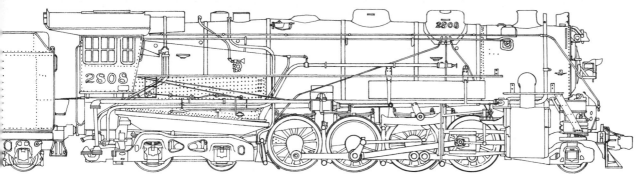

Chicago & North Western Railway Class J-4 *Because it was desired to augment the steaming capacity of the boiler for heavier trains, American locomotive practice in the 1920s was directed towards increasing the grate area. To carry the larger fireboxes a new wheel arrangement was devised, the 2-8-4 or Berkshire type. The bogie at the rear allowed the grate area to be increased by over 50 per cent and heating surface by over 10 per cent. Twelve highly-developed 2-8-4s were built in 1927 for the Chicago & North Western Railway, a road serving the states of Illinois, Wisconsin, Minnesota, Iowa, Nebraska and the two Dakotas. Two cylinders were 28in by 30in (711mm by 762mm), driving wheel diameter was 5ft 3in (1600mm), boiler pressure 245lb/in² (17.1kg/cm²) and grate area 100ft² (9.3m²). Tractive effort was 77 700lbf (35 250kgf) and weight in working order 216.9 tonnes. The class was used for Illinois' mineral trains.*

Boston & Albany Railroad Class D12 *This was one of the very few tank locomotives built for passenger service in the United States, designed expressly for the Boston-Brookline Junction suburban line where turntables were not available at the termini. Five of these 4-6-6 tanks (a very unusual wheel arrangement) were built in 1928, and arranged so that they could run equally well in either direction with their ten-coach loads. The two cylinders were 23½in by 26in (597mm by 660mm), driving wheels were 5ft 3in (1600mm) diameter and boiler pressure 215lb/in² (15kg/cm²). The locomotives carried 6 tonnes of coal and 4170 gallons of water (19m³). Weight in working order was 159.7 tonnes and tractive effort 41 700lbf (18 950kgf).*

Union Pacific Railroad *This road had freight locomotives with the exceptional wheel arrangement of 4-12-2. The design was a non-articulated freight locomotive and 88 of them were built 1926–1930. They were three-cylinder simples, with the two outside cylinders 24in by 32in (610mm by 813mm) and the single inside cylinder 25in by 31in (635mm by 787mm). Driving wheels were 5ft 7in (1702mm) diameter, boiler pressure 220lb/in² (15.4kg/cm²), grate area 107.6ft² (10m²), heating surface 5740ft² (543.74m²) and superheater surface 2560ft² (237.82m²). Coupled wheelbase was 30ft 10in (9347mm) and total wheelbase 52ft 4in (15 951mm). Weight in working order was 224.5 tonnes and maximum axle load 26.85 tonnes. The locomotives had exceptional performance and the designed maximum speed of about 40mph (64.5km/h) was put up to 55mph (89km/h) after traffic experience. Tractive effort was 90 900lbf (45 300kgf) and 150 wagons could be hauled with ease at about 50mph (80km/h).*

Paris, Lyons & Mediterranean *The increasing suburban traffic of the Paris region and the greater weight of the trains induced the PLM to build a four-cylinder compound 4-8-4 tank locomotive class. They were handsome machines and 351 were built between 1926 and 1932. Cylinders were 16½in and 25in by 25½in (420mm and 630mm by 650mm), the outside HP cylinders driving the second coupled axle and the inside LP the first coupled axle. Driving wheels were 5ft 5in (1650mm) diameter and the boiler pressure 228lb/in² (16kg/cm²). Some of the locomotives had the piston valves replaced by poppet valve gear. Weight in working order was 116 tonnes, the maximum axle load 16 tonnes, and 1750hp could be developed. Maximum speed exceeded 62mph (100km/h), but this was less important than the excellent acceleration, a quality very necessary for locomotives heading trains with frequent stops. When hauling local trains on the 37 miles (60km) Paris-Fontainbleau run, an average speed of 53¼mph (86km/h) was obtained, despite stops. These 4-8-4 tanks were used outside the Paris region, too: on the Côte d'Azur they handled a Cannes-Milan service made up of British-built Pullman cars, as well as the local trains.*

Federal Railway of Austria Class 629 *These two-cylinder 4-6-2 tanks first appeared on the old Südbahn in 1913, but it was on the Federal Railway that they were built in quantity for Vienna local trains and branch line duties, especially during 1926 and 1927. The firebox was between the last two driving axles and the rear carrying wheel took the weight of the coal bunker. The two cylinders were 18¾in by 28¼in (475mm by 720mm), driving wheel diameter was 5ft 2in (1570mm), boiler pressure 186lb/in² (13kg/cm²), grate area 29ft² (2.7m²), heating surface 1540ft² (142.8m²) and superheating surface 313ft² (29.1m²). Weight in working order was 83.8 tonnes and adhesive weight 45 tonnes. They developed 1200hp and passenger trains of 430 tonnes could be hauled up 1 in 330 (0.3 per cent) gradients at 37mph (60km/h). The Class 629 was useful and long-lived–apart from their more normal duties, the locomotives hauled the Orient Express from Vienna to the Hungarian border at Hegyshalom, and were to be seen shunting in marshalling yards on occasion. The illustration shows a member of the class as fitted with a Giesl ejector in post-1945 years.*

London, Midland & Scottish Railway (LMS) *After the grouping of railways in Great Britain it was found on many routes that there were not sufficient powerful freight locomotives. Double-heading of coal trains had to be resorted to, despite the expense of double locomotive crews which that entailed. On the LMS the problem was solved by adopting Beyer-Garratt locomotives (see page 156), which could be driven by a single locomotive crew but had the capacity of two ordinary locomotives. They were used between a marshalling yard at Toton (near Nottingham and Derby in the coalfield area) and Cricklewood marshalling yard in London, a distance of 121½ miles (196km). Beyer, Peacock & Co built the first three of these four-cylinder simple 2-6-6-2 Garratts in 1926 and another 31 were added in 1930. Cylinders were 18½in by 26in (470mm by 660mm), driving wheels 5ft 3in (1600mm) diameter, the Belpaire firebox had a grate area of 44.5ft² (4.13m²), boiler pressure was 190lb/in² (13.4kg/cm²), heating surface 2137ft² (198.61m²) and superheating surface 500ft² (4.65m²). The locomotives were 87ft 10½in long and the weight in working order was 151.2 tonnes. They were low-speed machines designed to run for considerable periods of time without replenishing coal and water, carrying 7 tonnes of the former and 4500 gallons of the latter (20.43m³).*

Chapelon Pacifics *In 1931 and 1932 the Paris-Orleans Railway introduced a fresh 4-6-2 type that outclassed anything else in France, even the recently introduced 4-8-2 type. It was the work of André Chapelon, one of the world's great locomotive engineers. He rebuilt 21 of the Paris-Orleans 4-6-2s of 1907–1909 (see page 158), which, after 20 years service, were no longer equal to traffic demands. In rebuilding, special attention was given to steam passageways and to superheater design, as well as to the blastpipe shape, the chimney in relation to it, and to valve events. Lentz rotary cam poppet valve gear was fitted. As four-cylinder de Glehn compounds the outside HP cylinders were 16½in by 25½in (420mm by 650mm) and the LP cylinders inside 25½in by 27¼in (650mm by 690mm). Driving wheel diameter was 6ft 4¾in (1950mm), boiler pressure 243lb/in² (17kg/cm²) and weight in working order 102.5 tonnes, with a 19.1 tonnes axle load. The rebuilds became famous very rapidly and more were built, not only for the Paris-Orleans, but also for the Northern and Eastern Railways. The class could maintain average speeds including stops of 62mph (100km/h) with 450 tonnes express trains, and could run up to 84mph (135km/h) while doing it. While on trial as late as 1956, one of the class took 225 tonnes at a continuous speed of 100 to 112½mph (160 to 180km/h) for many miles.*

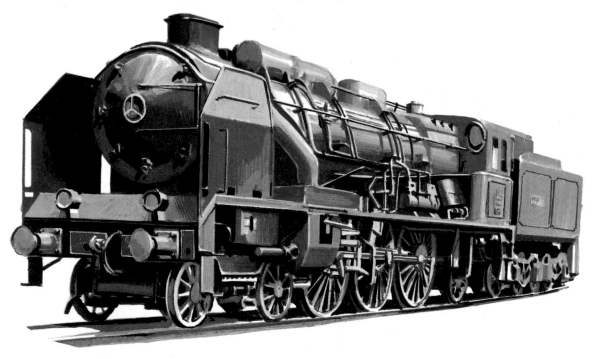

Italian State Class 691 *This four-cylinder simple 4-6-2 design was the queen of Italian locomotives for many years. It started with 33 locomotives of Class 690, built between 1911 and 1914. A single prototype that had been built previously was so unsatisfactory that it was broken up after a few months. During the 1920s a replacement three-cylinder 4-6-2 was designed, but due to the spread of electrification this Class 695 was not built. However the project was not entirely wasted, for Class 695 bogies were used each end under two classes of electric locomotive. As a substitute for the abortive new design, during the years 1928 to 1934 all 33 of Class 690 were rebuilt with a larger*

boiler (as used on a 2-8-2 locomotive of 1922) and with a rear truck with outside instead of inside bearings. As rebuilt they were known as Class 691, with four cylinders 17³⁄₄in by 26³⁄₄in (450mm by 680mm), driving wheel diameter 6ft 8in (2030mm), boiler pressure 200lb/in² (14kg/cm²) and a weight in working order of 96.5 tonnes. Tractive effort was 35 500lbf (16 130kgf) and 1750hp could be developed at 56mph (90km/h). For most of their lives Class 691 locomotives worked the Milan-Venice main line, until this was electrified and the class disappeared in the early 1960s. No 691.022 is now in the Museum of Science and Technology, Milan.

Swiss Federal Railway *This 0-8-0 tank is a typical heavy shunting locomotive for marshalling-yard work, such as the yard at Chiasso where many of the class spent their lives. From 1930 to 1933 SLM Winterthur built 17 of these two-cylinder simples and, unusually for shunting work, they were superheated. Cylinders were 22¹⁄₂in by 25¹⁄₄in (570mm by 640mm), driving wheel diameter was 4ft 4¹⁄₄in (1330mm), boiler pressure 171lb/in² (12kg/cm²), grate area 18.3ft² (1.7m²), heating surface 835ft² (77.7m²) and superheating surface 308ft² (28.6m²). Weight in working order was 68.4 tonnes and if the locomotives ever got out on the main line the maximum speed was 28mph (45km/h). Swiss railways were electrified extensively during the life of this class and electric locomotives did much of the shunting work except in special locations such as Chiasso. The last of the class were taken out of service in 1968.*

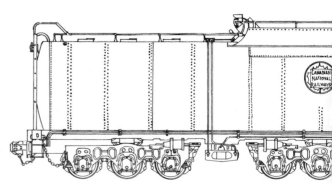

the law was used to confine the companies to specific areas in order to avoid wasteful spending of capital. Once capital is sunk into the infrastructure of a railway, most of it is lost for good should the line be driven into bankruptcy by the activities of a rival route competing for traffic.

Transport control is a powerful tool of good government administration, a concept expressed best by considering a simple country lane. It is clear that traffic carried by such a lane cannot begin to cover a return on the capital sunk in its construcion. Those using the lane regard it as essential, but nevertheless it is a non-commercial proposition. Because of the lane's existence there are profits, and they arise quite outside the transport field in the hands of the householders, landowners and such commercial concerns that are served. These profits are part of the nation's prosperity, which the government must encourage. Taxation is raised nationally to pay for roads to encourage prosperity, the government undertaking to

(continued on page 194)

Great Northern Railway *This Class S2 is considered by many to be the forerunner of a new style of American express locomotive built during the 1930s. It was with reluctance that, only 40 years or so earlier, the railroads had turned from two coupled axles to three for express work. Now the step was made to the four coupled axles that hitherto had been reserved for freight work only. Baldwin Locomotive Works produced 14 of the Class S2 in 1930, a magnificent two-cylinder simple 4-8-4 locomotive. Cylinders were 29in by 29in (737mm by 737mm), boiler pressure 225lb/in² (15.7kg/cm²), driving wheel diameter 6ft 8in (2032mm) and weight in working order 190.9 tonnes. Tractive effort reached 58300lbf (26400kgf). These locomotives worked express trains, including the Empire Builder, along the main line from Chicago to Portland and Seattle, a little way south of the Canadian border. They demonstrated that eight-coupled locomotives could attain the same maximum speeds as the Atlantic or Pacific types.*

Canadian National Railways Class K-5 *On the north American continent the 4-6-2 type needed even greater firebox sizes for maximum steam production, and to support them a bogie was substituted for the rear truck, thus evolving the Hudson or 4-6-4 type. The Montreal Locomotive Works built a two-cylinder 4-6-4 for the Canadian National from 1930, the locomotives being used on the Montreal-Chicago International Limited and on other express trains. Cylinders were 23in by 28in (584mm by 711mm), driving wheels 6ft 8in (2030mm) diameter and boiler pressure 225lb/in² (19.3kg/cm²). A large Vanderbilt tender on six-wheel bogies was fitted, with a capacity of 18 tonnes of coal and 11000 gallons of water (50m³), so that the total length of locomotive and tender was 92ft 6½in (28219mm) over couplers. Class K-5 stayed in service until the end of steam in Canada at the start of the 1960s.*

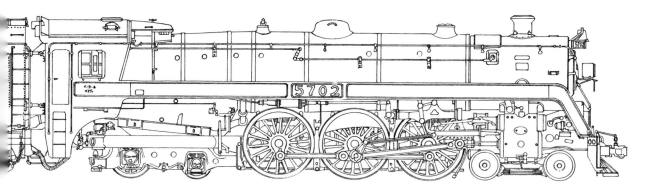

Federal Railway of Austria Class 214 *The ever-increasing weight of passenger trains in the new republic of Austria, particularly over the difficult 196½ miles (317km) between Vienna and Salzburg on which trains were frequently loaded to 700–800 tonnes, prompted the design of a 2-8-4 two-cylinder simple locomotive to work them at average speeds of about 62mph (100km/h). A prototype was built in 1931 and by 1936 another 12 had been added, all from Floridsdorf works. Cylinders were 25¾in by 28in (650mm by 710mm), driving wheels 6ft 2½in (1900mm) diameter, boiler pressure 214lb/in^2 (15kg/cm^2), grate area 51ft^2 (4.7m^2), heating surface 3450ft^2 (283.2m^2) and superheating surface 838ft^2 (77.8m^2). Lentz poppet valve gear was fitted, the first carrying axle was combined with the first driving axle in a Krauss-Helmholtz bogie, and the weight in working order was 118 tonnes. During first trials the output at 56mph (90km/h) was found to be 1980hp, but 2500hp was recorded several times and 2900hp on one occasion. The locomotives were able to haul 500 tonnes up a gradient of 1 in 100 (1.0 per cent) at a speed of 31mph (50km/h). The authorised maximum speed was 68mph (110km/h), but on trial one locomotive reached 97mph (156km/h). The last was withdrawn in 1956, but one is preserved in the Austrian Railway Museum at Vienna. Roumanian builders supplied 79 similar locomotives to the Roumanian State Railways between 1937 and 1940.*

Swedish State Railways *Two of these inside-cylinder 4-6-0 locomotives were built by Motola in 1930 for use on passenger trains of the Kalmar line. Cylinders were 20½in by 24in (520mm by 610mm), driving wheel diameter 5ft 7½in (1720mm), boiler pressure 171lb/in^2 (12kg/cm^2) and grate area 26.9ft^2 (2.5m^2). Weight in working order was 61.4 tonnes and adhesive weight 39 tonnes. The three-axle tender carried 5½ tonnes of coal and 3950 gallons of water (18m^3). Tractive effort was 21550lbf (9780kgf) and the design was a typical European second-line passenger locomotive, apart from the rather unusual appearance.*

Soviet Railways Class IS *This system adopted the 2-8-4 wheel arrangement for its principal class of express locomotive, a two-cylinder simple known as Class IS after Joseph (Iosip) Stalin. Kolomna works produced the prototype in October 1932 and others followed from there and from elsewhere to a total of about 640. Cylinders were 26½in by 30¼in (670mm by 770mm), driving wheels were 6ft 0¾in (1850mm) diameter, boiler pressure was 214lb/in^2 (15kg/cm^2), grate area 75.32ft^2 (7m^2), heating surface 3178ft^2 (295m^2) and superheating surface 1590ft^2 (148m^2). On trial the first locomotive developed 3200hp hauling a 998 tonnes train and the tractive effort was 52400lbf (23840kgf). Weight in working order was 133.6 tonnes.*

Superpacific—1931

Northern of France locomotives

The Northern continued to improve the four-cylinder de Glehn compound locomotive, especially for express trains. In 1931 they introduced the Superpacific 4-6-2, No 3.1251–1290, built by Cail, the firm which had designed the famous Crampton type for the same railway 72 years earlier. The outside HP cylinders were 17½in by 26in (440mm by 660mm) and the inside LP cylinders were 24½in by 27¼in (620mm by 690mm). Driving wheels were 6ft 2¾in (1900mm) diameter, boiler pressure 243lb/in^2 (17kg/cm^2), grate area 37.65ft^2 (3.5m^2), heating surface 2315ft^2 (214.8m^2) and superheating surface 614ft^2 (57.2m^2). De Glehn compounds were very flexible in service and the Superpacifics could be worked in five different ways according to the prevailing conditions and the wishes of the driver. These five were: full compound; full compound with additional reduced-pressure boiler steam supplied to the LP cylinders; and simple expansion with either pair of cylinders or with all four together. The locomotive could only work for short periods with all four cylinders on simple expansion, for otherwise the boiler would run short of steam. High capacity tenders were

fitted carrying 7 tonnes of coal and 8130 gallons of water (37m^3). Painted the traditional chocolate brown of the Northern Railway, these locomotives had a weight in working order of 100.5 tonnes, a maximum axle load of 18.9 tonnes, and they could develop 2700hp.

For the Northern Railway's Paris suburban services a two-cylinder simple 2-8-2 tank locomotive class was designed and built from 1932 to 1935. No 4.1201–1272 were designed to work pull-and-push trains with equal facility in either direction and, because of the short distances between stops, they were provided with high acceleration. Cylinders were 23in by 27½in (585mm by 700mm), driving wheel diameter 5ft 1in (1550mm) and the boiler pressure was 257lb/in^2 (18kg/cm^2). Cossart valves were fitted to the cylinders, actuated by levers and a camshaft. At this time electric light was being installed in locomotives, the current being supplied by a steam-driven dynamo. When travelling backwards with the driver at the rear of the train, elecricity was used to work the regulator and reversing lever on the footplate.

No 4.1201–1272–1932

Central Aragon Railway *This 5ft 6in (1674mm) railway had a Saragossa-Caminreal section with sharp curves and steep gradients which ran through dry country with very few watering points, while coal could only be picked up at those watering points. A Garratt articulated locomotive was just the thing for these conditions and Beyer, Peacock designed an enormous 4-6-2 + 2-6-4, six of which were built by Euskalduna of Bilbao and which were at the time the only passenger Garratts in Europe. The four simple cylinders were 19in by 26in (481mm by 660mm), driving wheels were 5ft 8¾in (1750mm) diameter, boiler pressure was 171lb/in² (12kg/cm²), grate area 52.7ft² (4.9m²), heating surface 3187ft² (293.2m²) and superheating surface 743ft² (69m²). Weight in working order was 184 tonnes and maximum axle load 15.83 tonnes. The coupled wheelbase of each of the engine groups was 12ft 10in (3810mm) and the total wheelbase 83ft 9in (25527mm). These locomotives hauled Calatayud-Saragossa-Valencia trains of 300 tonnes on gradients exceeding 1 in 50 (2.0 per cent) at a speed of 25mph (40km/h). They remained in service for many years and finished in 1966 on Barcelona to Seville trains, running via Tarragona and Valencia.*

provide an adequate road system. In effect the very profitable trunk roads provide a cross-subsidy to support all the necessary loss-making lanes.

Railways have their lanes as well – the loss-making branch lines and the unprofitable off-peak trains. Government's insist that these loss-making services continue, for they benefit the country as a whole and it is anticipated that the profitable main lines will make up for the losses. Indeed when a railway is state-owned it is immaterial to the government whether or not it runs at a profit, within certain limits. Any loss is regarded as part of the costs of good government. The catch comes in the definition of the words 'certain limits', a subject too complicated to pursue.

Because good government makes transport control a necessity, there has been a strong incentive always to combine all the railways of a country into one organisation. In Great Britain the grouping of the old railway companies into four companies only from the start of 1923 was one result of this incentive. Quite apart from simpler government control another incentive was the economies of scale that can be expected by operating in a large unit. The amalgamation of the different railways of Germany into the German State Railway in 1920 was an example of this.

Between the wars the two influences of state control and economy had combined the railways of most countries in Europe each into a single organisation, or at least into a minimal number of administrative units. Part of the

(continued on page 202)

State Railways of France No 241.101 *This French three-cylinder simple 4-8-2 broke away from the compound designs traditional for express locomotives in that country. A highly-developed example of functional locomotive design, it was built by Fives-Lille in 1932. The two outside cylinders were 21in by 22½in (530mm by 570mm) and the single inside cylinder was 30in by 25½in (760mm by 650mm). Driving wheels were 6ft 4¾in (1950mm) diameter and boiler pressure 286lb/in² (20kg/cm²). Renaud poppet valve gear was fitted. Grate area was 53.8ft² (5m²), heating surface 2888ft² (268m²), superheating surface 925ft² (86m²) and weight in working order 86 tonnes, with a 20 tonnes axle load. During first trials it developed 2800hp, but various design faults were exposed at the same time. The steam port area leading into the cylinders was insufficient, and the long wheelbase caused track deformation and excessive rail wear, problems which eventually led to costly modifications.*

Japanese National Railways Class C12 *Not until the 1930s was the 3ft 6in (1067mm) gauge track in Japan modernised for greater axle loads. This Class C12 two-cylinder 2-6-2 tank was designed with a 11 tonnes axle load limit in mind, and it was built by Kisha Seizo Kaisha in 1932. The class was used for light local and branch line trains and had a maximum speed of 43½mph (70km/h).*

Western of Spain *This line from Astorga to Palazuelo had one of the biggest 4-8-0 locomotives in Spain. Various Spanish builders produced 38 of them between 1932 and 1940. Two-cylinder simples and superheated, the cylinders were 24½in by 26in (620mm by 660mm), driving wheels 5ft 3in (1600mm) diameter, boiler pressure 200lb/in² (14kg/cm²) and grate area 48.7ft² (4.5m²). Tractive effort was 41500lbf (18750kgf). At first the class worked passenger trains, but the Spanish National Railways System put them on freights, working from the Salamanca depot.*

The Franco Locomotive *This 6-2 + 2-4-2-4-2 + 2-6 articulated monster with eight cylinders was built in Belgium by Tubize as an experiment in 1931, following the patents of an Italian, Attilio Franco. The aim was to cut unit fuel consumption. The central portion with four cylinders carried two boiler barrels disposed diagonally to the frames and sharing a central firebox. There were two grates and two firemen were needed, one on each side of the locomotive. Articulated ducts took combustion gases over to preheaters and chimneys on the units at either end. Feed water was fed to the preheater barrels and passed from them to the main boilers. Weight in working order was 248 tonnes and the axle load 16.3 tonnes. Tractive effort was 93600lbf (42500kgf). On trial on the Belgian National Railways' Luxembourg line, the locomotive took 1207 tonnes up 1 in 59 (1.7 per cent) gradients at 17mph (28km/h), but the load was limited by coupling strength and by the length of the sidings available. The locomotive was far too big and, in 1942, Tubize cut it in half in effect and produced a 6-2 + 2-6-2, but this disappeared during the 1939–1945 war. There were sequels to the experiment using single unit locomotives (see page 209).*

German State Class 05 – 1935

German State Class 61 – 1935

High speed records

By 1935 the railways had begun to suffer from the competition of other types of transport, which had an increasing amount of attention devoted to them. In various European countries railways had been electrified extensively, while the diesel railcar was being adopted by other lines. Nevertheless the steam locomotive was still the major method of traction and engineers devoted much time and energy towards its improvement and the betterment of its performance. From 1930 or so, there was rivalry over maximum speed, each railway striving towards 125mph (200km/h). The memorable day when this speed was at last attained came on 11 May 1936 in Germany. A 4-6-4 Class 05 streamlined locomotive hauling 297 tonnes was used, and during the course of much high speed running between Berlin and Hamburg, just touched 124½mph (200.4km/h). The locomotive developed 3400hp on this occasion. Class 05 was designed by Adolf Wolff and had been built by Borsig. Three cylinders were 17¾in by 26in (450mm by 660mm), driving wheels were 7ft 6½in

(2300mm) diameter, boiler pressure 286lb/in^2 (20kg/cm^2), heating surface 2750ft^2 (256m^2) and superheating surface 976ft^2 (90m^2). Another German streamlined locomotive had been built by Henschel in 1935. This was a 4-6-4 tank with two cylinders 18in by 29½in (460mm by 750mm), driving wheels 6ft 8in diameter and boiler pressure 286lb/in^2 (20kg/cm^2). It was intended to haul a Weymann light metal articulated train of 125 tonnes and at the head of this on the Berlin-Dresden route it reached 116mph (187km/h). Both these German locomotives had been designed for a maximum speed of 108½mph (175km/h) and in going so much faster they demonstrated the flexibility of steam.

Belgian National Railways also had speed aspirations and introduced a partially-streamlined four-cylinder simple 4-6-2 type in 1934, the Class 1. Fifteen were built, with cylinders 16½in by 28¼in (420mm by 720mm), driving wheel diameter 6ft 6in (1980mm) and a boiler pressure of 257lb/in^2 (18kg/cm^2). Class 1 developed 3400hp and could haul 450 tonnes on

Belgian National Railways Class 1 – 1934

London & North Eastern Railway Class A4 – 1935

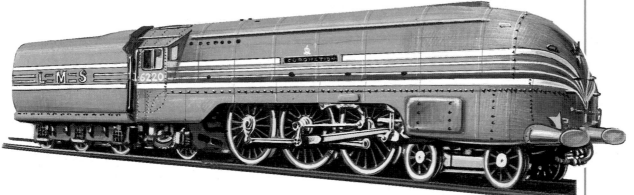

London Midland & Scottish Coronation class – 1937

the level at 87mph (140km/h) with a maximum of 93mph (150km/h).

In Britain, H N Gresley continued to perfect his three-cylinder simple Class A1 4-6-2s on the London & North Eastern Railway (see page 180) and designed the streamlined Class A4. Cylinders were 18½in by 26in (470mm by 660mm), driving wheels 6ft 8in (2030mm) diameter, boiler pressure 250lb/in^2 (17.5kg/cm^2), grate area 41.25ft^2 (3.84m^2), heating surface 2576ft^2 (249m^2) and superheating surface 749ft^2 (69.7m^2). Class A4 *Silver Link*, on a northbound special train from London, attained 112½mph (180km/h) on 30 September 1935, and on 3 July 1938 another of the class, *Mallard*, established the world speed record for a steam locomotive at 126mph (202.7km/h), while hauling a 240 tonnes train. The National Railway Museum at York now has *Mallard* in its collection.

On the London, Midland & Scottish Railway William Stanier built four-cylinder simple streamlined 4-6-2s for London-Glasgow trains, principally for the train Coronation Scot. Cylinders were 16½in by 28in (419mm by 711mm), driving wheels 6ft 9in (2057mm) diameter, boiler pressure 250lb/in^2 (17.5kg/cm^2), heating surface 2807ft^2 (261m^2) and superheating surface 830ft^2 (77.3m^2). On 29 June 1937 the locomotive *Coronation* achieved 114mph (184km/h).

In France, too, the urge for high speed was felt, especially on the Paris-Orleans where the Chapelon rebuilt 4-6-2s were regarded with enthusiasm (see page 189). In 1934 another ten 4-6-2s were rebuilt, with increased cylinder volume and increased admission and exhaust cylinder port area. These locomotives could haul 150 tonnes at between 96 and 100mph (155 and 160km/h). No 231.726 of this batch was fully-streamlined and valve events altered in 1937, with a view to attaining speeds of over 100mph (160km/h).

Paris-Orleans No 231.726 – 1937

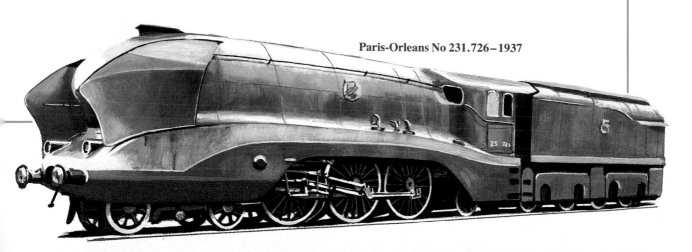

Kin-Han Tramways *In 1935 this standard gauge Chinese railway acquired some mixed-traffic two-cylinder simple locomotives from the Belgian builder Haine St Pierre. They were a follow-up to locomotives built in America and their design was pure American, with bar frames and a high-pitched boiler. Cylinders were 20in by 26in (508mm by 660mm), driving wheel diameter was 4ft 11½in (1510mm), boiler pressure 171lb/in² (12kg/cm²), grate area 32.28ft² (3m²), heating surface 1618ft² (150.3m²) and superheating surface 328.5ft² (30.5m²). Weight in working order was 73 tonnes, adhesive weight 48 tonnes, and maximum axle load 16 tonnes. Maximum speed was 50mph (80km/h).*

Federal Railways of Austria *To combat the spread of the diesel railcar, this railway tried out small two-cylinder 2-4-2 tank locomotives for light suburban and branch line work. Cylinders were 11½in by 22½in (290mm by 570mm), driving wheels 4ft 7½in (1410mm) diameter and boiler pressure 228lb/in² (16kg/cm²). Weight in working order was 45 tonnes and maximum speed 62mph (100km/h). During trials, a speed of 84mph (136km/h) was attained, an excellent result with a locomotive of only 400hp and with small-diameter driving wheels. Floridsdorf built 20 of this Class DT1 from 1935, and another six for the Slovakian Railways in 1940. These last were Class M273 with a boiler pressure of 257lb/in² (18kg/cm²) and could develop 500hp.*

Princess Royal Class *This four-cylinder simple 4-6-2 class was designed by William Stanier for the London, Midland & Scottish Railway. Crewe works built 12 of them from 1933 to 1935, the first of which had the name* Princess Royal. *Cylinders were 16¼in by 28in (413mm by 711mm), driving wheel diameter 6ft 6in (1981mm), boiler pressure 250lb/in² (17.5kg/cm²), grate area 45ft² (4.18m²), heating surface 2713ft² (252m²) and superheating surface 370ft² (34.37m²). Independent Walschaert's valve gear was fitted for each cylinder. A thirteenth locomotive was built in 1935 in which the cylinders were replaced by a steam turbine on the left-hand side, and by a smaller turbine on the right-hand side for backward movement (see page 184). The unit was known as the Turbomotive and worked successfully for many years, but was finally rebuilt in 1952 to conform with the rest of the class. It was then named* Princess Anne, *but was destroyed in an accident eight weeks later. The Coronation class (see page 197) was developed from the Princess Royal Class.*

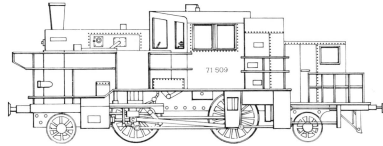

Paris, Lyons & Mediterranean (PLM) *From 1909, the 4-6-2 type was the most powerful express locomotive on the PLM in France. The type showed itself adaptable to improvement and rebuilding, so that the PLM always had up-to-date and high performance locomotives available for its principal main lines. A total of 412 of these 4-6-2s were built from 1909 to 1932, in classes 231A to 231E, some of which had been rebuilt from one class to another. From 1934 more modernisation took place, 50 of Class 231G being newly built, while Class 231D was rebuilt to Class 231G. Classes 231B and 231E were rebuilt to Class 231H and Class 231C was rebuilt to Class 231K. A modernised Class 231G is illustrated, a four-cylinder compound like all the rest, with HP cylinders outside and LP cylinders inside. Cylinders were 17$\frac{1}{4}$in and 25$\frac{1}{2}$in by 25$\frac{1}{2}$in (440mm and 650mm by 650mm), driving wheel diameter 6ft 6$\frac{1}{2}$in (2000mm), boiler pressure 228lb/in^2 (16kg/cm^2), grate area 46.3ft^2 (4.3m^2), heating surface 2215ft^2 (206m^2) and superheating surface 731ft^2 (68m^2). Class 231G developed 2800hp and on trial reached 93mph on several occasions.*

Belgian National Railways Class 7 *The Belgian State Railway acquired 75 de Glehn four-cylinder compound 4-6-0s between 1921 and 1924. These were Class 8 bis, latterly altered to Class 7 after the formation of the Belgian National Railways Co in 1926. Cylinders were 15$\frac{3}{4}$in and 23$\frac{1}{2}$in by 25$\frac{1}{4}$in (400mm and 600mm by 640mm), driving wheel diameter 5ft 10$\frac{1}{2}$in (1800mm), boiler pressure 228lb/in^2 (16kg/cm^2), grate area 33.1ft^2 (3.08m^2), heating surface 1810ft^2 (153.88m^2) and superheating surface 792ft^2 (73.5m^2). The class was subjected to a number of improvements and rebuildings over its years in service. Thus four were altered to four-cylinder simples, with no particular benefit, while most of the class if not all were fitted with feed water heaters and with either Lemaître or Legein blastpipes with necessary alteration to the chimneys. Compared with the normal single-jet blastpipe, the altered blastpipes had multiple jets with consequent major entrainment of combustion gases and more air drawn through the fire. Class 7 weighed 83.5 tonnes in working order, with an adhesive weight of 59.7 tonnes and a maximum axle load of near 20 tonnes. The class was regarded as a second rank express locomotive that was also useful on fast freights and local trains.*

American high speed

In the middle 1930s American railroads were competing with each other to reduce journey times over the great distances between major cities. Many companies acquired express locomotives that in normal daily service could be expected to run at up to 100mph (160km/h) or more. The first designed expressly for high speed were four Atlantic-type 4-4-2s which entered service on the Chicago, Milwaukee, St Paul & Pacific (the Milwaukee Road) in May 1935. They hauled a new train called the Hiawatha – it will be recalled that in Longfellow's poem there was a suggestion that the red indian hero of that name could run so swiftly that he could outpace an arrow shot by his own bow. The American Locomotive Co built these 4-4-2s, with cylinders 19in by 28in (483mm by 711mm), driving wheels 7ft (2134mm) diameter, boiler pressure 300lb/in^2 (21.1kg/cm^2), an oil-fired grate area of 68.8ft^2 (6.4m^2), a heating surface of 3250ft^2 (301.46m^2) and a superheating surface of 1035ft^2 (95.59m^2). The 409 miles (660km) between Chicago and St Paul were covered in 5 hours 5 minutes, at an average speed of 80.6mph (131.5km/h) with maximum speeds of 105mph (170km/h).

The Pennsylvania Railroad obtained excellent

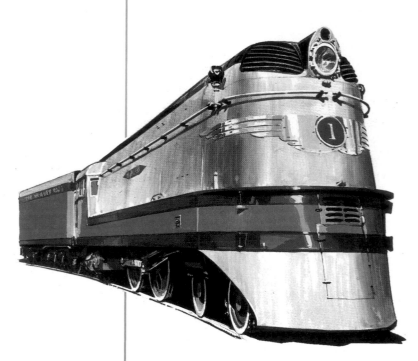

Milwaukee Road Class A – 1935

Pennsylvania Railroad Class K4s – 1939

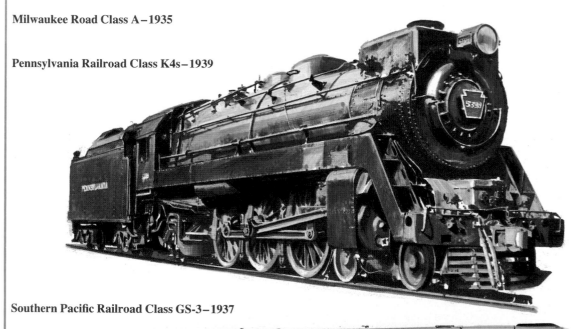

Southern Pacific Railroad Class GS-3 – 1937

results with improved Class K4s 4-6-2s (see page 169). With Lentz poppet valve gear fitted, these were able to develop 2800hp at 100mph (160km/h). On a trial run with 998 tonnes on 16 October 1939, an average speed of 85½mph (138km/h) was obtained, with a maximum speed of 97½mph (157km/h). The Southern Pacific Railroad was going for high speeds as well and had two-cylinder simple streamlined 4-8-4s, Class GS-3, built by the Lima Locomotive Works in 1937. Cylinders were 26in by 32in (660mm by 813mm), driving wheel diameter 6ft 8in (2032mm), boiler pressure 280lb/in^2 (19.6kg/cm^2), grate area 96.74ft^2 (9m^2), heating surface 4890ft^2 (454m^2) and superheating surface 2085ft^2 (194m^2). Weight in working order was 209 tonnes, adhesive weight 121.1 tonnes and maximum axle load 30.25 tonnes. Class GS-3 worked the Daylight Limited between San Francisco and Los Angeles, a train of 14 coaches weighing about 650 tonnes. In 1938 this train left San Francisco at 08.15 hours and after a run of 470 miles (758km) arrived in Los Angeles at 18.00 hours. There were five intermediate stops totalling 23 minutes and, excluding this stationary time, the average speed was 50.3mph (81.2km/h). Such a speed was remarkable, given the mountain gradients and curves of the route, which were such that the train was able to approach speeds of 100mph (160km/h) or more very rarely.

For express service on the other side of the United States the American Locomotive Co had built ten high-speed two-cylinder simple streamlined 4-6-4s for the New York Central in 1938, producing Class J-3a, derived from 4-6-4s already in service. Cylinders were 22½in by 29in (571mm by 737mm), driving wheel diameter 6ft 7½in (2017mm), boiler pressure 275lb/in^2

(19.25kg/cm^2), grate area 82ft^2 (7.62m^2), heating surface 3180ft^2 (288.97m^2) and superheating surface 1745ft^2 (162.11m^2). Baker valve gear was fitted. Weight in working order was 166 tonnes, maximum axle load 30.5 tonnes and at 77½mph (125km/h) the locomotives developed 4725hp. Class J-3a hauled the Twentieth Century Limited between New York and Chicago. This train loaded to about 1000 tonnes and the average speed for the journey was 59.8mph (96.5km/h) with maximum speeds of over 100mph (160km/h).

Not locomotives for high maximum speeds, but equally important for decreasing journey times, were the massive machines used by the Canadian Pacific Railway through the Rocky Mountains and to climb the gradients of the Selkirk range. These two-cylinder simple 2-10-4s were built by the Montreal Locomotive Works from 1938. Cylinders were 25in by 32in (635mm by 813mm), driving wheel diameter 5ft 3in (1600mm), boiler pressure 285lb/in^2 (20kg/cm^2), grate area 93.5ft^2 (8.69m^2), heating surface 5050ft^2 (469.52m^2) and superheating surface 2030ft^2 (188.71m^2). The weight in working order was 202.8 tonnes with an adhesive weight of 140.6 tonnes. Tractive effort was 77000lbf (34900kgf). The tender carried 3400 gallons of fuel (15.5m^3) and 9900 gallons of water (45m^3). Across the wide stretches of Canada, with trains of up to 1000 tonnes or more, it was possible for Class T1b to reach speeds of 74½mph (120km/h), but the class came into its own when climbing from Calgary to Field in the Rocky Mountains or up Beaver Hill in the Selkirks. Using two 2-10-4s, with perhaps another banking, they helped cut the time for the 2871 miles journey (4633km) from Montreal to Vancouver to 87 hours.

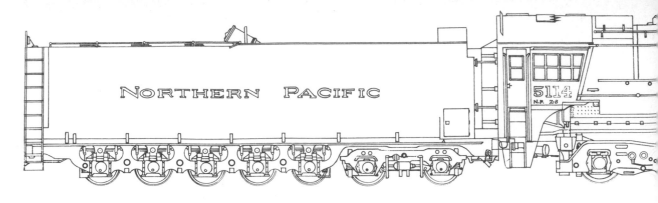

Northern Pacific Railway *The end of the era of the Mallet locomotive in the United States was first heralded by this gigantic 4-6-6-4 Challenger type machine, 47 of which were built by the American Locomotive Co for the Northern Pacific Railway between 1936 and 1944. A great deal of work had gone into the design to produce Mallets that were more stable when running, so that they could reach higher speeds. The Challengers could reach 74½mph (120km/h). Unlike the Mallet compound classes built previously, the Challengers were four-cylinder simples. Cylinders were 23in by 32in (584mm by 813mm), driving wheel diameter 5ft 9in (1753mm) and boiler pressure 250lb/in² (17.5kg/cm²). A design feature was the way that the boiler was carried on the frames to eliminate difficulties experienced with the previous Mallet compounds. With these Mallet compounds, difficulty had been experienced when running because the front engine unit tended to be unloaded so that the weight was thrown on to the rear engine unit. In consequence the front unit tended to oscillate dangerously at speed. In the Challengers, the frame supports were so arranged that more weight was thrown on the axles of the forward unit than on those at the rear. The Northern Pacific used a low-grade fuel, so the grate area was as large as 107.6ft² (10m²). Weight in working order was 283.3 tonnes and adhesive weight 193.2 tonnes. The locomotives were technically sophisticated with cast steel frames, roller bearing axle boxes, feed water heaters and disc driving wheels without spokes. The locomotives could exert 5500 to 6000hp and tractive effort was 104200lbf (47400kgf). It was found that the Challenger class stressed the track considerably, especially when the locomotives travelled at 68 to 74½mph (110 to 120km/h). Locomotive designers held that this was not because the class was a Mallet design–the rigid wheelbase of each engine unit was only 12ft 4in (3.76m)–but simply because a locomotive of almost 300 tonnes weight was used for the first time at these higher speeds. Trevithick could have said much the same thing when his pioneer steam locomotive of 1804 smashed its track (see page 10). The Vanderbilt tenders of the first Challengers carried 22 tonnes of coal and 15500 gallons of water (70.3m³). The class was designed in the first place for heavy freight trains, but came to be used on mountain passenger trains as well.*

economies of scale thus made possible was the provision of locomotive power. One locomotive design for service throughout a country could be used, instead of the wasteful proliferation of designs that had gone before. Economies are still being sought today and the European Economic Community has started to talk of a European State Railway, while under the auspices of the International Union of Railways, standard European diesel locomotives were being designed as long ago as the late 1950s. These, intended for all of Europe, were before their time, and they were abandoned after a minimal number had been built for Holland and Italy.

The concentration of engineering effort on relatively few locomotive designs made thorough research and testing possible to gain the best results. It was not by chance alone that Germany, France and Britain all produced more highly efficient steam locomotives in the period between the wars than had been seen before. Compounding was abandoned by the new German State Railway, which concentrated on new two- or three-cylinder simple designs. In Great Britain the splendid locomotives of Sir Nigel Gresley and Sir William Stanier broke fresh ground and took British locomotive design out of an unhealthy preoccupation with how things had been done in the past. In France the overall aim was to improve track and traction to allow the highest average speeds between large towns. There, the pre-eminent name was that of André Chapelon, who from the 1930s rebuilt certain existing types of compound locomotive so that they achieved truly extraordinary performances. The Chapelon-improved de Glehn compounds attracted the attention of the world's engineers in the 1930s because of the high speeds at which they could handle heavy loads with minimum coal and water consumption, although the higher maintenance costs of compound locomotives did not appeal to all. Chapelon had studied the

(continued on page 206)

Union Railroad Co Pittsburgh *This company worked the marshalling yards of Pittsburgh, and their 0-10-2 built by Baldwin in 1936 represented the latest American practice for steam shunting locomotives. It was designed for maximum tractive effort, while at the same time carrying as much coal and water as possible to allow it to stay at work in the yard for long periods. Because of the railway for which it was built, the unusual 0-10-2 wheel arrangement came to be known as the Union type. Cylinders were 28in by 32in (711mm by 813mm), driving wheel diameter 5ft 1in (1549mm), boiler pressure 260lb/in^2 (18.2kg/cm^2), weight in working order 191.4 tonnes and maximum axle load 31.7 tonnes. The front bogie of the tender was fitted with cylinders and motion for use as a booster. Tractive effort of the locomotive was 90700lbf (41200kgf), to which could be added the tractive effort of the booster at 17150lbf (7800kgf). Despite the size of the boiler it is doubtful if it could supply sufficient steam for runs of any length. Nevertheless, when these locomotives were sold to the Duluth, Missabe & Iron Range Railway in 1949, they were used for runs of about 7 miles (11km) from Proctor to the ore staithes at Duluth on Lake Superior.*

Central of Brazil Railway *The metre-gauge lines of this railway handled mineral traffic, and in 1937 Henschel designed and built four of these Mallet simple 2-8-8-2 locomotives for them. They were intended to work 500 tonnes over a route with a ruling gradient of 1 in 33 (3 per cent) and with particularly restrictive conditions for locomotive designers. The maximum axle load had to be held down to 12 tonnes, which was the reason for the considerable number of axles, while the locomotives could not be too long as they had to run through curves of 64 yards (58.5m) radius. Hence the length of the boiler and smokebox was limited, for on curves the combined barrel might be thrown out too far beyond the centre line of the front engine unit. Furthermore, the locomotives had to burn locally-available lignite fuel with an ash content as high as 30 per cent, which called for a large grate area and ashpan. Cylinders were 17in by 22in (431mm by 559mm), the molybdenum steel boiler (for lightness) carried a pressure of 210lb/in^2 (14.7kg/cm^2), driving wheel diameter was 3ft 10in (1070mm), grate area 75.3ft^2 (7m^2), heating surface 2495ft^2 (232m^2) and superheating surface 915ft^2 (85m^2). A mechanical stoker was fitted. Weight in working order was 117.7 tonnes and adhesive weight 95.7 tonnes. Tractive effort was 56700lbf (24100kgf).*

London Midland & Scottish Railway Duchess Class *The class name Duchess was given to ten locomotives built in 1938 that were similar to the Coronation class (see page 197) save that no streamlined casing was provided. The first locomotive of the batch was named* Duchess of Gloucester *and the rest named after other duchesses. These unstreamlined locomotives caused much controversy. It is probable that the streamlining of locomotives had little technical justification and that it was a response to the public taste of the day – and a reply by the publicists to the streamlined locomotives of the London & North Eastern Class A4, which rivalled those of the London, Midland & Scottish. It was true that the Coronation class looked very fine in their streamlined casing, but there were those who claimed the Duchess as one of the handsomest and most powerful-looking classes to run in Great Britain. The long boiler surmounted six large driving wheels 6ft 9in (2057mm) diameter, together with a bogie of 7ft 6in (2286mm) wheelbase to ensure good riding. Cylinders were 16½in by 28in (418mm by 711mm), grate area 50ft^2 (4.65m^2), heating surface 2867ft^2 (261m^2) and superheating surface 830ft^2 (77.3m^2). On occasion the Coronation and Duchess classes had an output exceeding 3000hp, and the tractive effort for each was 40000lbf (18150kgf). The tender carried 10 tonnes of coal and 4000 gallons of water (18.2m^3).*

German State Railway Class 45 *This was one of the largest and most powerful freight locomotives in Europe. Designed and built by Henschel for the German State Railway in 1937, it included many of the standard locomotive components and auxiliaries evolved by that railway since the 1920s. It was a three-cylinder simple, with cylinders 20½in by 28¼in (520mm by 720mm), driving wheel diameter 5ft 3in (1600mm), boiler pressure 286lb/in^2 (20kg/cm^2), grate area 53.8ft^2 (5m^2), heating surface 3,110ft^2 (289m^2) and superheating surface 1425ft^2 (132m^2). Maximum speed was 56mph (90km/h) and slightly over 3000hp could be developed. Weight in working order was 128 tonnes, of which 100 tonnes was adhesive, with a maximum axle load of 20 tonnes. The design was excellently adapted to the widest range of duties and its robustness allowed the locomotives to perform in a capable manner. A ten-wheeled tender carried 10 tonnes of coal and 8360 gallons of water (38m^3), weighing over 81 tonnes when loaded.*

Japanese National Railways Class D51 *The D51 class was the most typical locomotive of the modern 3ft 6in gauge (1067mm) railways of Japan. No less than 1151 of these two-cylinder 2-8-2s were built between 1936 and 1945; they were very popular and were used on every sort of train, although they were not really suitable for expresses, being incapable of high speed. In some ways the design was derived from American practice, but the locomotives were nonetheless typically Japanese. Cylinders were 21¾in by 26in (550mm by 660mm), driving wheel diameter 4ft 7in (1400mm), boiler pressure 200lb/in² (14kg/cm²) and grate area 35.5ft² (3.27m²). Weight in working order was 76.8 tonnes, adhesive weight 57.2 tonnes and maximum axle load 14.3 tonnes. Tractive effort was 37 400lbf (16 950kgf). The tender carried 8 tonnes of coal and 4400 gallons of water (20m³). There was a shortage of steel in Japan after 1943 and locomotives built in that year and afterwards used thinner steel and had smoke deflectors and tender coal space built up of timber. Adhesive weight was made up with concrete ballast.*

United States Army *When the United States came into the Second World War late in 1941, it was seen that its overseas operations must be supported by additional railway motive power. Consequently a two-cylinder simple 2-8-0 was designed for the 4ft 8½in (1435mm) gauge of such dimensions that it could run on most railways in the world. Some were built for the 5ft (1524mm) and 5ft 6in (1676mm) gauges as well. From 1942 to 1945 a total of 2386 of the class were built. Cylinders were 19in by 26in (483mm by 660mm), driving wheel diameter 4ft 9in (1448mm), boiler pressure 225lb/in² (15.7kg/cm²) and grate area 41ft² (3.81m²). Weight in working order was 73.2 tonnes and the maximum axle load 15.9 tonnes. Tractive effort was 31500 (14250kgf), maximum speed 43½mph (70km/h) and they could develop 1250hp. The list of countries in which they worked is long, from South Korea to Peru, and the list of railways that included them in their stock after 1945 is almost as long. Illustrated is one of them as Italian State Railways Class 736. Some were still at work in 1980 in Poland and Turkey, while still others existed in Greece and Italy although laid aside.*

Belgian National Railways Class 12 *Still interested in high speeds, the Belgian National had six inside-cylinder simple streamlined 4-4-2 locomotives built in 1939. With light, 160 tonnes trains the acceleration was such that 87mph (140km/h) could be attained within 3 minutes of a start, while one of them reached 102¼mph (165km/h) on trial. Four of the class had normal piston valves and two Dabeg or Caprotti poppet valves. Cylinders were 19in by 28¼in (480mm by 720mm), driving wheels 6ft 10½in (2100mm) diameter, boiler pressure 257lb/in² (18kg/cm²) and grate area 39.75ft² (3.7m²). Weight in working order was 89 tonnes and the maximum axle load 23 tonnes. In the ordinary way the locomotives were limited to a maximum speed of 87mph (140km/h).*

use of steam throughout the locomotive and obtained his success by precise design of detail. Thus the steam pipes from boiler to cylinders were of ample size and were free of sharp bends; the exhaust system from the cylinders up the chimney was given attention and a multiple jet blastpipe called the Kylchap was designed, Chapelon basing this work on previous blast-pipe designs by a Finn called Kylälä. The blastpipe ensured maximum flow of combustion gases and thus maximum air flow through the fire, combined with minimum back pressure on the pistons. In addition, the superheater was carefully designed for the precise conditions anticipated in the superheater flues, and to give the required steam temperatures. Auxiliary apparatus such as feedwater heaters and boiler feed pumps also came under examination and they were altered where necessary for maximum output. Interest in locomotive streamlin-

ing revived in all three countries as a result of the higher speeds.

Steam locomotives do not exist in a vacuum and they must be serviced. Between the wars, along with advances in locomotive design, great economies were made in servicing arrangements. One of the results of boiling water is that scale forms on the hot surfaces of containers, as most users of kettles will have noticed. In a locomotive boiler this scale is removed by regular washing out, at intervals of less than a week in hard water areas, and perhaps a fortnight at more favoured places. The scale comes from chemicals dissolved in the water, which can be removed by a water softening process. From the 1920s, strange-looking water-softening plants were erected by the lineside to treat locomotive water in quantity. An alternative method favoured by some

(continued on page 212)

Bulgarian State Railways Class 11 *German builders supplied locomotives to Bulgaria (as their design showed clearly) and Henschel built this fine three-cylinder simple 4-10-0 for the State Railways in 1939. Cylinders were 20½in by 27½in (520mm by 700mm), driving wheel diameter was 4ft 9in (1450mm) and the boiler pressure was 228lb/in² (16kg/cm²). Weight in working order was 109.6 tonnes and maximum axle load 17 tonnes. The tractive effort was 58500lbf (26,600kgf).*

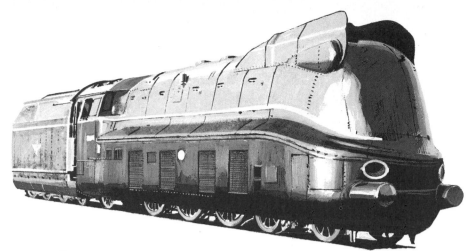

German State Railway Class 03¹⁰ *During 1939, both on 4-6-2 Class 01 and on Class 03, various streamlined casings were tried out, designed by various locomotive builders and with good aerodynamic results. The Class 03^{10} shown was similar to the three-cylinder simple Class 03 with cylinders 18½in by 26in (470mm by 660mm), boiler pressure 228lb/in^2 16kg/cm^2) and 6ft 6½in (2000mm) driving wheels. Grate area was 41.9ft^2 (3.89m^2), heating surface 2,185ft^2 (203m^2) and superheating surface 77.4ft^2 (72m^2). The class could develop 1790hp and the designed maximum speed was 87mph (140km/h). By 1941, the DR had 60 of Class 03^{10} in service and on the Berlin-Hamburg run they were attaining speeds of 87–93mph (140–150km/h) daily with six-coach, 286 tonnes, trains. Weight in working order was 103 tonnes with a maximum axle load of 18.4 tonnes. A streamlined tender was attached, carrying 11 tonnes of coal, 7475 gallons of water (34m^3) and weighing 76 tonnes loaded.*

Merchant Navy class *The Southern Railway in England christened these new 4-6-2 three-cylinder simple locomotives the Merchant Navy class. They were designed by O V Bullied and introduced in 1941, with a new type of valve gear for the three cylinders that was chain-driven and worked in an oil bath. Cylinders were 18in by 24in (457mm by 610mm), driving wheel diameter 6ft 2in (1880mm) and boiler pressure 280lb/in^2 (19.6kg/cm^2). Weight in working order was 94 tonnes and the maximum axle load 22 tonnes. The streamlined casing incorporated the usual smoke deflector plates, but from 1955 to 1959 British Railways removed this casing from 30 locomotives to produce a handsome and powerful-looking locomotive in the traditional style.*

French National Railways Class 141P *After the formation of the French National Railways Co in 1938, André Chapelon sought standard locomotive designs. The 141P class four-cylinder compound 2-8-2 was derived from the Paris, Lyons & Mediterranean 141C class and was intended for express passenger work on steeply-graded routes and for fast freight trains. From 1942 to 1952 a total of 318 Class 141P were built. Cylinders were 16¼in and 25¼in by 27½in (410mm and 640mm by 700mm), driving wheel diameter was 5ft 5in (1650mm), boiler pressure 286lb/in^2 (20kg/cm^2), grate area 46.2ft^2 (4.28m^2), heating surface 2168ft^2 (201.8m^2) and superheating surface 937ft^2 (86.9m^2). Weight in working order was 111.6 tonnes and maximum axle load 19 tonnes. A high-capacity tender was fitted carrying 12 tonnes of coal and 7475 gallons of water (34m^3). The 141P class developed 3120hp heading a 700 tonnes train while travelling at a steady 62mph (100km/h).*

German war locomotives

The German State Railway's war locomotives represent one of the greatest efforts of the locomotive building industry in its 150 year history. Between 7,000 and 8,000 locomotives of two types of two-cylinder 2-10-0 were produced in 2½ years. Class 52 appeared first at the end of 1942, a development of the Class 50 standard 2-10-0 that had been built since 1938. Class 52 represented a peak of standardisation and simplification, both in the production of individual components and in the use of many different manufacturers, great and small, for all the auxiliary apparatus and lesser fittings. Everything was subordinated to building a type as quickly as possible that was easy to maintain and repair. An urgent need had to be filled, for the territories occupied by the Germany armies needed a single type which could run anywhere, while in Germany itself traffic had increased. Not only German builders were involved – works in Poland, Austria, Belgium and France were all drawn in, and it was not at all uncommon for a boiler built in one country to be taken a few hundred miles for use in a locomotive built in another. Class 52 cylinders were 23½in by 26in (600mm by 660mm), driving wheel diameter 4ft

7in (1400mm), boiler pressure 228lb/in^2 (16kg/cm^2), grate area 41.9ft^2 (3.9m^2), heating surface 1910ft^2 (177.6m^2) and superheating surface 686ft^2 (63.7m^2). Tractive effort was 50075lbf (23050kgf). Weight in working order was 85 tonnes and to give widespread route availability the maximum axle load was only 15.3 tonnes. Maximum speed was 50mph (80km/h) officially, although the locomotives could and did run faster than that where the line was suitable.

For service on railways where a higher axle load was permitted, 837 of Class 42 were built with a larger boiler, the first appearing from the Floridsdorf Works, Vienna in August 1943. Cylinders were 25in by 26in (630mm by 660mm), driving wheel diameter 4ft 7in (1400mm), boiler pressure 228lb/in^2 (16kg/cm^2), grate area 50.6ft^2 (4.7m^2), heating surface 2105ft^2 (199.6m^2) and superheating surface 816ft^2 (75.8m^2). Tractive effort was 56000lbf (25,450kgf). Weight in working order was 96.5 tonnes and maximum axle load 18 tonnes. Tenders fitted to many of these locomotives were semi-cylindrical and indeed appeared to be derived from standard oil tank wagons with the top of the tank removed. Where axle loading limits permitted, they could carry 10 tonnes of coal and 7030 gallons of water (32m^3).

Class 42 – 1943

Franco-Crosti boilers

When Attilio Franco, who had designed a
locomotive with a preheater (see page 195), died,
Piero Crosti carried on his work. It was he who
avoided complication by placing the preheater
barrels on either side of the main boiler of a
locomotive with chimneys towards the rear. From
1942, a total of 94 of the standard Italian State
Railways' two-cylinder simple 2-8-0s–Class 740–
were rebuilt with Franco-Crosti boilers to
become Class 743. Cylinders were 21¼in by
27½in (540mm by 700mm), driving wheel
diameter was 4ft 6in (1370mm), grate area 30.1ft²
(2.8m²), preheater heating surface 1180ft²
(109.6m²), heating surface of main boiler 1088ft²
(101.2m²) and superheating surface 473ft²
(44m²). Weight in working order was 72.7
tonnes. Class 743, compared with Class 740,
consumed 25 per cent less fuel. Another 81 of
Class 740 were later rebuilt to Class 741 with a
Crosti boiler between 1955 and 1958, a boiler in
which a single preheater was placed under the
barrel, with a single chimney to one side. Crosti
boilers were used also by the German Federal
Railway and British Railways.

Pennsylvania Railroad Class T-1 *During 1942 the
Pennsylvania put into service two prototypes of a new
4-4-4-4 express locomotive. It was a four-cylinder
simple with the peculiarity that two cylinders drove
the front pair of driving wheels while another two
cylinders drove the rear pair. The streamlined casing
of the locomotive was designed by R Loewy.
Cylinders were 19¾in by 26in (502mm by 660mm),
driving wheels 6ft 8in diameter (2030mm), boiler
pressure 300lb/in² (21kg/cm²) and weight in working
order 226 tonnes, of which 122 tonnes was adhesive.
During road and test plant trials the prototypes
developed more than 6580hp, but several design
faults were revealed that had to be corrected before
Class T-1 was built in quantity. Eventually the
company's own shops at Altoona (which had built
the prototypes) and the Baldwin Locomotive Works
built another 50 of the class between 1945 and 1946.
Class T-1 could exceed 100mph (160km/h) at the
head of passenger trains of more than 1000 tonnes
and one attained 120mph (193km/h). Unfortunately,
at the highest speeds one or other of the driving wheel
sets were apt to lose their footing and slip badly.
Nevertheless the class put in a great deal of hard
work, taking over the working of such trains as the
Broadway Limited, the Manhattan Limited and the
Admiral from the old Class K-4s Pacifics.*

Norfolk & Western Railway *The
Roanoke shops of this railway built
some giant two-cylinder simple 4-8-4
locomotives from 1941 to 1943.
Cylinders were 27in by 32in (686mm
by 813mm), driving wheels were 5ft
9½in (1765mm) diameter, boiler
pressure 275lb/in² (19kg/cm²), grate
area 108ft² (10m²) and weight in
working order 224 tonnes. Maximum
axle load was 32.77 tonnes and the
tractive effort 80 000lbf (36 300kgf).*

Union Pacific Railroad – 1941

High technology locomotives

During the Second World War, the north American locomotive industry produced many very advanced machines incorporating the latest technology, machines that marked the last step in the evolution of the steam locomotive. The many different railroads still competed with each other to acquire the best locomotives and designs multiplied as each was directed towards fulfilling specific needs. Four examples of the period are shown here.

The climax of the Mallet type came in 1941, when Union Pacific No 4000-4019 were built by the American Locomotive Co, to be followed by another five in 1944. A Mallet simple 4-8-8-4, this class was a development of the Challenger class of the Northern Pacific (see page 202) and the Union Pacific class became known as the Big Boys because they were the largest, most powerful and heaviest locomotives that the world had seen and was to see, a fitting end to the American drama of giant steam locomotives. The four cylinders were 23¾in by 32in (603mm by 813mm), driving wheel diameter was 5ft 8in (1727mm), boiler pressure 300lb/in^2 (21kg/cm^2), grate area 152ft^2 (14m^2), heating surface 5940ft^2 (547m^2) and superheating surface 2465ft^2

Nickel Plate Road – 1942

Louisville & Nashville Railroad – 1942

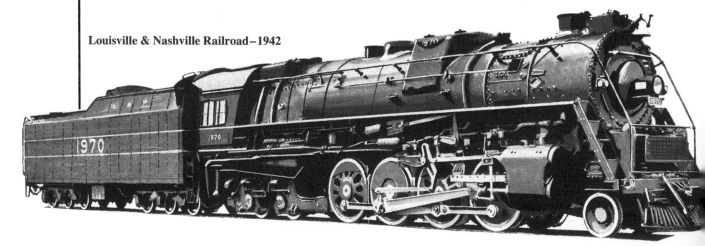

(229m²). Tractive effort was 136000lbf (61750kgf). Weight in working order was 346 tonnes and the maximum axle load 30.6 tonnes. The tender was on seven axles and carried 28 tonnes of coal and 21000 gallons of water (95.4m³). The locomotives could develop about 6300hp and could take up to 4000 tonnes up the 1 in 91 gradients (1.1 per cent) between Ogden and Green River at 25mph (40km/h). Fittingly, one of these tremendous machines has been preserved.

The 2-8-4 or Berkshire type was the type most highly developed for fast freight work and the occasional passenger train. The New York, Chicago & St Louis Railroad (Nickel Plate Road) had introduced the Berkshire type in the 1930s and ordered 55 more of an improved class that were delivered in between 1942 and 1949. They were built by the Lima Locomotive Works and the last of them was the final locomotive that this works built. The two cylinders were 25in by 34in (635mm by 864mm), driving wheel diameter was 5ft 9in (1753mm) and boiler pressure 245lb/in² (17.2m²). They weighed 191 tonnes in working order and they had a 29.3 tonnes axle load. In the same year (1942) that saw the first of the Nickel Plate locomotives, the Baldwin Locomotive Works delivered 14 of a very similar design to the

Louisville & Nashville Railroad. Boiler pressure was higher at 265lb/in² (18.7kg/cm²), which gave a tractive effort of 65600lbf (28750kg/cm²). The class was put to work on mineral trains between De Courcey and Ravenna in eastern Kentucky, could develop 4500hp at 42mph (68km/h) and they were able to haul trains of up to 9500 tonnes, needing banking locomotives up the steepest gradients only. The class was replaced by diesels in 1956.

Despite the development of other means of transport the Shay locomotive (see page 149) was still being built in the 1940s for the lumber and mineral railway duties for which they were suited. Lima Locomotive Works built its last and most sophisticated Shay in 1945. As it happened, this was delivered to a minor railway, the Western Maryland Railway, for duties on one of its mineral branches in West Virginia. It had a traffic life of five years only, and was replaced by diesel locomotives in 1950, three years later going to the Mount Clare Museum of the Baltimore & Ohio Railroad for preservation. It was a 4-4-4 and the three vertical cylinders were 17in by 18in (432mm by 457mm), driving wheel diameter was 4ft 3in (1219mm), weight in working order was 147 tonnes and, aided by the gearing, the tractive effort was 63500lbf (27100kgf).

Western Maryland Railway – 1945

Spanish National Railways System (RENFE) *Locomotives of this class were the most advanced of the 4-8-2 type to run in Spain, and they were the first class to be built for the new RENFE after its formation in 1941. The design was intended to meet the need for better motive power on the Madrid-Alicante and Seville main line of the old Madrid-Saragossa-Alicante Railway. La Maquinista built two prototypes in 1944 and 1946 and thereafter another 55 were delivered between 1946 and 1952. The two cylinders were 25¼in by 28in (640mm by 710mm), Lentz poppet valve gear was fitted, driving wheel diameter was 5ft 8¾in (1750mm), boiler pressure 228lb/in² (16kg/cm²) and grate area 57ft² (5.3m²). Weight in working order was 204 tonnes and length over the buffers, including the tender, reached 83ft 7in (25500mm). The locomotives were not suited to high speeds, but they could haul almost any load demanded. Tractive effort was 49700lbf (22550kgf).*

railways was to introduce water-softening chemicals direct into the tenders and tanks. By such means intervals between boiler washouts could be extended to perhaps as much as a month.

For many years coal supplies were moved by hand from coal wagons to locomotive tenders. Later coal stages were built, the coal wagons being pushed up to a level above that of the locomotive which was to be coaled. Coal from a wagon was shovelled downwards into a skip and the skip pushed a few yards before being tipped into the locomotive's tender. Another innovation of the 1920s was a coal bunker holding 100 tonnes or more astride a coaling track. A complete railway wagon went up in a lift alongside this and was tilted bodily at the top to empty its contents into the bunker. Measured quantities of coal could be dropped into the tenders of locomotives under the bunker. By 1939 such bunkers towered over many locomotive depots and in the United States they even straddled running lines to replenish coal supplies without taking locomotives off trains. Ash disposal was another tiresome manual task, the ash being raked out of fireboxes and ashpans into pits between the rails. Many of these pits came to be equipped with conveyor belts to take the ash out of the pit and to lift it into waiting railway wagons.

South African Railways & Harbours *Around 1400 locomotives with the 4-8-2 wheel arrangement were built for the South African Railways, of 26 major classes and over a period of 42 years. One of the most important and popular was Class 15, introduced as Class 15CA for the Cape Town to Johannesburg expresses (see page 186). A variant of the class was known as 15F, designed by W A J Day and built just before the Second World War, but not produced in quantity until after 1945. The first locomotives of Class 15F came from Germany in 1938, seven from Schwartzkopff and 11 from Henschel. Another 160 were built from 1945 to 1948 in Great Britain by Beyer, Peacock & Co and by the North British Locomotive Co. Eventually the class totalled 255. Class 15F had two cylinders 24in by 28in (610mm by 711mm), driving wheels 5ft (1524mm) diameter and a boiler pressure of 210lb/in² (14.7kg/cm²). A mechanical stoker was provided and the tractive effort was 48000lbf (21800kgf). Weight in working order was 111 tonnes with a maximum axle load of 19 tonnes. Some of Class 15F were in service still during 1980.*

Pennsylvania Railroad Class S2 *In the search for higher steam locomotive efficiency and spurred on by the competition of the newly-emergent diesel-electric locomotive, Baldwin and Westinghouse, together with the Pennsylvania Railroad, designed and built a steam turbine locomotive in 1944. Among their objectives were the elimination of reciprocating parts, uniform distribution of power to the driving wheels and, of course, reduced fuel consumption. The primary turbine when running at 9000rpm had a 6900hp output, while a lesser 1500hp turbine provided for backwards locomotive movements. During tests it was found that maximum efficiency was obtained at a speed of 71mph (115km/h), although the locomotive was perfectly capable of speeds in excess of 100mph when needed. Class S2 was enormous, with the 6-8-6 wheel arrangement and trailed a gigantic tender with two eight-wheeled bogies so that together the length over couplers reached 147ft 1½in (37370mm). The design was well-conceived and successful as far as it went, but the turbine locomotive came too late to the American scene to be followed up.*

New York Central Railroad *This 4-8-4 Niagara type locomotive was the last of the giant American steam express locomotives. The class appeared at the end of the Second World War just as the diesel-electric locomotive started to sweep the steam locomotive off the United States' tracks. The New York Central had used the 4-8-4 wheel arrangement for a compound locomotive in 1931, but the new design exceeded the dimensions of the latter in every way when the American Locomotive Co built them in 1945 and 1946. Despite the massive size, the design was notable for its pleasing and clean appearance, and it was one of the more successful efforts of the American locomotive industry in this respect. The two simple cylinders were 25in by 32in (635mm by 813mm), driving wheel diameter was 6ft 6½in (2001mm), boiler pressure 290lb/in^2 (20.3kg/cm^2) and grate area 100ft^2 (9.3m^2). Weight in working order was 214 tonnes and the maximum axle load was just over 31 tonnes. The locomotives could develop 6300hp and the tractive effort was 74000lbf (33600kgf). A train of over 1000 tonnes weight could be hauled at over 100mph (160km/h), while thanks to good design and construction, the locomotives were economical to work and easy on maintenance cost. Two European features were adopted: smoke deflector plates and a water scoop on the tender. Together with the necessary water troughs between the tracks, the water scoop allowed elimination of water stops and hence lessened the time taken to run from New York to Chicago.*

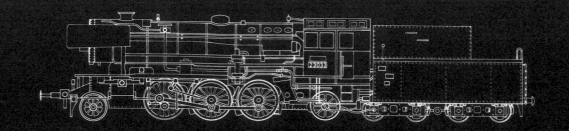

The Fires
Go Out

The last years of the steam locomotive were packed with technical development and experiment, just as in all the previous decades, and the engineers engaged in building and operating the machines can perhaps be forgiven their supposition that there were many years to come for steam. What other explanation can be given of the large investments made in new steam power in North American during the 1940s and for the fresh designs tried out during the same period? Europe at that time was engaged in war and its aftermath and, although plans were made for the coming years of peace with the steam locomotive in mind, progress was not apparent. Nevertheless the cheaper diesel locomotive, and in North America the diesel-electric locomotive in particular, was fast becoming the preferred railway motive power. This occurred despite the diesel being incapable of matching steam power outputs (unless several diesel locomotives were used for each train) and

Belgian National Railways Class 29 *After both the end of the First World War and that of the Second, the Belgian railways were damaged and in need of new motive power. New 2-8-0 locomotives came from the United States, 150 of Class 38 from 1920, and 300 of Class 29 from 1946, the latter built in both the United States and Canada. Class 29's two simple cylinders were 22in by 28in (559mm by 711mm), driving wheel diameter was 5ft (1524mm), weight in working order 93 tonnes and they could develop 2000hp. The class worked all over Belgium and became known popularly as the Jeep. With their robust design and construction, the class made a notable contribution to train services, although as passenger locomotives they were hampered by their top speed of only 60mph (97km/h). The steam locomotive vanished long ago from the Belgian railway scene, but at least one Class 29 survives and is still used on occasional special trains.*

despite the diesel's failure to match steam locomotive maximum speeds. This fact is still largely true today in North America, although in Europe both electric traction and the diesel-electric have shown that they can now far surpass steam in tonnage hauled and in maximum speeds. The difference between the thinking in the two continents is due not so much to technical development as to social customs. The North Americans still call for some half-a-dozen men to man each train, so that lengthy and weighty trains with several locomotives are run to save on wage costs, even if overall speeds are reduced. On the other hand, European freight trains of 1000–2000 tonnes are run in some cases with only one man in charge, while only two men (one of whom is engaged partially with other duties) take care of passenger trains running consistently at 100mph (160km/h).

Turkish State Railways *The German locomotive industry that had supplied Turkey was disorganised after the Second World War and the Turkish State Railways turned to the United States for modern motive power. The Vulcan Iron Works, Wilkes-Barre, Pennsylvania, supplied 88 freight 2-10-0s in 1947 and 1948. They had larger boilers than had been used hitherto in Turkey, and the class was particularly useful over the long mountain gradients and near desert upland plains of that country. Two simple cylinders were 23½in by 28in (597mm by 711mm) and the driving wheels were 4ft 9in (1450mm) diameter. A mechanical stoker was fitted and the tractive effort was 57300lbf (26440kgf). The locomotives are readily recognisable (some were still in traffic in 1980) by the continuous casing running along the top of the boiler, enclosing the chimney and the other boiler mountings, a form of construction then fashionable in the United States.*

Lighter trains in Europe aid the achievement of much higher speeds, both for freight and passengers. During 1980, experiments in Europe presage a time when electrically-powered trains will be controlled entirely automatically, with no one at all in charge on board.

The final North American steam express locomotive designs were ambitious in the extreme. The Duplex 4-4-4-4 type of the Pennsylvania Railroad (see page 209) perhaps did not meet all the hopes of the designers, possibly because war conditions did not allow sufficient time to be devoted to the type to get them right. Other railroads had more orthodox 4-8-4 locomotives of very advanced design (see that of the New York Central, page 213) which amply demonstrated that by increased performance and by reduction of running costs the steam locomotive could still hold its own in terms of power, speed and mechanical reliability. Although development in Europe was held back by the war, German designers produced a scheme for a 4-8-4 locomotive suitable for hauling special passenger coaches at speeds up to 155mph (250km/h) in 1942. This proposed locomotive was enclosed in streamlined coachwork, with a cab for the driver at the leading end, and was to have been a five-cylinder compound.

Steam turbine locomotives had been tried spasmodically since before the First World War with no lasting success, although a Swedish railway had steam turbine geared-drive locomotives in service for many years. The steam turbine shares a difficulty with the diesel engine, in that both are at their most efficient when running at a constant speed far in excess of the speed of the driven wheels on the track. To cope with the varying speed of the train and the constantly varying power outputs needed, some form of transmission must be provided. The pioneer steam turbine driven locomotive in Great Britain in 1914 had an electric transmission just like a diesel-electric locomotive; so

(continued on page 224)

Polish State Railways Class Pt47 *One of the best-looking and efficient post-war locomotive classes in Poland was this 2-8-2, of which Cegielski produced 60 and Chrzanow 120 from 1948. The design was a development of the pre-war Pt31 class and included some traces of German locomotive practice, for the Poles had been building German locomotives during the war. Class Pt47 had two simple cylinders 24¾in by 27½in (630mm by 700mm), driving wheels 6ft 0¾in diameter and a boiler pressure of 214lb/in² (15kg/cm²). The class was used extensively on express trains and also gave good results on local and suburban trains in non-electrified areas. The class exemplified later Polish locomotive practice, strongly influenced by the German Democratic Republic and later by the Soviet Union. Some Class Pt47 were in traffic still during 1980.*

Class 141R – 1945

Last French designs

Reconstruction and continuing modernisation of the French National Railways after the Second World War necessitated the building of many new locomotives. For speed, orders were placed with North American locomotive builders, both in the United States and Canada, and 1340 of the Class 141R (also known non-officially as the Liberation class) were built between August 1945 and July 1947. Two simple cylinders were 23½in by 28in (597mm by 711mm), driving wheels were 5ft 5in diameter (1650mm) and boiler pressure 220lb/in² (15.4kg/cm²). Weight in working order was 115.5 tonnes and maximum axle load 20 tonnes. The class was not fast, but one of them could haul a sleeping car train of 800 tonnes at over 62mph (100km/h) or 1500 tonnes of freight at 31mph (50km/h). Passenger trains on steeply-graded routes were within their capabilities, and they were used also along the French Riviera between Marseilles and Ventimiglia.

Among locomotives rebuilt, was the old Paris, Lyons & Mediterranean 241A class, a four-cylinder compound 4-8-2. As rebuilt to the 241P class (which work was undertaken by Schneider, between 1948 and 1952), the HP cylinders were 17½in by 25½in (446mm by 650mm) and the LP cylinders 26½in by 27½in (674mm by 700mm). Driving wheel diameter was 6ft 6½in (2000mm), boiler pressure 286lb/in² (20kg/cm²) and 3200hp could be developed. Another streamlined rebuild

Class 241P – 1948

was a 4-6-0 de Glehn compound of the turn of the century, that had been built for the old Eastern Railways. As rebuilt to the 230K class in 1947, the cylinders were 14½in and 23¼in by 26¾in (370mm and 590mm by 680mm), driving wheel diameter was 6ft 10in (2090mm), boiler pressure 257lb/in² (18kg/cm²) and weight in working order 84 tonnes. The 230K class ran expresses from Paris to Strasbourg in 5 hours 15 minutes.

Class 230K – 1947

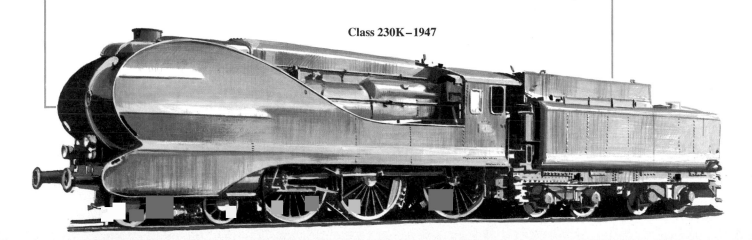

Chesapeake & Ohio Railway *This railway was very forward-looking at the end of the Second World War and designed a very advanced locomotive for its heavy coal traffic from the Pocahantas coalfield, a design that, while burning coal, was intended to compete with burgeoning diesel traction. It was also laid down that the locomotives should haul passenger express trains from Cincinnati to Washington. Baldwin and Westinghouse prepared a design for a gigantic articulated steam turbine locomotive, with electric transmission (instead of the mechanical transmission of the two previous steam turbine locomotives—see pages 185 and 213). The boiler and turbine could generate 6000hp when the latter was running at 6000rpm, and there were eight traction motors of 620hp each. Continuous tractive effort of 106000lbf (48000kgf) could be exerted, and the maximum tractive effort was 216000lbf (98000kgf). The streamlined casing, while not otherwise remarkable, covered the front and coal bunker, the driver's cab, and the boiler, the turbine and its control gear. A water tank tender on six-wheel bogies was trailed behind and, including this, the total length over couplers was 154ft 2in (47m), while the total number of wheels was 40. From 1947 three of these locomotives were built, unkindly nicknamed the Sacred Cows by railwaymen, for none of them had any success. Frequent failures occurred in use and although they were supposed to be capable of speeds of over 100mph (160km/h), none of them got anywhere near this. The three unfortunates were scrapped in 1950.*

Indian Railways Class WP *This 4-6-2 is the fastest and most powerful steam locomotive class on the 5ft 6in (1676mm) gauge Indian Railways. During 1980, a great many of the class were still hard at work. The first of the class were built by Baldwin in the United States and delivered to the then East Indian Railway in 1947, but many more have been built since both in Europe and in India itself. The locomotives are modern two-cylinder Pacifics with decorative semi-streamlining. Cylinders are 20¼in by 28in (514mm by 711mm), driving wheels 5ft 7in (1705mm) diameter, boiler pressure 210lb/in² (14.7kg/cm²), grate area 46ft² (4.27m²), weight in working order 89 tonnes and maximum axle load 18.3 tonnes.*

New Zealand Government Railways *This 3ft 6in (1067mm) railway had 35 Class Ja locomotives built at its Hillside Locomotive Works from 1946. The design was a modernisation of R J Gard's 4-8-2 Class J, built by the North British Locomotive Co in 1939. During 1951 the same North British Locomotive Co built an additional 15 of Class Ja, this time equipped for oil firing. The locomotives were two-cylinder simples, with cylinders 18in by 26in (457mm by 660mm), driving wheels 4ft 6in (1370mm) diameter and a boiler pressure of 200lb/in^2 (14kg/cm^2). Weight in working order was 70.2 tonnes and the maximum axle load was 11.7 tonnes. Class Ja was intended principally for freight trains of up to 800 tonnes on secondary routes, but the class showed itself to be equally at home on fast passenger trains running at up to 74^1/$_2$mph (120km/h) and indeed the locomotives might have run faster if the layout of the railway had allowed.*

Swedish State Railways Class E10 *This secondary line 4-8-0 locomotive was put into service by the Swedish State in 1947. Built by Nydquist & Holm, the two-cylinder simple had cylinders 17^3/$_4$in by 24in (450mm by 610mm), driving wheels 4ft 7in (1400mm) diameter, boiler pressure 200lb/in^2 (14kg/cm^2), a weight in working order of 74.2 tonnes and a maximum axle load of 13 tonnes. Tractive effort was 23142lbf (10500kgf). The cab was totally enclosed against the Swedish winter and the six-wheel tender carried 7 tonnes of coal, together with 3630 gallons of water (16.5m^3). The locomotives worked the Östersund-Mora and Bollnäs-Orsa lines.*

Hungarian State Railways Class 303 *A pair of two-cylinder simple 4-6-4s were built by Mávag, Budapest, and put into service in 1951. Cylinders were 21^3/$_4$in by 27^1/$_2$in (549mm by 699mm), driving wheel diameter was 6ft 6^1/$_2$in (2000mm) and boiler pressure 257lb/in^2 (18kg/cm^2). Weight in working order was 114 tonnes and the maximum axle load 17.5 tonnes. A mechanical stoker was fitted, the locomotives developed over 2000hp and 500 tonnes could be hauled at over 74^1/$_2$mph (120km/h). Once again the cab was completely enclosed against winter weather. One of the locomotives has been preserved.*

French National Railways Class 232U *This 4-6-4 four-cylinder compound locomotive was built in 1949. Cylinders were 17¾in and 26¾in by 27½ (450mm and 680mm by 700mm), driving wheels were 6ft 6½in (2000mm) diameter and boiler pressure 286lb/in² (20kg/cm²). The locomotive could develop 3000hp to haul 710 tonnes at about 74½mph up a gradient of 1 in 250 (0.4 per cent). Maximum speeds of over 100mph (160km/h) were possible, weight in working order was 130.7 tonnes and maximum axle load 23 tonnes.*

Soviet Railways Class P36 *There were 251 of this two-cylinder simple 4-8-4 type, built by Kolomna Locomotive Works from 1951 to 1956. Cylinders were 22¾in by 31½in (575mm by 800mm), driving wheel diameter was 6ft 0¾in (1850mm) and weight in working order 135 tonnes. Tractive effort was 40100lbf (18200kgf).*

South African Railways & Harbours Class 25
Finding copious and continuing water supplies for steam locomotives can be a problem in dry areas. One solution is the condensing locomotive, in which all exhaust steam is led to the tender. Tender-mounted rotary fans reduce the steam temperature so that it condenses into water for re-use in the boiler. South African Railways introduced their Class 25 two-cylinder simple 4-8-4 condensing locomotives in 1953, and a total of 90 were built. They had 24in by 28in (610mm by 711mm) cylinders, driving wheels 5ft (1524mm) diameter and a 225lb/in² (15.7kg/cm²) boiler pressure. Tractive effort was 51300lbf (11300kgf). The tender mounted five large condensing fans on its roof and had a 18 tonnes coal capacity, although only 3300 gallons of water could be carried (15m³).

Czechoslovakian State Railways Class 498.1 *Skoda built 15 of this three-cylinder simple 4-8-2 class in 1954, the design being derived from the 498.0 class of 1948-1949. Cylinders were 19¾in by 26¾in (500mm by 680mm), driving wheels 6ft (1830mm) diameter and the boiler pressure 228lb/in² (16kg/cm²). The locomotives had bar frames, roller bearings, mechanical stokers and Kylchap blastpipes. Weight in working order was 116.6 tonnes and the maximum axle load was 18.3 tonnes.*

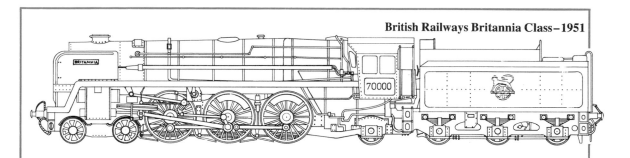

British Railways Britannia Class – 1951

British Rail standard designs

Crewe works delivered a mixed traffic two-cylinder simple 4-6-2 named *Britannia* on 2 January 1951, the first of British Railways' standard steam locomotive designs. In a dark green livery, it was the first of 55 Britannia class locomotives built from 1951 to 1954. Cylinders were 20in by 28in (508mm by 711mm), driving wheel diameter 6ft 2in (1880mm) and boiler pressure 250lb/in² (17.5kg/cm²). Weight in working order was 95.5 tonnes and maximum axle load 20.5 tonnes. Tractive effort was 32 100lbf (14 600kgf) and the locomotives showed themselves capable of hauling 320 tonnes at 93mph (150km/h). Another standard design was

a heavy freight two-cylinder simple 2-10-0, of which 251 were built between 1953 and 1958. Cylinders were 20in by 28in (508mm by 711mm), driving wheels 5ft (1524mm) diameter and boiler pressure 250lb/in² (17.5kg/cm²). Weight in working order was 88 tonnes and maximum axle load 17¾ tonnes. No 92220 of this class was the last steam locomotive built for British Railways, emerging from Swindon works in a special dark green livery and named nostalgically *Evening Star*. Both the locomotives shown are now preserved, the last in the National Railway Museum, York.

British Railways Class 9F – 1953

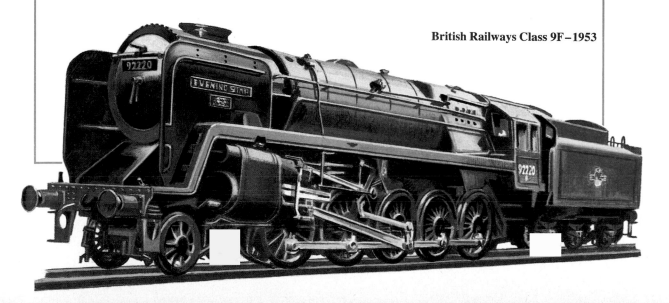

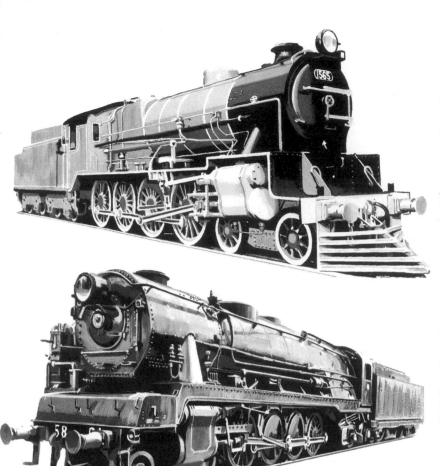

General Roca National Railway Class 15B *This 5ft 6in (1676mm) gauge railway, known formerly as the Buenos Aires Great Southern, had this two-cylinder simple mixed traffic 4-8-0 class built by Vulcan Foundry in England in 1949. Cylinders were 19½in by 28in (495mm by 711mm), driving wheels 5ft 8in (1727mm) diameter and boiler pressure 225lb/in^2 (15.7kg/cm^2). Weight in working order was 82.4 tonnes and the maximum axle load 16 tonnes. The timber-built cowcatcher was typical of Argentinian locomotive practice.*

New South Wales Government Railway Class D58 *This three-cylinder simple 4-8-2 locomotive was built for freight work, particularly on the famous Zig-Zag inclines where they worked in pairs or even threes. Thirteen of the class were built in Australia in 1950, with a weight in working order of 141 tonnes and a maximum axle load of 23.3 tonnes. Previous three-cylinder locomotives for the line had Gresley derived motion, but motion for the D58 inside cylinder's valve was obtained by a rack gear.*

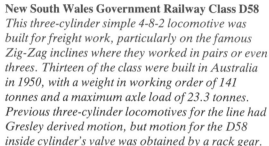

Hellenic State Railways Class M∝ *Twenty of these two-cylinder simple 2-10-2 locomotives were built by Breda and Ansaldo in Italy in 1953 and 1954. Half of them were coal burners and half were arranged for oil, and they were used on the Athens-Salonika main line, which has a ruling gradient of 1 in 50 (2 per cent). The class had bar frames, cylinders 26in by 27½in (660mm by 700mm), driving wheels 5ft 3in (1600mm) diameter and a 257lb/in^2 (18kg/cm^2) boiler pressure. Weight in working order was 134 tonnes with a maximum axle load of 20 tonnes. Tractive effort ws 64200lbf (29100kgf).*

Jugoslav Railways Class 38 *Ten of this class were built by Djuro Djaković, Slavonski Brod, in 1957, These followed the design of 65 two-cylinder simple 2-8-0s supplied from Great Britain as post-war aid in 1946. There were minor differences, principally the addition of a Heinl feed water heater. Cylinders were 21¾in by 28in (550mm by 711mm), driving wheel diameter was 4ft 9in (1450mm) and boiler pressure 228lb/in^2 (16kg/cm^2).*

Rhodesia Railways Class 15 *Many African railways favoured the Beyer-Garratt articulated locomotive for their trains over tortuous and heavily-graded routes on which water supplies were difficult. Furthermore powerful locomotives were needed, and articulation allowed the power to be provided without exceeding the often low axle load limit. Class 15 was built from 1940, a four-cylinder simple 4-6-4 + 4-6-4 Garratt type. Cylinders were $17\frac{1}{2}$in by 26in (444mm by 660mm), driving wheel diameter 4ft 9in (1450mm) and boiler pressure 180lb/in^2 (12.6kg/cm^2). The class was able to run 500 tonnes passenger trains at more than 50mph (80km/h) or alternatively to work 900 tonnes freight trains. The length over couplers was 92ft 11in (28194mm), but the locomotives could run through curves readily, as the fixed wheelbase of each unit was 9ft 9in (3200mm) only. Class 15 locomotives, together with other Beyer-Garratt classes, were being refurbished during 1980 for further service on Zimbabwe Railways, successor to the old Rhodesia Railways.*

Spanish National Railways System *La Maquinista of Barcelona built ten of this two-cylinder simple 4-8-4 class in 1955 and 1956. Cylinders were $25\frac{1}{4}$in by 28in (640mm by 710mm), driving wheel diameter 6ft $2\frac{3}{4}$in (1900mm), boiler pressure 214lb/in^2 (15kg/cm^2) and grate area 57ft^2 (5.3m^2). Lentz poppet valves were fitted, the locomotives were oil-fired, and a steam turbo-generator provided electric current for locomotive lights and additionally for lighting the coaches of the train. Weight in working order was 162 tonnes and adhesive weight 76 tonnes. Originally put on to Madrid-Irun trains, the class worked Avila-Miranda de Ebro trains latterly.*

Finnish State Railways Class Tr1 *This class was built over a long period, the first batch by Tampella in 1940, and the class total of 67 was made up by other batches from Jung in Germany and from Lokomo, while Tampella built a last one in 1957. The locomotives were mixed traffic 2-8-2s, able to run at 50mph (80km/h) on passenger trains, as well as being able to handle heavy freights. Cylinders were 24in by $27\frac{1}{2}$in (610mm by 700mm), driving wheel diameter was 5ft 3in (1600mm), weight in working order was 95 tonnes and the maximum axle load 17 tonnes. The large tender fitted weighed 62 tonnes fully-loaded with 9 tonnes of coal and 5940 gallons of water (27m^3).*

German Federal Railway Class 10 – 1956

Last German Pacifics

Germany at the end of the Second World War was divided into two, and two railways were formed, that in the west being called the German Federal Railway and that in the east retaining the name German State Railway. Both provided the 4-6-2 type for express trains and two of Class 10 were built for the German Federal by Krupp in 1956. They were three-cylinder simples with cylinders 19in by 28½in (480mm by 720mm), driving wheels 6ft 6½in (2000mm) diameter, boiler pressure 257lb/in^2 (18kg/cm^2), weight in working order 114.5 tonnes and with a 21.5 tonnes maximum axle load. For several years they worked on the Kassel to Frankfurt-am-Main line and were withdrawn in 1967. On the German State Railway it was preferred to rebuild the existing Class 01 (see page 184) from 1962. A more striking outward appearance was provided and the blastpipe was modified for a freer exhaust. Cylinders became 23½in by 26in (600mm by 660mm), driving wheels were 6ft 6½in (2000mm) diameter, weight in working order was 111 tonnes and the maximum axle load was 20.2 tonnes. The Class 01^5 could attain 100mph (160km/h) or more, and a number of them were still in service in the German Democratic Republic during 1980.

**German State Railway
Class 01^5 – 1962**

did the last three steam turbine locomotives built for the Chesapeake & Ohio Railroad in 1947 (see page 218). In passing it may be noted that the transmission problem is accentuated by using gas turbines, which is why the gas turbine has had no lasting success in railway motive power.

The steam locomotive has now passed from the scene in western Europe, and in North America. The familiar sounds and smell of coal smoke are unfamiliar to more and more people, unless they happen to see some preserved steam locomotive and its nostalgic train. Economic conditions are different elsewhere, and the steam locomotive is still in limited use. It has been estimated that as many as 26000 were running in the world during 1980, but even for these time is running out; only China still builds new steam locomotives. The Advance Forward class 2-10-2 was being built for Chinese Railways during 1980, and an entirely new Red Flag class heavy freight locomotive is due to be built. China has an estimated 8000 steam locomotives in traffic, but extensive railway electrification programmes are being pushed ahead with. Just as in the rest of the world, where electricity does not take over the diesel locomotive may.

Appendices

Wheel arrangements Leading dimensions of nearly all the locomotives described in this book are set out in the following pages. A bibliography is then given of the books from which the leading dimensions have been taken. The wheel arrangement column needs special mention, for in this book the Whyte system is used. This was devised in the United States about 1900, and notes the number of locomotive wheels, first the leading carrying wheels, then the driving wheels and lastly the rear carrying wheels. Thus a six-coupled locomotive with no carrying wheels is an 0-6-0, while the Pacific type with a leading four-wheel bogie, six driving wheels and a rear two-wheel truck is a 4-6-2. The system can be used readily enough for articulated locomotives, eg 2-6-6-2, but where there is doubt as to which figures show the driving wheels it is customary to put in a plus sign between the articulated units, eg 2-6-0 + 0-6-2. The Whyte system is used in Great Britain, North America, Belgium and in countries that have been under their railway influence.

In France, other Latin countries and in Russia, instead of counting wheels the number of axles is noted. Thus the Whyte system 4-6-2 becomes 2-3-1 in France, frequently condensed to 231. Germany Central and eastern Europe and the Scandinavian countries use yet another system, similar to the French, but using a letter to show the driving wheels. Thus the Whyte 4-6-2 becomes 231 in France and 2C1 in Germany. The International Union of Railways (UIC) has standardised the German system internationally, and it is now used for electric and diesel locomotives. Thus an electric locomotive with two four-wheel bogies and all axles driven is a B-B or BB, while if each axle is driven by a separate electric motor the letter 'o' is added to make Bo-Bo. The German system is elaborated by more signs and letters, but space does not allow description here. The opposite page sets out various wheel arrangements in the different systems, the left-hand column showing the locomotive wheels symbolically.

Tractive efforts The power of steam locomotives can be compared by calculating the maximum tractive effort, the force exerted against the rails. This is expressed in pounds force (lbf) – as distinct from pounds weight – or kilograms force (kgf) or, nowadays increasingly, in kilonewtons (kN), a new international unit. Unfortunately railway systems have never agreed on a common basis for calculating tractive effort and all tractive efforts quoted in this book have therefore been re-calculated using the equations set out below. These equations are in common use in Great Britain and in North America, but the results they give may differ from 'official' figures in some cases, although it is helpful that all tractive efforts given are comparable directly.

For a two-cylinder non-superheated simple locomotive the tractive effort is given by: $TE = c^2 \times S \times 0.75 P/D$, where TE = tractive effort in lbf, c = diameter of cylinder in inches, S = stroke of cylinder in inches, P = boiler pressure in lb/in^2 and D = diameter of driving wheel in inches. For a superheated locomotive $0.85P$ is substituted for $0.75P$ in the equation to cover the greater effectiveness of superheated steam. For three-cylinder locomotives the result is multiplied by 1.5 and for four-cylinder by 2.0. By substituting centimetres for inches and kg/cm^2 for lb/in^2 the equation will give tractive effort in kgf, and can be converted to lbf by multiplying by 2.204.

Compound locomotives are another thing again and there are various equations. Among others one for a four-cylinder compound is as follows $TE = 1.7P \times c^2 \times S/(c^2/C^2 + 1) \times D$. Letter equivalents are as before, save that c = diameter of the HP cylinder and C = diameter of the LP cylinder. The equation will allow fair comparisons to be made between compound locomotives, but the results are not comparable with those for simple locomotives, unless an allowance of plus or minus 5 per cent is made. No allowance is made for superheating on compound locomotives.

Locomotive wheel arrangements

Wheels	French system	Whyte system	Name in the United States	German system
Oo	011	0-2-2		A1
oO	110	2-2-0		1A
oOo	111	2-2-2		1A1
ooO	210	4-2-0	Jervis	2A
ooOo	211	4-2-2	Bicycle	2A1
OO	020	0-4-0	Four-wheel switcher	B
OOo	021	0-4-2		B1
oOO	120	2-4-0		1B
oOOo	121	2-4-2	Columbia	1B1
ooOO	220	4-4-0	American	2B
ooOOo	221	4-4-2	Atlantic	2B1
ooOOoo	222	4-4-4	Reading	2B2
OOO	030	0-6-0	Six-wheel switcher	C
oOOO	130	2-6-0	Mogul	1C
oOOOo	131	2-6-2	Prairie	1C1
oOOOoo	132	2-6-4		1C2
ooOOO	230	4-6-0	Ten-wheeler	2C
ooOOOo	231	4-6-2	Pacific	2C1
ooOOOoo	232	4-6-4	Hudson	2C2
OOOO	040	0-8-0	Eight-wheel switcher	D
oOOOO	140	2-8-0	Consolidation	1D
oOOOOo	141	2-8-2	Mikado	1D1
oOOOOoo	142	2-8-4	Berkshire	1D2
ooOOOO	240	4-8-0	Mastodon	2D
ooOOOOo	241	4-8-2	Mountain	2D1
ooOOOOoo	242	4-8-4	Niagara	2D2
OOOOO	050	0-10-0	Ten-wheel switcher	E
oOOOOO	150	2-10-0	Decapod	1E
oOOOOOo	151	2-10-2	Santa-Fe	1E1
oOOOOOoo	152	2-10-4	Texas	1E2
ooOOOOO	250	4-10-0		2E
ooOOOOOo	251	4-10-2	Union Pacific	2E1
OOOOOO	060	0-12-0		F
oOOOOOO	160	2-12-0	Centipede	1F
ooOOOOOOo	261	4-12-2	Union Pacific	2F1

Articulated locomotive wheel arrangements

Wheels	French system	Whyte system	Name in the United States	German system
OOO-OOO	030 + 030	060 + 060	Erie	C + C
oOOO-OOOooo	130 + 033	260 + 066	Allegheny	1C + C3
ooOOO-OOOo	230 + 031	460 + 062	Southern Pacific (Cab Forward)	2C + C1
ooOOO-OOOoo	230 + 032	460 + 064	Challenger	2C + C2
oOOOO-OOOOoo	140 + 042	280 + 084	Yellowstone	1D + D2
ooOOOO-OOOOoo	240 + 042	480 + 084	Big Boy	2D + D2

LEADING DIMENSIONS

Page	Locomotive	Country	Year	Builder	Railway
10	Trevithick's	GB	1804	R. Trevithick	Pen-y-Daren Railway
10	Prince Royal	GB	1812	Fenton & Murray	Middleton Railway
11	Puffing Billy	GB	1813	W. Hedley	Wylam
11	Locomotion	GB	1825	R. Stephenson & Co.	Stockton & Darlington Railway
12	Killingworth	GB	1816	G. Stephenson	Wylam colliery
12	Royal George	GB	1827	Shildon	Stockton & Darlington Railway
12	Lancashire Witch	GB	1828	R. Stephenson & Co.	Bolton & Leigh Railway
13	Agenoria	GB	1829	Foster, Rastrick	Shutt End colliery
13	Novelty	GB	1829	Braithwaite	Liverpool & Manchester Railway
14	Sanspareil	GB	1829	Shildon	Liverpool & Manchester Railway
14	Rocket	GB	1829	R. Stephenson & Co.	Liverpool & Manchester Railway
15	—	F	1827	R. Stephenson & Co.	St Etienne - Andrézieux
15	—	F	1829	M. Seguin	St Etienne - Andrézieux
17	Tom Thumb	USA	1830	P. Cooper	Baltimore & Ohio Railroad
18	Best Friend of Charleston	USA	1830	West Point Foundry	South Carolina & Hamburg Railroad
19	De Witt Clinton	USA	1831	West Point Foundry	Mohawk & Hudson Railroad
20	John Bull	USA	1831	R. Stephenson & Co.	Camden & Amboy Railroad
20	Experiment	USA	1831	West Point Foundry	Mohawk & Hudson Railroad
21	Monster	USA	1834	R. Stevens & I. Dripp	Camden & Amboy Railroad
21	Atlantic	USA	1832	R. Winans	Baltimore & Ohio Railroad
21	Mazeppa	USA	1837	R. Winans	Baltimore & Ohio Railroad
21	Buffalo	USA	1842	Baldwin	Western Railroad of Massachusetts
22	Cambell	USA	1837	Brooks	Philadelphia, Germanstown & Norriston Railroad
23	George Washington	USA	1834	W. Norris	Philadelphia & Reading Railroad
23	Lafayette	USA	1837	W. Norris	Baltimore & Ohio Railroad
23	Virginia	USA	1842	W. Norris	Winchester & Potomac Railroad
24	Hercules	USA	1837	Garrett & Eastwick	Beaver Meadow Railroad
24	Gowan & Marx	USA	1839	Eastwick & Harrison	Philadelphia & Reading Railroad
24	—	USA	1842	Baldwin	Central of Georgia Railway
25	—	USA	1846	Baldwin	Camden & Amboy Railroad
25	Atlas	USA	1846	Baldwin	Philadelphia & Reading Railroad
25	Chesapeake	USA	1847	S. Norris	Philadelphia & Reading Railroad
26	—	USA	1848	Swinburne	New York & Erie Railroad
27	Camel	USA	1848	R. Winans	Baltimore & Ohio Railroad
27	—	USA	1850	Baldwin	Various
27	—	USA	1851	Amoskeag Manufacturing	Chicago & Aurora Railroad
30	Planet	GB	1830	R. Stephenson & Co.	Liverpool & Manchester Railway
30	Austria	A	1837	R. Stephenson & Co.	Kaiser Ferdinands Nordbahn
31	Liverpool	GB	1830	E. Bury	Liverpool & Manchester Railway
31	—	GB	1837	E. Bury	London & Birmingham Railway
32	Hercules	GB	1833	R. Stephenson & Co.	Stanhope & Tyne Railway
32	Atlas	GB	1834	R. Stephenson & Co.	Leicester & Swannington Railway
32	Lion	GB	1838	Todd, Kitson & Laird	Liverpool & Manchester Railway
33	Patentee	GB	1833	R. Stephenson & Co.	Liverpool & Manchester Railway
33	Nordstern	A	1838	G & J Rennie	Kaiser Ferdinands Nordbahn
34	Adler	D	1835	R. Stephenson & Co.	Nuremburg-Fürth Railway

Wheel arrange-ment	Cylinders diam by stroke (mm)	Boiler pressure (kg/cm²)	Driving wheel diam (mm)	Grate area (m²)	Heating surface (m²)	Weight		Coupled wheel-base (mm)	Total wheel-base (mm)	Length over buffers (mm)	Page
						Work order (tonnes)	Adhesive (tonnes)				
0-4-0	1/210 × 1372	2·8	1092			5·1	5·1	1600	1600		10
0-4-0	2/203 × 610	3·9			5·56	4·1		2438	2438		10
0-4-0	2/229 × 914	3·3	991	0·56	7·15			1900	1900		11
0-4-0	2/241 × 610	1·7	1219		5·56	6·7	~ 6·7	1578	1578	7315	11
0-4-0	2/229 × 610		965								12
0-6-0	2/279 × 508	3·5	1219	0·52	13·10						12
0-4-0	2/229 × 610		1219	1·12	6·08	7·0	~ 7·0	1524	1524		12
0-4-0	2/216 × 914		1238			11·0					13
2-2-0	2/152 × 305		1270	0·17	3·95	3·1					13
0-4-0	2/178 × 483		1372	0·93	8·36	4·9					14
0-2-2	2/203 × 432	3·5	1435	0·56	13·28	4·3	2·5		2184	6558	14
0-4-0	2/220 × 660	3·5	1219			9·4	9·4				15
0-4-0	2/230 × 590	3·0	1213	0·65	22·18	6·0	6·0		1473		15
2-2-0	2/ 89 × 356					~ 1·0					17
0-4-0	2/152 × 406	3·5	1371			~ 4·5	~ 4·5				18
0-4-0	2/140 × 406		1372								19
0-4-0	2/279 × 508	2·1	1372	0·93	27·85	~ 10·5	~ 10·5	1524	1524	11278	20
4-2-0	2/241 × 406		1524			~ 7·0					20
0-8-0	2/457 × 762		1219			27·6	27·6				21
0-4-0	2/318 × 610	5·5	914			~ 12·0	·~ 8 6				21
0-8-0	2/432 × 610					23·5					21
0-4-0	2/305 × 559	5·2	889			~ 8·5	~ 8·5	1245	1245		22
4-4-0	2/356 × 406	6·3	1372		67·17	~ 12·0	~ 8·0				22
4-2-0	2/260 × 448	4·2	1219			6·8	4·1		2413		23
4-2-0	2/267 × 457	4·2	1220	0·80	37·62	12·5	5·8			9250	23
4-4-0	2/318 × 508		1219			13·5	9·0				23
4-4-0	2/305 × 457	6·3	1117			14·0					24
4-4-0	2/305 × 406	5·6	1067			~ 11·0	~ 9·0				24
0-6-0	2/381 × 457					8·3	6·8	1844	1844		24
4-4-0	2/349 × 457		1524								25
0-8-0	2/445 × 457		1066			22·5	22·5				25
4-6-0	2/368 × 559		1168			19·9	14·5				25
4-4-0	2/419 × 508	5·6	1829			20·9	13·1				26
0-8-0	2/432 × 559		1092	2·50		21·8	21·8	3505	3505		27
0-8-0	2/457 × 510		1016			32·4	32·4	5921	5921		27
4-4-0	2/356 × 508	4·9	1219			17·2	12·2				27
2-2-0	2/279 × 406		1524			8·0	5·0				30
2-2-0	2/254 × 406	3·5	1524	0·54	28·12	9·1			1524	8900	30
0-4-0			1830								31
2-2-0	2/280 × 415		1546	0·66	33·18	10·0	5·7				31
0-4-2	2/356 × 457	3·5	1372	0·87	47·18	14·0	9·6	3022			32
0-6-0	2/406 × 508	3·5	1372	0·95	61·20	17·0	17·0	3543	3543		32
0-4-2	2/305 × 457	3·5	1524								32
2-2-2	2/279 × 457	3·5	1676	0·85	33·82	11·6	4·4		3048		33
2-2-2	2/351 × 435	5·4	1831	0·88	49·74	14·5	6·4		3372	10200	33
2-2-2	2/229 × 406	3·3	1372	0·48	18·20	14·2	6·0				34

LEADING DIMENSIONS

Page	Locomotive	Country	Year	Builder	Railway
34	Le Belge	B	1835	J. Cockerill	Belgian State Railway
35	Bayard	I	1839	Longridge & Starbuck	Bayard Co Railway
35	Gironde	F	1840	Le Creusot	Paris-Versailles rive droite
35	Der Münchener	D	1841	Maffei	Munich-Augsburg Railway
36	No 3	F	1838	Sharp, Roberts & Co.	Northern Railways
36	Phoenix	A	1841	E. Kessler	Kaiser Ferdinands Nordbahn
36	Badenia	D	1839	Sharp, Roberts & Co.	Baden State Railway
36	Sharp-type	GB	1843		Sheffield & Manchester
37	Odin	DK	1846	Sharp, Roberts & Co.	The Zealand Railway
38	North Star	GB	1837	R. Stephenson & Co.	Great Western Railway
38	Iron Duke	GB	1847	Swindon Works	Great Western Railway
38	Lord of the Isles	GB	1851	Swindon Works	Great Western Railway
39	L'Aigle	F	1846	R. Stephenson & Co.	Avignon-Marseilles Railway
39	Sézanne	F	1847	A. Hallette	Montereau-Troyes Railway
40	Tarasque	F	1846	Le Benet	Avignon-Marseilles Railway
40	No 17-50	F	1846	Cail	Northern Railways
40	Ernst August	D	1846	G. Egestorff	Hanover State Railway
41	No 345	F	1846	Schneider	Centre Railway
41	Glück Auf	D	1848	R. Hartmann	Saxony-Bavaria Railway
42	No 19	GB	1845	Crewe Works	London & North Western Railway
42	Saint Pierre	F	1844	Buddicom & Allcard	Paris-Rouen Railway
42	Perraches	F	1847	Cail	Lyons Railway
43	Jenny Lind	GB	1847	E.B. Wilson	London, Brighton & South Coast Railway
43	Prussia	D	1839	W. Norris	Berlin-Potsdam Railway
44	Columbus	A	1838	W. Norris	Kaiser Ferdinands Nordbahn
44	Ganymed	A	1846	W. Günther	Kaiser Ferdinands Nordbahn
44	Koloss	A	1844	W. Günther	Kaiser Ferdinands Nordbahn
45	—	D	1846	E. Kessler	Wurtemburg State Railway
45	No 61	I	1846	W. Norris	Royal Neapolitan Railroad
46	Borsig	D	1841	Borsig	Berlin-Anhalt Railway
46	Beuth	D	1843	Borsig	Berlin-Anhalt Railway
46	Drache	D	1848	Henschel	North Hesse Railway
47	Steinbrück	A	1848	Haswell	Southern State Railway
47	Limmat	CH	1847	E. Kessler	Zurich-Baden Railway
48	Namur	B	1845	Tulk & Ley	Namur-Liège Railway
48	Liverpool	GB	1848	Bury, Curtis & Kennedy	London & North Western Railway
48	John Stevens	USA	1849	W. Norris	Camden & Amboy Railroad
49	No 165-170	F	1849	Cail	Northern Railways
49	Le Continent	F	1852	Cail	Eastern Railways
49	Die Palfz	D	1853	Maffei	Palatinate Railway
51	Matarò	E	1848	Jones & Potts	Barcelona-Matarò Railway
52	Chiabrera	I	1853	J. Cockerill	Piedmont State Railways
52	L'Auroch	F	1854	Ivry Works	Paris-Orleans Railway
53	Bloomer	GB	1854	Sharp, Roberts & Co.	London & North Western Railway
53	No 215	GB	1853	R. & W. Hawthorn	Great Northern Railway
53	No 2002	GB	1868	Bristol Works	Bristol & Exeter Railway

Wheel arrange-ment	Cylinders diam by stroke (mm)	Boiler pressure (kg/cm²)	Driving wheel diam (mm)	Grate area (m²)	Heating surface (m²)	Weight		Coupled wheel-base (mm)	Total wheel-base (mm)	Length over buffers (mm)	Page
						Work order (tonnes)	Adhesive (tonnes)				
2-2-2	2/279 × 457	5·0	1520	0·86	33·59	12·0	4·8				34
2-2-2	2/356 × 425	3·5	1680	0·98	37·32	13·0					35
2-2-2	2/330 × 460		1670	1·02	50·48	15·5	7·3				35
2-2-2	2/306 × 457	6·0	1524	0·90	46·00	14·3	5·9		3200	5817	35
2-2-2	2/406 × 508	5·2	1676	1·17	85·41	12·5					36
2-2-2	2/327 × 461	5·4	1700	1·03	45·10	15·6	8·0		3470	9100	36
2-2-2	2/330 × 457	4·5	1680	0·90	42·50	16·2	6·1		3354		36
2-2-2											36
2-2-2	2/381 × 508	5·0	1524	1·00	77·20	20·0	12·5		3861	11650	37
2-2-2	2/406 × 406	4·2	2448	1·25	66·05	21·1	9·8		4064		38
4-2-2	2/457 × 610	7·0	2438	2·14	165·80	36·0	12·5			14066	38
4-2-2	2/457 × 610	7·0	2438	2·00	166·31	38·8	14·2				38
2-2-2	2/330 × 610	6·0	1700	0·83	58·00	22·1	10·1		3150	6966	39
2-2-2	2/340 × 550	6·0	1690	0·86	62·90	26·1	8·4			7115	39
4-2-0	2/380 × 560	6·0	1650	0·83	58·00	26·8	12·7		4050		40
2-2-2	2/360 × 560	6·5	1680	0·91	75·50	23·7	11·2		4600		40
2-2-2	2/356 × 559	4·7	1524	0·80	78·00	21·8	8·8				40
2-4-0	2/380 × 600	7·0	1600	0·84	78·84	22·7	22·7		3300		41
2-4-0	2/356 × 560	5·5	1500	1·0	80·62	24·0		1600	3181	6705	41
2-2-2	2/330 × 508	4·6	1829	0·97	73·54	16·2					42
2-2-2	2/318 × 533		1600	0·86	48·52	18·9	6·6		3377		42
2-2-2	2/380 × 600	6	1800	0·92	79·00	25·3	11·4		4010		42
2-2-2	2/381 × 508	8·4	1829	1·13	74·35	24·2	8·7		4115		43
4-2-0	2/267 × 457	3·2	1219	0·80	37·62	12·5	5·8			6187	43
4-2-0	2/267 × 406	3·5	1219	0·80	37·62	12·5	5·8		2750	9250	44
4-2-0	2/369 × 553	5·4	1264		59·90	17·6	10·4			10800	44
2-4-0	2/382 × 562	5·4	1185		68·10	28·9	17·4	2400	3529	12150	44
4-4-0	2/354 × 561	6·3	1380	0·81	59·06	22·0	11·0	1665	4455	7275	45
4-4-0	2/356 × 558	6	1527	0·88	66·46	21·8	15·9	1600	5505	12790	45
4-2-2	2/279 × 457	5·8	1372	0·85	36·24	19·2	9·6		4200		46
2-2-2	2/330 × 558	5·5	1525	0·83	46·60	18·5	9·1		3813		46
4-4-0	2/381 × 610	6·3	1524								46
4-4-0	2/368 × 579	5·5	1422	0·94	70·60	22·7	15·0		3872		47
4-2-0	2/362 × 559	6	1320	0·91	57·36	29·8	9·1	2490	2800	11810	47
4-2-0	2/406 = 508	6	2134	1·35	91·88	22·0	10·5		3962		48
6-2-0	2/457 × 610	8·4	2438	2·00	212·75	35·6	12·2		5639		48
6-2-0	2/330 × 965		2438	1·84		25·0			5050		48
4-2-0	2/400 × 500	6·5	2100	1·42	98·40	28·9	12·6		4860		49
4-2-0			2300			27·3	10·3			13515	49
4-2-0	2/356 × 610	6·3	1830	0·98	68·60	24·2	9·2		3962		49
2-2-2	2/350 × 500	6·0	1823			26·0				11880	51
4-4-0	2/406 × 610	7	1265	1·00	82·80	27·3	21·2	1505	3700	13362	52
0-6-0	2/420 × 650	8	1390	1·21	133·14	30·6	30·6	3660	3660		52
2-2-2	2/406 × 559	10·5	2134		134·51	30·9	12·5		5081		53
4-2-2	2/431 × 610	8·4	2286	1·88	159·80	37·5	14·0		6616		53
4-2-4	2/457 × 610		2743	2·15	114·60	50·8	18·8		7772		53

LEADING DIMENSIONS

Page	Locomotive	Country	Year	Builder	Railway
54	Lüneburg	D	1863	G. Egestorff	Brunswick State Railway
54	Corsair	GB	1849	Swindon Works	Great Western Railway
54	Heidelberg	D	1854	Esslingen	Wurtemburg State Railway
55	Kufstein	D	1853	Maffei	Bavarian State Railway
55	Toess	CH	1854	Maffei	North Eastern Railway
55	Dx class	GB	1855	Crewe Works	London & North Western Railway
56	Sampierdarena	I	1854	Ansaldo	Piedmont State Railways
56	Raigmore	GB	1855	R. & W. Hawthorn	Inverness & Nairn Railway
56	L'Aigle	F	1855	Gouin	Western Railway
57	Express	IND	1856	Kitson, Thompson & Hewittson	East Indian Railway
57	No 61-68	I	1858	Gouin	Victor Emanuel Co.
57	No 1224-1243	F	1856	Nîmes Works	Paris, Lyons & Mediterranean Railway
57	No 246-313	E	1857	E.B. Wilson	Madrid, Saragossa & Alicante Railway
58	No 720-791	F	1855	Paris-Orleans Works	Paris-Orleans Railway
58	General	USA	1855	Rogers	Western & Atlantic Railroad
59	Allan type	GB	1855	Crewe Works	London & North Western Railway
59	Chillon	CH	1857	Karlsruhe Works	Western Railway
59	Phantom	USA	1857	Mason	Toledo & Illinois Railroad
60	No 81-100	F	1857	Koechlin	Bourbonnais Co.
60	No 501-540	CH	1858	Cail	Western Railway
60	Einkorn	D	1859	Esslingen	Wurtemburg State Railway
61	Prins August	S	1856	Beyer, Peacock	Södra Railway
61	Zürich	D	1858	Borsig	Leipzig-Dresden Railway
61	No 9-14	E	1859	Slaughter, Gruning	Tarragona, Barcelona & France Railway
62	Olten	CH	1854	Esslingen	Swiss Central Railway
62	Nembo	I	1857	Beyer, Peacock	Lombardy-Venetian Railroad
62	Lady of the Lake	GB	1862	Crewe Works	London & North Western Railway
63	Atlanta	GB	1859	Nine Elms Works	London & South Western Railway
63	Connor single	GB	1859	St Rollox Works	Caledonian Railway
63	—	USA	1858	Danforth, Cooke	Delaware, Lackawanna & Western Railroad
64	No 467-539	A	1859	Esslingen	Südbahn
64	Class 29	A	1860	StEG	Südbahn
64	Kopernicus	D	1860	Esslingen	Hesse Railway
65	Romont	CH	1862	Esslingen	Lausanne-Freiberg-Berne Railway
65	No 236-250	F	1862	Paris-Orleans Works	Paris-Orleans Railway
66	No 1-150 (Byciclette)	F	1855	Cail	Western Railway
66	Rahuenstein	A	1857	StEG	Südbahn
66	Ilmarinen	SF	1860	Canada Works	Helsinki-Hämeenlinna Railway
67	Caroline	N	1861	R. Stephenson & Co.	Norwegian Trunk Railway
67	—	GB	1862	R. Stephenson & Co.	Great North of Scotland Railway
68	Rakete II	A	1862	G Sigl	Kaiser Ferdinand Nordbahn
68	Munin	S	1864	Beyer, Peacock	Swedish State Railway
68	Rigi	CH	1863	Esslingen	Zurich-Zug-Lucerne Railway
69	No 624 (RA 3202)	I	1873	Pietrarsa Works	Roman Railroad
69	Class 28	B	1864	Cockerill	Belgian State Railway
69	Hertha	DK	1864	Esslingen	The Zealand Railway

Wheel arrangement	Cylinders diam by stroke (mm)	Boiler pressure (kg/cm²)	Driving wheel diam (mm)	Grate area (m²)	Heating surface (m²)	Weight		Coupled wheel-base (mm)	Total wheel-base (mm)	Length over buffers (mm)	Page
						Work order (tonnes)	Adhesive (tonnes)				
2-2-2	2/381 × 559	7	1830	1·19	91·24	27·7	12·8		4467		54
4-4-0	2/432 × 610	8·4	1824	1·77	117·0	36·4	21·6	2335	5537		54
4-4-0	2/381 × 561	7	1842	0·89	67·82	27·8	14·3				54
2-2-2	2/301 × 559	7	1694	1·10	78·00	23·0	9·5				55
4-4-0	2/381 × 559	9	1676	1·10	83·00	43·7	14·2	1830	4710	12980	55
0-6-0	2/432 × 610	8·4	1575	1·39	102·90	27·4	27·4	4724	4724		55
0-4-2	2/406 × 559	7·0	1555	1·10	83·4	27·4	20·3	2132	7239	12700	56
2-2-2	2/381 × 508		1829								56
2-4-0	2/420 × 826		2840								56
2-2-2	2/305 × 559	8·4	1803	1·12	71·80		10·0				57
2-4-0	2/420 × 600	9	1680	1·21	93·00	27·3	19·2		3300	7980	57
0-6-0	2/430 × 640	8·0	1390	1·14	111·00	32·0	32·0	3430	3430	8020	57
0-6-0	2/440 × 600	8	1430	1·32	111·13	28·2	28·2	3430	3430		57
0-6-0	2/420 × 650	7·5	1390	1·21	135·60	30·5	30·5	3520	3520		58
4-4-0	2/381 × 610	6	1727			26·3	18·1				58
2-4-0	2/387 × 508	7	1860	1·23	74·88	23·4	16·5	2337	4115		59
2-4-0	2/408 × 612	8	1690	1·0	95·0	40·2	18·1		3585	13650	59
4-4-0	2/381 × 559		1680					2133	6317	12865	59
0-6-0	2/450 × 650	8	1300	1·32	166·0	31·5	31·5	3370	3370	8540	60
0-6-0	2/450 × 650	9	1320	1·40	133·5	50·3	32·3	3370	3370	14550	60
4-4-0	2/410 × 610										60
2-4-0	2/394 × 508	7	1684	1·38	66·60	23·2	18·3		4141	12714	61
2-2-2	2/380 × 560	7	1830	1·10	83·09	27·8	11·6				61
4-4-0	2/420 × 560	10	1920	1·35	95·54	36·1	22·4	2660	5930		61
0-4+6	2/408 × 561	9	1375	0·90	100·90	45·0	26·0		2250	10941	62
2-2-2	2/400 × 508	7	1885	1·31	91·5	29·5	13·2		4585	13500	62
2-2-2	2/406 × 610	8·4	2324	1·39	102·00	27·4	11·7		4674		62
2-4-0	2/381 × 533		1981	1·49	71·44	28·9	9·6				63
2-2-2	2/444 × 610	8·4	2489	1·41	100·46	30·7	14·6		4775		63
4-4-0	2/432 × 559		1680			21·7	14·5	2184	6312	14430	63
2-4-0	2/411 × 632	6·5	1500	1·38	180·00	32·5	22·5		3477		64
0-6-0	2/460 × 632	9	1245	1·59	109·00	38·0	38·0	2950	2950		64
2-2-2	2/381 × 561	7	1680	0·90	77·50	25·0	11·5				64
4-4-0	2/410 × 612	8	1374	1·20	103·8	41·0	27·0		6090	10120	65
2-2-2	2/400 × 650	7·5	2040	1·34	105·46	29·5	12·9		4300		65
2-4-0	2/420 × 560	8·5	1660	1·04		37·0			3440	8125	66
4-4-0	2/395 × 580	6·5	1580	1·10	94·00	31·0					66
4-4-0	2/406 × 508	8·5	1524	1·11	89·70	28·9	17·8		11861	14360	66
2-4-0	2/305 × 508		1435								67
4-4-0	2/406 × 559	9·8	1689								67
2-2-2	2/395 × 632	5·4	1982	1·20	106·70	31·5	14·2		4584	14253	68
2-2-2	2/381 × 508	7·0	1874	1·30	77·30	24·8	12·0		4268	12470	68
0-4+6	2/431 × 686	10·0	1370	1·40	106·20	52·0 *	26·0	2438	2438	12770	68
0-6-0	2/450 × 650	9·0	1330	1·35	126·58	34·8	34·8	3470	3470	14227	69
0-6-0	2/450 × 600	8·3	1450		109·38	38·8	38·8	4000	4000	9338	69
2-4-0	2/381 × 610	9·0	1638	1·20	73·90	30·7	19·1	2400	4200	13144	69

LEADING DIMENSIONS

Page	Locomotive	Country	Year	Builder	Railway
70	—	GB	1865	Ashford Works	South Eastern Railway
71	Class A	GB	1864	Beyer, Peacock	Metropolitan Railway
72	No 201-212	F	1864	Ivry Works	Paris-Orleans Railway
72	No 2451-2551	F	1867	Fives Lille	Northern Railways
72	Herford	D	1866	Haswell	Cologne-Minden Railway
73	No 401-426	F	1867	Epernay Works	Eastern Railways
73	Landwürhden	D	1867	Krauss	Oldenburg State Railway
73	Class A3	SF	1869	Dübs & Co.	Rühimäki-Linjalla Railway
73	Class D	IND	1867	Neilson & Co.	East Indian Railway
74	800 class	GB	1870	Neilson & Co.	Midland Railway
74	8 ft singles	GB	1870	Doncaster Works	Great Northern Railway
75	Ventnor	GB	1868	Beyer, Peacock	Isle of Wight Railway
75	Jura	GB	1866	Neilson & Co.	London, Chatham & Dover Railway
77	Alb	D	1849	Esslingen	Wurtemburg State Railway
78	Bavaria	D	1851	Maffei	Southern State Railway
78	Vindobona	A	1851	Haswell	Southern State Railway
78	Seraing	A	1851	Cockerill	Southern State Railway
79	Wiener Neustadt	A	1851	W. Günther	Southern State Railway
79	Mastadons of the Giovi	I	1853	Cockerill	Piedmont State Railways
80	Kapellen	A	1853	Cockerill	Southern State Railway
80	—	CH	1854	Esslingen	Swiss Central Railway
80	No 360-399	F	1856	Schneider	Northern Railways
81	La Rampe	F	1859	Koechlin	Paris, Lyons & Mediterranean Railway
81	Petiet type	F	1862	Gouin	Northern Railways
82	Steyerdorf	H	1862	StEG	Austrian State Railways Co.
82	No 2571-2590	E	1865	Avonside Engine Co.	Barcelona-Saragossa-Pamplona Railway
82	Cantal	F	1867	Ivry Works	Paris-Orleans Railway
83	—	GB	1885	Boston Lodge Works	Festiniog Railway
83	Escalador de Montes	PE	1873	Avonside Engine Co.	Chimbote-Huallanca Railway
83	Class R	NZ	1877	Avonside Engine Co.	Dunedin & Port Chalmers Railway
84	—	E	1878	Sharp, Stewart	Tarragona, Barcelona & France Railway
84	No 2205-2210	ZA	1874	R. Stephenson & Co.	Cape Government Railway
85	—	CH	1872	SLM Winterthur	Gotthard Railway
85	—	CH	1871	Esslingen	Swiss Central Railway
85	—	CH	1882	Maffei	Gotthard Railway
86	No 4001-4165	F	1868	Various	Paris, Lyons & Mediterranean Railway
86	Class A	IND	1881	Sharp, Stewart	Darjeeling Himalayan Railway
87	No 1-2	CH	1870	Olten Works	Rigi Railway
87	Class Bhm	CH	1886	SLM Winterthur	Pilatus Railway
89	William Crooks	USA	1861	New Jersey Locomotive	St Paul & Pacific Railroad
90	Pennsylvania	USA	1863	Railway's Shops	Philadelphia & Reading Railroad
90	Consolidation	USA	1866	Baldwin	Lehigh Valley Railroad
91	America	USA	1867	Grant Locomotive	Chicago, Rock Island & Pacific Railroad
91	Seminole	USA	1867	Rogers Locomotive	Union Pacific Railroad
92	Genoa	USA	1872	Baldwin	Virginia & Truckee Railroad
93	San Juan	USA	1878	W Mason	Denver, South Park & Pacific Railroad

Wheel arrangement	Cylinders diam by stroke (mm)	Boiler pressure (kg/cm^2)	Driving wheel diam (mm)	Grate area (m^2)	Heating surface (m^2)	Weight Work order (tonnes)	Adhesive (tonnes)	Coupled wheelbase (mm)	Total wheelbase (mm)	Length over buffers (mm)	Page
2-2-2	2/432 × 559	9·1	2133			33·5	12·5		5258		70
4-4-0	2/432 × 610	9·1	1753	1·76	94·20	42·7	32·9	2692	6325	9527	71
2-4-0	2/420 × 650	8·5	2026	1·40	136·00	34·0	29·8	2100	4000		72
0-4-2	2/420 × 560	8·0	1800	1·52	82·37	32·4	23·0	2150	4400		72
2-4-0	2/457 × 610	8·0	1581	1·58	120·11	34·7	26·1				72
0-6-0	2/440 × 660	8·0	1400	1·31	121·05	33·0	33·0	3580	3580		73
0-4-0	2/360 × 560	10·0	1520	1·00	75·00	27·0	27·0	2660	2660	7537 □	73
4-4-0	2/406 × 508	8·5	1705	1·24	81·75	35·4	22·8		11125	13688	73
0-6-0	2/432 × 610	8·2	1524	1·67	117·20	34·5	34·5				73
2-4-0	2/457 × 610	9·8	2057	1·63	113·80	40·5		2591	5029	15244	74
4-2-2	2/457 × 711	9·8	2463	1·64	108·23	39·1			6985	15608	74
2-4-0	2/381 × 508	8·4	1524			30·9					75
0-4-2	2/432 × 610		1676			42·1					75
0-6-0	2/447 × 612	7·0	1270	0·90	97·00	33·5	33·5	3580	3580		77
0-8-0	2/510 × 760	6·8	1070	1·80	157·54	44·0	44·0	6335	11992		78
0-8-0	2/421 × 580	6·8	957	1·45	159·44	45·5	45·5	4742	4742		78
0-4-4-0	4/407 × 711	5·8	1049	2 × 1·00	2 × 170·95	49·4	49·4	2 × 2134	8204		78
0-4-4-0	4/329 × 632	6·8	1120	1·66	175·12	44·0	44·0	2 × 2312	8159		79
0-4+4-0	4/335 × 559	7·0	1075	2 × 1·08	2 × 65·4	2 × 28·0	2 × 28·0	2 × 2590	10148	14502	79
0-6+2	2/475 × 610	7·4	1068	1·28	140·50	56·0	39·0	2292	5997	10399	80
0-4+6	2/408 × 561	9·0	1375	0·90	100·90	45·0	26·0	2250	6525	10941	80
0-8+4	2/500 × 660	8·0	1258	1·94	197·00	62·8	42·3	3950	8700	13193	80
0-8+6	2/540 × 560	7·0	1200	1·89	172·93	70·8	47·3	3900	9600		81
2-6-2	4/360 × 340	8·5	1600	2·61	166·00	49·0	23·0				81
0-6+4	2/461 × 632	7·0	1000	1·44	121·50	42·5	42·5	10500	10500	17093	82
0-8-0	2/505 × 610		1295			74·8 ★				15400 □	82
0-10-0	2/500 × 600	8·0	1070	2·08	227·48	59·6	59·6	4532	4532	10126	82
0-4-4-0	4/229 × 355	11·2	844	1·12	82·6	28·7	28·7	2 × 1424	6009		83
0-6-6-0	4/439 × 457					46·0	46·0				83
0-6-4	2/311 × 406	9·1	914	1·11	56·50	30·5		2057	6502		83
0-8-0	2/508 × 660	8·0	1388	2·61	137·14	47·7	47·7	4615	4615		84
2-6-2	2/381 × 508	9·1	970	1·02	69·68	29·2		2438	3734	8230	84
0-4-0	2/360 × 600	10·0	1330	1·10	80·50	29·0	29·0	2600	2600	8612	85
0-6-0	2/421 × 632	9·0	1265	1·70	127·90	52·0 ★	35·6	3320	3320	14220	85
0-8-0	2/520 × 610	10·0	1170	2·10	158·00	79·1 ★	52·8	3900	3900	14870	85
0-8-0	2/540 × 660	9·0	1260	2·08	199·00	51·7	51·7	4050	4050	10090	86
0-4-0	2/203 × 356	9·8	660	0·50	24·50	11·0	11·0	2514	2514	6426	86
0-4-0	2/270 × 400	10·0	637	0·90	39·50	12·5		3000	3000	6375	87
0-4-0	2/220 × 300	12·0	409	0·40	19·30	12·0		6120	6120	10300	87
4-4-0	2/305 × 559	7·7	1600			46·3		2134	6071	15310 □	89
0-12-0	2/508 × 660		1092	2·90	130·00	50·0	50·0	5969	5969		90
2-8-0	2/508 × 610		1219	2·32		39·0		4005	6095		90
4-4-0	2/406 × 539	8·5	1702	1·45	88·24	28·8	18·6	2482	6794		91
4-4-0	2/406 × 559	9·1	1372	1·35	92·50	27·0					91
4-4-0	2/432 × 559	9·5	1448			31·7	20·4	2438	4160	15291	92
2-6-6	2/330 × 406		940			19·9					93

LEADING DIMENSIONS

Page	Locomotive	Country	Year	Builder	Railway
93	Uncle Dick	USA	1878	Baldwin	New Mexico & Southern Pacific Railroad
93	No 5000	USA	1880	Baldwin	Philadelphia & Reading Railroad
94	El Gobernador	USA	1884	Sacramento Works	Central Pacific Railroad
94	No 7	USA	1884	Baldwin	New York, Philadelphia & Norfolk Railroad
95	Class R	USA	1885	Altoona Works	Pennsylvania Railroad
95	Mogul Type	USA	1888	Baldwin	Atchison, Topeka & Santa Fe Railway
95	Buena Vista	USA	1887	Baldwin	Denver & Rio Grande Railroad
96	No 293	USA	1887	Baldwin	Pennsylvania & New York Railroad
96	No 23	USA	1887	Schenectady	Colorado Midland Railway
97	Compound	USA	1889	Schenectady	Chicago, Milwaukee & St Paul Railway
97	No 593	USA	1890	Baldwin	Philadelphia & Reading Railroad
97	No 999	USA	1893	Railway's Shops	New York Central & Hudson River Railroad
99	—	IRL	1866	Inchicore Works	Great Southern & Western Railway
100	Pythagoras	A	1870	G. Sigl	Austrian North Western Railway
100	Metz	D	1871	Borsig	Cologne-Minden Railway
101	Humboldt	A	1871	Floridsdorf	Austrian North Western Railway
101	No 224	GB	1871	Cowlairs Works	North British Railway
101	Class 901	GB	1872	Gateshead Works	North Eastern Railway
102	Wörth	D	1872	Hartmann	Saxon State Railway
102	—	CH	1870	Schwartzkopff	Swiss North Eastern Railway
102	Rittinger	A	1873	G. Sigl	Austrian North Western Railway
102	Weipert	D	1872	Hartmann	Saxon State Railway
103	Class A4	SF	1872	Baldwin	Hyvinkää-Hanko Railway
103	'Terrier' Class	GB	1872	Brighton Works	London, Brighton & South Coast Railway
104	Minos	A	1873	Floridsdorf	Kaiser Ferdinands Nordbahn
104	Andaluces	E	1877	Hartmann	Andalusian Railway
105	—	GB	1873	Kilmarnock Works	Glasgow & South Western Railway
105	Europe	GB	1873	Sharp, Stewart	London, Chatham & Dover Railway
105	Livingstone	A	1874	Floridsdorf	Austrian North Western Railway
106	Anglet	F	1873	Schneider	Bayonne-Biarritz Railway
106	Ardross	GB	1876	Inverness Works	Highland Railway
107	Gylfe	DK	1875	Esslingen	The Zealand Railway
107	Sträken	S	1874	Borsig	Swedish State Railways
107	Webb's Precursor Class	GB	1874	Crewe Works	London & North Western Railway
108	No 265-390	F	1876	Ivry Works	Paris-Orleans Railway
108	Outrance	F	1877	Société Alsacienne	Northern Railways
109	Class 79	AUS	1877	Beyer, Peacock and Dübs	New South Wales Government Railway
109	Class P2	D	1877	Various	Royal Prussian Union Railway
110	Jungfrau Class	CH	1878	SLM Winterthur	Swiss Central Railway
110	Class 150	I	1881	Various	Adriatic System
110	No 31-90	F	1876	Railway's Works	Paris, Lyons & Mediterranean Railway
111	Class T3	D	1878	Various	Royal Prussian Union Railway
111	—	D	1880	Schichau	Royal Prussian Union Railway

Wheel arrange-ment	Cylinders diam by stroke (mm)	Boiler pressure (kg/cm²)	Driving wheel diam (mm)	Grate area (m²)	Heating surface (m²)	Weight Work order (tonnes)	Adhesive (tonnes)	Coupled wheel-base (mm)	Total wheel-base (mm)	Length over buffers (mm)	Page
2-8-0	2/508 × 660	9·8	1067			65·0					93
4-2-2	2/457 × 610	9·1	1981	5·00	130·10	38·6	15·9				93
4-10-0	2/533 × 660		1448			67·0			7607		94
4-4-0	2/457 × 610	9·6	1570	1·64		38·6					94
2-8-0	2/508 × 610	9·8	1270	2·90	160·90	51·9	45·6	4216	6629		95
2-6-0	2/457 × 610	10·2	1448			40·8		4577	7087	17018	95
4-6-0	2/457 × 610	9·8	1370			54·4					95
4-8-0	2/508 × 660	9·2	1280			50·9					96
4-6-0	2/457 × 660		1448			53·1		3657	6654	17513	96
4-6-2	HP 553 × 660	14·0	1981	3·10		66·0	40·8	4114	9227		97
	LP 787 × 660										
2-8-0	2/559 × 711	10·2	1283	7·06	126·07	66·5					97
4-4-0	2/483 × 610	12·7	2184	2·85	179·00	56·2	38.1	2591	7290	21239	97
0-6-0	2/457 × 610	11·2	1568			38·3					99
4-4-0	2/410 × 632	8·5	1580	1·70	133·00	36·0	24·0	1660	4175	14481	100
2-4-0	2/420 × 508	10·0	1981	1·57	124·43	42·0	26·0	2500	5690	15900	100
0-6-0	2/435 × 632	8·0	1185	1·70	137·00	34·1	34·1	3300	3300	14552	101
4-4-0	2/432 × 610	9·8	1981	1·58	93·38	37·6	24·6	2311			101
2-4-0	2/430 × 610	9·8	2156	1·50	111·56	40·1	27·5	2057	4902		101
2-4-0	2/407 × 560	8·5	1556	1·60	91·70	37·7	26·4				102
0-4-0	2/400 × 620	12·0	1580	1·50	87·60	44·7	25·2	2500	2500	12360	102
4-4-0	2/411 × 632	10·0	1900	1·64	107·60	39·5	23·0	2400	5370	14554	102
2-4-0	2/381 × 559	8·5	1390	1·13	88·90	35·5	27·1		3575		102
4-4-0	2/381 × 508	8·5	1575	1·21	67·10	30·0	18·2		12555○	14710	103
0-6-0	2/330 × 508	9·8	1194	0·93	48·12	31·3	31·3	3658	3658	7936	103
2-4-0	2/382 × 632	8·6	1976	1·90	115·20	31·2	12·3	2528	4425	14855	104
0-6-0	2/450 × 650		1300			56·3 ★					104
4-4-0	2/457 × 660	10·5	1829	1·42		40·6					105
2-4-0	2/432 × 610	9·8	1981	1·53	109·62	36·8		2515	4877	15261	105
4-4-0	2/410 × 632	10·0	1900	1·80	111·00	40·5	24·0	2300	5900	14866	105
0-4-2	HP 240 × 450	10·0	1200	1·00	45·10	19·3	15·2	1300	2700		106
	LP 400 × 450										
4-4-0	2/457 × 610	10·0	1905	1·50	112·87	43·7	28·1	2667	6556		106
0-4-2	2/406 × 559	9·0	1630	1·30	76·20	29·3	24·0	1778	3810	12950	107
2-4-0	2/394 × 559	10·0	1570	1·70	76·10	32·2	21·1	2071	3900	13290	107
2-4-0	2/432 × 610	9·8	1676	1·59	99·8	31·9	21·3	2515	4775	14341	107
2-4-2	2/440 × 650	9·0	2040	1·62	142·84	42·6	25·4	2100	5700	15800	108
4-4-0	432 × 610	10·0	2130	2·31	100·00	43·2	26·9	2500	6230		108
4-4-0	457 × 610	9·8	1676	1·86		75·4 ★					109
2-4-0	2/420 × 600	10·0	980	1·73	95·36	36·7	24·5	2500	4500	10645	109
2-6-0	2/420 × 600	10·0	1280	1·60	108·00	52·1	41·4	3400	5850	10865	110
4-4-0	2/432 × 610	10·0	1850	2·05	92·00	40·8	25·6	2450	6275	14993	110
2-4-2	2/500 × 650	9·0	2100	2·21	126·00	49·7	27·1	2097	5900		110
0-6-0	2/350 × 550	12·0	1100	1·35	60·00	32·3	32·3	2919	2919	3546	111
2-2-0	HP 200 × 400	12·0	1130	0·52	22·79	18·2	9·7		4000	8170	111
	LP 300 × 400										

LEADING DIMENSIONS

Page	Locomotive	Country	Year	Builder	Railway
111	Valkyrian	S	1886	Nydquist & Holm	Swedish State Railways
112	Gladstone Class	GB	1882	Brighton Works	London, Brighton & South Coast Railway
112	Class G	GB	1881	Brighton Works	London, Brighton & South Coast Railway
113	Southend	GB	1880	Sharp, Stewart	London, Tilbury & Southend Railway
113	Class K	NZ	1877	Rogers Locomotive	New Zealand Government Railways
114	Parthenay	F	1880	Schneider	State Railway, France
114	—	CH	1882	Olten Works	Swiss Central Railway
114	—	I	1882	Borsig	Meridionali Railroad
115	Class TO	D	1883	Henschel	Royal Prussian Union Railway
115	Class I	A	1882	StEG	Austro-Hungarian State Railway Co.
115	—	ZA	1882	Kitson & Co.	Natal Government Railways
116	'Dean Goods'	GB	1883	Swindon Works	Great Western Railway
116	No 1904-2244	F	1883	Société Alsacienne	Western Railways
116	'Webb Coal Tank'	GB	1881	Crewe Works	London & North Western Railway
117	Class N	NZ	1885	Baldwin	New Zealand Government Railways
117	Class A	AUS	1884	Beyer, Peacock	Victoria Government Railways
117	Class S1	D	1885	Borsig	Royal Prussian Union Railway
118	—	RA	1884	Neilson & Co.	Central Argentine Railway
118	Vittorio Emanuele III	I	1884	Turin Works	Upper Italy Railways
118	Class F1	SF	1885	SLM Winterthur	Finnish State Railways
118	Class Xc	A	1884	StEG	Austrian North Western Railway
119	—	CH	1885	Olten Works	Swiss Central Railway
119	'Tennant' class	GB	1885	Darlington Works	North Eastern Railway
120	'Spinners'	GB	1887	Derby Works	Midland Railway
120	No 701	F	1892	Société Alsacienne	Northern Railways
121	No 1801-1831	F	1885	Ivry Works	Paris-Orleans Railway
121	Class 12	B	1888	Cockerill	Belgian State Railway
121	No 123	GB	1886	Neilson & Co.	Caledonian Railway
122	No 1701-1731	I	1889	Turin Works	Mediterranean System
122	No 1865-1900	I	1899	Ansaldo	Adriatic System
122	No 51-68	I	1888	StEG	Sicilian System
123	'Jubilee' Class	GB	1887	Nine Elms Works	London & South Western Railway
123	Class P	DK	1882	Esslingen	Thyland Railway
123	Class BX	D	1890	Krauss	Bavarian State Railway
124	Class C1	F	1888	Paris Works	Paris, Lyons & Mediterranean Railway
124	—	GB	1889	Horwich Works	Lancashire & Yorkshire Railway
125	Teutonic Class	GB	1890	Crewe Works	London & North Western Railway
125	Class J	GB	1889	Gateshead Works	North Eastern Railway
125	—	NL	1889	Sharp, Stewart	Dutch Rhenish Railway
127	No 801-840	F	1890		Eastern Railways

Wheel arrange- ment	Cylinders diam by stroke (mm)	Boiler pressure (kg/cm²)	Driving wheel diam (mm)	Grate area (m²)	Heating surface (m²)	Weight Work order (tonnes)	Adhesive (tonnes)	Coupled wheel- base (mm)	Total wheel- base (mm)	Length over buffers (mm)	Page
4-4-0	2/419 × 559	10·0	1878	2·12	81·30	40·5	25·5		5900	14754	111
0-4-2	2/464 × 660	9·8	1981	1·89	137·86	39·3	28·7	2305	4750	15761	112
2-2-2	2/432 × 610	10·5	1981	1·58	110·04	33·0	13·7		4851	15539	112
4-4-2	2/432 × 660	11·2	1854	1·60	94·85	56·1	32·1	2592	8941	11201	113
2-4-2	2/305 × 508	9·1	1219	0·82		43·2		3650	6782	13995	113
2-4-0	2/440 × 650	10·0	2020	1·33	118·95	36·8	26·0	2100	4000	15378	114
2-6-2	2/450 × 600	12·0	1510	1·30	140·20	65·7	43·5	3400	8400	11150	114
4-4-0	2/450 × 600	10·0	1850	2·05	92·00	40·0	27·0	2430	6270	15625	114
2-2-0	HP 270 × 420	12·0	1130	0·80	34·50	20·0	10·6		3500	6402	115
	LP 410 × 420										
2-4-2		9·0	1800	2·30	143·00	50·0	26·7				115
4-6-2	2/356 × 533	12·3	991	1·02	62·15	29·1		2362	5086	7932	115
0-6-0	2/444 × 610	11·2	1575	1·42	103·61	37·4	37·4	4724	4724	15915	116
0-6-0	2/460 × 640	11·0	1440	1·48	154·71	40·6	40·6	3700	3700	14361	116
0-6-2	2/432 × 610	9·8	1359	1·59	99·81	43·8					116
2-6-2	2/381 × 508	9·4	1245	1·47		45·5					117
4-4-0	2/432 × 660	10·5	1830								117
2-4-0	2/420 × 600	12·0	1980	2·07	94·23	41·3	27·6	2500	4500	10645	117
4-6-0	2/457 × 610	10·5	1372	1·58	110·74	45·7	34·2	3937	7137	17221	118
4-6-0	2/470 × 620	10·0	1675	2·20	124·00	58·3	48·0	3760	7260	16500	118
0-4-4	2/310 × 510	10·5	1250	0·90	40·0	26·1	15·5	1766	4960	8600	118
0-6-0	2/342 × 500	10·0	1015	1·22	70·3	36·5	36·5	2900	2900	8406	118
2-6-0	2/500 × 630	10·0	1280	1·80	136·1	76·1 ∗	42·0	3700	6300	14167	119
2-4-0	2/457 × 610	9·8	2134	1·58	113·62	42·2	29·5	2645	5080	17636	120
4-2-2	2/457 × 660	11·2	2230	1·83	115·25	44·9	18·8		6667	16038	120
4-4-0	2 HP 330 × 610	11·0	2110	2·27	101·00	38·3	28·6	2500	6800	15630	120
	2 LP 460 × 610										
2-6-0	2/480 × 600	10·0	1540	1·74	175·00	51·5	39·1	3509	5800		121
2-4-2	2/500 × 600	10·0	2100	4·71	124·68	42·2	26·3	2165	6565	17040	121
4-2-2	2/457 × 660	10·5	2134	1·62	100·80	42·5	17·3		6426	15947	121
4-4-0	2/450 × 600	12·0	2100	2·30	163·90	49·8	31·4	2600	6800	16740	122
4-4-0	2/480 × 600	12·0	1920	2·30	163·90	48·3	29·5	2430	6700	16083	122
4-4-0	2/420 × 600	10·0	1800	2·10	107·62	43·6	27·0	2500	6400	16176	122
0-4-2	2/457 × 660	11·2	1829	1·58	115·95	43·0	32·2	2450	5131	15200	123
0-4-4	2/305 × 406	10·0	1092	0·70	29·40	23·3	14·3	1600	5700	8900	123
2-4-0	HP 430 × 610	12·0	1870	1·95	99·00	44·2	29·8				123
	LP 610 × 610										
2-4-2	2 HP 310 × 620	15·0	2000	2·34	128·03	53·5	29·6	2160	5860	2880 □	124
	2 LP 500 × 620										
2-4-2	2/457 × 660	11·2	1727	1·74	113·00	56·8	34·2	2738	7417	11203	124
2-2-2-0	2 HP 356 × 610	12·3	2159	1·90	130·20	46·2	31·5	2946	5512	15552	125
	1 LP 762 × 610										
4-2-2	HP 457 × 610	12·3	2166	1·92	105·81	43·17	18·3		6880	16449	125
	LP 660 × 610										
4-4-0	2/457 × 660	10·3	2020	2·15	113·0	50·0				16593	125
4-4-0	2/470 × 660	8·5	2130	2·42	168·30	56·8	33·4	3000	7450		127

LEADING DIMENSIONS

Page	Locomotive	Country	Year	Builder	Railway
128	—	CH	1890	Maffei	Gotthard Railway
128	Class B6	J	1890	Various	Tokyo-Osaka Railway
129	—	CH	1890	SLM Winterthur	United Swiss Railway
129	No B111-400	F	1891	Paris Works	Paris, Lyons & Mediterranean Railway
129	Wigmore Castle	GB	1894	Swindon Works	Great Western Railway
130	Class XIII	A	1891	StEG	Austrian North Western Railway
130	Greater Britain Class	GB	1891	Crewe Works	London and North Western Railway
131	Class N	Russia	1892	Kolomna	Novisibirsk-Tashkent Railway
131	Class T19	GB	1886	Stratford Works	Great Eastern Railway
131	—	CH	1892	SLM Winterthur	Jura-Simplon Railway
132	Class S3	D	1893	Various	Royal Prussian State Railway
132	Class P6	AUS	1891	Beyer, Peacock	New South Wales Government Railway
132	Class T3	GB	1892	Nine Elms Works	London & South Western Railway
133	No 694	USA	1893	Baldwin	Philadelphia & Reading Railroad
133	Columbia	USA	1893	Baldwin	
133	No 650	USA	1893	Brooks Locomotive	Great Northern Railway
134	Class IVe	D	1894	Société Alsacienne	Baden State Railway
134	—	CH	1894	SLM Winterthur	Gotthard Railway
134	No 860	J	1893	Kobe Works	Kyoto-Osaka Railway
135	Duke of Cornwall Class	GB	1895	Swindon Works	Great Western Railway
135	Class Ad	Russia	1896	Hanomag	Vladicaucasus Railway
136	Grande C Class	F	1898	Paris Works	Paris, Lyons & Mediterranean Railway
136	Dunalastair Class	GB	1896	St Rollox Works	Caledonian Railway
137	Class 5500	J	1894	Beyer, Peacock	Japanese National Railways
137	Class T15	D	1897	Henschel	Royal Prussian Union Railway
137	Class B2	GB	1895	Brighton Works	London, Brighton & South Coast Railway
138	Class 270	I	1898	Various	Adriatic System
138	—	GB	1898	Stratford Works	Great Eastern Railway
139	Class 6	A	1893	Floridsdorf	Austrian State Railway
139	Class 60	A	1895	Various	Austrian State Railway

Wheel arrangement	Cylinders diam by stroke (mm)	Boiler pressure (kg/cm²)	Driving wheel diam (mm)	Grate area (m²)	Heating surface (m²)	Weight Work order (tonnes)	Adhesive (tonnes)	Coupled wheel-base (mm)	Total wheel-base (mm)	Length over buffers (mm)	Page
0-6-6-0	2 HP 400 × 640	12·0	1230	2·20	154·30	87·2	87·2	2 × 2700	8130	13776	128
	2 LP 580 × 640										
0-6-2	2/406 × 610	12·6	1250	1·31	84·40	51·2	38·2	3810	6020	10371	128
2 6 0	HP 450 × 650	12·0	1590	1·70	138·60	74·6	37·7	3520	6000	13380	129
	LP 640 × 650										
4-4-0	2/500 × 620	11·0	2000	2·32	142·50	50·9	32·4	2970	7510	10013□	129
4-2-2	2/483 × 610	11·2	2350	1·93	145·05	49·0	18·0		7163	17662	129
0-6-0	2/470 × 632	11·0	1195	1·91	148·90	41·2	41·2	3300	3300	10650	130
2-2-2-2	2 HP 381 × 610	12·3	2159	1·90	139·88	52·9	31·5	2515	7214	16194	130
	1 LP 762 × 610										
2-6-0	HP 540 × 648	12·0	1702	2·19		54·8					131
	LP 749 × 648										
2-4-0	2/457 × 610	11·2	2134	1·67	113·07	42·0		2667	5029	14681	131
4-4-0	HP 450 × 650	12·0	1830	2·00	129·30	82·1 *	29·8	2600	7100	15785	131
	LP 670 × 650										
4-4-0	HP 460 × 600	12·0	1980	2·27	118·43	50·5	30·4	2600	7400	17561	132
	LP 680 × 600										
4-6-0	2/508 × 660	11·2	1524	2·51		90·0					132
4-4-0	2/483 × 660	12·3	2007	1·83	122·64	49·3	31·1	2362	7163	14331	132
2-4-2	2 HP 330 × 610	12·6	1981	7·10	134·30	68·5	37·2	2027	6818	11241□	133
	2 LP 559 × 610										
2-4-2	HP 330 × 660	12·6	2134	2·30	138·20	57·0	36·0	2300	7597	12091□	133
	LP 559 × 660										
4-6-0	2/483 × 660	12·6	1854	2·37	167·00	62·3					133
4-6-0	2 HP 350 × 640	13·0	1600	2·10	129·40	58·8	41·7	2600	7000	17590	134
	2 LP 550 × 640										
4-6-0	2 HP 458 × 600	14·0	1610	2·30	165·50	100·2 *	48·8	3520	7470	16320	134
	2 LP 498 × 600										
2-4-2	HP 381 × 508		1346	1·11	71·48			2286	5944	9652	134
	LP 572 × 508										
4-4-0	2/457 × 600	12·6	1727	1·60	104·38	46·5	29·0	2591	6782	18844	135
4-6-0	HP 502 × 660		1850		151·00						135
	LP 737 × 660										
4-4-0	2 HP 340 × 620	15·0	2000	2·48	189·50	56·3	34·1	3000	7250	18992	136
	2 LP 540 × 620										
4-4-0	2/464 × 660	11·2	1981	1·91	130·36	47·7	31·7	2743	6731	16402	136
4-4-0	2/406 × 559	12·0	1395	1·33	73·00	31·6	20·0	2540	6578	13910	137
0-6-4-0	2/520 × 630	12·0	1200	2·37	137·40	69·8	69·8	6860	6860	12084	137
4-4-0	2/457 × 660		2056	1·74	124·68	43·1	29·2	3277	7290	17929	137
0-6-0	2/430 × 580	12·0	1510	1·53	94·16	44·0	44·0	4000	4000	9000	138
4-2-2	2/457 × 660	11·2	2134	1·98	120·09	50·0	18·3		6934	16923	138
4-4-0	HP 500 × 680	13·0	2100	2·90	140·00	55·4	28·8	2800	7300	16480	139
	LP 740 × 680										
2-6-0	HP 520 × 632	13·0	1258	2·70	131·00	54·0	43·0	2900	5500	9473	139
	LP 740 × 632										

LEADING DIMENSIONS

Page	Locomotive	Country	Year	Builder	Railway
139	Class 170	A	1897	G. Sigl	Austrian State Railway
140	Class P4	D	1898	Henschel	Royal Prussian Union Railway
140	Class Cc	S	1892	Nydquist & Holm	Swedish State Railways
140	—	CH	1897	SLM Winterthur	Swiss Central Railway
141	'Klondyke' Class	GB	1898	Doncaster Works	Great Northern Railway
141	Class P3[1]	D	1898	Krauss	Palatinate Railway
141	Class DXII	D	1897	Krauss	Bavarian State Railway
142	No 2801-2805	F	1899	Baldwin	State Railway, France
142	No 640	USA	1899	Brooks Locomotive	Illinois Central Railroad
143	No 3101	I	1898	Ansaldo	Mediterranean System
143	Class 500	I	1900	Florence Works	Adriatic System
143	Class 180	A	1901	G. Sigl	Austrian State Railway
144	—	GB	1896	Gateshead Works	North Eastern Railway
144	No 1015	USA	1900	Schenectady	Chicago & North Western Railway
144	Class AD	D	1899	Esslingen	Wurtemburg State Railway
145	—	NL	1899	Beyer, Peacock	State Railways Co
145	No 580	F	1899	Ivry Works	Paris-Orleans Railway
145	Class K	DK	1894	Neilson, Reid	Danish State Railways
146	Precursor Class	GB	1904	Crewe Works	London & North Western Railway
146	No 21	CH	1903	SLM Winterthur	Thun Lake Railway
146	Class Q	NZ	1901	Baldwin	New Zealand Government Railways
147	'Nord Atlantic'	F	1900	Société Alsacienne	Northern Railways
147	No 3001-3014	F	1903	Société Alsacienne	Paris-Orleans Railway
147	No 2971-2990	F	1906	Paris Works	Paris, Lyons & Mediterranean Railway
148	Class Hk	SF	1898	Baldwin	Finnish State Railways
148	Class XVIb	A	1901	StEG	Austrian North Western Railway
149	Shay 2T	USA	1902	Lima Locomotive	Various
149	No 4530	I	1902	Breda	Mediterranean System
149	Class B/2	IND	1904	Vulcan Foundry	Great Indian Peninsula Railway
149	Class VIb	D	1900	Maffei	Baden State Railway
150	Class B	GB	1905	Beyer, Peacock	Metropolitan Railway
150	Class S9	D	1904	Henschel	Royal Prussian Union Railway
151	City Class	GB	1903	Swindon Works	Great Western Railway
151	Saint Class	GB	1902	Swindon Works	Great Western Railway

Wheel arrange-ment	Cylinders diam by stroke (mm)	Boiler pressure (kg/cm²)	Driving wheel diam (mm)	Grate area (m²)	Heating surface (m²)	Weight Work order (tonnes)	Adhesive (tonnes)	Coupled wheel-base (mm)	Total wheel-base (mm)	Length over buffers (mm)	Page
2-8-0	HP 540 × 632 LP 850 × 632	14.0	1258	3.90	227.00	68.0	57.0	4300	6800	19295	139
4-4-0	2/460 × 600	12.0	1750	2.30	65.08 + 21.00	49.3	31.0	2600	7400	17611	140
4-4-0	2/420 × 559	11.0	1880	1.97	97.00	41.1	26.5	2 × 1900	5900	15305	140
0-4-4-0	2 HP 355 × 640 2 LP 550 × 640	14.0	1280	2.00	130.00	90.6	57.2	2083	6200	16230	140
4-4-2	2/483 × 610	12.0	2032	2.48	133.97	58.9	31.5	2050	8026	17748	141
4-4-2	2/490 × 570	13.0	1980	2.70	168.60	59.6	30.0	2050	8700		141
2-4-4	2/450 × 560	13.0	1640	1.96	104.63	68.8	28.8	2050	8000	11850	141
4-4-0	HP 330 × 660 LP 558 × 660	15.0	2140	2.38	168.00	55.0	32.8		8120		142
4-8-0	2/584 × 762	13.6	1435	3.49	324.70	105.0	87.5				142
4-6-0	HP 500 × 640 LP 730 × 640	13.0	1675	2.4	125.75	62.5	45.0	3950	1850	17020	143
4-6-0	2 HP 370 × 650 2 LP 580 × 650	14.0	1920	3.00	166.60	69.0	43.0	4100	8350	24135	143
0-10-0	HP 560 × 632 LP 850 × 632	14.0	1260	3.00	184.00	69.0	69.0	5600	5600	17286	143
4-4-0	2/508 × 660	12.3	2315	1.93	112.97	51.9	34.5	2896	7239	17096	144
4-4-2	2/508 × 660	14.0	2030			72.6					144
4-4-0	HP 450 × 560 LP 670 × 560	14.0	1800	2.04	129.0	50.0	29.0	2700	6983	9931 □	144
4-4-0	2/508 × 660	11.0	2150	2.10	73.50 + 29.00	53.0	31.0			16455	145
4-4-2	2/420 × 650	15.0	1840	2.11	173.68	52.7	32.0	2033	8377	18109	145
4-4-0	2/430 × 610	12.0	1866	1.80	70.4 + 19.0	44.2	26.2	2600	6750	14820	145
4-4-0	2/483 × 660	12.3	2057	2.08	186.70	41.3	19.4	3048	7658	17445	146
2-6-0	2/360 × 500	12.0	1320	1.40	94.00	44.0	35.7	3000	5300	9500	146
4-6-2	2/406 × 559	14.0	1245	3.72		73.3	30.9	2442	5207	16872	146
4-4-2	2 HP 390 × 640 2 LP 560 × 640	16.0	2040	2.76	137.84 + 38.98	67.0	35.5	2150	8500	18247	147
4-4-2	2 HP 360 × 640 2 LP 600 × 640	16.0	2040	3.10	239.40	74.0	36.0	2150	8700	19070	147
4-4-2	2 HP 340 × 650 2 LP 560 × 650	16.0	2000	2.98	214.00	69.7	34.1	2187	8180	20875	147
4-6-0	2/406 × 609	12.0	1575	1.35	79.8 + 21.8	44.5	31.5	3798	12177 ★	14997	148
4-4-2	HP 500 × 650 LP 760 × 650	13.0	1920	2.88	178.30	61.5	28.0	2220	8630	17853	148
0-4-4-0	3/254 × 305	12.6	673			34.5	34.5	2 × 1270	6045	9804	149
4-8-0	HP 540 × 680 LP 800 × 680	12.0	1400	4.80	178.46	75.4	58.3	4560	8060	17432	149
4-4-0	2/470 × 660	11.2	2007	2.00	116.13		29.7				149
2-6-2	2/435 × 630	13.0	1480	1.83	116.20	64.5	41.7	3400	8400	11760	149
4-4-0	2/432 × 610	9.1	1753	1.67	90.67	45.9	34.5	2692	6096	9717	150
4-4-4	3/524 × 630	14.0	2200	4.39	260.00	89.5	36.6	2560	11485	25158	150
4-4-0	2/457 × 660	14.0	2040	1.91	168.90	56.2	36.7	2438	6858	17189	151
4-6-0	2/470 × 762	15.8	2040	2.51	171.07 + 24.40	73.1	55.7	4496	8255	19209	151

LEADING DIMENSIONS

Page	Locomotive	Country	Year	Builder	Railway
151	La France	GB	1902	Société Alsacienne	Great Western Railway
152	Class XIX	A	1904	StEG	Austrian North Western Railway
152	Class 18	B	1905	Tubize	Belgian State Railway
152	—	E	1905	Henschel	Madrid-Saragossa-Alicante Railway
153	Class 0	USA	1904	Schenectady	Baltimore & Ohio Railroad
153	—	CH	1906	Maffei	Gotthard Railway
154	No 3201	D	1906	Maffei	Bavarian State Railway
154	Class P8	D	1906	Various	Royal Prussian Union Railway
155	Star Class	GB	1907	Swindon Works	Great Western Railway
155	Class 640	I	1907	Schwartzkopff	Italian State Railways
155	Class 470	I	1907	Maffei and Breda	Italian State Railways
156	Class P	DK	1907	Hanomag	Danish State Railways
156	Garratt	AUS	1909	Beyer, Peacock	Tasmania Government Railways
157	—	NL	1907	Werkspoor	Holland Iron Railway
157	—	CH	1907	SLM Winterthur	Swiss Federal Railways
157	Class Shch	Russia	1907	Various	Various
158	No 4501-4570	F	1907	Société Alsacienne	Paris-Orleans Railway
158	No 5301-5490	F	1911	SLM Winterthur	Paris-Orleans Railway
158	Class 310	A	1908	Floridsdorf	Austrian Federal Railway
159	'Bavarian Pacific'	D	1908	Maffei	Bavarian State Railway
159	Class CC	USA	1909	Baldwin	Little River Railroad
159	'Nord 4-6-0'	F	1908	Various	Northern Railways
160	George the Fifth Class	GB	1911	Crewe Works	London & North Western Railway
160	Class C	D	1909	Esslingen	Wurtemburg State Railway
160	Class T12	D	1902	Various	Royal Prussian Union Railway
161	—	P	1910	Henschel	South & South Eastern State Railway
161	Class A3	USA	1910	Baldwin	Baltimore & Ohio Railroad
161	Class ITv	D	1910	Hartmann	Saxon State Railway

Wheel arrange-ment	Cylinders diam by stroke (mm)	Boiler pressure (kg/cm²)	Driving wheel diam (mm)	Grate area (m²)	Heating surface (m²)	Weight		Coupled wheel-base (mm)	Total wheel-base (mm)	Length over buffers (mm)	Page
						Work order (tonnes)	Adhesive (tonnes)				
4-4-2	2 HP 360 × 640	16·0	2045	3·10	256·13	72·8	37·8	2150	8700	20413	151
	2 LP 600 × 640										
4-6-0	2 HP 350 × 650	13·5	1770	3·10	198·6	63·9	42·0	4000	8300	18322	152
	2 LP 600 × 650										
4-4-0	2/482 × 660	13·5	1980	2·07	127·62	53·3	36·3		7187		152
4-6-0	2 HP 350 × 650	14·0	1750	2·70		112·5 ★				16000	152
	2 LP 550 × 650										
0-6-6-0	2 HP 508 × 813	16·5	1422	6·71	518·94	151·3	151·3	2348	9347	24214	153
	2 LP 813 × 813										
2-8-0	2 HP 395 × 640	15·0	1350	4·10	278·10	115·3 ★	62·4	3300	7520	16802	153
	2 LP 635 × 640										
4-4-4	2 HP 410 × 640	14·0	2200	4·70	214·50 + 37·50	83·0	32·0	2320	11700	21182	154
	2 LP 610 × 640										
4-6-0	2/590 × 630	12·0	1750	2·60	150·16 + 49·38	69·5	47·7	4500	8350	18592	154
4-6-0	4/381 × 660	15·8	2045	2·51	171·07 + 24·40	73·1	55·7	4496	8306	19558	155
2-6-0	2/540 × 700	12·0	1850	2·42	108·30 + 33·50	54·0	44·3	4200	6750	16530	155
0-10-0	2 HP 375 × 650	16·0	1360	3·50	212·57	74·8	74·8	6000	6000	20565	155
	2 LP 610 × 650										
4-4-2	2 HP 340 × 600	13·0	1984	3·20	204·50	69·0	33·0	2100	8950	18515	156
	2 LP 570 × 600										
0-4-4-0	2 HP 279 × 406	13·7	800	1·38	58·34	34·0	34·0	2 × 1219	8153	10325	156
	2 LP 432 × 406										
4-4-0	2/500 × 660	10·5	2016	2·04		91·4 ★				16830	157
4-6-0	2 HP 425 × 660	14·0	1780	2·80	160·60 + 42·40	114·8 ★	48·0	4350	8650	18740	157
	2 LP 630 × 660										
2-8-0	HP 540 × 700	14·0	1310	2·80		77·0					157
	LP 762 × 700										
4-6-2	2 HP 390 × 650	16·0	1850	4·27	257·25 + 63·50	90·0	52·3	3900	10500	20790	158
	2 LP 640 × 650										
2-8-2	2/600 × 650	12·0	1400	2·77	166·22 + 41·00	92·7	68·0	5000	9700	13450	158
2-6-4	2 HP 390 × 720	15·0	2140	4·62	212·90 + 43·40	86·0	44·1	2220	10450	21404	158
	2 LP 660 × 720										
4-6-2	2 HP 425 × 610	15·0	1870	4·50	218·40 + 50·00	88·0	48·0	4020	11365	21396	159
	2 LP 650 × 670										
2-4-4-2	2 HP 381 × 559	14·0	1220			64·5	53·5	1620	1620	20061	159
	2 LP 584 × 559										
4-6-0	2 HP 380 × 640	16·0	1750	2·80	140·70 + 40·03	71·0	50·2	4300	8450	19520	159
	2 LP 550 × 640										
4-4-0	2/521 × 660	12·3	2057	2·08	143·64 + 28·10	41·4	19·4	3048	7658	17445	160
4-6-2	2 HP 420 × 612	15·0	1800	3·95	208·00 + 53·00	87·3	47·5	3800	11040	21855	160
	2 LP 620 × 612										
2-6-0	2/540 × 630	12·0	1500	1·73	103·36 + 29·50	62·9	48·7	3850	6350	11800	160
4-6-0		14·0	1540	2·90							161
4-4-2	2/559 × 660	14·4	2032	5·20	218·30	86·0	52·3	2134	8306		161
0-4-4-0	2 HP 360 × 630	13·0	1260	1·60	99·30	60·2	60·2	2 × 2000	7700	11624	161
	2 LP 570 × 630										

LEADING DIMENSIONS

Page	Locomotive	Country	Year	Builder	Railway
162	Class 10	B	1910	Various	Belgian State Railway
162	—	NL	1910	Various	State Railway Co. Holland
163	Class S10	D	1911	Schwartzkopff	Royal Prussian Union Railway
163	—	CH	1910	Maffei	Bodensee-Toggenburg Railway
163	Abergavenny	GB	1910	Brighton Works	London, Brighton & South Coast Railway
164	—	CH	1913	SLM Winterthur	Swiss Federal Railways
164	—	TR	1912	Maffei	Smyrna-Cassaba Railway
165	Class K3	USA	1912	American Locomotive	New York Central Railroad
165	Class E6	USA	1910	Altoona Works	Pennsylvania Railroad
166	Class S	Russia	1911	Sormovo	Various
166	Class 685	I	1912	Various	Italian State Railways
166	Class G8[1]	D	1912	Schichau	Royal Prussian Union Railway
167	Class T18	D	1912	Vulkan	Royal Prussian Union Railway
167	—	D	1913	Maffei	Bavarian State Railway
167	Class Mc2	USA	1910	Baldwin	Southern Pacific Railroad
168	Class J	S	1914	Motala	Swedish State Railways
168	Class F	S	1915	Nydquist & Holm	Swedish State Railways
168	—	NL	1913	Beyer, Peacock	State Railway Co. Holland
169	Class K4	USA	1914	Baldwin	Pennsylvania Railroad
169	Class J1	USA	1912	American Locomotive	Wabash Railroad
169	No 800-809	USA	1913	American Locomotive	Virginian Railway
170	No 140.101-170	F	1913	Various	State Railways, France
170	Class 324	H	1909	Budapest	Hungarian State Railways
170	—	E	1914	Hanomag	Madrid-Saragossa-Alicante Railway
171	Class 880	I	1915	Breda	Italian State Railways
171	Class S3	USA	1915	Baldwin	Chicago, Burlington & Quincy Railroad
172	Class EL-1	USA	1916	Baldwin	Baltimore & Ohio Railroad
172	Class P1	USA	1914	Baldwin	Erie Railroad
172	Class D	USA	1916	Baldwin	St Louis & South Western Railroad
173	—	USA	1917	Baldwin	Union Pacific Railroad
173	Class J-1	USA	1917	South Louisville Works	Louisville & Nashville Railroad
174	Class XVIII H	D	1917	Hartmann	Saxon State Railway
174	Class IVh	D	1918	Maffei	Baden State Railway
174	Class C51	J	1919	Various	Japanese National Railways
175	Class G12	D	1917	Henschel	Royal Prussian Union Railway
175	Class 735	I	1917	American Locomotive	Italian State Railways

Wheel arrange-ment	Cylinders diam by stroke (mm)	Boiler pressure (kg/cm²)	Driving wheel diam (mm)	Grate area (m²)	Heating surface (m²)	Weight Work order (tonnes)	Adhesive (tonnes)	Coupled wheel-base (mm)	Total wheel-base (mm)	Length over buffers (mm)	Page
4-6-2	4/500 × 660	14·0	1980	4·58	232·28 + 75·79	112·0	66·0	4100	11425	15011 □	162
4-6-0	4/400 × 660	12·0	1850	2·84		116·0 *				18480	162
4-6-0	4/430 × 630	12·0	1980	2·86	156·86 + 53·00	77·7	50·9	4700	9100	20750	163
2-6-2	2/540 × 600	12·0	1540	2·40	139·50 + 34·20	74·3	47·4	3800	8700	12320	163
4-6-2	2/533 × 660	11·9	2018	2·34	147·35 + 33·17	90·4	53·3	4420	10744	14105	163
2-10-0	2 HP 470 × 640	14·0	1330	3·70	211·30 + 54·50	126·6 *	75·0	2900	8800	19195	164
	2 LP 690 × 640										
0-6-0	2/430 × 630	12·0	1250								164
4-6-2	2/597 × 660	14·0	2001	5·40	318·43 + 77·37	134·0	88·2	4267	11125		165
4-4-2	2/597 × 660	14·6	2032	5·13	269·00 + 56·95	109·4	61·7	2261	9068	21808	165
2-6-2	2/549 × 700	13·0	1829	3·79		76·5	48·1				166
2-6-2	4/420 × 650	12·0	1850	3·50	190·40 + 52·40	72·7	46·8	3950	8451	20575	166
0-8-0	2/600 × 660	14·0	1350	2·63	144·43 + 51·88	67·8	67·8	4700	4700	17968	166
4-6-4	2/560 × 630	12·0	1650	2·44	131·39 + 40·90	105·0	51·1	4100	11700	14800	167
0-8-8-0	2 HP 520 × 640	15·0	1216	4·25	230·89 + 55·39	121·6	121·6	2 × 4500	12200	17700	167
	2 LP 800 × 640										
2-8-8-2	2 HP 600 × 762	14·1	1448	6·40	480·57 + 113·34	198·2	179·0	2 × 4572	17247	41627	167
	2 LP 1020 × 762										
2-6-4	2/420 × 580	12·0	1300	1·40	69·30 + 20·40	62·0	33·0		8960	11900	168
4-6-2	2 HP 420 × 660	13·0	1880	3·60	189·30 + 68·00	87·8	48·0	3950	11100	21265	168
	2 LP 630 × 660										
4-6-4	2/508 × 650	12·0	1850	2·40		92·0				14625	168
4-6-2	2/686 × 711	14·3	2032	6·44	374·94 + 107·21	138·1	90·5	4216	11024	25086	169
4-6-2	2/610 × 660	15·0	1880	5·80	415·00	112·0		3912	10363	20516	169
2-10-10-2	2 HP 762 × 813	15·0	1422	10·10	800·40 + 192·20	310·5	280·0	2 × 6070	19583	32341	169
	2 LP 1217 × 813										
2-8-0	2/590 × 650	12·0	1450	3·16	172·00 + 49·00	76·0	66·0	5100	7600	18970	170
2-6-2	HP 460 × 650	15·0	1440	3·15	213·60	58·1	41·7	3590	8310	10974 □	170
	LP 490 × 650										
4-8-0	2 HP 420 × 640	16·0	1600	4·10	201·13 + 57·00	88·0	60·0	5700	9700		170
	2 LP 640 × 640										
2-6-0	2/450 × 580	12·0	1510	1·53	79·60 + 29·00	50·9	39·1	3900	6200	9172	171
4-6-2	2/686 × 711	12·6	1880	5·50							171
2-8-8-0	2 HP 635 × 813	14·7	1474	8·10	541·00 + 131·00	219·5	208·0				172
	2 LP 1041 × 813										
2-8-8-2 + 8-2	2 HP 914 × 813	14·7	1600	10·00	640·00 + 143·00	390·0	351·3	3 × 5029	27432	32309	172
	4 LP 914 × 813										
4-6-0	2/559 × 711	14·0	1753	4·60	229·90 + 49·90	95·0	75·0	4420	8001		172
2-10-2	2/749 × 762	14·1	1600	7·80	478·25 + 108·23	167·1	129·9	6858	12624	28768	173
2-8-2	2/698 × 762	13·0	1524			227·2 *	115·7	4877	10617	22679	173
4-6-2	3/500 × 630	14·0	1905	4·50	215·00 + 72·00	93·0	50·0	4100	10375	22200	174
4-6-2	2 HP 440 × 680	15·0	2100	5·00	221·00 + 82·00	97·0	54·0	4630	12310	23050	174
	2 LP 680 × 680										
4-6-2	2/530 × 660	13·0	1750	2·53	168·80 + 41·40	69·6	44·6	3800	10000	19994	174
2-10-0	3/570 × 660	14·0	1400	3·25	194·96 + 68·42	95·7	82·5	6000	8500	18495	175
2-8-0	2/540 × 700	12·0	1370	2·86	152·60 + 42·68	63·7	55·9	4500	7100	19462	175

LEADING DIMENSIONS

Page	Locomotive	Country	Year	Builder	Railway
177	Class H4 (laterK3)	GB	1920	Doncaster works	Great Northern Railway
178	Class Hv2	SF	1919	Schwartzkopff	Finnish State Railways
178	Class 33	B	1921	Tubize	Belgian State Railway
178	Class G3c	CND	1923	Montreal Locomotive	Canadian Pacific Railway
178	Class HG	IND	1919	Vulcan Foundry	North Western Railway
179	Class 365	CS	1921	ČKD Prague	Czechoslovakian State Railways
179	No 231.001-040	F	1921	Franco Belge	Eastern Railways
179	No 2068-2504	E	1921	Various	Northern of Spain Railways
180	Class A1	GB	1922	Doncaster works	Great Northern Railway
180	Class E	SU	1921	Various	Soviet Railways
180	Class 940	I	1921	Various	Italian State Railway
181	Class P10	D	1922	Borsig	Royal Prussian Union Railway
181	Class 231	R	1922	Maffei and Henschel	Roumanian State Railways
182	Class Ok22	PL	1922	Chrzanow	Polish State Railways
182	Class 387	CS	1925	Škoda	Czechoslovakian State Railways
182	Class S	DK	1924	Borsig and Frichs	Danish State Railways
183	Castle class	GB	1923	Swindon works	Great Western Railway
183	No 241.001	F	1925	Epernay works	Eastern Railways
184	Class 01	D	1925	Various	German State Railway
184	Class T18	D	1926	Maffei	German State Railway
185	Class Ps-4	USA	1923	American Locomotive	Southern Railway
185	—	E	1925	Hanomag	Northern of Spain Railways
185	Royal Scot Class	GB	1927	North British Locomotive	London, Midland & Scottish Railway
186	Class 15CA	ZA	1926	American Locomotive	South African Railways
186	—	TR	1926	Henschel	Turkish State Railways
187	Class J-4	USA	1927	American Locomotive	Chicago North Western Railway
187	Class 9000	USA	1926	American Locomotive	Union Pacific Railroad
187	Class D12	USA	1928	American Locomotive	Boston & Albany Railroad
188	Class 629	A	1927	StEG	Federal Railway of Austria
188	Class 242AST	F	1926	Paris works	Paris, Lyons & Mediterranean Railway
189	No 4997	GB	1926	Beyer, Peacock	London, Midland & Scottish Railway
189	'Chapelon Pacifics'	F	1929	Fives Lille	Paris-Orleans Railway
	—				
190	Class 691	CH	1939	SLM Winterthur	Swiss Federal Railways
190	Class S2	I	1928	Florence works	Italian State Railways
191	Class K-5	USA	1920	Baldwin	Great Northern Railway
191	Class 214	CND	1930	Montreal Locomotive	Canadian Pacific Railway
191	—	A	1931	Floridsdorf	Federal Railway of Austria
192	Class IS	S	1930	Motala	Swedish State Railways
192		SU	1932	Kolomna	Soviet Railways

Wheel arrangement	Cylinders diam by stroke (mm)	Boiler pressure (kg/cm²)	Driving wheel diam (mm)	Grate area (m²)	Heating surface (m²)	Weight Work order (tonnes)	Adhesive (tonnes)	Coupled wheelbase (mm)	Total wheelbase (mm)	Length over buffers (mm)	Page
2-6-0	3/470 × 660	12.7	1727	2.60	176.60 + 37.81	73.7	60.9			18136	177
4-6-0	2/510 × 600	12.0	1750	1.96	109.80 + 30.70	57.1	38.4		12935	15814	178
2-8-0	2 HP 420 × 660	16.0	1520	3.24	179.30 + 59.50	85.0	75.1		8560		178
	2 LP 600 × 660										
4-6-2	2/635 × 762	14.0	1905					4013	10592	24800	178
2-8-0	2/559 × 660	12.6	1435	2.97	195.55		65.8	5218	8088	19568	179
2-6-2	2/570 × 680	13.0	1780	4.00	258.60 + 44.50	73.2	45.4	4000	9950	19102	179
4-6-2	2 HP 420 × 650	17.0	1950	4.27	195.81 + 80.00	97.0	55.0	4100	10900	22975	179
	2 LP 640 × 650										
2-8-0	2/610 × 650	12.0	1560	3.05	184.50 ⊗	70.5	64.5	5200	7850	18400	180
4-6-2	3/508 × 660	12.6	2032	3.81	272.01 + 48.77	93.9	60.9	4420	10897	21466	180
0-10-0	2/620 × 700	12.0	1320	4.46	188.80 + 47.70	81.5	81.5	5780	5780	20686	180
2-8-2	2/540 × 700	12.0	1370	2.80	152.92 + 41.23	87.3	61.6	4700	9900	13178	181
2-8-2	3/520 × 660	14.0	1750	4.00	238.00 + 77.20	110.4	75.7	6000	11600	22980	181
4-6-2	4/420 × 650	13.0	1855	4.00	254.50 + 60.50	89.0	48.0	4081	11779	22260	182
4-6-0	2/575 × 630	12.0	1750	4.01	184.20 ⊗						182
4-6-2	3/525 × 680	13.0	1950	4.80	226.00 + 64.40	89.6	50.2	4100	11000	23370	182
2-6-4	2/430 × 670	12.0	1730	2.40	118.20 + 46.00	97.0	50.1	4050	11450	14860	183
4-6-0	4/406 × 660	15.75	2045	2.73	187.70 + 24.40	81.1	59.7	4496	8306	19863	183
4-8-2	2 HP 450 × 720	16.0	1950	4.43	217.60 + 92.57	114.7	74.9	6150	12970	26275	183
	2 LP 660 × 720										
4-6-2	2/650 × 660	16.0	2000	4.50	238.00 + 100.00	109.8	60.0	4600	12400	23940	184
4-6-2	turbine	22.0	1750	3.50	160.00 + 51.00	104.0	60.0			24135	184
4-6-2	2/686 × 711	14.3	1854	6.50	295.00 ⊗	154.0		3962	10998	24092	185
4-8-2	2 HP 460 × 680	16.0	1750	5.00	224.00 + 99.85	113.1	70.0	5550	12675	23030	185
	2 LP 700 × 680										
4-6-0	3/457 × 660	17.6	2057	2.90	193.33 + 37.07	86.3	63.5	4674	8382	19315	185
4-8-2	2/584 × 711	14.0	1448	4.49	257.80 + 64.10	107.8	72.3	4801	10871	22333	186
4-8-0	2/630 × 660	12.0	1650	3.03							186
2-8-4	2/711 × 762	17.1	1600	9.30	671.00 ⊗	216.9		5105	12090	28619	187
4-12-2	2/610 × 813	15.4	1702	10.06	543.74 + 237.82	224.5	161.0	9347	15951	31436	187
	1/635 × 787										
4-6-6	2/597 × 660	15.0	1600			159.7		4572	13005	16529	187
4-6-2	2/475 × 720	13.0	1574	2.70	142.80 + 29.10	83.8	45.0	3600	9590	13268	188
4-8-4	2 HP 420 × 650	16.0	1650	3.08	173.00 + 45.50	116.5	64.0	5910	14360	17825	188
	2 LP 630 × 650										
2-6-6-2	4/470 × 660	13.4	1600	4.13	229.54 + 53.8	158.0	124.6	2 × 5029	24080	26784	189
4-6-2	2 HP 420 × 650	17.0	1950	4.33	198.00 + 80.00	102.5	57.3	3900	10700	21285	189
	2 LP 650 × 690										
0-8-0	2/570 × 640	12.0	1330	1.70	77.70 + 28.60	68.4	68.4	3050	3050	11770	190
4-6-2	4/450 × 680	14.0	2030	4.30	237.00 + 67.00	96.5	60.0	4300	10365	22590	190
4-8-4	2/737 × 737	15.7	2032			19.09					191
4-6-4	2/584 × 711	19.3	2032					4267	12243	28219	191
2-8-4	2/650 × 710	15.0	1900	4.72	283.20 + 77.80	124.0	72.0	6210	12635	22640	192
4-6-0	2/520 × 610	12.0	1720	2.50	116.00 + 36.40	61.4	39.0		8575	17700	192
2-0-4	2/670 × 770	15.0	1850	7.04	295.00 + 148.00	133.6	80.7	6210	12635	15347 □	192

LEADING DIMENSIONS

Page	Locomotive	Country	Year	Builder	Railway
193	No 3.1251-1290	F	1931	Cail	Northern Railways
193	No 4.1201-12172	F	1932	Cail	Northern Railways
194	No 101-106	E	1930	Euskalduna	Central Aragon Railway
194	No 241.101	F	1932	Fives Lille	State Railways of France
195	Class C12	J	1932	Kisha Seizo Kaisha	Japanese National Railways
195	No 1001-1038	E	1932	Various	Western of Spain
196	Class 05	D	1935	Borsig	German State Railway
196	Class 61	D	1935	Henschel	German State Railway
196	Class 1	B	1934	Various	Belgian National Railways
197	Class A4	GB	1935	Doncaster Works	London & North Eastern Railway
197	Coronation Class	GB	1935	Crewe Works	London, Midland & Scottish Railway
197	No 231.726	F	1937	Tours Works	Paris-Orleans Railway
198	Princess Royal Class	GB	1933	Crewe Works	London, Midland & Scottish Railway
198	Class DT1	A	1935	Floridsdorf	Federal Railways of Austria
198	No 544-546	RC	1935	Haine St Pierre	Kin-Han Tramways
199	Class 231G	F	1934	Various	Paris, Lyons & Mediterranean Railway
199	Class 7	B	1934	Various	Belgian National Railways
200	Class A	USA	1935	American Locomotive	The Milwaukee Road
200	Class K4s	USA	1939	Altoona Works	Pennsylvania Railroad
200	Class GS-3	USA	1937	Lima Locomotive	Southern Pacific Railroad
201	Class J-3a	USA	1938	American Locomotive	New York Central System
201	Class T1b	CND	1938	Montreal Locomotive	Canadian Pacific Railway
202	Challenger Class	USA	1936	American Locomotive	Northern Pacific Railway
203	Class S7	USA	1936	Baldwin	Union Railroad
203	—	BR	1937	Henschel	Central of Brazil Railway
204	Duchess Class	GB	1938	Crewe Works	London, Midland & Scottish Railway
204	Class 45	D	1937	Henschel	German State Railway
205	Class D51	J	1936	Various	Japanese National Railways
205	—	—	1942	Various USA	United States Army
205	Class 12	B	1939	Various	Belgian National Railways
206	Class 11	BG	1939	Henschel	Bulgarian State Railways
206	Class 03^{10}	D	1939	Krauss-Maffei	German State Railway
207	Merchant Navy Class	GB	1941	Eastleigh Works	Southern Railway
207	Class 141P	F	1942	Various	French National Railways
208	Class 52	D	1942	Various	German State Railway
208	Class 42	D	1943	Various	German State Railway
209	Class T-1	USA	1942	Baldwin	Pennsylvania Railroad
209	Class J	USA	1941	Roanoke Works	Norfolk & Western Railway
209	Class 743	I	1942	Various	Italian State Railways
210	Big Boy Class	USA	1941	American Locomotive	Union Pacific Railroad

Wheel arrangement	Cylinders diam by stroke (mm)	Boiler pressure (kg/cm²)	Driving wheel diam (mm)	Grate area (m²)	Heating surface (m²)	Weight Work order (tonnes)	Adhesive (tonnes)	Coupled wheelbase (mm)	Total wheelbase (mm)	Length over buffers (mm)	Page
4-6-2	2 HP 440 × 660	17·0	1900	3·50	214·80 + 57·20	100·5	56·8	4020	10420	22458	193
	2 LP 620 × 690										
2-8-2	2/585 × 700	18·0	1550	3·09	181·50 + 64·20	122·5	85·0	5400	11400	15150	193
4-6-2 + 2-6-4	4/481 × 660	14·0	1750	4·90	293·20 + 69·00	184·0	95·0	2 × 3810	25527	28548	194
4-8-2	2/530 × 570	20·0	1950	5·00	268·00 + 86·00	116·0	80·0		13050		194
	1/760 × 650										
2-6-2	2/400 × 610	14·0	1400	1·30	54·40 + 19·80	50·5	33·0				195
4-8-0	2/620 × 660	14·0	1600	4·50		148·5				16120	195
4-6-4	3/450 × 660	20·0	2300	4·71	255·52 + 90·00	127·0	57·0	5100	13900	26265	196
4-6-4	2/460 × 750	20·0	2300	2·80	151·00 + 69·00	128·3	55·6	5100	14350	18505	196
4-6-2	4/420 × 720	18·0	1980	5·00	234·78 + 111·70	126·0	72·0				196
4-6-2	3/470 × 660	17·5	2032	3·83	239·03 + 69·58	104·6	67·1	4420	10897	21652	197
4-6-2	4/419 × 711	17·5	2057	4·65	260·67 + 77·3	110·0	68·6	4420	11278	22498	197
4-6-2	2 HP 420 × 650	17·0	1950	4·33	198·00 + 80·00	103·4	57·8	3900	10700	21345	197
	2 LP 650 × 690										
4-6-2	4/413 × 711	17·5	1981	4·18	252·04 + 34·37	106·0	68·0	4648	11506	22663	198
2-4-2	2/290 × 570	16·0	1410	0·80	42·00 + 21·00	45·0	26·0	3200	7660	11200	198
2-6-2	2/508 × 660	12·0	1512	3·00	150·30 + 34·50	73·0	18·0	4234	9677	12247 □	198
4-6-2	2 HP 440 × 650	16·0	2000	4·28	206·00 + 67·70	97·6	56·1	4193	11230	19995	199
	2 LP 650 × 650										
4-6-0	2 HP 400 × 640	16·0	1800	3·08	153·88 + 73·50	83·5	59·7	4859	8880	12147 □	199
	2 LP 600 × 640										
4-4-2	2/483 × 711	21·1	2134	6·40	301·46 + 95·59	127·0	63·5	2591	11455	27026	200
4-6-2	2/686 × 711	14·4	2032	6·49	375·32 + 87·60	154·5	98·4	4216	11024	25086	200
4-8-4	2/660 × 813	19·6	2032	9·00	454·00 + 194·00	209·0	121·1	6553	13894	33680	200
4-6-4	2/571 × 737	19·3	2017	7·62	388·97 + 162·11	165·8	91·4	4267	12294	29517	201
2-10-4	2/635 × 813	20·0	1600	8·69	469·52 × 188·77	202·8	140·6	6706	14033	29836	201
4-6-6-4	4/584 × 813	17·5	1753	10·00	653·38 ⊗	283·3	193·2	2 × 3759	18948	38462	202
0-10-2	2/711 × 813	18·2	1549	7·92	443·78 + 126·34	191·4	158·8	6706		26378	203
2-8-8-2	4/431 × 559	14·7	1070	7·00	232·00 + 85·00	117·7	95·7			24765	203
4-6-2	4/419 × 711	17·5	2057	4·65	260·67 + 77·3	107·0	68·0	4420	11278	22498	204
2-10-2	3/520 × 720	20·0	1600	5·00	289·00 + 132·50	128·0	100·0	5550	13600	25645	204
2-8-2	2/550 × 660	14·0	1400	3·27	242·10 ⊗	76·8	57·2	4650	9450	12180 □	205
2-8-0	2/483 × 660	15·7	1448	3·81	164·30 + 43·70	73·2	63·6	4725	7087	18385	205
4-4-2	2/480 × 720	18·0	2100	3·70	160·60 + 63·00	89·0	46·0		9887		206
4-10-0	3/520 × 700	16·0	1450	4·87	224·10 + 80·00	109·6	85·0		10900		206
4-6-2	3/470 × 660	16·0	2000	3·89	203·00 + 72·00	103·0	55·0	4500	12000	23905	207
4-6-2	3/457 × 610	19·6	1880	4·50	227·70 + 61·78	94·0	64·0	4572	11201	21298	207
2-8-2	2 HP 410 × 700	20·0	1650	4·28	201·80 + 86·90	111·6	76·0	5600	11050	23940	207
	2 LP 640 × 700										
2-10-0	2/600 × 660	16·0	1400	3·90	177·60 + 63·70	84·7	75·5	6600	9200	23055	208
2-10-0	2/630 × 660	16·0	1400	4·70	199·60 + 75·80	96·5	85·5	6600	9200	23000	208
4-4-4-4	4/502 × 660	21·0	2030	8·50	391·85 + 156·07	226·0	122·0	7722	15824	37433	209
4-8-4	2/686 × 813	19·0	1765	10·00	489·68 + 202·24	224·0	131·0	5715	14414	33280	209
2-8-0	2/540 × 700	12·0	1370	2·80	152·30 + 43·30	72·7	62·2	4700	11040	19885	209
4-8-8-4	4/603 × 813	21·0	1727	14·00	547·09 + 229·09	345·6	247·2	2 × 5563	22085	40488	210

LEADING DIMENSIONS

Page	Locomotive	Country	Year	Builder	Railway
210	No 715-729	USA	1942	Lima Locomotive	Nickel Plate Road
210	Class M1	USA	1942	Baldwin	Louisville & Nashville Railroad
211	Shay 3T	USA	1945	Lima Locomotive	Western Maryland Railway
212	No 2201-2257	E	1944	La Maquinista	Spanish National Railways System
212	Class 15F	ZA	1945	Beyer, Peacock	South African Railways
212	Class S2	USA	1944	Baldwin	Pennsylvania Railroad
213	Class S-1a	USA	1945	American Locomotive	New York Central System
217	Class 141R	F	1945	Baldwin	French National Railways
217	Class 241P	F	1948	Schneider	French National Railways
217	Class 230K	F	1947	Epernay works	French National Railways
218	Class WP	IND	1947	Baldwin	Indian Railways
218	Class M-1	USA	1947	Baldwin	Chesapeake & Ohio Railway
219	Class Ja	NZ	1946	Hillside Works	New Zealand Government Railways
219	Class E10	S	1947	Nydquist & Holm	Swedish State Railways
219	Class 303	H	1951	Mávag	Hungarian State Railways
220	Class 232U	F	1949	Société Alsacienne	French National Railways
220	Class 25	ZA	1953	Henschel	South African Railways
220	Class P36	SU	1951	Kolomna	Soviet Railways
221	Class 498.1	CS	1954	Škoda	Czechoslovakian State Railways
221	Britannia Class	GB	1951	Crewe Works	British Railways
221	Class 9F	GB	1953	Crewe Works	British Railways
222	Class 15B	RA	1949	Vulcan Foundry	General Roca National Railway
222	Class D58	AUS	1950	Everleigh Works	New South Wales Government Railway
222	Class Mα	GR	1953	Breda and Ansaldo	Hellenic State Railways
223	No 2001-2010	E	1955	La Maquinista	Spanish National Railways System
223	Class Tr1	SF	1953	Tampella	Finnish State Railways
223	Class 15	RSR	1952	Beyer, Peacock	Rhodesian Railways
224	Class 10	D	1956	Krupp	German Federal Railways
224	Class 01⁵	RDT	1962	Various	German State Railway

□ Excluding the tender
★ Including the tender
⊗ Superheated locomotive
◇ Rack locomotive
☆ Rack railcar

Wheel arrange-ment	Cylinders diam by stroke (mm)	Boiler pressure (kg/cm^2)	Driving wheel diam (mm)	Grate area (m^2)	Heating surface (m^2)	Weight Work order (tonnes)	Adhesive (tonnes)	Coupled wheel-base (mm)	Total wheel-base (mm)	Length over buffers (mm)	Page
2-8-4	2/635 × 864	17·2	1753	8·39	443·32 + 179·48	191·0	117·0	5563	12802	30846	210
2-8-4	2/635 × 813	18·7	1753	8·39	432·08 + 177·25	203·3	121·3	5563	12903	32214	210
0-4-4-4-0	3/432 × 457	14·1	1219	4·50	171·80 + 39·90	147·0	147·0	3 × 1727	10719	19997	211
4-8-2	2/640 × 710	16·0	1750	5·30		204·0 ∗				25500	212
4-8-2	2/610 × 711	14·7	1524	5·85	315·86 + 62·80	111·0	73·7	4801	10871	22403	212
6-8-6	turbine	21·8		10·8	389·70 + 183·90	267·9	123·2	5944	16154	37370	213
4-8-4	2/635 × 813	20·3	2001	9·3	447·69 + 192·58	214·0	125·0	6248	14706	35194	213
2-8-2	2/597 × 711	15·4	1650	5·16	250·74 + 65·40	115·5	80·0	5181	10870	24663	217
4-8-2	2 HP 446 × 650 2 LP 674 × 700	20·0	2020	5·05	244·57 + 108·38	131·4	81·6	6300	13460	27418	217
4-6-0	2 HP 370 × 680 2 LP 590 × 680	18·0	2090	3·16	135·50 + 54·20	84·0	58·0	4950	8890	21870	217
4-6-2	2/514 × 711	14·7	1705	4·27	286·32	89·0	55·0				218
4-8 + 4-8-4	turbine	21·8	1016			559·7 ∗		2 × 5309	27610	46958	218
4-8-2	2/457 × 660	14·0	1370	3·62	135·82 + 25·18	70·2	46·8	4343		20403	219
4-8-0	2/450 × 610	14·0	1400	2·80	138·70 + 51·00	74·2	50·8		8600	18085	219
4-6-4	2/549 × 699	18·0	2000	5·50	259·84 + 77·94	114·0	51·9	4500	12920	25455	219
4-6-4	2 HP 450 × 700 2 LP 680 × 700	20·0	2000	5·17	195·00 + 63·96	130·7	69·0	4390	11990	26634	220
4-8-4	2/610 × 711	15·7	1524	6·50	292·60 + 58·50	124·6	74·8	4801	11582	32768	220
4-8-4	2/575 × 800	15·0	1850	6·75	243·20 + 131·70	134·9	74·0	5850	13450	29809	220
4-8-2	3/500 × 680	16·0	1830	4·90	228·40 + 72·80	116·6	74·4	5790	12550	25594	221
4-6-2	2/508 × 711	17·5	1880	3·90	229·83 + 65·40	95·5	61·7	4267	10897	20955	221
2-10-0	2/508 × 711	17·5	1524	3·73	187·10 + 49·70	88·0	79·7	6604	9195	20168	221
4-8-0	2/495 × 711	15·7	1727	3·03	162·76 + 32·33	82·4	64·0	5639		21215	222
4-8-2	3/546 × 711	14·0	1524	6·94	314·93 + 71·81	141·0	93·1	4801		26673	222
2-10-2	2/660 × 700	18·0	1600	5·60	312·05 + 125·04	134·0	100·0	5919		25000	222
4-8-4	2/640 × 710	15·0	1900	5·30	293·56 + 104·51	142·0	76·0	6652		27000	223
2-8-2	2/610 × 700	15·0	1600	3·54	195·40 + 68·00	95·0	68·0		18910 ∗	22250	223
4-6-4 + 4-6-4	4/444 × 660	12·6	1450	4·60	217·01 + 45·89	182·3	80·8	2 × 3200	25679	28194	223
4-6-2	3/480 × 720	18·0	2000	4·0	206·50 + 96·00	114·5	64·5	4600	12500	26503	224
4-6-2	2/600 × 660	16·0	2000	4·88	229·17 + 97·90	111·0	60·5				224

253

Index

ABDILL G.: *Rails West*. New York, Bonanza Books – 1960

ADAMS K.: *Logging Railroads of the West*. New York, Bonanza Books – 1961

AHRONS E.L.: *The Development of British Locomotive Design*. London, 1914

ALEXANDER E.: *Iron Horses: American Locomotives 1829–1900*. New York, 1941. *American Locomotives 1900–1950*. New York, Bonanza Books – 1950

ALLEN P.C. - MAC LEOD A.B.: *Rails in the Isle of Wight*. London, George Allen and Unwin Ltd. – 1967

BARBIER F. - GODFERNAUX: *Les Locomotives à l'Exposition de 1900*. Paris, 1902

BAY W.: *Danmarks Damplokomotiver*. Hamlet, Herluf Andersens Forlag – 1977

BINUS D.: *Articulated Locomotives of the World*. Truro (England), Bradford Barton Ltd. – 1975

BORN E.: *2C1, Entwicklung und Geschichte der Pazifik Lokomotiven*. Stuttgart, Franckh'sche Verlagshandlung – 1964 *Die Regel – Dampflokomotiven der Deutschen Reichsbahn und der Deutschen Bundesbahn*. Frankfurt am Main – 1953

BRATÉ T.: *The Steam Locomotives of Yugoslavia*. Wien, Verlag, Josef Otto Slezak – 1971

BUCHMANN H.: *Dampflokomotiven in den USA*. Basel, Birkäuser Verlag – 1977

CARTER E.: *Unusual Locomotives*. London, Frederick Muller Ltd. – 1960

CASSERLEY H.C.: *The Historic Locomotive Pocketbook*. London, B.T. Batsford Ltd. – 1960 *Preserved Locomotives*. Shepperton, Ian Allan – 1976

CHAPELON A.: *La locomotive à vapeur*. Paris – 1938

DAMBLY P.: *Nos inoubliables «vapeur»*. Bruxelles, Le Rail – 1968

DAMEN A. - NAGLIERI V. - PIRANI P.: *Italia – Locomotive a vapore*. Parma, Ermanno Albertelli Editore – 1971

DIEHL - FJELD - NILSSON: *Normalspäriga änglok Vid Statens Järnvägar*. Växjö C. Davidson Boktryckeri / Offset AB – 1973

DEWHURST P.C.: *The Norris Locomotives*. Boston – 1950

DÜRING T.: *Schnellzug – Dampflokomotiven der deutschen Länderbahnen 1907–1922*. Stuttgart, Franckh'sche Verlagshandlung – 1972

DURRANT A.E.: *The Steam Locomotives of Eastern Europe*. Newton Abbot, David & Charles – 1966

EONSUU T. - HONKANEN P. - KILPINEN T. – PÖLHÖ E.: *Suomen veturit die Lokomotiven Finlands*. Malmö, Verlag Frank Stenvall – 1975

FENTON W.: *Nineteenth Century Locomotive Engravings*. London, Hugh Evelyn – 1964 *Locomotives in retirement*. London, Hugh Evelyn – 1958

FLEMING LE H. - PRICE J.H.: *Russian Steam Locomotives*. Newton Abbot, David & Charles, 1968

FLURY P.F.: *Dampflokomotiven und ihre Bauteile*. Düsseldorf, Alba Buchverlag, 1976

FOURNEREAU J.: *Les locomotives à vapeur de la SNCF*. Mont chauvet – 1947

GARBE R.: *Die Dampflokomotiven der gegenwart*. Berlin, 1ª ed. 1907

GARRATT C.: *Steam Safari*. London, Blandford Press Ltd – 1974

GIESL - GIESLINGEN: *Lokomotiv – Athleten*. Wien, Verlag Josef Otto Slezak – 1976

GILLOT J.: *Les locomotives à vapeur de la S.N.C.F. Région Est*. Levallois-Perret, Editions Picador – 1976

GLOVER G.: *British Locomotive Design 1825–1960*. London, George Allen and Unwin Ltd. – 1967

GRIEBL H.: *CSD – Dampflokomotiven (Teil 1 – Teil 2)*. Wien, Verlag Josef Otto Slezak – 1969

HAMILTON ELLIS C.: *The Lore of the Train*. New York Grosset & Dunlap Inc. – 1971 *The Pictorial Encyclopedia of Railways*. London, Hamlyn – 1968

HARDER K.J.: *Die P8*. Stuttgart, Franckh'sche Verlagshan-Ian Allan Ltd. – 1969

HARRISON M.: *Indian Locomotives of Yesterday. Bracknell (Berks.), Town and Country Press* – 1972

HARESNAPE B.: *Railway Design since 1830* (I-II). Shepperton, Ian Allan Ltd. – 1969

HENSCHEL LOKOMOTIVFABRIK: *125 Jahre Henschel*. Kassel, Henschel & Sohn – 1935

HERMANN O.: *Lokomotiven der Gotthardbahn*. Basel, Birkäuser Verlag – 1971

HIROTA N.: *Steam Locomotives of Japan*. Tokyo, Kodausha International Ltd. – 1972

HOECHERL - KRONAWITTER - TAUSCHE: *S 3/6 – Star unter den Dampflokomotiven*. Stuttgart, Franckh'sche Verlagshandlung – 1971

HOLLAND D.F.: *Steam Locomotives of the South African Railways*. Newton Abbot, David & Charles – 1971

HORN A.: *Die Bahnen in Bosnien und Herzegowina. 1964 Die Österreichische Nordwestbahn*. Wien Heidelberg, Bohmann Verlag – 1967 *Die Kaiser - Ferdinands - Nordbahn*. Wien Heidelberg, Bohmann Verlag – 1971

HORNSTEIN VON A.: *Einsenbahnmuseen Denkmalloks Touristikbahnen*. Zürich, Orell Füssli Verlag – 1973

JOHNSTON H.: *Thunder in the Mountains*. California, Trans-Anglo Books – 1968

JONES K.W.: *Steam in the Landscape*. London, Blandford Press Ltd. – 1971

JURRIAANSE VAN WIJCK: *Stoomlocomotieven van de Nederlandse Spoorwegen*. Rotterdam, Uitgevers WYT – 1973 *De Nederlandsche Central Spoorwegmaatschappy*. Rotterdam, Uitgevers WYT – 1973

KINERT - REED: *Early American Steam Locomotives, First Seven Decades 1830–1900*. New York – 1962

KRONAWITTER L.B.: *Die bayerischen S 3/6 – Locomotiven der Baureihen 18⁴, 18⁵ und 18⁶, Krauss - Maffei - Informationen Nr. 213*. Separata de «Der Eisenbahnen» – 1959

KUBINSZKY M.: *Ungarische Lokomotiven und Triebwagen*. Basel, Birkäuser Verlag – 1975

LEGGET F.R.: *Railways of Canada*. Newton Abbot, David & Charles – 1973

LEITCH D.B.: *Railways of New Zealand.* Newton Abbot, David & Charles – 1972

MAEDEL K.E.: *S10¹, Geschichte der letzten preussischen Shenellzug – Dampflokomotiven.* Stuttgart, Franckh'sche Verlagshandlung – 1967

Geliebte Dampflok. Stuttgart, Franckh'sche Verlagshandlung – 1967

Dampflokomotiven geliebt und unvergessen. Stuttgart, Franckh'sche Verlagshandlung – 1976

Die Dampflokzeit. Stuttgart, Franckh'sche Verlagshandlung – 1968

Liebe alte Bimmelbahn. Stuttgart, Franckh'sche Verlagshandlung – 1967

Unvergessene Dampflokomotiven. Stuttgart, Franckh'sche Verlagshandlung – 1966

Die Königlish Sächsischen Staatseisenbahnen. Stuttgart, Franckh'sche Verlagshandlung – 1977

Die deutschen Dampflokomotiven gestern und heute. Berlin, VEB Verlag Technik – 1965

MARISTANY M.: *Adios Viejas Locomotoras.* Barcelona, J.M. Casademont – 1973

MARSHALL J.: *The Lancashire & Yorkshire Railway.* Newton Abbot, David & Charles – 1969

MARSHALL L.G.: *Steam on the RENFE.* London, MacMillan & Co Ltd. – 1965

MASKELYNE J.N.: *Locomotives I have known.* London, Percival Marshall – 1959

MESSERSCHMIDT W.: *1C1, – Entstehung und Verbreitung der Prärie – Lokomotiven.* Stuttgart, Franckh'sche Verlagshandlung – 1966

Dampflok - Raritäten. Stuttgart, Franckh'sche Verlagshandlung – 1974

1D1 – Erfolg und Schicksal der Mikado-Lokomotiven. Stuttgart, Franckh'sche Verlagshandlung – 1963

Von Lok zu Lok. Stuttgart, Franckh'sche Verlagshandlung – 1969

Geschichte der italienischen Dampflokomotiven. Zürich, Orell Füssli Verlag – 1968

MORGAN D.: *Canadian Steam!* Milwaukee, Kalmbach Publishing Co. – 1961

MOSER A.: *Der Dampfbetrieb der Schweizerischen Eisenbahnen 1847–1966.* Basel, Birkäuser Verlag – 6ª ed. 1975

MÜHL A. - SEIDEL K.: *Die Württembergischen Staatseisenbahnen.* Stuttgart – 1970

NAVÉ H.: *Dampflokomotiven in Mittel und Oesteuropa.* Stuttgart, Franckh'sche Verlagshandlung, 1977

NOCK O.S.: *The Dawn of World Railways – 1800–1850.* London, Blandford Press Ltd. – 1972

Railways in the Formative Years – 1851–1895. London, Blandford Press Ltd. – 1973

Railways at the Turn of the Century – 1895–1905. London, Blandford Press Ltd. – 1969

Railways in the Years of Pre-Eminence – 1905–1919. London, Blandford Press Ltd. – 1971

Railways at the Zenith of Steam – 1920–1940. London, Blandford Press Ltd. – 1970

Railways in the Transition from Steam – 1940–1965. London, Blandford Press Ltd. – 1974

LNER Steam. Newton Abbot, David & Charles – 1969

Steam Railways of Britain. London, Blandford Press Ltd. – 1967

60 years of Western Express Running. Shepperton, Ian Allan Ltd. – 1973

The LNWR Precursor Family. Newton Abbot, David & Charles – 1966

Steam Locomotive. London, George Allen & Unwin Ltd. – 1957

Railways of Australia. London, Adam & Charles Black – 1971

Great Steam Locomotives of All Time. Poole (Dorset), Blandford Press – 1976

British Steam Locomotives in colour. London, Blandford Press Ltd. – 1964

The Premier Line, the Story of London & North Western Locomotives. London – 1952

The Great Western Railway in the Nineteenth Century. London – 1962

OBERMAYER J.H.: *Taschenbuch Deutsche Dampflokomotiven.* Stuttgart, Franckh'sche Verlagshandlung – 1969

OSTENDORF R.: *Ungewöhnliche*

Dampflokomotiven von 1803 bis Heute. Stuttgart, Motorbuch Verlag – 1975

PHILLIPS L.: *Yonder comes the train.* A.S. Barnes and Co. Inc. – 1965

RANSOME - WALLIS P.: *The Concise Encyclopaedia of World Railway Locomotives.* London, Hutchinson – 1959

The last steam Locomotives of Eastern Europe. Shepperton, Ian Allan Ltd. – 1974

The last steam Locomotives of Western Europe. Shepperton, Ian Allan Ltd. – 1963

REDER G.: *Le Monde des Locomotives à vapeur.* Friburg, Office du livre – 1974

REED B.: *Locomotives in Profile.* Windsor – 1971

ROBERT G.: *Le Ferrovie nel Mondo.* Milano, Vallardi – 1964

ROGERS H.C.B.: *Französische Dampflokomotiven des 20 Jahrhunderts.* Stuttgart, Franckh'sche Verlagshandlung – 1974

ROWE TREVOR D.: *Railway Holiday in Spain.* Newton Abbot, David & Charles – 1966

SAGLE W.L.: *B & O Power.* Medina (Ohio), Alvin Staufer – 1964

SAUTER A.: *Die Königlich Preussischen Staatseisenbahnen.* Stuttgart, Franckh'sche Verlagshandlung – 1974

SCHEINGRABER G.: *Die Königlich Bayerischen Staatseisenbahnen.* Stuttgart, Franckh'sche Verlagshandlung – 1975

SLEZAK J.O.: *Die Lokomotiven der Republik Österreich.* Wien, Verlag Joseph Otto Slezak – 1973

Die Lokomotivfabriken Europas. Wien – 1963

STAFFELBACH H.: *Vitznau-Rigi.* Zürich, Orell Füssli Verlag – 1972

STUFER A.F.: *Steam Power of the New York Central System.* Medina, (Ohio), Alvin Staufer – 1961

SWENGEL F.M.: *The American Steam Locomotive.* Davenport (Iowa), Midwest Rail Publications Inc. – 1967

TUPLIN W.A.: *Great Western Steam.* London – 1958

North Western Steam. London – 1963

VALLANCE H.A.: *Railway Holiday in Northern Norway &*

Sweden. David & Charles (Dawlish), MacDonald (London) – 1964
The Highland Railway. Newton Abbot, David & Charles – 1969 (3rd ed.)
VILAIN L.M.: *La Locomotive à vapeur et les grandes vitesses.* Paris, Editions Dominique Vincent – 1972
Les Locomotives à vapeur françaises à grande vitesse et à grande puissance du Type «Pacific». Vigot Frères. Paris – 1959
Un siècle (1840–1938) de matériel et traction le réseau d'Orléans. Paris, Editions Vincent. Fréal et Cie. – 1970

L'évolution du matériel moteur et roulant à la Cie du Midi, des origines (1855) à la fusion avec le P.O. (1934) et à la S.N.C.F. (1938). Paris, Les Presses Modernes – 1965
L'évolution du matériel moteur et roulant des Chemins de Fer de l'Etat. Paris, Editions Vincent, Fréal et Cie. – 1967
L'évolution du matériel moteur et roulant de la Cie Paris-Lyon-Méditerranée (PLM) des origines (1857) à la S.N.C.F. (1938). Paris, Editions Vincent, Fréal et Cie – 1971
Les locomotives articulées du sys-

tème Mallet dans le Monde. Paris, Editions Vincent, Fréal et Cie – 1969
WAGNER L.: *Sächsische Lokomotiven.* VdEF, Mitteilungen – Wuppertal. pl. n. 1971–73
WHITE J.H. Jnr.: *Early American Locomotives.* New York, Dover Publications inc. – 1972
WHITEHOUSE F.B.: *World of Trains.* London, Hamlyn – New English Library – 1976
ZIEL R. - EAGLESON M.: *The twilight of world steam.* New York, Grosset & Dunlap – 1973